CONSEQUENCES OF RAPID POPULATION GROWTH IN DEVELOPING COUNTRIES

CONSEQUENCES OF RAPID POPULATION GROWTH IN DEVELOPING COUNTRIES

Proceedings of the United Nations/
Institut national d'études démographiques
Expert Group Meeting, New York, 23–26 August 1988

Published for and on behalf of the United Nations

Routledge
Taylor & Francis Group

LONDON AND NEW YORK

First published 1991 by Taylor & Francis

2 Park Square, Milton Park, Abingdon, Oxon OX14 4RN
711 Third Avenue, New York, NY 10017, USA

Routledge is an imprint of the Taylor & Francis Group, an informa business

First issued in paperback 2016

CONSEQUENCES OF RAPID POPULATION GROWTH IN DEVELOPING COUNTRIES

Cover design by David Lunn.
A CIP catalog record for this book is available from the British Library.

Library of Congress Cataloging-in-Publication Data

Consequences of rapid population growth in developing countries.
    p.   cm.
    "Published for and on behalf of the United Nations."
    Includes index.

    1. Developing countries—Population—Economic aspects.
    2. Population forecasting—Developing countries. 3. Economic forecasting—Developing countries. 4. Developing countries—Economic conditions. I. United Nations.
HB884.C65   1990
304.6'2'091724—dc20   90-43692
                                       CIP

ISBN 978-0-8448-1566-4 (hbk)
ISBN 978-1-138-97155-4 (pbk)

Contents

Preface

More than 30 years ago, a number of studies appeared on both sides of the Atlantic, which were to leave a lasting imprint on ideas concerning the relationship between population and development in countries which at the time were called, not very diplomatically, "underdeveloped countries".

In 1953, at United Nations Headquarters in New York, the Population Division, at the urging of its supervisory body, the Population Commission, published the first edition of what, 20 years later, was to become a monumental work, *Causes et conséquences de la croissance démographique.* In 1958, Ansley Coale and Edgar Hoover published, in turn, a work which was to have a profound influence among both researchers and politicians. The work was entitled *Population Growth and Economic Development in Low-income Countries: A Case Study of India's Prospects.*

In 1956, on the other side of the Atlantic, the Institut national d'études démographiques (National Institute for Population Studies) published, at the initiative of Alfred Sauvy, *Tiers Monde : sous développement et développement,* which was in those days a provocative title. In France, this work, which was original for its multidisciplinary viewpoint, among other things, was one of the first attempts to fathom fully the issue of development in the poor countries. However, it refrained—quite properly, given the times—from broaching the question of population policies. Even so, the expression "third world" was destined to become tremendously popular, so well did it express, by analogy with 1789, the "pre-revolutionary" state in which the newly decolonized countries found themselves in 1956.

The 1960s and 1970s was to be a time of prolific writing on the issues of population growth in the countries which the United Nations had at last decided to designate by the term "developing countries". That same period saw an increase in governmental activities expressly designed to reduce fertility. At last, in 1974, at Bucharest, the international community took a decisive step by adopting the World Population Plan of Action, whose title alone reflected a veritable revolution in the thinking of the international community.

In the 1970s, there were many specialized works on the determinants of population growth, but far less research on the consequences of that growth. Overall, except for the second edition of the *Determinants and Consequences of Population Growth* in 1974, which presented a finely tuned analysis of the effects of population growth, the tone of these works was decidedly Malthusian.

The picture was to alter radically in the 1980s. In the United States, a bastion of Malthusian orthodoxy, authors who were typically branded "revisionists" questioned certain Malthusian postulates. Admittedly, the disastrous consequences of the oft-announced third world population explosion had not materialized. The third world, as a whole, made remarkable strides on the demographic, scientific and social fronts, which frequently went unrecognized. A growing number of developing countries entered the demographic transition and in some of them, particularly in Asia, fertility rates experienced an unprecedented decline. At the same time, life expectancy at birth rose from 40 years to 59 years between 1950 and 1985. The under-five mortality rate was reduced by half and the percentage of couples using modern methods of birth control rose from next to nothing in 1950 to over 40 per cent in the early 1980s. As a counterbalance to this demographic progress, it should be remembered that between 1950 and 1985 per capita food production rose by 20 per cent, while the population of the third world increased by two billion.

This overall progress, however, should not cause us to overlook the delays, failures and even the instances of regression. According to the World Bank, more than one billion persons live in a state of abject poverty, 900 million are illiterate and 800 million are undernourished. The situation is even more disturbing in sub-Saharan Africa where many indicators of economic and social well-being have remained the same or have regressed. Also according to the World Bank, the number of persons in this region who are living in absolute poverty increased by 60 per cent over the past two decades.

The picture is therefore one of contrasts and the situation is ripe for a reassessment of the effects of population growth on development. In that connection, two recent reports have had a great impact. The first, the 1984 World Bank report, entitled *World Development Report,* on demographic trends and development issues, was a bold and stimulating effort to cast a somewhat different perspective on the World Bank's traditionally Malthusian approach to the problem: that of the effects of population growth on the development of human resources. The 1986 report by the United States National Research Council, entitled *Population Growth and Economic Development: Policy Questions,* offered a very detailed analysis of the effects of population growth, contrasting with the extremely pessimistic conclusions of a report it had published in 1971.

Despite these recent publications and repeated appeals from a variety of forums to advance scientific knowledge on the complex relationships between population, resources, the environment and development, much still remains to be done in order to achieve an understanding of how population growth influences the rate of economic growth. It is the intention of this publication to make a contribution, which does not purport to be exhaustive but is, on the contrary, limited, to certain aspects of the debate as it has been revived by empirical and theoretical research in recent years.

One of the primary concerns of the United Nations, as a partner of the Institut national d'études démographiques (INED) in this project—and it does not exclude other, more research-oriented concerns—resides in the potential political implications of its work. At the international level—largely as a result of determined action by the United Nations—world opinion on population issues has gradually taken shape. The United Nations, therefore, has the duty, in collaboration with such prestigious research centres as INED, to provide international public opinion-makers, politicians and researchers with the bases for an earnest debate on an issue which cannot be resolved by slogans or *a priori* ideological positions.

In the tradition established by the publication of its work on the third world, INED was duty-bound to play a creative role in the debate. This debate is of great interest to the French-speaking, and particularly the African community, in view of the specific problems posed by very rapid population growth in a region so fragile economically and politically.

As a means of partially fulfilling this expectation, the Population Division of the Department of International Economic and Social Affairs of the United Nations Secretariat and INED jointly organized a colloquium on the consequences of rapid population growth in developing countries. At the conclusion of that meeting, which was held at United Nations Headquarters in New York, from 23 to 26 August 1988, a decision was taken to publish the most important findings of the colloquium in English and in French. This publication was prepared under the supervision of G. Tapinos, D. Blanchet and D. Horlacher. The French edition, to be published in the INED series *Cahiers de travaux et documents* with the collaboration of the Presses universitaires de France, was issued in late 1990.

Jean-Claude Chasteland
Gérard Calot

PART ONE

Introduction

● **G. Tapinos and D. Blanchet***

The economic consequences of population growth, which have preoccupied economists off and on in the past, have now, with the exceptionally high rates of population increase observed in the less developed countries, become a recurrent theme throbbing at the heart of demo-economic analysis. The doctrines of Malthus – and his followers – served as reference for many years, until their underlying theoretical propositions and their predictive value were eventually strongly challenged. The meeting which has led to the present publication was intended to bring light to the main lines of reflection that have emerged in recent years, in opposition to the simplistic approaches sometimes engendered by the debate.

Four main themes are presented. The first recalls the necessity to take the statistical measure of the problem. The magnitude and rapidity of present–day population growth makes it unique, compared with all historic world population trends in general and with the demographic changes observed during the Industrial Revolution in particular (El Badry). D. Weir and D. Blanchet respectively study the meaning of the elasticity of wage growth to population growth over the very long term, and the correlation – or lack of it – between the rates of population growth and per capita income growth in a period analysis of the whole world.

Before discussing more specifically the effects of population growth on certain key variables of development, it was appropriate to examine how the economic system can adapt and react to such effects, and its capacity to diminish or even radically transform them. This second theme was dealt with by J. Coussy and V. Ruttan–Y. Hayami, who investigate the mechanisms by which population growth may stimulate induced technical progress and modify the structure of international exchanges.

In the third section, recent analytical developments concerning the environment, health and development - fields in which population growth plays a particularly significant role – are explored. B. Commoner, A. S. Oberai and J. Potter discuss the impact of demographic variables on problems of the environment, employment and poverty in the cities, on the standard of health and the quality of medical care. It is shown that environmental degradation can be attributed first and foremost to technological options, that population growth is not the only factor accountable for employment problems and poverty, and that birth spacing improves the health of mother and child, which in turn favours the introduction of family planning and thus contributes to reducing fertility. E. A. Hammel and others throw light on an often neglected aspect of the problem, the consequences of rapid population change on kinship networks, as seen through the Chinese data.

---

* Professors, Institut national d'études démographiques (INED), Paris.

The normative aspect of population growth are analysed by A. Berry, F. Bourguignon and C. Morrison on the one hand and R. Lee and N. Cohen on the other. The former examine its impact on world income distribution, while the latter, taking the case in India, propose to identify and measure the externalities related to population growth (they are cautious in their conclusions; however, the visions of catastrophe are not confirmed).

Finally, D. Horlacher and L. Heligman set the different papers in the context of the intellectual debate of the past twenty years, also referring to other contributions to the Expert Group Meeting.

The agenda of the Meeting, the list of documents and the list of participants appear as annexes I, II ad III, respectively to this introduction.

The intention of the present volume is not to take stock of the costs and benefits of population growth, but to show the limits of the "catastrophic" approach that some have inferred from the Malthusian model and to pinpoint themes of research that seem the most promising for analysing the problem.

<u>Annex I</u>

AGENDA

1.   Opening of the meeting

2.   Adoption of the agenda

3.   Overview

   (a)   Population growth and structure in the less developed
          regions of the world according to the 1988 United Nations
          assessment

   (b)   Rapid population growth: a historical perspective

   (c)   Rapid population growth and socio-economic development in
          socialist developing countries

4.   Economic consequences of rapid population growth

   (a)   Estimating the relationship between population growth and
          aggregate economic growth in LDC's: methodological problems

   (b)   The world distribution of income: evolution over the recent
          period and effects of population growth

   (c)   Relations economiques internationales et croissance
          démographique rapide des economies dependantes

5.   Effects of rapid population growth on resources for development

   (a)   Rapid population growth, the quality of health, and the
          quality of health care in developing countries

   (b)   Population growth and common property resources: micro-level
          evidence from India

   (c)   Rapid population growth and environmental stress

6. Rapid population growth, rural-urban migration and urbanization

    (a)   Rapid population growth, migration and development in the
           African context

    (b)   Urban population growth, employment and poverty in
           developing countries: a conceptual framework for policy
           analysis

7. Rapid population growth as a cause of family and institutional
    change

    (a)   Micro-simulation as a tool in exploring social and
           demographic interrelationships with an example from China,
           1850-2200 or how tradition is achieved by modernity

    (b)   Rapid population growth and technical and institutional
           change

8. Rapid population growth and development planning

    (a)   Rapid population growth and economic development in Latin
           America

    (b)   Population growth and regional development planning in China

    (c)   Evaluating externalities to child-bearing in developing
           countries: the case of India

9. The consequences of rapid population growth as a basis for policy

    Panel discussion on the foundations of population growth policy

10. Closing of the meeting

Annex II

LIST OF DOCUMENTS

Symbol	Agenda item	Title/Author
IESA/P/AC.26/1		Provisional agenda
IESA/P/AC.26/2	3	Population growth and structure in the less developed regions of the world according to the 1988 United Nations Assessment (United Nations Secretariat)
IESA/P/AC.26/3	3	A historical perspective on the economic consequences of rapid population growth (David Weir)
IESA/P/AC.26/4	3	Rapid population growth and socio-economic development in socialist developing countries (Zdenek Pavlik)
IESA/P/AC.26/5	4	Estimating the relationship between population growth and aggregate economic growth in LDC's : methodological problems (Didier Blanchet)
IESA/P/AC.26/6	4	The world distribution of income: evolution over the recent period and effects of population growth (A. Berry, F. Bourguignon and C. Morrisson)
IESA/P/AC.26/7	4	International economic relations and rapid demographic growth in dependent countries (Jean Coussy)
IESA/P/AC.26/8	5	Rapid population growth, the quality of health, and the quality of health care in developing countries (Joseph Potter)
IESA/P/AC.26/9	5	Population growth and common property resources: micro-level evidence from India (Narpat Jodha)

<u>Annex II</u>

LIST OF PARTICIPANTS

<u>Experts</u>

Lawrence Adeokun	Department of Demography and Social Statistics Obafemi Awolowo University, Nigeria
Didier Blanchet	Institut national d'études démographiques Paris, France
François Bourguignon	Ecole des hautes études en sciences sociales Paris, France
Gerard Calot	Institut national d'études démographiques Paris, France
Barry Commoner	Center for the Biology of Natural Systems Queens College, New York, United States of America
Jean Coussy	Ecole des hautes études en sciences sociales Paris, France
Paul Demeny	The Population Council New York, United States of America
Eugene A. Hammel	University of California Berkeley, California, United States of America
Zhenghua Jiang	Population Research Institute Xi'an Jiaotong University Xi'an, The People's Republic of China
Narpat S. Jodha	International Center for Integrated Mountain Development Kathmandu, Nepal
Allen C. Kelley	Duke University Durham, North Carolina, United States of America
Ronald D. Lee	University of California Berkeley, California, United States of America

Paulo Paiva   Centro de Desenvolvimento e Planejamento
                                       Regional
                                      Belo Horizonte, Brazil

Zdenek Pavlik   Charles University
                                      Prague, Czechoslovakia

Joseph Potter   Harvard University
                                      Boston, Massachusetts, United States of America

Vernon W. Ruttan   University of Minnesota
                                      Minneapolis, Minnesota, United States of America

Ismail Sirageldin   The Johns Hopkins University
                                      Baltimore, Maryland, United States of America

Georges Tapinos   Institut national d'études démographiques
                                      Paris, France

Jacques Veron   Centre francais sur la population
                                        et le développement
                                      Paris, France

David Weir   Yale University
                                      New Haven, Connecticut, United States of America

George Zeidenstein   The Population Council
                                      New York, United States of America

United Nations

Department of International Economic and Social Affairs (DIESA)

Population Division

Jean-Claude Chasteland   Director
Shunichi Inoue   Assistant Director
Donald Heisel   Assistant Director
David Horlacher   Chief, Population and Development Section
Larry Heligman   Population Affairs Officer, Population and
                              Development Section

Economic and Social Commission for Asia and the Pacific (ESCAP)

Srawooth Paitoonpong   Population Affairs Officer
                            Population Division

Economic and Social Commission for Western Asia (ESCWA)

George Kossaifi   Population Affairs Officer
                            Population Division

United Nations Population Fund (UNFPA)

Paul Shaw   Senior Population Economist
                            Technical and Evaluation Division

United Nations Institute for Training and Research (UNITAR)

Philippe de Seynes   Senior Special Fellow

Specialized agencies

International Labour Organisation (ILO)

A. S. Oberai   Economist, Employment Planning and
                               Population Branch
                           Employment and Development Department

Food and Agriculture Organization of the United Nations (FAO)

Alain Marcoux   Senior Population Officer
                           Economic and Social Policy Department

World Bank

Susan Cochrane   Principal Population Economist
                           Population, Health and Nutrition Division
                           Population and Human Resources Department

PART TWO

Global trends in population growth and economic growth

Chapter 1

The growth of world population :
past, present and future

● M. A. El-Badry*

Global concern about population trends is a recent phenomenon in the history of mankind. In fact, the current accelerated growth, whose magnitude is both unprecedented on a large geographic scale and unlikely to be experienced again by future generations, is a unique demographic feature of the third quarter of the present century. It is expected to continue for some time into the next century while the demographic transition, which is currently under way in the developing countries, runs its course. The turning point came with the dramatic mortality decline in developing countries beginning at mid-century that was brought about by modern advancements in public health technology. It was this decline in mortality, unaccompanied by an equivalent fertility decline, that caused the post-war acceleration in the growth of world population and consequently a mounting concern about its implications for the countries involved and for the world as a whole. Before this dramatic turn of demographic events, population growth was hardly a subject for international attention and debate. Change in the trend of world population growth has been appreciable only since the eighteenth century as a result of demographic changes taking place in the then-industrializing countries of Europe, USSR, and North America.

This paper aims at incorporating and summarizing the work that has already been done on estimating the population of the world and its major geographic areas at different times in history. The presentation is divided into the following stages: (a) ancient times, from the beginning of agriculture to the middle of the eighteenth century; (b) more modern times, from the middle of the eighteenth century to the middle of the twentieth century; (c) the second half of the twentieth century; and (d) the twenty-first century. This division is made partly because it represents stages in the availability of information on population growth and distribution and partly because it defines approximate phases in the trends of population growth. Since the present-day developed countries have nearly completed their demographic transition, the emphasis in the latter part of the paper is on currently developing countries.

*Senior Advisor, Population Division, Department of International Economic and Social Affairs, United Nations Secretariat.

Population growth in ancient times

For centuries and millennia, world population has experienced fluctuations around a slowly increasing secular trend. There were periods of increase resulting from better living conditions, others of near stagnation, and yet others of decline caused by calamities of one kind or another. Assessments of these historical changes are not abundant. The uncertainty of information and the scarcity of data have made the exercise difficult as well as hazardous. Among the few available estimates of pre-historic world total population is that given by Durand (1977) of 5–10 million around the period 10,000–8000 B.C. at the dawn of the agricultural age, when human societies first began to turn to agriculture for food production. This estimated range is based on available information about the population densities of primitive societies observed in various parts of the world during more recent times (table 5) (United Nations, 1973, chap. II, pp. 11–12), which is obviously uncertain, and also on other assessments. Biraben (1979) gives a range of 5–8 million for about the same period. 1/ Both authors make it clear that these estimates are highly tentative.

Several attempts have been made at estimating world and regional population since the time of Christ. These attempts usually piece together available information, direct or indirect, about the total population of areas of population concentration, primarily China, the Indian sub-continent, Europe (including the USSR), and the Middle East. (These areas have together always contained between two thirds and three quarters of humankind, thus largely determining its evolution.) The information is then assessed and either accepted, modified, or replaced by the author's own estimates. There are three main comprehensive sets of estimates, of which the most analytically detailed and thorough is that prepared by Durand in 1967 and then revised by him in 1974 and again in 1977 (Durand, 1967, 1974, and 1977). The other two are the set prepared by Colin Clark in connection with his study on population growth and land use (Clark, 1968) and a set by Biraben (1979). The latter agrees closely with Durand's, except for minor differences, mainly for China, France, and Italy. It also gives estimates at more even intervals than those of Durand. The three sets are summarized in table 1. Durand gives his 1977 estimates in the form of "indifference ranges", which define limits within which in his judgement there is little ground for preference. It goes without saying that the three studies entail a lot of analytical and geographic detail that cannot be covered here and for which the interested reader is referred to the three main references.

None of the figures in table 1 has an absolute claim to accuracy. This applies particularly to the early estimates, which are derived from indirect and uncertain sources. However, it can perhaps be safely noted that:

(a) World population has had a tiny net secular rate of increase of roughly 0.04 or 0.05 per cent annually between the onset of settled agriculture and the time of Christ.

(b) The first thousand years after Christ were a period of near-stagnation in world and regional population growth, with likely losses in the populations of China, Southwestern Asia, and North Africa. All available

Table 1.   Estimates of world population by region, A.D. 0–1900
(millions)

Region[a]	Set	A.D. 0[b]	1000	1500	1750	1900
World Total	D	270-330	275-345	440-540	735-805	1650-1710
	C	256	280	427	731	1668
	B	255	254	460	770	1633
Northern Africa	D	10-15	5-10	6-12	10-15	53-55
	C	11	4	6	5	27
	B	14	9	9	10	43
Remainder of Africa	D	15-30	20-40	30-60	50-80	90-120
	C	12	46	79	95	95
	B	12	30	78	94	95
China	D	70-90	50-80	100-150	190-225	400-450
	C	73	60	100	207	500
	B	70	56	84	220	415
Indian Sub-Continent [c]	D	50-100	50-100	75-150	160-200	285-295
	C	70	70	79	100	283
	B	46	40	95	165	290
Southwestern Asia	D	25-45	20-30	20-30	25-35	40-45
	C	34	22	15	13	38
	B	49	34	23	27	38
Japan	D	1-2	3-8	15-20	29-30	44-45
	C	2	10	16	26	44
	B	2	4	10	26	45
Remainder of Asia excl. USSR	C	5	10	15	32	120
	B	5	19	33	61	115
	D	8-20	10-25	15-30	35-55	110-125
Middle & South America	D	6-15	20-50	30-60	13-18	71-78
	C	-	-	40	13	63
	B	8	14	34	15	75
Northern America	D	1-2	2-3	2-3	2-3	82-83
	C	-	-	1	2	81
	B	1	2	3	3	90
Europe excl. USSR	D	30-40	30-40	60-70	120-135	295-300
	C	37	32	62	102	284
	B	35	30	66	109	294
USSR	D	5-10	6-15	10-18	30-40	130-135
	C	8	12	12	34	127
	B	12	13	17	35	127
Oceania	D	1-2	1-2	1-2	2	6
	C	1	1	2	2	6
	B	1	1	3	3	6

Sources: J. D. Durand, "The modern expansion of world population", Proceedings of the American Philosophical Society, vol. III, No. 3., table 1 and appendix table A; World Population Prospects, 1988 (United Nations publication, Sales No. E.88.XIII.7).

Notes:
a/ D_1, D_2, D_3 are consecutively Durand's low, medium and high variants. CS – Carr–Saunders estimates, W – Willcox's estimates.
b/ Figures for 1950 are United Nations estimates as revised in 1988.
c/ Europe, USSR, Northern America, Japan, Australia and New Zealand.
d/ Asia excluding Japan, Africa, Latin America, Micronesia and Melanesia.

estimates show that the total world population hardly changed during this millennium.

(c) There was an upward turn in the growth curve around the year 1000 A.D. Between the years 1000 and 1750 the world population increased at an overall annual growth rate of about 0.13 or 0.14 per cent. The growth is known to have fluctuated during this period, the first three centuries of which witnessed expansion in the populations of China, Europe, and the USSR (see table 1). The losses of life caused by the Black Death and its sequel of plague epidemics in the fourteenth century caused a decline in the populations of Europe, North Africa, and Southwest Asia and other Asian regions.

Population growth in early modern times

There was another distinct upward turn in the growth curve at some point in the eighteenth century (possibly somewhat earlier in China), indicating the ascent that continued and gained momentum over the last two and a half centuries. This clear upturn took place not only in Europe (excluding the USSR), where the demographic expansion was associated with the beginnings of industrialization and modernization, but also in China, where such developments started much later, and in the USSR and East Europe, where they were minimal. Upturns also took place in the nineteenth century in the growth of the developing regions of North Africa, Southwest Asia and the Indian sub-continent, and Latin America. The lack of a clear association between the upturn and trends in industrialization and modernization provides one more indication of the need for a clearer understanding of the relationships between population growth and development factors.

Durand (1967) expressed the opinion that an explanation may be found in the economic and epidemiological repercussions of the European voyages and conquests that started in the fifteenth century. The strengthening of agriculture by the exchange of food plants was an important outcome. On the other hand, this contact had a negative epidemiological effect in some regions, including America, until growing natural resistance to the new diseases opened the way for an upturn of the population trend.

Here, again, there are two classical series of estimates for world and regional population during 1750-1900, namely, Carr-Saunders (1936) and Willcox (1940). 2/ Durand (1967) prepared a new set of estimates in which he made a critical evaluation of these two works and added the findings of new historical studies and newly available demographic statistics. His revised series is given in the form of low, medium, and high estimates. Like the United Nations population projection variants, the low and high variants are intended to indicate the plausible range of variation; accordingly, they differ from the indifference limits given in table 1.

These works made use of the increasingly available results of census counts and other official statistics. For several regions Durand used the early census figures as the "low" variant, due to the likely existence of underenumeration; for the "medium" and "high" variants he added "more or less arbitrary allowances for possible deficiencies in the census counts". Where firm statistical foundations were lacking, Durand used backward extrapolation from the earliest reliable benchmarks, with assumed rates of population growth appropriate to the circumstances and history of the area. Details of the estimation procedures are given in the sources, and a critical evaluation is available in the appendix to Durand's paper. The three series are shown here in table 2, in which United Nations estimates for 1950 as derived in the 1988 revision of the estimates and projections were added (United Nations, 1989).

There is no doubt that the population estimates during the eighteenth and part of the nineteenth centuries are still based on shaky grounds in most regions and that the early estimates can be considered as only rough approximations. However, the approximately 800 million people existing in the middle of the eighteenth century were increasing at a rate which, though quite modest by today's standards, was several times higher than the average rate experienced earlier. As table 3 shows, the rate of growth of the world population was stable or had a very slowly rising trend during 1750–1900, reaching a little over one half of 1 per cent towards the end of the nineteenth century.

It is necessary, however, to take a closer look at the regional patterns of growth during this period. The rate of growth of Europe, which was leading in industrialization, was not higher than that of the world in the second half of the eighteenth century, and during the nineteenth century the rate was only modestly higher in absolute terms, averaging less than 0.7 per cent. Due to immigration, much higher rates, averaging about 2.5 per cent through the nineteenth century, existed in North America, and to a smaller extent in Latin America. The latter was growing at perhaps 0.8–0.9 per cent annually during 1750–1850 and at 1.3 per cent in the second half of the nineteenth century. The area now occupied by the Soviet Union, which was far behind Europe in industrialization, had growth rates equal to or larger than those of Europe during 1750–1850 and much larger during 1850–1900 (table 3). China also appears to have experienced rapid population growth in the eighteenth century and equaled the European rate of 0.6 per cent during the first half of the nineteenth century.

On the other hand, Africa seems to have had hardly any expansion until the second half of the nineteenth century, when its population grew at about 0.4 per cent annually. The Indian sub-continent had somewhat higher, though still modest, rates. China's population estimates, which may well be deficient, do not seem to indicate any tangible increase during the second half of the nineteenth century.

It is thus clear that during 1750–1900 the rates of growth of the developed and the developing groups of countries, 3/ which are given in table 3, were influenced by several different regional trends. The rising trends of population growth in Europe, the area now occupied by the Soviet Union, and Northern America led to the clear difference between the rates of the two groups of countries during the nineteenth century.

Around the beginning of the present century the general picture of the growth curves began to take the shape with which we are familiar at present. The improvement in mortality conditions had an obvious impact on the growth rates of Africa, Asia, and (particularly) Latin America (table 3), all of which experienced considerable increases in their populations during

Table 2.   Estimates of world population by region, 1750–1950
(millions)

Region	Set[a]	1750	1800	1850	1900	1950[b]
World Total	D1-D3	629-961	813-1,125	1,128-1,402	1,550-1,762	
	D2	791	978	1,262	1,650	2,515
	CS	728	906	1,171	1,608	
	W	694	919	1,091	1,571	
Developed countries[c]	D1-D3	180-222	231-262	333-352	555-568	
	D2	201	247	343	562	832
Developing countries[d]	D1-D3	450-738	583-862	795-1,049	995-1,194	
	D2	590	731	919	1,088	1,683
Africa	D1-D3	60-153	69-142	81-145	115-154	
	D2	106	107	111	133	224
	CS	95	90	95	120	
	W	100	100	100	141	
Asia	D1-D3	408-595	524-721	711-893	853-1,006	
excl. USSR	D2	498	630	801	925	1,375
	CS	475	597	741	915	
	W	437	595	656	857	
Latin America	D1-D3	12-20	20-29	34-42	71-78	
	D2	16	24	38	74	165
	CS	11	19	33	63	
	W	10	23	33	63	
Northern America	D1-D3	2-3	6-7	26-26	82-82	
	D2	2	7	26	82	166
	CS	1	6	26	81	
	W	1	6	26	81	
Europe & USSR	D1-D3	146-187	193-223	274-293	423-436	
	D2	167	208	284	430	572
	CS	144	192	274	423	
	W	144	193	274	423	
Oceania	D1-D3	2-2	2-2	2-2	6-6	
	D2	2	2	2	6	13
	CS	2	2	2	6	
	W	2	2	2	6	

Sources: J. D. Durand, "The modern expansion of world population",
Proceedings of the American Philosophical Society, vol. III, No. 3.,
table 1 and appendix table A; World Population Prospects, 1988 (United
Nations publication, Sales No. E.88.XIII.7).

Notes:
a/ D_1, D_2, D_3 are consecutively Durand's low, medium and high
variants. CS – Carr-Saunders
estimates, W – Willcox's estimates.
b/ Figures for 1950 are United Nations estimates as revised in 1988.
c/ Europe, USSR, Northern America, Japan, Australia and New Zealand.
d/ Asia excluding Japan, Africa, Latin America, Micronesia and
Melanesia.

Table 3. Estimated average annual rates of growth for the world and
major regions, fifty-year Periods, 1750–1950
(per cent)

Region	1750-1800	1800-1850	1850-1900	1900-1950
World	0.42	0.51	0.54	0.84
Developed countries	0.41	0.66	0.99	0.78
Developing countries	0.43	0.46	0.34	0.87
Africa	0.01	0.07	0.37	1.04
Asia (excluding USSR)	0.47	0.48	0.29	0.79
Latin America	0.81	0.92	1.33	1.62
North America	2.51	2.62	2.30	1.41
Europe (excluding USSR)	0.39	0.63	0.71	0.57
USSR	0.58	0.61	1.13	0.59
Oceania	-	-	2.20	1.55

Source: Calculated from the "medium" estimates given in table 2.
Separate growth rates were calculated for Europe (excluding USSR) and the
USSR using the "medium" estimates given by Durand for 1750–1900 and the
United Nations for 1950.

1900–1950. In Europe, the Soviet Union, and Northern America, on the other hand, fertility decline more than offset the increases due to further mortality decline, and growth rates substantially declined during this period. As a consequence, the growth rates of the developing countries as a group showed an increasing trend in the first half of the twentieth century and a level already higher than that of the developed countries, while in the latter group these rates showed a declining trend.

The growth rate of the developed countries declined from 1.2 per cent in the 1920s to 0.8 per cent in the 1930s due to the economic depression; this rate further declined to 0.4 per cent in the 1940s due to impact of the Second World War. Indeed, the population of the Soviet Union declined from 195 million in 1940 to 180 million in 1950. As far as can be determined from available reliable estimates, Europe had the lowest rates of population growth during this period, namely 0.9, 0.7, and 0.3 per cent during the 1920s, 1930s and 1940s, respectively, while Latin America had the highest rates, which increased slowly from 1.8 per cent in the 1920s to 1.9 per cent in the 1930s and then more rapidly to 2.2 per cent in the 1940s. The developing countries as a group, with unreliable data in most cases, may have had an increase in their rate of population growth from about 1 per cent in the 1920s to 1.2 per cent in the 1930s and 1940s rates were derived from estimates given in United Nations (1966, table A3.6).

The second half of the twentieth century

Availability of estimates and projections has improved dramatically since the middle of the present century. Demographers prepared world, regional, and country estimates and projections of the population by basic characteristics, namely, age and sex, and then later by other characteristics, notably urban, rural, and city residence, labour force participation, and school enrolment. The United Nations took the lead in this work, with contributions made by the specialized agencies and others. This work started with a study entitled World Population Trends, 1920–1947 (United Nations, 1949), followed by a number of regional assessments (United Nations, 1954, 1956, 1959, and 1959a). These were followed by reports on the future growth of world population (United Nations, 1959b, 1966). The computerization of work on projections in the mid-1960s made it possible to prepare them on a country-by-country basis and in four variants for each country starting with the 1968 revision (United Nations, 1972). Since then, the estimates and projections have been revised more frequently, with the most recent revision carried out in 1988 using 1985 as the base year. In each revision since 1968, estimates going back to 1950 were prepared either by using available figures when these were deemed reliable or by projecting backward the population of the base year. The results of the median variant of this last revision are summarized in tables 4–9, on the basis of which the following discussion is developed. More data can be found in the source (United Nations, 1989).

The decade of the 1950s witnessed accelerated growth in all major areas. The acceleration in the developed countries, resulting in an average growth rate of 1.3 per cent, is characterized by a relatively high birth rate and a slowly declining death rate. This acceleration did not last very long, however, and already in the 1960s the growth rate of the developed countries

Table 4. Estimates and projections of total population and annual rate
of growth (medium variant), world and major areas, 1950–2025
(millions)

	1950	1965	1975	1985	1990	1995	2000	2025
	Estimates and projections of total population							
World	2,515	3,336	4,080	4,854	5,292	5,766	6,251	8,467
Developed countries	832	1,003	1,096	1,174	1,205	1,235	1,262	1,352
Developing countries	1,683	2,333	2,984	3,680	4,087	4,531	4,989	7,114
Africa	224	318	415	557	648	753	872	1,581
Asia	1,375	1,860	2,353	2,834	3,108	3,404	3,698	4,889
Latin America	165	250	323	404	448	494	540	760
Northern America	166	214	239	265	276	286	295	333
Europe	393	445	474	492	498	503	509	512
USSR	180	231	255	277	288	298	308	351
Oceania	13	18	21	25	26	28	158	39
	Annual rates of growth							
	1950–1955	1965–1970	1975–1980	1985–1990	1990–1995	1995–2000	2000–2005	2020–2025
World	1.80	2.06	1.74	1.73	1.71	1.62	1.47	0.98
Developed countries	1.28	0.91	0.73	0.53	0.48	0.45	0.38	0.18
Developing countries	2.05	2.54	2.10	2.10	2.06	1.92	1.74	1.13
Developing countries (excluding China)	2.13	2.50	2.39	2.38	2.33	2.20	2.04	1.32
Africa	2.18	2.63	2.95	3.00	3.01	2.95	2.84	1.85
Asia	1.90	2.44	1.86	1.85	1.82	1.66	1.44	0.87
Latin America	2.74	2.60	2.28	2.09	1.94	1.78	1.63	1.12
Northern America	1.80	1.13	1.06	0.82	0.71	0.62	0.56	0.35
Europe	0.79	0.67	0.45	0.22	0.22	0.21	0.13	-0.06
USSR	1.71	1.01	0.82	0.78	0.68	0.64	0.61	0.47
Oceania	2.25	1.97	1.51	1.44	1.34	1.26	1.18	0.85

Source: World Population Prospects, 1988 (United Nations publication,
Sales No. E.88.XIII.7), pp. 74–75, table 1.

Table 5. Crude birth and death rates world and major areas,
1950-2025, medium variant crude birth rates

	1950-1955	1965-1970	1975-1980	1985-1990	1990-1995	1995-2000	2000-2005	2020-2025
				Crude birth rates				
World	37.4	33.9	28.4	27.1	26.3	24.8	22.9	17.4
Developed countries	22.6	17.9	15.6	14.6	14.0	13.5	13.1	11.9
Developing countries	44.6	40.4	32.9	30.9	29.8	27.7	25.3	18.5
Developing countries (excluding China)	45.1	42.1	38.0	35.0	33.5	31.2	28.8	20.1
Africa	48.9	47.7	46.4	44.7	43.3	41.4	39.0	25.5
Asia	42.9	38.4	29.7	27.6	26.7	24.5	21.8	16.0
Latin America	42.5	37.9	32.4	29.1	27.0	24.9	23.2	18.5
Northern America	24.6	18.0	15.1	15.0	14.0	13.1	12.6	11.8
Europe	19.8	17.7	14.4	13.0	12.8	12.4	11.9	10.9
USSR	26.3	17.9	18.3	18.4	16.7	15.9	15.7	14.1
Oceania	27.6	24.5	21.3	20.1	19.1	18.4	17.6	14.9
				Crude death rates				
World	19.7	13.3	11.1	9.9	9.3	8.7	8.3	7.7
Developed countries	10.1	9.2	9.4	9.8	9.6	9.5	9.7	10.6
Developing countries	24.3	15.1	11.7	9.9	9.2	8.5	7.9	7.1
Developing countries (excluding China)	24.0	16.9	13.6	11.2	10.1	9.1	8.3	6.8
Africa	27.0	21.1	17.6	14.9	13.4	12.0	10.7	7.0
Asia	24.1	14.1	10.7	9.1	8.5	7.9	7.5	7.3
Latin America	15.3	10.9	8.7	7.5	7.0	6.7	6.6	7.0
Northern America	9.4	9.3	8.5	8.6	8.7	8.7	8.8	9.9
Europe	11.0	10.4	10.4	10.7	10.6	10.3	10.6	11.5
USSR	9.2	7.8	10.0	10.6	9.9	9.5	9.6	9.4
Oceania	12.4	10.3	8.8	8.0	8.0	7.9	7.8	8.0

Source: World Population Prospects, 1988 (United Nations publication,
Sales No. E.88.XIII.7), pp. 118-125, tables 6 and 9, and pp. 134-141.

Table 6. Total fertility rates and life expectancy at birth
world and major areas, 1950-2025, medium variant

	1950-1955	1965-1970	1975-1980	1985-1990	1990-1995	1995-2000	2000-2005	2020-2025
				Total fertility rates				
World	5.00	4.88	3.84	3.44	3.29	3.13	2.96	2.27
Developed countries	2.84	2.44	2.03	1.90	1.89	1.90	1.91	1.94
Developing countries	6.18	5.99	4.54	3.92	3.69	3.45	3.21	2.33
Developing countries (excluding China)	6.15	5.99	5.25	4.61	4.35	4.02	3.68	2.45
Africa	6.61	6.71	6.52	6.23	6.00	5.66	5.25	3.05
Asia	5.92	5.67	4.06	3.45	3.23	2.99	2.76	2.07
Latin America	5.86	5.00	4.38	3.61	3.30	3.04	2.84	2.39
Northern America	3.47	2.54	1.91	1.81	1.83	1.86	1.88	1.94
Europe	2.59	2.50	1.98	1.74	1.72	1.75	1.78	1.86
USSR	2.82	2.42	2.34	2.38	2.30	2.25	2.20	2.10
Oceania	3.83	3.54	2.85	2.57	2.47	2.43	2.41	2.13
				Life expectancy at birth				
World	45.90	54.90	58.10	61.50	63.00	64.50	65.90	71.30
Developed countries	65.70	70.30	71.70	73.40	74.50	75.40	76.20	78.70
Developing countries	41.00	52.10	55.80	59.70	61.50	63.10	64.60	70.40
Developing countries (excluding China)	41.20	49.10	53.40	57.50	59.40	61.30	63.10	69.30
Africa	38.00	44.10	48.10	51.90	53.80	55.70	57.60	65.20
Asia	41.10	53.30	57.50	61.70	63.60	65.50	67.10	72.80
Latin America	51.20	58.70	62.80	66.00	67.50	68.70	69.80	72.80
Northern America	69.00	70.50	73.30	75.50	76.30	77.00	77.70	79.70
Europe	65.30	70.60	72.30	74.20	75.10	75.90	76.60	79.10
USSR	64.10	69.30	67.90	69.50	70.90	72.10	73.20	76.70
Oceania	60.80	64.20	66.30	68.80	69.80	70.80	71.70	75.60

Source: World Population Prospects, 1988 (United Nations publication, Sales No. E.88.XIII.7), pp. 166-189, table 15.

Table 7. Aging indicators for the World and Major Areas, 1950–2025

Area	Median age				Per cent aged 65 +			
	1950	1975	2000	2025	1950	1975	2000	2025
World	23.4	21.9	26.0	31.1	5.1	5.7	6.8	9.7
Developed countries	28.2	30.4	36.3	40.7	7.6	10.7	13.7	18.9
Developing countries	21.2	19.3	23.8	29.7	3.8	3.8	5.0	8.0
Africa	18.7	17.5	17.7	22.6	3.3	3.1	3.1	4.1
Asia	21.8	20.1	25.8	32.5	4.0	4.1	5.8	9.6
Latin America	19.7	19.1	24.1	30.2	3.3	4.1	5.3	8.5
Northern America	30.0	28.6	36.5	40.8	8.1	10.3	12.8	19.7
Europe	30.5	32.4	37.5	42.9	8.7	12.3	14.9	20.1
USSR	24.7	25.7	33.0	36.4	6.1	9.5	11.7	14.8
Oceania	27.9	29.1	30.5	34.5	7.5	7.5	9.5	13.4

Source: World Population Prospects, 1988 (United Nations publication, Sales No. E.88.XIII.7), pp. 200–554, table 17–A.

Table 8.   Total population of the world and major areas three variants,
            in 2025, 2050, 2075 and 2100
                              (Millions)

Area	Variant	2025	2050	2075	2100
World	M	8125	9513	10097	10185
	G	9135	11690	13642	14927
	D	7168	7667	7562	7247
Developed countries	M	1377	1402	1419	1421
	G	1488	1625	1758	1858
	D	1251	1190	1137	1102
Developing countries	M	6818	8111	8677	8764
	G	7647	10065	11884	13069
	D	5917	6477	6425	6145
Africa	M	1542	2166	2507	2591
	G	1850	2998	3966	4575
	D	1109	1341	1385	1333
East Asia	M	1712	1765	1762	1763
	G	1825	1958	2038	2123
	D	1610	1594	1525	1465
South Asia	M	2819	3198	3306	3284
	G	3116	3814	4227	4491
	D	2548	2772	2724	2596
Latin America	M	865	1096	1215	1238
	G	984	1424	1787	2019
	D	761	868	883	841
Northern America	M	344	364	378	382
	G	366	409	449	477
	D	301	291	279	266
Europe	M	522	509	503	504
	G	572	603	640	674
	D	476	433	407	404
USSR	M	355	375	384	381
	G	381	436	481	511
	D	332	336	328	311
Oceania	M	36	40	43	42
	G	40	48	53	56
	D	32	33	32	30

Source: "Long-range global population projections as assessed in
1980", Population Bulletin, No. 14, United Nations publication, Sales
No. E.82.XIII.6), pp. 22-23, table 4.

Table 9.   Projected annual rate of growth, crude birth rate and crude
           death rate, world and major areas, medium variant 2025--2105

Major areas	2025-2030	2050-2055	2075-2080	2100-2105
	Annual rate of growth (per cent)			
World	0.82	0.36	0.10	-0.03
Developed countries	0.15	0.07	0.02	-0.01
Developing countries	0.96	0.41	0.11	-0.03
Africa	1.70	0.84	0.31	-0.03
East Asia	0.33	-0.03	-0.04	0.01
South Asia	0.77	0.30	0.01	-0.04
Latin America	1.25	0.52	0.20	-0.06
Northern America	0.32	0.22	0.06	0.03
Europe	-0.08	-0.08	-0.00	0.01
USSR	0.38	0.16	-0.00	-0.06
Oceania	0.64	0.19	0.07	0.00
	Crude birth rate			
World	16.9	13.8	13.0	12.9
Developed countries	13.3	13.0	12.9	13.0
Developing countries	17.6	14.0	13.0	12.9
Africa	23.2	15.2	13.2	12.8
East Asia	13.7	12.9	12.8	12.9
South Asia	16.0	13.8	13.0	12.9
Latin America	19.9	13.8	12.8	12.8
Northern America	13.4	13.2	13.1	13.0
Europe	12.5	12.8	13.0	13.0
USSR	14.5	13.0	12.7	12.9
Oceania	14.9	13.2	13.0	13.0
	Crude death rate			
World	8.7	10.3	12.0	13.1
Developed countries	12.2	12.6	12.8	13.0
Developing countries	8.0	9.9	11.8	13.2
Africa	6.2	6.8	10.2	13.1
East Asia	10.4	13.1	13.2	12.8
South Asia	8.3	10.8	12.8	13.3
Latin America	7.1	8.5	10.8	13.4
Northern America	11.3	12.1	12.5	12.8
Europe	13.3	13.7	13.0	12.9
USSR	10.7	11.4	12.7	13.5
Oceania	9.6	11.4	12.3	13.0

Source: "Long-range global population projections, as assessed
in 1980", Population Bulletin, No. 14 (United Nations publication,
Sales No. E.82.XIII.6), p. 23, table 5.

was declining (1.2 per cent during 1960-1965 and 0.9 per cent during 1965-1970) as the result of declining birth rates and increasing death rates due to changes in the age structure of their populations. This trend has continued since then. In the developing countries, on the other hand, the acceleration continued through the 1960s (2.1 per cent in 1950-1955 and 2.5 per cent in 1965-1970) as the consequence of a faster decline in the death rate than in the birth rate. Population growth has slowed since then, as the fertility decline has become more effective. As a result of these different trends in the two groups of countries, the rate of growth of the world population escalated until it peaked to about 2.1 per cent in the second half of the 1960s; it has been declining since then, reaching about 1.7 per cent in the 1980s. The world population, which stood at about 2,500 million in 1950, reached about 5,100 million in 1988.

Thus, two different situations existing in industrialized and developing countries underlie the global trends and patterns. In 1950, the former had one third of the world population, which was growing at about 1.3 per cent annually, while the latter's rate of growth was 50 per cent higher. By 1985, the share of the industrialized countries declined to one quarter and their population was growing at only 0.5 per cent, while the third world's rate of growth, although back to its 1950 level after peaking in the late 1960s, was four times as high as that of the industrialized countries.

The patterns of growth in Latin America and Asia in the second half of the twentieth century are similar. Both areas experienced accelerating growth that peaked in the 1960s, after which the rate of growth declined to about 2.1 per cent in Latin America and 1.9 per cent in Asia in 1985 (2.2 per cent in Asia excluding China and 1.3 per cent in China). Africa is the only major area maintaining an escalating growth rate, estimated to be 3.0 per cent at present. This latter pattern can be seen in Eastern, Central, and Western Africa but not in North Africa, where some countries, notably Tunisia, have experienced a recent decline in their growth rate.

Changes in fertility since mid-century can be presented by the trends of the total fertility rate (TFR). In the developed countries there was very little change in the 1950s, during which time the TFR remained virtually constant at 2.8 births per woman. A decline started by the end of the decade and continued monotonically, bringing the TFR down from 2.7 in 1960-1965 to 1.9 in 1985-1990, with a decline of 30 per cent over this 25-year period. In the developing countries, on the other hand, the sustained decline started in the second half of the 1960s when the TFR was 6.0 and reached 3.9 in 1985-1990, thus declining by about 35 per cent over this period. It should be noted that about 40 per cent of this decline was caused by trends in China alone and 60 per cent by those in the rest of the developing countries.

Mortality decline since the middle of the century has added almost 19 years to the life expectancy at birth in the third world (from 41 years in 1950-1955 to a little under 60 years in 1985-1990). Two and a half of these 19 years were brought about by the faster mortality decline in China. During the same period mortality decline in the developed countries, though naturally much slower, has added eight years to the life expectancy at birth, bringing it to over 73 years.

Apart from sub-Saharan Africa and Western Asia, the general picture of fertility is one of sustained decline, although this decline is faster in some regions than in others. Rather dramatic declines that started in the mid-1960s in several East and Southeast Asian countries have brought fertility down to near or even below replacement. China's fertility decline from a TFR of 6.0 to 2.4 over the past 20 years is the most significant, but highly impressive declines to below-replacement levels took place in a number of other countries, including the Republic of Korea; the decline in Thailand is also substantial. The decline of the Indonesian TFR to about 3.3 at present should be highlighted in view of the fact that it is the largest Muslim country. Available estimates indicate that fertility declined by 25 per cent in India over the past 20 years, and in Bangladesh the estimates indicate a limited decline, though the current level is still quite high. Over the same period total fertility has declined from 5 to 3 in the Caribbean, with some countries, notably Cuba, reaching below-replacement levels. In Northern Africa, some decline is observed in Morocco, Algeria, Egypt, and particularly Tunisia, where the current TFR level is nearly 4 live births per woman.

On the other hand, available estimates of the TFR do not show decline in Eastern, Middle, and Southern Africa (excluding South Africa). Furthermore, there is evidence that fertility may have even increased in Kenya and some other countries. In Arab Western Asia, while considerable decline is observed in such small countries as Bahrain, Kuwait, Lebanon, and the United Arab Emirates, little change is reported in Saudi Arabia, Oman, or Yemen. There is likewise little evidence of a decline in Pakistan in South Asia.

Latin America as a whole has gained almost 15 years of life expectancy at birth over the past 35 years and reached a life expectancy of 66 years, which is the highest among major developing areas, although still several years below that of the developed countries. It should be noted in this regard that while several small countries in the Caribbean have actually reached developed-country mortality levels and the countries of Temperate South America are not far from this level, life expectancy is still below 55 in Haiti and Bolivia. Even more impressive is the progress in China, where life expectancy increased from 40.8 years in 1950-1955 to 69.4 years in 1985-1990, a level close to that of the advanced countries. Elsewhere in Asia, as in Latin America, while developed-country levels have been reached or approached in small Gulf countries and in Hong Kong, Singapore, and Sri Lanka, levels near 50 years are still observed in Yemen, Democratic Yemen, Nepal, Bhutan, and Afghanistan. Sub-Saharan Africa still has the lowest subregional levels despite a gain of 13 or 14 years in life expectancy since mid-century. The averages in Eastern, Middle, and Western Africa are still about 50 years, with levels in the 40-45 years range estimated for Ethiopia, Somalia, Angola, Central African Republic, and Chad.

The year 2000 is so close to the base year of the 1988 revision of the United Nations projections that the error due to assumptions about demographic trends in the 1990s is probably insubstantial. The medium variant estimates that at the end of this century the world population will reach 6,250 million. By this time the global rate of population growth will probably have declined to about 1.5 per cent annually as a result of a continuing decline in fertility which will bring the TFR down to about 3.0 per cent   It is also expected that by the turn of the century life expectancy will have risen to about 65 years.

Although the advanced countries will still have during the 1990s a growth rate a little below one half of 1 per cent, their share of the world population will decline from one fourth in 1985 to one fifth in 2000 due to the expected continuation of their below-replacement fertility level of about 1.9 per cent. On the other hand, the TFR of the developing countries is expected to continue its slow decline to about 3.5 per cent, and the growth rate would similarly decline to about 1.8 per cent. The influence of the expected Chinese demographic trends on these figures can be seen from the corresponding figures for the developing countries (excluding China), namely, a TFR of about 4.0 per cent and a growth rate about 2.1 per cent. Mortality is also expected to continue its decline in the developing countries, reaching a life expectancy level of a little under 64 years at the turn of the century, which is still 12 years below that of the industrialized countries.

Variations in the demographic situation in the year 2000 among the major areas are perhaps what one would expect in the light of current trends: a TFR of about 5.5 per cent in Africa compared with 2.9 per cent in Asia and Latin America and 1.8 per cent in Europe and a growth rate of 2.9 per cent in Africa compared with 1.6 per cent or 1.7 per cent in Asia and Latin America and less than 0.2 per cent in Europe. A gain of 5 years of life expectancy in Africa would still leave the mortality level almost 10 years behind Asia and almost 13 years behind Latin America.

The aging phenomenon

Aging is a fairly recent phenomenon in the world's demographic history, arising as a population moves along the path of demographic transition. The main influencing demographic factor has been fertility, whose decline reduces the proportion of the young and consequently increase the proportion of the old. In 1950, the population of the developed countries was already older than that of the developing countries, whose median ages were 28.2 and 21.2 years respectively. The proportion of the population aged 65 and over was also 7.6 per cent in the former, which is twice the corresponding proportion in the latter (table 7). The developed countries continued their aging trend as both fertility and mortality continued to decline, reaching a present median age of about 33.0 years and a percentage of about 12 aged 65 and over; by 2025 the median age may be 40 years and the proportion aged 65 and over may reach 20 per cent. The population of the developing countries, on the other hand, first became younger before slowly starting its aging trend. The juvenation took place approximately between 1950 and 1970, with the median age declining by over two years as a consequence of a rapid mortality decline that was most effective among infants and children. Fertility decline then began to reduce the proportion of children and initiate the aging process, while mortality, which had already attained more moderate levels, was such that its further decline was less concentrated in young ages. The median age is currently a little above its 1950 level and is expected to be slightly below 24 years at the turn of the century and to gain momentum thereafter. The percentage aged 65 and over remained constant or declined slightly up to 1970, is currently a little over 4.0, is expected to be about 5.0 in 2000, and should increase more rapidly in the first quarter of the next century.

While the aging gap between the industrialized countries and the third world is substantial, there are some developing countries where this gap is narrowing. In Eastern Asia, the median age was less than 21 years in 1970, exceeds 26 years at present, and is expected to exceed 30 years by the turn of the century; soon afterward, this region will attain the median age prevalent in developed countries. Similarly the population aged 65 and over, which was only 5 per cent of the total population as recently as 1980, may well be about 14 per cent in 2025. A comparison between these figures and those calculated for Africa would show the extent of the demographic gap between developing countries as a result of high fertility and relatively high mortality. The median age in Africa is at present about nine years below that of Eastern Asia and has been declining slightly but consistently for a fairly long time; although it may soon start increasing slowly due to fertility and infant and child mortality decline, even by the end of the first quarter of the twenty-first century this median age may not be much higher than the current median age for the third world as a whole. Barely 3 per cent of the African population is aged 65 and above, and it may take to 2020 or 2025 before this percentage increases to four.

The twenty-first century

It must be emphasized that this exploratory look at the prospects for the coming century is based on long-range projections prepared in 1981 by the Population Division as an extension of the 1978 revision of the United Nations projections (United Nations, 1982) and not on the latest 1988 revision whose results were discussed above. In the earlier revision, the age-sex country projections were prepared as usual in three variants extending up to 2025. Projections for the rest of the twenty-first century were then prepared for the eight major areas of the world in the usual medium, high, and low variants as well as in two additional "growth" and "decline" variants. In the usual three variants, fertility is assumed to remain constant after reaching the replacement level of TFR = 2.1, or a net reproduction rate equal to unity to be exact. Since it is highly unlikely that the population would remain stationary for a long time after it had stabilized, the "growth" and "decline" variants were introduced, as fertility increases or decreases very slowly after it stabilizes.

The fertility assumptions are such that its decline in areas with above-replacement fertility would continue at a speed determined by past demographic trends, expected social and economic progress, ongoing population policies, and prevailing public attitudes towards population issues. It was assumed on the basis of the experience of countries that currently have below-replacement fertility levels that the momentum of decline will not suddenly cease as the replacement level is reached but will continue to the rather arbitrary level of TFR = 1.84. Fertility would then increase again to the replacement level. For the areas in which fertility is currently below replacement, it was assumed in this exercise to increase gradually until it reaches replacement. The assumptions of the "growth" and "decline" variants are the same as those of the high and low variants except that the very small increase in the "growth" variant is achieved by keeping the net reproduction rate constant at 1.05 rather than at 1.00; similarly in the "decline" variant, fertility, as it increases from the minimum level, remains constant at a net reproduction level of 0.95. Only one mortality assumption is employed for each major area after 2025. Expectation of life was assumed in these long-range projections to increase to 75 years for males and 80 years for females. The Coale-Demeny model life tables were used in making the projections, with model North used for Africa and West for all other areas. Limited declining and eventually terminating interregional migration was assumed, but the impact on totals and trends is of little significance.

One need not emphasize the uncertainties encountered in this necessary exercise; indeed, the results convey this message when for the year 2100 the "growth" or highest variant gives a global estimate of 14.9 billion and the "decline" or lowest variant gives only 7.2 billion - a range as large as the lowest estimate itself. The numerically convenient net reproduction rate of unity is usually assumed as the ultimate reproductive level, although it is perhaps impractical to maintain this level for any length of time. The same objection arises about any other value like 1.05 or 0.95 if it is maintained for a long time. A more plausible anticipated trend would perhaps be one that has limited secular fluctuations combined with more minor oscillations, but the obvious difficulty is how to make assumptions about the parameters of such a trend. There may be reason to expect on the basis of trends in technological progress that there will be larger gains in life expectancy in the course of the coming century than assumed by the projections, but there is little basis at present for quantifying this expectation. It looks as though international migration is presently dwindling, but it is unclear whether there might later be a change in demand for labour force caused by substantial aging in some regions. We should also keep in mind that no allowance is made for possible massive famines, global wars, or other catastrophes.

The tentative and illustrative nature of the projections is therefore obvious. The results are summarized in tables 8 through 10. It should be pointed out that the medium-variant data for 2025 in table 8 are somewhat different from those given in table 4 because the latter are the results of the most recent (1988) revision, while those given in table 8 are the results of the 1978 revision.

According to the medium variant, world population would stabilize by the end of the twenty-first century, with a total of 10.2 billion persons. After reaching 9.5 billion at mid-century, the total population shows a clear asymptotic approach to stabilization, reaching 10.1 billion in 2075. The annual growth rate would decline from less than 0.4 per cent at mid-century to 0.1 at the end of the third quarter and to 0.0 at the end of the century. Both the crude birth and death rates would stabilize at about 13 per thousand. The high value of the death rate (relative to its present value) is, of course, due to the aging of the population. In fact it is to be expected that the crude death rate will be increasing throughout the twenty-first century despite the assumed mortality decline.

Only a slight total population increase is expected to occur in the developed countries, which are assumed to regain replacement level early in the coming century; their total population would increase only by 12 per cent during the entire century and only by 3 per cent (44 million) between 2025 and 2100 (table 8). Their share of the world population, which is expected to be

Table 10. Projected median age and proportion aged 65+ in the twenty first century in the world and major areas, as assessed in 1980

Major area	Median age				Proportion 65+ (per cent)			
	2025	2050	2075	2100	2025	2050	2075	2100
World	30.8	35.7	39.1	39.5	9.3	13.2	17.1	19.0
Developed countries	38.2	38.8	39.3	39.1	16.7	17.8	18.1	18.4
Developing countries	29.5	35.2	39.1	39.6	7.8	12.5	17.0	19.1
Africa	22.8	31.0	38.2	40.3	4.3	8.0	15.1	19.8
East Asia	37.7	39.6	39.3	39.1	13.6	18.2	18.7	18.4
South Asia	30.4	37.3	39.9	39.4	6.9	13.1	18.0	18.9
Latin America	27.4	33.0	38.7	39.6	7.2	10.8	15.6	19.1
Northern America	37.5	38.2	38.7	38.9	15.9	17.1	17.7	18.0
Europe	40.4	39.6	39.1	39.1	18.2	19.2	18.3	18.2
USSR	35.2	37.9	40.1	39.4	14.4	16.0	18.1	19.1
Oceania	34.0	37.1	39.0	39.0	12.5	15.5	17.4	18.4

Source: "Long-range global population projections, as assessed in 1980", Population Bulletin, No. 14 (United Nations publication, Sales No. E.82.XIII.6), pp. 25-26, table 6.

one fifth in 2000, would decline to one sixth in 2025 and to less than one seventh in the last quarter of the century. The developing countries, on the other hand, would still be increasing at an annual rate of 1 per cent in 1925 and 0.4 per cent at mid-century even though the median variant assumes that the net reproduction rate would reach 1.0 in the year 2035 and remain constant thereafter. Their crude birth rate, still exceeding 18 per thousand in 2025, would rapidly approach the stable level of 13 per thousand in the third quarter of the century. The death rate, reaching a minimum of about 7 per thousand early in the second quarter, would gradually ascend with aging until it reached the stable value of 13 per thousand around the end of the century (table 9).

With the different tempos of development envisaged for the early part of the century, different demographic situations are to be expected in the major developing areas in the first half of the century, followed by gradual convergence to stabilization. At one end would be Africa, whose declining birth rate would still be about 24 per thousand by the end of the first quarter and, though the net reproduction rate would reach unity in 2045, the birth rate would still be a little higher than that of other areas for some years beyond mid-century. The continent's death rate, which may reach the minimum value of 6 per thousand early in the second quarter, would start a slow increase thereafter, but would still have the lowest values of about 7 per thousand at mid-century and about 10 per thousand by the end of the third quarter. As may well be expected, Africa would maintain the highest growth rate almost throughout the century. Even at mid-century, Africa's projected annual rate of growth of over 0.8 per cent equals that expected for the developing countries as a whole at the beginning of the century.

At the other end of the spectrum is East Asia, which may reach replacement level in the 1990s. Its rapidly declining fertility is expected to bring the birth rate down to near stabilization level early in the second quarter of the coming century, and its relatively early aging would cause the death rate to increase in the first half of the century, after which the death rate would stabilize. Its rapidly declining growth rate would be almost nil (0.3 per cent) by the end of the first quarter and nil from mid-century onwards.

As may be expected, the aging process would continue through the first half of the twenty-first century, albeit very slowly in the currently developed countries. By mid-century, the difference in the median age between developed and developing countries is expected to have narrowed to less than four years, and the aged population (65 and over) may have reached 12.5 in the latter as against almost 18 in the former (table 10). Evidently, while the bulk of the transition is being completed within the first half of the century, Africa's population will remain the youngest and East Asia's the oldest among the major developing areas of today. By 2050, East Asia's population will be as old as that of Europe, while the gap in median age between Africa and East Asia may have narrowed to less than nine years. However, all gaps are expected to have all but vanished by 2075.

Concluding remarks

It would not be difficult to criticize the available estimates of population in the remote past: after all, many of them are based on shaky estimates of inhabited areas and their density or of cultivated land and number of persons that the unit can support. Even later, when taxes were levied and records of such taxes were kept, one could easily question the plausibility, at least in some cases, of using the total revenue and a per capita average to derive population estimates. When censuses were used in more recent times to arrive at population figures, these censuses had their own problems of coverage, and it was only quite recently that all countries finally had at least one census taken.

However, assuming that the historical figures given here are simply orders of magnitude, it is easy to see that the historical secular trend of world population was one that reflected a very limited growth over time, until about the middle of the eighteenth century. World population growth then started escalating for the world as a whole, albeit still moderately by current standards. In fact, it was sometime near the turn of the nineteenth century that human numbers reached their first billion, after centuries of staggering against disease, epidemics, famines, and wars, during which time there was little regard for population other than as a body of taxpayers and labourers. The second billion was accumulated much faster, in about 120 years.

What brought about the upturn in demographic growth about two and a half centuries ago? Was it due to access to more food or a better ability to deal with disease and control epidemics, or, more generally and vaguely stated, social and economic progress? The term "industrialization and modernization" is also often used in this regard. It is true that this term applied in Europe, but it is also true that acceleration of the tempo of population took place about the same time in the USSR, where little development was under way and also, perhaps even earlier, in China, where no tangible change towards industrialization and modernization was under way at that time. Even within Europe, the fact that declines in fertility and mortality differed in their relative dates of commencement in each country naturally broadens the package of possible specific factors behind the initiation of demographic transition. Needless to say, this widely discussed situation, together with the transition currently under way in developing countries, clearly demonstrates the need for better understanding of the relations between population and development, a need that has gained wider and more emphatic expression during the last two decades.

The third billion was accumulated in only 35 years, i.e., by 1960, when developing countries with little modernization and industrialization dominated demographic events. Indeed, interpretation of the transition experienced by developed countries meant that a period of rapid growth in the third world was to be expected, since mortality was generally easier to reduce than fertility. While this interpretation was quite valid, the decline of mortality was much faster than could have been foreseen from the experience of the industrialized world. Hence, there was an urgent need for population policies aimed at closing the gap between the fall in the death rate and the potential fall in the birth rate anticipated as a phase of the transitional experience, particularly since the decline in mortality was much faster than could have been anticipated on the basis of past experience. International concern in this regard found wide and often anxious expression in the second half of the 1960s as well as in the 1970s for well-known economic, social, and political reasons. This concern was justified as demographic statistics showed that the fourth billion was attained by 1975 in just 15 years and that 85 per cent of the increase occurred in the developing world.

Many developing countries subsequently experienced substantial decline in fertility even with modest or limited degrees of modernization. Though transition theory does not enable demographers to predict the timing and tempo of fertility transition, it is by now clear that substantial decline is under way in such large countries as China, India, Indonesia, Brazil, and Mexico and also in most of Latin America and in several of the smaller countries of East- and South-East Asia. Naturally, the growth potential is still considerable due to the young age structure prevalent in developing countries; indeed, the fifth billion was reached in 1987, or in 12 years, and the sixth is expected to be attained in just 11 years. The United Nations figures show that although the growth rate of developing countries may decline significantly in the 1990s, the total annual increase in world population is not expected to decline before the turn of the century. It is true that fertility transition is still under way and that it probably will take until the end of the first quarter of the coming century before the fertility level in developing countries as a whole is not far above replacement. Nevertheless, it is probably correct to say that the disquieting situation existing in the 1970s is significantly different as perceived at present.

Long-range projection through the twenty-first century is more than an intellectual endeavour. A baby born today is expected to live through the middle of that century, and some of the children of this baby will survive to century's end. Planning for these and subsequent generations is clearly a necessary exercise, and planning for the first is even imminent. However, as the authors of the above discussed long-range projections indicate, preparing these projections is a risky task that faces several imponderables, particularly regarding the plausible assumptions to be made for the second half of the century.

Optimism requires that we forget about catastrophes altogether. The ceiling of attainable life expectancy, including the one used above, is continually transcended, a fact that raises a certain degree of uncertainty about the exact future course and pattern of mortality decline. Is it really safe to assume that interregional migration, at least movement among the major areas discussed here, is terminating, or is it possible that economic, demographic, and political factors will revitalize migratory trends, particularly in the existence of differential aging? These factors may well have only a limited impact on future demographic trends regardless of the techniques applied. The influencing assumptions in the long-range projection process, at least as far as developing countries are concerned, remain those concerning future fertility trends. A commonly used approach is to assume that fertility will decline to replacement level, either by a certain assumed date or in accordance with an assumed pattern of decline. Stabilization thereafter is usually assumed not just for convenience but obviously because neither an increasing nor a declining trend can be maintained indefinitely. Nevertheless, it seems difficult to envisage at present the feasibility of maintaining an exact replacement level of reproduction on a largely voluntary basis. Perhaps it would be more plausible, therefore, to assume fluctuations around replacement level. The United Nations long-range projections incorporate this idea. Further elaboration in this direction may well be worthwhile.

Assuming that the medium assumptions will turn out to be true, perhaps one can say that in a sense it is auspicious to see that transition will finally be completed, in the sense of reaching replacement level for the first time, by 2035 in the third world as a whole. Even in Africa, where fertility decline is assumed to be lagging behind other major areas, the transition would be completed before the middle of the century. On the other hand, still in the realm of the medium assumption, one can only invite the attention of analysts to the economic, social, and policy implications of the figures reproduced in tables 8 through 10, particularly the potential population increase in certain regions of the world after the replacement level is reached. A leading, though most dramatic, question concerns what Africa needs in order to accommodate population increases from 650 million today to 1.5 billion in 2025, 2 billion in mid-century, and 2.5 billion in 2075.

Notes

1/ A range of 5-10 million for the period 7000-6000 B. C. is given in United Nations (1973), p. 10, table II.1, and in Ohlin (1965).

2/ In fact, Carr-Saunders estimates are a revision of estimates prepared by Willcox in 1929. Willcox then revised some of his earlier estimates.

3/ Developing countries are those in Africa, Latin America, Asia (excluding Japan), Micronesia, and Melanesia. Developed countries are those in Europe, Soviet Union, North America, Japan, Australia, and New Zealand.

References

Biraben, Jean–Noël (1979). Essai sur l'evolution du nombre des hommes. Population, vol. 34, No. 1, pp. 13–24.

Carr–Saunders, A. M. (1936). World Population: Past Growth and Present Trends. Oxford: Norwood Editions.

Clark, Colin (1968). Population Growth and Land Use, 2nd ed. New York: St. Martin's Press.

Durand, J. D. (1967). The modern expansion of world population. Proceedings of the American Philosophical Society, vol. 111, No. 3, pp. 136–159.

_____ (1974). Historical estimates of world population: an evaluation. Analytical and Technical Reports, No. 10. Philadelphia: Population Studies Center, University of Pennsylvania.

_____ (1977). Historical estimates of world population: an evaluation. Population and Development Review, vol. 3, No. 3, pp. 253–296.

Ohlin, G. (1965). Historical outline of world population growth. Background paper presented to the World Population Conference, Belgrade, 30 August–10 September.

United Nations (1949). World Population Trends, 1920–1947. Sales 1949.XIII.3.

_____ (1954). Future Population Estimates by Sex and Age. Report I: The Population of Central America, 1950–1980. Sales No. 1954.XIII.3.

_____ (1956). Future Population Estimates by Sex and Age. Report II: The Population of South America, 1950–1980. Sales No. 56.XIII.2.

_____ (1959). Future Population Estimates by Sex and Age. Report III: The Population of South–East Asia, 1950–1980. Sales No. 59.XIII.2.

_____ (1959a). Future Population Estimates by Sex and Age. Report IV: The Population of Asia and the Far East, 1950–1980. Sales No. 59.XIII.3.

_____ (1959b). The Future Growth of World Population. Sales No. 59.XIII.2.

_____ (1966) World Population Prospects as Assessed in 1963. Sales No. 66.XIII.2.

_____ (1971). The Determinants and Consequences of Population Trends, vol. 1. Sales No. E.71.XIII.5.

_____ (1972). <u>World Population Prospects as Assessed in 1968</u>. Sales No. 72.XIII.4.

_____ (1982). Long-range global population projections, as assessed in 1980. <u>Population Bulletin</u>, No. 14. Sales No. E.82.XIII.6.

_____ (1988). <u>World Population Prospects, 1988</u>. Sales No. E.88.XIII.7.

Willcox, Walter F. (1940). <u>Studies in American Demography</u>. Ithaca, New York: Russell.

Chapter 2

A historical perspective on the economic consequences of rapid population growth

● D. R. Weir*

Simon Kuznets has defined modern economic growth as simultaneous growth in population and income per capita (Kuznets, 1966). This was for him the characteristic which distinguished the modern world from the premodern Malthusian world in which population growth led to falling per capita incomes and eventually to a slowdown in population growth itself.

When Malthus wrote, modern economic growth seemed a utopian concept, divorced from the reality of historical experience. Most of us living today have experienced modern economic growth as a personal reality and not merely a theoretical possibility. And yet we remain concerned about the possibility of extending the process forward in time and outward to all the globe. We feel some discomfort at the cheery optimism of those who say rapid population growth can only spur the process on.

That discomfort arises because we have a less-than-perfect understanding of how modern economic growth works and why it is that population growth does not bring it to a halt. Economic historians have an important role to play in this discussion: to show us which changes in economic institutions and demographic behaviours first allowed modern economic growth in Europe. Answering the questions of how and why requires first an answer to the question of when. When did Europe escape the Malthusian trap? Recent historiography has pushed back the starting point of the Industrial Revolution. This paper will explore the possibility that the structural break in the economic consequences of rapid population growth occurred earlier than is commonly believed.

Traditionally, Europe's history has been divided into two periods characterized by very different consequences of rapid population growth. According to the consensus view, before the Industrial Revolution, Europe was strongly Malthusian: living standards moved in inverse rhythm with the level

*Department of Economics, Yale University, New Haven, Connecticut, USA.

41

of population. During Europe's nineteenth-century development, population growth was neutral or perhaps even beneficial to the rate of economic growth. As Keynes described it, the Malthusian devil had been chained.

This consensus is of recent origin and is not without its critics. In this paper I will pursue some doubts about the Malthusian consensus, especially for the early modern era (1500-1800). Industrialization after 1800 certainly altered economic and demographic life. But so too did the discovery of the New World, the invention of the printing press, and the Protestant Reformation, to name only a few of the momentous changes that separate the early modern period from medieval Europe. Economic change, never really absent in Europe's history, accelerated and accumulated in the three centuries before rapid industrialization, raising the possibility that the economic consequences of population growth might have changed as well. The best empirical tests of the economic consequences of population growth before 1800 also raise doubts because the consequences appear to have been too severe. Thus, there is ample motivation for a reappraisal of the Malthusian consensus. We can begin by reviewing the evidence on which the consensus has been built.

Historical overview

The evidence that the nineteenth century fits Kuznets's definition of modern economic growth is overwhelming, as indeed it should be since it was the basis for his generalization. The irrelevance of population growth rates for modern economic development can be seen in figures I and II, based on the work of Paul Bairoch. Figure I plots rates of growth of per capita income against rates of population growth in nine West European countries in two-time periods, 1830-1860 and 1860-1913. The absence of any relationship between the two is confirmed by a regression of per capita income growth on population growth. The coefficient is .44, with a standard error of .52. The R-squared was only 4 per cent. The relationship is similarly absent when the time periods are examined separately or when country changes between periods are used.

Another way to view the matter is to compare specific country experiences. The most telling comparison is between the United Kingdom and France. Figure II shows the growth paths of the United Kingdom and France from 1700 to 1910, in both the population and per capita income dimensions. At the beginning of the eighteenth century, France was three times the size of the United Kingdom. Over the next two centuries, Britain managed to maintain its lead in per capita income while expanding its population to overtake France. Per capita income grew .65 per cent per year in the United Kingdom and .62 per cent per year in France. Population grew .88 per cent in Britain and only .31 per cent per year in France. In a Malthusian world, British economic welfare would have suffered for its exuberant demographic growth.

Europe from 1250 to 1800 has been described as precisely that sort of Malthusian world. Figures III and IV show the course of population and real wage growth in the United Kingdom and France over that time period. Historians and economists have elaborated cyclical models to describe the six or seven centuries preceding the Industrial Revolution. Figures III and IV

Figure I. Nine European countries, 1830–60 and 1860–1913

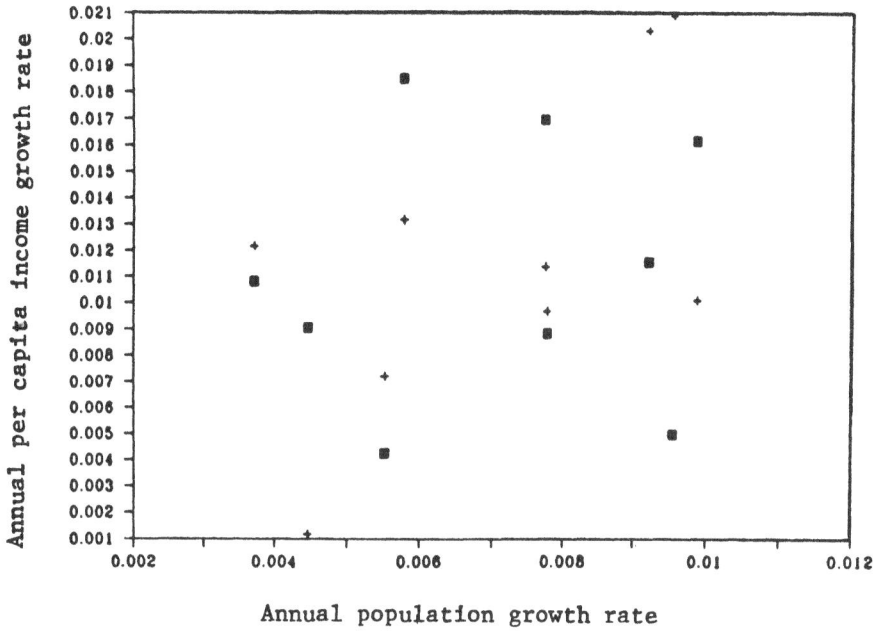

Figure II. Growth in the United Kingdom and France, 1700–1910

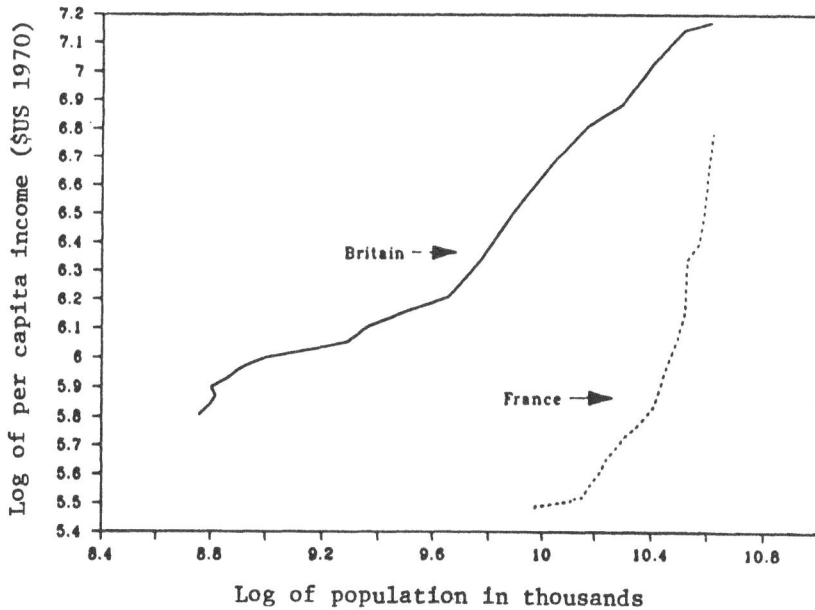

serve as a useful reminder that the number of "cycles" is not sufficient to prove such theories. What we have are a few periods of demographic expansion or decline, each separated by many decades of economic, social, and political change.

The first period was the demographic expansion from 1100 to 1348. We do not have much evidence on wages and prices from this period in which feudalism remained important, but what there is consistent with diminishing returns.

In 1347–1350 the Black Death, a pandemic of bubonic plague, reduced Europe's population by about one third. Estimates for the United Kingdom suggest an even worse situation (Hatcher, 1977). Repeated outbreaks held down population growth for most of the fifteenth century in England. The hypothesis of growth for France after 1400 is purely guesswork on the part of McEvedy and Jones (1978). By 1400, real wages had climbed appreciably above their pre–plague levels. In the United Kingdom they continued to climb slowly until 1450 and then held steady until 1500. The French data show wide movement in the fifteenth century because of the English occupation of northern France and the resulting disruption of agricultural production.

The third period involved renewed demographic expansion from 1500 to about 1650. In France, the expansion may have halted by 1590. Population regained or surpassed its pre–plague levels, while real wages fell to what they had been in 1340. This was also the period of European exploration and conquest of other continents.

Demographic stagnation followed until the early eighteenth century. Real wages recovered somewhat, but never approached the heights of the fifteenth century. Renewed population growth then halted the rise in living standards.

In all, there were five periods: three expansions, one stagnation, and one decline. In using this historical record to test hypotheses about the economic–demographic system, it is important to recall the enormous potential for coincidence.

The Malthusian orthodoxy and its critics

Although Malthus advanced his theories early in the nineteenth century and attempted to illustrate them with historical evidence, Malthusian thinking did not come to dominate historical writing until a century or so after his death. A major pioneer of the Malthusian revival was Postan, a British medieval historian (cf. Postan, 1966). He challenged an earlier paradigm that gave primacy to commercialization, urbanism, and the money supply as the dynamic forces of European history. He pointed out that for the late medieval period (1200–1500), relative prices (especially real wages) changed in ways that were consistent with population movements but could not be explained by inflation alone.

The Malthusian model has subsequently been extended to all of European history before the Industrial Revolution by historians like Le Roy Ladurie (1966), who describes the movement of population, prices, and wages as the "respiration" of a giant social structure, and Habakkuk, whose succinct

Figure III.   Real wages in the United Kingdom and France, 1275–1789

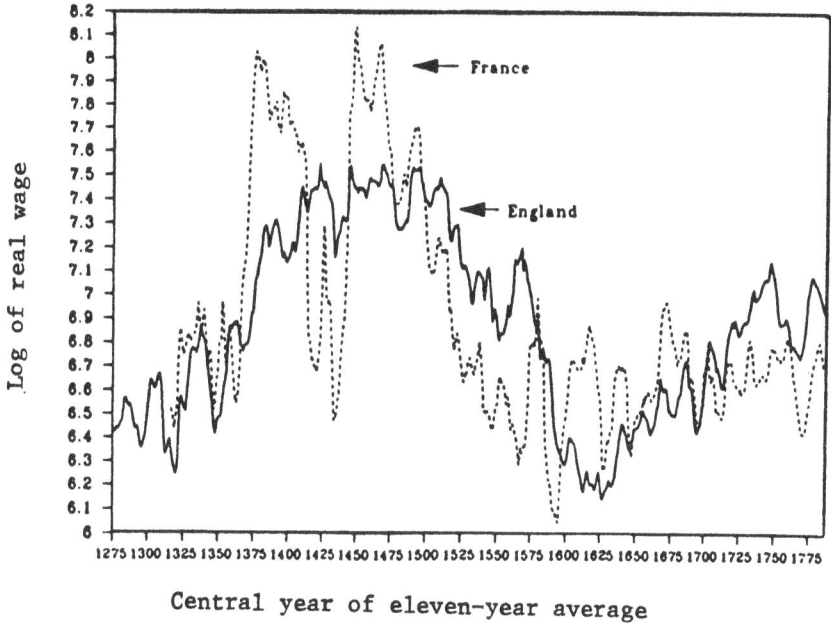

Central year of eleven-year average

Figure IV.   Population in France and the United Kingdom, 1250–1800

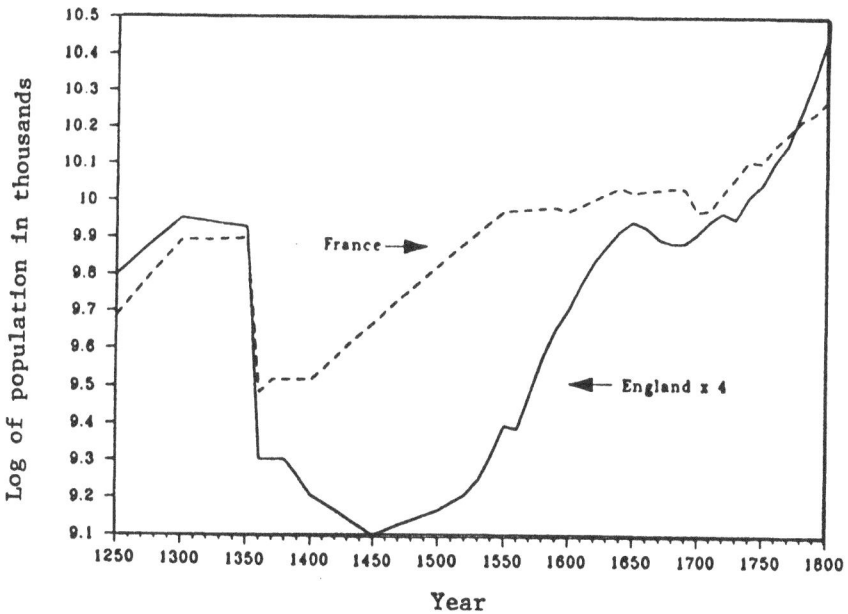

Year

Malthusian summary has been widely quoted. New population estimates for the United Kingdom by Wrigley and Schofield (1981) have strengthened the case. The model has been given more formal and explicit theoretical and empirical expression in the work of Ronald Lee. So strong is the consensus that one can now find chapter titles like "Economic evidence of population change" (Hatcher, 1977), in which the course of population growth is inferred from the path of real wages.

Population has gone from being overlooked to being the single dynamic element in European history. Historians have, therefore, sought to explain many of the observed changes as consequences of population growth or decline. These include urbanization, income distribution, and inflation. Attempts to endogenize other features of the historical landscape besides real wages have not always been successful.

Malthus was reviled by Marx, and the strongest critique of the Malthusian historical paradigm has come from a Marxist historian, Robert Brenner. Just as Postan derailed the commercialization paradigm by pointing to a previously ignored set of facts, Brenner (1976) challenges the Malthusians by pointing out things they cannot explain. He argues that technological stagnation, the foundation of diminishing returns, is itself a product of the structure of class relations. Moreover, changes in income distribution are, in his view, driven by class struggle and not by land/labour ratios. Postan shifted the emphasis from one set of measurable variables to another. Brenner offers no new strategies to solve the intractable problem of measuring class power independently of the outcomes of class struggle. Thus, the Marxist critique cannot itself be put to an empirical test except to the extent that the failure of specifiable alternatives raises questions about its own credibility.

Another challenge might be seen as a resurrection of the earlier paradigm. Peter Lindert (1985) has argued that inflation's correlation with population growth and real wage declines suggests that some mechanism other than simple diminishing returns was at work. He suggests that inflation may have been endogenous to population growth. We can consider this challenge in more detail in the context of empirical specifications.

Formal applications of the model: time-series data

The consensus view is neatly summarized in Ronald Lee's (1977, 1980, 1987) econometric model of long-run population and wage growth. In its typical form, the model consists of a regression of real wages on population and a time trend. Real wages and population are measured in natural logarithms, so the estimated coefficients are elasticities: the per cent change in real wages due to a 1 per cent change in population. The simplest interpretation of the model is that mortality and technological change are the two main exogenous forces. Technological change is assumed to occur smoothly and gradually and can therefore be captured by a time trend. The level of population at any time is treated as exogenous to the current standard of living, mainly because it reflects past values of exogenously varying mortality. The regression model is thus a formal representation of Le Roy Ladurie's description of European history as Malthusian equilibrium with "drift".

So simple a model can naturally be challenged on many grounds. We will pursue some objections in detail below. Some others will not be explored here, mainly for lack of data. The wage data generally come from construction work, while our models emphasize the much larger agricultural sector for which wage data are sparse. In using mason's wages as "the wage", we assume that the labour market was sufficiently competitive that wages in all sectors moved in parallel, even if there were persistent differentials. The level of population may not be truly exogenous in this equation, for two reasons. First, the full Malthusian model includes a feedback response in which higher real wages will raise the rate of population growth. This might create a bias against finding negative economic consequences of population growth. Lee has shown that the impact of the feedback response must have been too slow and too small to cause serious problems for a regression of current wages on the current level of population. A second problem is that the amount of labour supplied by a given population may depend on the level of the real wage. The direction of the bias will depend on the slope of the labour supply curve. If the population supplies more labour when wages are higher, the population elasticity will be biased towards zero. On the other hand, if income effects dominate the labour supply decision so that lower wages lead to more labour supplied per person in a given population, then the population elasticity will be too large.

The constant term in this regression has no particular meaning; its value is determined by the units of measurement of the variables in the model. The coefficient on time tells us how fast (in per cent per year) real wages would rise (or fall) over time if population size remained constant. The coefficient on population size is the elasticity of real wages with respect to population size. This tells us what percentage change in real wages is produced by a given percentage change in population. Using the coefficients on time and population we can calculate a third measure of interest: the absorption rate. This is the rate of population growth over time that would just offset the underlying economic growth trend and leave real wages constant, or, in other words, the rate of population growth that the economy can absorb.

The rate of growth of real wages over time will be equal to the time trend coefficient plus the rate of growth of population times the population coefficient. For it to be zero, the rate of population growth must be equal to minus the time coefficient divided by the population coefficient. In models that include higher-order polynomials of time, the absorption rate is not a constant. Over long-time periods, this rate is essentially determined by the difference between the growth rate of real wages and the growth rate of population. Lee's model attempts to divide up the absorption rate between the effects of technological improvements and population growth by looking at the effects of deviations from trend in population growth on deviations from trend in real wages.

Table 1 reports estimates of this simple model for France and the United Kingdom in two-time periods. We report versions with no-time trend, a single (log-linear) time trend, and a quadratic in time. The English results are similar to those obtained by Lee (1977, 1980) using essentially the same data and a variety of alternative specifications. The population coefficient for the early period, 1300–1500, is smaller than Lee found. This is due to the use of Hatcher's more recent estimates of population which make the magnitude of the plague declines greater than those in the estimates used by Lee. Both countries show population elasticities greater than one for the period after the year 1500. In the United Kingdom the coefficients are between 2 and 3, depending on the detrending.

According to the linear time-trend models, the absorption rate in France was .37 per cent per year before 1500 and .07 per cent per year after 1500. For the same periods in the United Kingdom, the absorption rate was .49 per cent and .33 per cent. The declining absorption rate in France is attributed by the model mainly to a decline in the trend rate of economic growth, while the effects of population remained constant. By contrast, the United Kingdom's smaller decline in the absorption rate is attributed to a large increase in the negative consequences of population growth, which offset an increase in the underlying trend economic growth rate.

More recently, Lee (1987) has extended the analysis to other European countries. In almost every case, the estimated elasticity of real wages with respect to population is below -1. This appears to indicate a strong confirmation of the Malthusian point of view. The problem is that it may be too strong.

The Malthusian model is based on a simple production function with the principle of diminishing returns to labour in the context of fixed supplies of land. The size of the regression coefficient should correspond to the strength of diminishing returns in the production function. In the most commonly used production function, the Cobb-Douglas function, the elasticity of labour's marginal product with respect to labour input is equal to the share of labour in total output minus one. If labour's share was around one half, then the coefficient should be minus one half. It would be impossible for a Cobb-Douglas production function to produce an elasticity below minus one, and yet most of the regression estimates are well below that.

Lee (1980) is well aware of this difficulty. He elaborates a two-sector general equilibrium model with a different type of production function for agriculture that could allow a wage-population elasticity as large as his estimates. The crucial characteristic of the production function is the degree of substitutability between land and labour (elasticity of substitution). A low degree of substitutability implies more sharply diminishing returns and more severe economic consequences of population growth. The Cobb-Douglas production function assumes rather high substitutability (the elasticity of substitution is fixed at unity). Other production functions allowing for much less substitutability could produce results similar to those estimated previously. Two facts suggest caution about this interpretation. The degree of substitutability implied by Lee's model is lower than that observed in direct studies of agricultural production. Moreover, Lee was unable to estimate the more complex specifications required by the alternative production functions because "the computer program encountered nearly singular matrices it could not invert" (Lee, 1980). In other words, population growth was too highly correlated with the time trend in early modern United Kingdom to allow the estimation of more complex models.

Table 1. Population and real wages; regression results for
France and the United Kingdom

	1300–1500					
	France			England		
Constant	23.408 (6.711)	2.288 (6.999)	-20.541 (87.777)	15.410 (0.760)	7.718 (2.420)	-21.621 (21.102)
Population (log)	-1.670 (0.691)	-1.134 (0.625)	-0.845 (1.001)	-1.037 (0.095)	-0.586 (0.158)	-0.402 (0.202)
Year		0.0042 (0.0015)	0.0470 (0.1140)		0.0029 (0.0009)	0.0419 (0.0279)
Year squared (divided by 1000)			-0.0152 (0.0405)			-0.0136 (0.0097)
R-squared	0.226	0.454	0.459	0.857	0.909	0.918

	1500–1800					
	France			England		
Constant	12.702 (4.366)	18.867 (8.097)	58.199 (17.564)	10.840 (1.543)	15.724 (1.031)	74.936 (5.609)
Population (log)	-0.604 (0.436)	-1.365 (0.948)	-1.622 (0.873)	-0.487 (0.184)	-3.000 (0.326)	-1.920 (0.371)
Year		0.0009 (0.0010)	-0.0442 (0.0183)		0.0098 (0.0012)	-0.0695 (0.0196)
Year squared (divided by 1000)			0.0138 (0.0056)			0.0230 (0.0057)
R-squared	0.066	0.095	0.272	0.205	0.775	0.864

Notes: Standard errors are in parenthesis. The dependent variable
is the log of nominal wages minus the log of wheat prices. The unit of
observation is a decade average.

There are other possible explanations that do not require such extreme assumptions about the production function. Three seem worthy of special notice. Labour markets might not work in the way the model assumes. De Vries (1984) has found evidence for the eighteenth-century Netherlands of institutional resistance to changing nominal wages, but side payments to labour were adjusted when the cost of living changed. If this was a general feature of early modern labour markets, then the real wage-population elasticity exaggerates the economic consequences of population growth. If the supply curve for labour were backward-bending (i.e., adults worked more days or hours per year to make up for lower wages), then the real wage-population elasticity gives an exaggerated measure of diminishing returns in the production function and an exaggerated measure of the decline in consumption of goods. Finally, we have no direct knowledge of what happened to investment and the capital stock over the population cycle. With cheaper labour and more valuable output, the incentives for making improvements like drainage or fencing must have increased. On the other hand, if a larger, hungrier population diverted more of its annual output to consumption, there may have been less capital in the form of seed, livestock, etc.

The most useful feature of Lee's general equilibrium model is that it generates predictions for quantities other than the real wage, such as urbanization and land rents. We can therefore test its credibility outside the real wage regressions. Before doing so, we need to consider a line of criticism suggesting that the real wage-population regression is so poorly specified as to produce sharply diminishing returns when there was in fact no Malthusian response at all.

Inflation and population growth

General equilibrium models of the real economy generally ignore the price level, and Lee's model is no exception. But one of the strongest features of Europe's economic-demographic history is the close correlation between population growth and inflation. Peter Lindert (1985) notes this pattern; he reestimates Lee's real wage regressions for the United Kingdom (1541-1800), including terms for lagged inflation rates, and finds that the coefficient on population falls to zero.

The statistical underpinnings of his results can be seen in table 2, which shows the correlations of prices, wages, and population. After detrending, population and prices were very weakly correlated in the late medieval period. After 1500, however, they became positively correlated, especially in the United Kingdom, where the correlation coefficient was .89.

This is an important and puzzling fact. The United Kingdom and France used specie money at this time. The quantity theory of money would predict that an increase in population would lead to a decline in prices, because of the larger volume of real output and transactions. Goldstone (1984), for example, has suggested mechanisms by which population growth might increase the velocity of circulation of money, but there is no evidence to confirm that changes in financial practices were sufficiently great to offset the inherent deflationary tendency. Lindert (1983) offers an alternative explanation: historical coincidence, or "impish Clio," to use his phrase. Perhaps it is

Table 2. Correlations of variables with time, and correlation matrix of detrended variables in France and the United Kingdom in time periods

	1300–1500							
	France				England			
	Popu-lation	Wheat Price	Money Wage	Real Wage	Popu-lation	Wheat Price	Money Wage	Real Wage
Time	-.30	-.01	.80	.60	-.87	-.31	.91	.92
Population	1.00	-.04	-.78	-.38	1.00	-.16	-.83	-.65
Wheat Price	-.04	1.00	.28	-.85	-.16	1.00	.37	-.49
Money Wage	-.78	.28	1.00	.27	-.83	.37	1.00	.63
Real Wage	-.38	-.85	.27	1.00	-.65	-.49	.63	1.00

	1500–1790							
	France				England			
	Popu-lation	Wheat Price	Money Wage	Real Wage	Popu-lation	Wheat Price	Money Wage	Real Wage
Time	.89	.87	.92	-.15	.95	.80	.97	-.20
Population	1.00	.20	.09	-.27	1.00	.89	.56	-.87
Wheat Price	.20	1.00	.88	-.73	.89	1.00	.69	-.96
Money Wage	.09	.88	1.00	-.31	.56	.69	1.00	-.48
Real Wage	-.27	-.73	-.31	1.00	-.87	-.96	-.48	1.00

Notes: The first row in each quadrant shows the correlation with time of the original variables (in logarithms). The square matrices show the correlations among the variables after a (log-linear) time trend (for each sub-period) has been removed. All variables are decade averages.

just a historical accident that phases of population growth coincided with the importation of silver and gold into Europe from the New World. Lindert (1985) considers some alternative systematic sources of the correlation.

Although these questions about the origins of the correlation of population growth and inflation are interesting and worthy of future research, they are not crucial to the problem at hand. To put it simply, for the purposes of estimating the real wage consequences of population growth, the correlation of prices and population is not a problem in and of itself, but it does interact with other problems to worsen their effects. This is true whatever the source of the correlation of prices and population. Two potential problems that might be exacerbated are measurement error in data on prices and wages, and what we might call "Keynesian" properties of labour markets, i.e., a tendency for nominal wages to be "sticky" and not adjust instantaneously to changes in the price level.

Lee (1985) discusses more fully the model of wage determination. In a neoclassical labour market, the nominal wage will be set equal to the marginal physical product of labour times the expected price level. In logarithms, the log of the nominal wage equals the log of marginal physical product plus the log of expected prices. The marginal physical product of labour should be determined by the time trend and population size terms.

One simple assumption is that observed prices are equal to expected prices. If so, then a regression of the log of nominal wages on the log of population, log prices, and a time trend should yield a coefficient of one on log prices and the same coefficient on population as found in the real wage regressions. Table 3 shows that this is far from true. The coefficient on prices is far below one, and the coefficient on population drops to near zero.

Lee (1985) showed that Lindert's regression model was equivalent to the regressions in table 3, so his discussion of Lindert's results applies equally well here. Both Lindert and I "expressed the log of nominal wages as a time trend, and found it insensitive to the price level or population". Lee went on to say that "it may be debatable whether population growth depresses real wages, but it seems unlikely that the money wage level should be completely independent of the level of prices, even when this level increased by a factor of 10; and equally unlikely that the money wage should have risen by a factor of six or seven over this period, apparently independently of any real or monetary influences".

I agree that these conclusions are unlikely in the extreme. I have tried various specifications for expected prices using lagged prices or prices in other countries, or other price series, but the results are generally similar. The statistical results of tables 1–3 indicate that some of the assumptions underlying Lee's real wage model must be violated. Some possible violations are more serious than others, but in all cases they pose serious problems only because of the background positive correlation of prices and population.

One possibility that cannot be ruled out is that the nominal wage series is worthless for the purpose of estimating Malthusian effects. Even if money

Table 3.   Population, prices and nominal wages: regression
results for France and the United Kingdom

| | 1300–1500 | | | |
	France		England	
Constant	11.132	-36.096	6.872	-17.797
	(5.981)	(23.871)	(1.261)	(19.786)
Population	-0.646	0.038	-0.308	-0.082
(log)	(0.692)	(0.734)	(0.386)	(0.423)
Prices	0.644	0.444	0.274	0.102
(log)	(0.069)	(0.118)	(0.092)	(0.165)
Year	0.0031	0.0534	0.0050	0.0341
	(0.0008)	(0.0248)	(0.0009)	(0.0233)
Year squared		-0.0150		-0.0088
(divided by 1000)		(0.0074)		(0.0070)
R-squared	0.963	0.969	0.970	0.971

Notes: Dependent variable is the log of nominal wages.   Standard
errors in parenthesis.

wages have the right trend, they will be of no use in a detrended model like the one we have been estimating unless they also move correctly over the cycle. Both the nature of the basic sources of wage data and the methods of construction of the published series make it likely that the timing of changes is poorly gauged. In the extreme, our real wage measure may simply subtract the log of prices from a series that is just noise around trend. Since prices are strongly positively correlated with population for reasons that remain mysterious, the estimated elasticity of real wages with respect to population growth may be nothing more than minus the regression coefficient of prices on population growth. Lindert (1985) thinks this the most likely alternative. It is a hard criterion, however, because it rests not merely on some element of measurement error but on the complete absence of any systematic component to the fluctuations of nominal wages around trend. In principle, any "signal" in the dependent variable should lead to unbiased parameter estimates, albeit with larger standard errors.

A second possibility is that nominal wages are reliably measured but that observed prices measure expected prices with error. There are really two variants to this case. In the first, the error (difference between observed prices and expected prices) is uncorrelated with population. If so, then Lee's real wage model is appropriate for estimating population's effects. The nominal wage regression on prices and population will bias both coefficients towards zero when population is correlated with expected prices. The coefficient on observed prices will be less than one because of the measurement error in prices. The coefficient on population will then be influenced by its correlation with expected prices.

The second variant is what we might call cyclically "sticky" nominal wages. It may be that nominal wages do not respond fully to deviations in prices around their trend. One way to describe this is that the expected prices used to set nominal wages heavily discount deviations from trend, whatever their source. If so, then the difference between observed and expected prices could well be positively correlated with population. Lee's real wage model would exaggerate the negative consequences of population growth.

The time-series studies of real wages in England, which form the empirical basis for the Malthusian consensus, are evidently fraught with difficulties of interpretation. There is no definitive indication that population growth did not have negative consequences, but the evidence that it had very large effects is subject to dispute. Quite possibly the data are inadequate to support conclusive results. We, therefore, move now to a consideration of other approaches to the problem that rely on other data, other variables, and other dimensions of variation in population growth.

Country variation

One way to avoid the identification problems of single-country time-series data is to use mixed cross-section time-series or "panel" data. In this section we use data drawn from six countries (the United Kingdom, the Netherlands, France, Federal Republic of Germany, Italy, and Spain) observed at 50-year intervals (1500, 1550,...1800). For each country at each point in time we have a population total (Vries, 1984) and an average real wage for the 20-year period centred on the "census "year. (We have constructed these figures from published data on prices and wages). Because we are interested in explaining the effects of population growth on the movement of real wages and not in the relationships between the absolute size of population in different countries and their different levels of real wages, we will work with percentage changes in variables between the half-century benchmarks. We construct the percentage change measures as the difference in logarithms of the original values.

Table 4 presents results of regression estimates. The basic model is in column 1. We regress the percentage change in real wages on a constant and the percentage change in population (the first difference of logarithms). The constant term in these regressions is like the time trend term in the time-series regressions. It tells us the percentage change that would occur in real wages over 50 years if there were no population growth. The most likely sources of a positive constant term are capital accumulation and technical progress. The coefficient on population growth is the elasticity of real wages with respect to population growth. Combining all the countries and time periods, the estimate was -1.18. While this is not as dramatic as the -2 found for some of the English time-series results, it is larger than the -.5 we would expect from a simple Cobb-Douglas production function.

The absorption rate (the rate of population growth that can be sustained with constant real wages) can be calculated by dividing the constant term by the coefficient on population growth and reversing the sign. Because the data are for 50-year time periods, we must divide again by 50 to obtain the absorption rate as an annual rate of growth. From Model 1 we would estimate the absorption rate to be .08 per cent per year, considerably less than the .4 per cent per year that Lee estimated for the United Kingdom.

The basic model assumes that the absorption rate was constant in all countries and all time periods. If it was not, our estimate of the consequences of population growth could be biased. It would also be of interest to know about differences in the absorption rate over time and between countries. We can accomplish this by including dummy variables for countries (Model 2), time periods (Model 3), or both (Model 4). These dummy variables allow the constant term to differ between countries or time periods. This allows for the absorption rate to differ because of different underlying rates of technical progress but retains the assumption that the effect of population growth was the same.

Our estimate of the consequences of population growth does not change much when we add these controls for fixed effects of country or time period. This ust be considered strong confirmation of the general conclusions of the time-series real-wage models. Population growth in early modern Europe evidently had not only negative consequences for real wages but consequences greater in magnitude than would be produced by simple changes in the land/labour ratio along a flexible production function.

The country effects reveal a sharp distinction between the "successful" countries of the United Kingdom and the Netherlands and the other four. Note that when using dummy variables, one category must be left out. (The constant

Table 4.   The effect of population growth on real wages, 1500–1800:
a mixed cross-section time series approach

	1.	2.	3.	4.	5.
Constánt	0.048	0.001	0.088	0.040	0.055
	(0.057)	(0.111)	(0.087)	(0.112)	(0.107)
Pop. Growth	-1.184	-1.379	-0.990	-1.258	-1.463
	(0.316)	(0.340)	(0.304)	(0.328)	(0.334)
Pop. Growth 1700-50					-0.140
					(2.457)
Pop. Growth 1750-1800					1.842
					(0.848)
England		0.202		0.186	0.153
		(0.158)		(0.124)	(0.119)
Holland		0.198		0.193	0.206
		(0.153)		(0.118)	(0.118)
Germany		0.040		0.036	-0.002
		(0.153)		(0.117)	(0.113)
Italy		-0.021		-0.020	0.010
		(0.152)		(0.117)	(0.112)
Spain		-0.001		0.000	0.015
		(0.152)		(0.117)	(0.112)
1500-1550			-0.378	-0.355	-0.338
			(0.122)	(0.120)	(0.114)
1550-1600			-0.208	-0.192	-0.179
			(0.121)	(0.119)	(0.113)
1600-1650			0.077	0.057	0.042
			(0.121)	(0.119)	(0.113)
1700-1750			0.121	0.136	0.164
			(0.120)	(0.118)	(0.312)
1750-1800			0.012	0.061	-0.355
			(0.131)	(0.131)	(0.228)
R-squared	.29	.38	.62	.70	.75

Notes: Standard errors are in parenthesis. The sample consists of
six countries observed over six 50-year time intervals for a total of 36
observations. The dependent variable is the percentage change in real
wages over a 50-year time period (the log of real wages at the endpoint
minus the log of real wages at the start).

term represents the effect of this excluded category). France was excluded in these regressions. The coefficients for the other countries therefore measure the extent to which they differed from France. The absorption rate calculated from the constant term of Model 2, corresponding to France, is nearly zero. The coefficients for the Federal Republic of Germany, Italy, and Spain are nearly zero, indicating that they had absorption rates nearly identical to that of France, so in all four countries the absorption rate was close to zero. The dummy variables for the United Kingdom and the Netherlands had coefficients around .2. Adding these to the constant, we find absorption rates of about .3 per cent per year. Thus, any positive population growth in most of Europe had negative consequences, while in the United Kingdom and the Netherlands economic growth allowed for modest growth without declines in real wages.

The dummy variables for time periods are the most important for solving the problems of the simple time-series models. Because prices and population were highly collinear in the United Kingdom and France after 1500 and because both are measured with some error, we could not determine whether the estimated effect of population on real wages was a real consequence of population growth or an artifact of historical coincidence. By allowing for different underlying growth rates of real wages in each time period, we can eliminate the effects of any coincidence in the timing of European inflation and population growth. Model 3 estimates the consequences of population growth from the variation across countries only. The estimated effect is only slightly smaller than in the first two models and is still around -1. The excluded time category is 1650-1700. In that period the absorption rate was about .18 per cent per year. The other periods after 1600 were not significantly different in a statistical sense, but the large coefficient for 1700-1750 does imply an absorption rate of .42 per cent per year. The negative coefficients in the sixteenth century imply that the absorption rate was lower than in the later years. Indeed, since they are greater in absolute value than the estimated constant, they imply that the absorption rate itself was negative. Population would have had to decline in absolute size in order to maintain real wages at a constant level during the years of the Price Revolution.

Model 4 includes both the country and time effects simultaneously. The results are not greatly changed from the separate models.

It is also possible to estimate different coefficients for population growth in different countries or different time periods by using interaction terms. The most appropriate hypothesis for the purposes of this paper is to test whether the impact of population growth declined in the eighteenth century. Model 5 therefore adds two new terms to the regression for the interaction of population growth with dummy variables for 1700-1750 and 1750-1800. The estimated coefficient on population growth corresponds to the years before 1700. For the two eighteenth-century periods the effect of population growth is the sum of the population coefficient and the interaction term. The coefficient on the 1700-1750 interaction is small with a very large standard error and has a negative sign; there was clearly no change in the basic Malthusian structure in those years. But for the last half of the eighteenth century the interaction term is positive and large enough to cancel out the base-line effect of population growth.

In other words, there appears to have been a transition to the "modern" pattern of very little cross–sectional correlation of population growth and economic growth in the second half of the eighteenth century. It is important to note, however, that when the interaction term is included, the fixed effect of the 1750-1800 time period becomes large and negative, indicating that there was downward pressure on real wages throughout Europe that was not related to population growth.

Further implications

The main virtue of Lee's general equilibrium model is that it generates predictions for quantities other than the real wage. Given his estimated wage–population elasticity, the magnitudes of other relationships can be predicted. The most important of these predictions bring us right back to our earlier theoretical discussion about the issues of urbanization, income distribution, and inflation.

Lee adopts a constant elasticity of substitution (CES) production function. A Cobb–Douglas production function is a special case of the CES with an elasticity of substitution between land and labour equal to one. Solving the equations of the general equilibrium model for a wage–population elasticity of –2.2, Lee finds that the elasticity of substitution would have to be .16. That implies very low substitutability between land and labour, lower than has been found in any direct study. Lee does not discuss this at any length, but by accepting the CES specification he is implicitly arguing that inflexible technology in agriculture is the root cause of all the other apparent consequences of rapid population growth.

Given the limited ability to absorb labour in agriculture, the model predicts that the agricultural labour force grows less quickly than does total population. The predicted elasticity is .66. If the agricultural labour force were about 75 per cent of the total, then only about half of population growth would be absorbed by agriculture. That implies that the rest must join the urban population, meaning that the elasticity of urban population with respect to total population would be around 2. In other words, urbanization would increase rapidly during periods of rapid population growth.

A second implication concerns the distribution of income. When wages fall at a faster rate than population grows, the total wage bill falls. Total output is rising, so the non–labour share of output is growing. Lee considers the ratio of rents to wages rather than rents alone. The point is that under a Cobb–Douglas Malthusian specification the elasticity of rents with respect to population would be less than one, while in Lee's CES model it must be greater than one.

Urbanization and population growth

Lee's two–sector neoclassical model suggests that agriculture had limited employment opportunities for "excess" population, so rapid population growth must lead to an even more rapid growth of urban population. Lee's model predicted an elasticity of .66 for rural population and perhaps 2 for urban population. We can look at the urbanization–population relationship using the data base recently constructed by De Vries (1984). For 16 territorial groupings, he has constructed estimates of total and urban population at 50–year intervals from 1500 to 1800. In his own appraisal of the relationship of population growth and urbanization he concludes that rapid urban growth "was at least as much a phenomenon of demographic stagnation and decline as it was of demographic expansion". In other words, the rate of urbanization (growth of the percentage urban) was independent of the growth rate of population.

After some necessary consolidations, I retained 13 regions and the six half–century time periods for a total of 78 observations. The dependent variable was change in the log of rural population or change in the log of urban population. The independent variable was change in the log of total population. I also experimented with dummy variables for countries and time periods. The estimated elasticities are shown in table 5.

It appears that rural population absorbed far more of population growth, and urban population less, than is suggested by Lee's model. The elasticity on rural population was never below .9.

It is of interest to compare these results with the work of Preston (1979) on the growth of cities in developing countries. His unit of observation was the city, not urban populations of countries, and he included controls for income level, initial size, and other characteristics of the city and country. He found a coefficient of 1.002 relating national population growth to the growth of cities. It would appear that early modern Europe had a stronger pro–urbanization tendency for rapid population growth. On the other hand, urban growth in De Vries's data includes the addition of new cities as they cross the minimum 10,000 population threshold, which might exaggerate the estimate. In any case, it appears that population growth was and is not a significant factor in determining the urban percentage.

Income distribution and population growth

A useful complement to the study of population's effect on real wages is a study of its effect on land rents. If population growth was very bad for real wages, it ought to have been very good for real rents. If agriculture had as limited a capacity to absorb labour as posited by Lee, then the elasticity of real land rents with respect to population growth should be much greater than one.

A decadal series of land rents in the United Kingdom from 1500 was constructed using data in Kerridge (1953) and Allen (1988). An index for France was constructed from several local studies (Blouin, 1972; Deyon, 1967; Veyrasset–Herren and Le Roy Ladurie, 1968; Zolla, 1893). In principle, the rent data represent the price of new leases on existing agricultural land of fixed quality. They should bear the same relation to the marginal product of land as the wage data bear to the marginal product of labour.

Regression results for France and the United Kingdom are presented in table 6. Whereas the real wage results were broadly similar for the two

Table 5. Urbanization and population growth in Europe, 1500–1800

Additional controls	Dependent variable	
	Rural population	Urban population
None	.944 (.046)	1.30 (.222)
Country effects	.954 (.041)	.99 (.215)
Time period effects	.915 (.052)	1.54 (.243)
Time and country effects	.924 (.047)	1.18 (.242)

Notes: Standard errors in parenthesis. The unit of observation is the change over a 50-year period in one country or region (N–78). All variables have been measured in logs so the regression coefficient is an elasticity measure.

Table 6. Population and real rents: regression results for France and the United Kingdom

	1500–1800					
	France			England		
Constant	.446 (3.763)	-4.384 (6.999)	44.982 (7.526)	-14.247 (0.971)	-11.918 (0.935)	-31.448 (16.631)
Population (log)	0.634 (0.376)	1.231 (0.819)	0.908 (1.502)	1.255 (0.116)	0.056 (0.295)	-0.301 (0.422)
Year		-0.0007 (0.0008)	-0.0572 (0.0135)		0.0047 (0.0011)	0.0309 (0.0223)
Year squared (divided by 1000)			0.0136 (0.0097)			-0.0076 (0.0064)
R-squared	0.095	0.118	0.483	0.812	0.890	0.895

Notes: Standard errors in parenthesis. The dependent variable is the log of the ratio of nominal rents to nominal wages. "Prices" are wheat prices.

countries, the real rent results are very different. Population growth in France had a large effect on rents: The elasticity was around one, although the large standard error means we cannot reject the hypothesis that the true effect was zero (or two). In England the effect of population growth on real rents disappears once we allow for time trends.

We can address the issue of income distribution in another way by using the ratio of rents to wages. This ratio has the advantage of not including output prices in its construction. In a Cobb-Douglas production function, the elasticity of the ratio of rents to wages with respect to labour input should be one. For production functions with less substitutability, it will be greater than one. Regression results for France and the United Kingdom are shown in table 7. They look very similar for the two countries, with a population coefficient between 2.5 and 3. The results reveal again theseverity of data problems for the United Kingdom. The relative price of land and labour should not depend on the price level. In France it did not; adding prices to the regression scarcely changed the estimates. In the United Kingdom, on the other hand, the price level completely determined the distribution of income, eliminating any influence of population or the time trend.

The English rent results do not lend any new confidence in the time-series real wage regressions discussed previously. They are completely consistent with the hypothesis that the English nominal wage data are meaningless after detrending, while the rent data track price movements closely. They are not consistent with the other explanation advanced in the discussion of real wages, namely, that prices might have been measured with error around their systematic correlation with population. That hypothesis would be consistent with the French results in which the addition of prices did not affect the regression of income distribution on population.

We are a long way from having a satisfactory knowledge of the movements of rents in the early modern period. Based on the results presented here, we can at least consider the hypothesis that population growth's strongly negative consequences for real wages were balanced by equally strong positive consequences for rents. A production function with inelastic substitution possibilities between land and labour could produce this pattern. Historians will no doubt want to consider other possibilities such as changes in the relative political power of landlords and labourers that may have magnified the effect of population growth on marginal products.

Conclusions

The Malthusian devil was chained in Europe sometime before the nineteenth century. The difficulty historians face is that there are too few long-run episodes and too many multi-collinear movements during these episodes to be confident of identifying the effects of population growth on the economy. These problems are especially severe in the available time series data for early modern United Kingdom, which has heretofore served as the main laboratory for testing the Malthusian model. Comparable data for France

Table 7. Population and income distribution: regression results
for France and the United Kingdom

	1500–1800					
	France			England		
Constant	-12.256 (3.486)	-23.251 (6.045)	-23.259 (6.374)	-25.088 (0.971)	-27.642 (0.935)	-17.789 (6.370)
Population (log)	1.238 (0.348)	2.596 (0.708)	2.597 (0.737)	1.742 (0.160)	3.05 (0.456)	0.060 (0.748)
Year		-0.0016 (0.0007)	-0.0016 (0.0009)		-0.0051 (0.0017)	0.0003 (0.0018)
Prices (log)			-0.0004 (0.0074)			0.8084 (0.1791)
R-squared	0.319	0.423	0.423	0.815	0.863	0.924

Notes: The dependent variable is the log of nominal rents minus the
log of wheat prices. Standard errors in parenthesis.

confirm the negative consequences of population growth, but they may suffer from some of the same problems of coincidence in the historical timing of population growth and price changes.

Using a data set that combines cross-section and time-series evidence on the six leading economies of Western Europe, we have found substantial negative consequences of population growth for real wages, at least up through 1750. Although the magnitude of the effect (around -1.2) was smaller than estimates produced by Lee, it was larger than would have been expected from a simple Cobb-Douglas production function. In light of the very real possibility of measurement error in the cross-section population data, the true effect may have been even larger.

Changes in the rate of population growth had little effect on the rate of urbanization in early modern Europe. If weak substitutability in the agricultural production function were the source of the large wage effect, we would expect to see large increases in urbanization during rapid population growth. This result also goes against Goldstone's (1984) explanation of inflation as a consequence of rapid urbanization during rapid population growth. The true mechanism linking population growth and inflation remains obscure.

Real returns to land apparently rose rapidly when population grew. It is possible that total output rose, as classical production theory says it should. The question is whether the large swings in income distribution were produced by a market mechanism (factors paid their marginal products) or by some other form of bargaining or persuasion.

Future studies will need to take a closer look at the operation of labour markets. Institutional arrangements that might violate the neoclassical assumption that labour is paid its marginal product in all sectors of the economy are the foundation of the labour surplus models of economic development (Lewis, 1954; Fei and Ranis, 1964). They are also the basis of such historical concepts as the moral economy. Undoubtedly some variants of these models could explain the aggregate results without the same harsh implications about the consequences of population growth for the consumption levels of the labouring population. Perhaps indirect measures of changes in real incomes, like the patterns of demand for different types of goods, might help determine what really happened to consumption when population grew too quickly.

References

Allen, Robert (1988). The price of freehold land and the interest rate in the 17th and 18th centuries. Economic History Review , vol. 41, No.1, pp. 33–50.

Bairoch, Paul (1976). Europe's gross national product: 1800–1975. Journal of European Economic History, vol. 5, pp. 273–240.

Blouin, D. (1972). Aux confins de la Normandie: la rente foncière en pays chartrain. Annales de Normandie, vol. 22, pp. 133–145.

Brenner, Robert (1976). Agrarian class structure and economic development in pre-industrial Europe. Past and Present, vol. 70, pp. 30–75.

de Vries, Jan (1984). European Urbanization, 1500–1800. London: Methuen.

Deyon, Pierre (1967). Contribution à l'étude des revenus fonciers en Picardie: Les fermages de l'Hotel Dieu d'Amiens et leurs variations de 1515 à 1789. Lille, France: Reni Giard.

Fei, John and Gustav Ranis (1964). Development of the Labor Surplus Economy: Theory and Policy. Homewood, Illinois: Richard D. Irwin.

Goldstone, Jack (1984). Urbanization and inflation: lessons from the English price revolution of the sixteenth and seventeenth centuries. American Journal of Sociology, vol. 89, No. 1, pp. 1,122–1,160.

Goy, Joseph, and Emmanuel Le Roy Ladurie (1982). Préstations paysannes, dîmes, rente foncière, et mouvement de la production agricole à l'époque préindustrielle. Paris: EHESS.

Habakkuk, J. (1958). The economic history of modern Britain. Journal of Economic History, vol. 28, pp. 487.

Hatcher, John (1977). Plague, Population, and the English Economy. London: Macmillan.

Henry, Louis and Yves Blayo (1975). La population de la France de 1740 à 1860. Population, vol. 30, pp. 71–122.

Kelley, A. C. (1988). Economic consequences of population change in the Third World. Journal of Economic Literature, vol. 26, pp. 685–1,728.

Kelley, A. C. and J. G. Williamson (1984). Population growth, industrial revolutions, and the urban transition. Population and Development Review, vol. 10. No. 3, pp. 419–441.

Kerridge, E. (1953). The movement of rent, 1540–1640. Economic History Review, 2nd ser., vol. 6, No. 1, pp. 16–34.

Kuznets, Simon (1966). Modern Economic Growth: Rate, Structure, and Spread.
New Haven: Yale University Press.

Le Roy Ladurie, Emmanuel (1966) Les paysans de Languedoc. Paris: Mouton.

Lee, Ronald D. (1977). Methods and models for analyzing historical series of
births, deaths, and marriages. In Population Patterns in the Past,
Ronald Lee, ed. New York: Academic Press.

_____ (1980). A historical perspective on the economic aspects of the
population explosion: the case of pre-industrial England. In Population
and Economic Change in Developing Countries, Richard A. Easterlin, ed.
Chicago: University of Chicago Press.

_____ (1985). Population homeostasis and English demographic history.
Journal of Interdisciplinary History, vol. 15, No. 4, pp. 635–660.

_____ (1987). Population dynamics of humans and other animals.
Demography, vol. 24, No. 4, pp. 443–466.

Lewis, W. A. (1954). Economic development with unlimited supplies of labour.
Manchester School of Economic and Social Studies, vol. 22, pp. 139–191.

Lindert, Peter H. (1983). English living standards, population growth, and
Wrigley-Schofield. Explorations in Economic History, vol. 20,
pp. 131–155.

_____ (1985). English population, wages, and prices: 1541-1913. Journal
of Interdisciplinary History, vol. 115, No. 4, pp. 609-634.

McEvedy, C. and C. Jones (1978). Atlas of World Population History. New
York: Penguin Books.

Mitchell, B. R. (1980). European Historical Statistics, 1750–1975. London:
Macmillan.

Phelps-Brown, H. and S. Hopkins (1962). Seven centuries of the prices of
consumables, compared with builders' wage rates. In Essays in Economic
History, E. Carus-Wilson, ed. London: Arnold.

Postan, M. M. (1966). Medieval agrarian society in its prime: England. The
Cambridge Economic History of Europe, vol. 1. Cambridge: Cambridge
University Press.

Preston, S. H. (1979). Urban growth in developing countries: a demographic
reappraisal. Population and Development Review, vol. 5, No. 2,
pp. 195–215.

Tugault, Yves (1975). Fécondité et Urbanisation. Institut National d'Etudes
Dimographiques, Cahier 74. Paris: Presses Universitaires de France.

Veyrasset-Herren, B. and E. Le Roy Ladurie (1968). La rente foncière autour
    de Paris. _Annales_, vol. 23, No. 3.

Williamson, J. G. (1985). The historical content of the classical labour
    surplus model. _Population and Development Review_, vol. 11, No. 2,
    pp. 171-191.

Wrigley, E. A. and Roger Schofield (1981). The population history of England,
    1541-1871: a reconstruction. Cambridge: Cambridge University Press.

Zolla, D. (1893, 1894). Les variations du revenu et du prix des terres e
    France aux 17e et 18e siècles. _Annales de l'Ecole Libre des Sciences
    Politiques 1893_, pp. 299-326, 439-461, 686-705; 1894, pp. 194-216,
    417-438.

Chapter 3

Estimating the relationship between population growth and aggregate economic growth in developing countries : methodological problems

● D. Blanchet*

A well-known result concerning the relationship between population growth and economic growth in developing countries is the apparent lack of any negative impact of the former on the latter when tested through simple correlation analysis. This finding has been established by a large number of studies, including some by Easterlin (1967), Kuznets (1971), or Sauvy (1972), and it seems to be confirmed regardless of the sample used, the data source, or whether we consider global economic growth or only the growth of agricultural gross domestic product (GDP).

This result is at variance with what can be found from historical records in presently developed countries, 1/ and it has been perceived in various ways in the profession. On the one hand, some authors think that the statistical validity of this result is not to be questioned and that it shows without doubt that Malthusian or neo-Malthusian views of development problems are wrong. Indeed, this kind of empirical evidence has played some role in the emergence of the so-called "revisionist approach", which denies any responsibility for population trends in the persistence of underdevelopment (Hodgson, 1988). On the other hand, other authors refuse to abandon their Malthusian paradigm and prefer to think that this result is an artifact due either to the imperfection of data or to the fact that simple correlation analysis is an improper tool for analysing the problem. However, most of the arguments that are generally invoked to support this point of view are informal and of a purely ad hoc nature. For instance, a popular explanation for this non-significant correlation is the heterogeneity that exists among developing countries. In fact, it is clear that such a general and vague statement cannot be taken for an explanation; the real problem is not heterogeneity per se, but whether the heterogeneity is or is not of the kind that is properly dealt with by our statistical methods.

The aim of this paper will therefore be to review the relevance of these correlation results from a more analytical perspective. We will do so in three steps, corresponding to the three sources of regression bias as they can

---

*Professor, Institut national d'etudes demographiques (INED), Paris.

be listed in any manual of elementary econometrics. These three sources are:

(a) Measurement errors, i.e., the fact that population growth and/or economic growth are improperly measured by the indicators used in the regressions, either in a random or in a systematic fashion;

(b) Specification bias, i.e., the fact that simple correlation analysis does not control variables other than current population growth that might affect economic growth;

(c) Simultaneous equation bias, i.e., the fact that the analysis must also take into account the reverse effects that economic growth has on demographic growth.

But before coming to this discussion, we will briefly review the various regression results that have been produced up to now in the field and try to actualize them. Most of these results were published before 1980 and, due to delays in the publication of world statistics, generally pertain to the pre-crisis period, i.e., before 1975. Now, this actualization will produce an interesting surprise, for the past 10 or 15 years show that non-significant correlation is no longer the rule and that a negative relation could be emerging. This result has already been found by some other authors. It needs further confirmation and suffers, perhaps from the same problems of interpretation as the previous ones, but it could give a renewed importance to the question, so we will try to take it into account, even cautiously, in the rest of the paper.

**Earlier results and their actualization:
emergence of a negative correlation?**

Table 1, reprinted from Sagnier (1979), gives most of the results that were published prior to 1980. At this stage the overwhelming majority of studies showed no negative correlation between population and economic growth, regardless of the time period, the data source, the sample of countries, or consideration of either total GDP per capita or only the growth of agricultural GDP (the only studies showing a negative correlation being the early ones by Stockwell, which relied on very small samples). 2/

More recent results are given in table 2. Some of these results are still non-significant, but it is either because they do not include data later than 1975 (Simon and Gobin, Bairoch, 1981), or because they consider the whole period 1960-1980. By contrast, a significantly negative correlation coefficient was obtained with OECD data for 1970-1980 by an author who cannot be suspected of a Malthusian bias (Chesnais, 1985). The same result holds for the same period with data from the United Nations and from the World Bank (Blanchet, 1988), at least with a weighted regression and considering growth of global GDP per capita as well as growth of agricultural GDP. 3/

Table 3 examines whether this downturn is confirmed when using more recent data taken exclusively from the World Bank Report, 1986. We see that there is indeed a confirmation when considering a large sample including some

Table 1. Results established before 1980

Reference	time period	Number of countries	Correlation coefficient	Significance at the 5% level
Stockwell (1962)	1950-1960	16	-0.710	S.
Stockwell (1966)	1955-1961	37	-0.580	S.
Easterlin (1967)	1957/58-1963/64	37	0.002	N.S.
Kuznets (1971)	1950-1964	21	0.036	N.S.
Thirlwall (1972)	1950-1966	32	0.907	S.
Sauvy (1972)	1959-1969	35	-0.120	N.S.
Stockwell (1972)	1960-1969	26	-0.370	N.S.
Sauvy and Chesnais (1973)	1960-1970	76	0.040	N.S.
	1959/61-1969/71	51	0.110	N.S.
Hagen (1975)	1960-1965	76	0.160	N.S.
Chesnais (1975)	1960-1972	77	-0.035	N.S.
Klatzmann (1975)	1961/65-1970/75*	50	0.001	N.S.
Lefebvre (1977)	1960-1974	100	-0.055	N.S.
	1961/65-1974*	90	-0.012	N.S.
Guillaumont and Bara (1978)	1960-1973	70	0.184	N.S.
Lefebvre (1978)	1960-1975	96	-0.114	N.S.
	1961/65-1971/75*	90	-0.038	N.S.
Lefebvre (1979)	1960-1976	79	0.052	N.S.
	1960/65-1974/76*	81	0.051	N.S.

* Growth of agricultural product.

Table 2. Results established after 1980

Reference	Data source	Number of countries	Time period	Weighting	Correlation coefficient	Regression coefficient	t-ratio	Significance at 5% level
Simon and Gobin, 1980	U.N. and World Bank	50	1960-1970	NW			1.3	NS
		66	1960-1970	NW			-0.2	NS
		54	1950-1970	NW			1.5	NS
Bairoch, 1981	Morawetz, 1977	76	1950-1960	NW	-0.173			NS
		89	1960-1970	NW	0.004			NS
Chesnais, 1985	OECD, 1981	77	1960-1970	NW	0.185			NS
		"	1970-1980	NW	-0.287			S
Blanchet, 1985	World Bank, 1982	78	1960-1980	NW		0.138	0.296	NS
	"	"		W		0.623	1.290	NS
Blanchet, 1988a	U.N., 1980 and World Bank, 1982	77	1960-1970	NW	0.151	0.466		NS
		"		W	0.083	0.263		NS
		"	1970-1980	NW	-0.122	-0.596		NS
		"		W	-0.322	-1.361		S
Blanchet, 1988b *	U.N., 1980 and World Bank, 1982	42	1960-1980	NW	0.077	0.168	0.34	NS
		"		W	-0.031	-0.062	-0.18	NS
		"	1960-1970	NW	0.192	0.422	1.31	NS
		"		W	0.498	1.008	3.82	S
		70	1970-1980	NW	-0.089	-0.350	-0.75	NS
		"		W	-0.322	-1.307	-3.86	S
U.N., 1988	U.N.	58	1960-1983	NW	0.200	-0.700	-1.480	NS
		"	1960-1973	NW	0.200	0.750	1.510	NS
		"	1973-1983	NW	0.510	-2.430	-4.580	S

* Growth of agricultural product.

Table 3. Results derived from World Bank data

Data	Number of countries	Time period	Weighting	R^2	Regression coefficient	t-ratio	Significance at 5% level
Growth of global GDP, total sample	86	1965-1973	NW	0.0114	-0.346	-0.98	NS
	84	"	W	0.0037	0.275	0.55	NS
	82	1973-1984	NW	0.0767	-0.869	-2.57	S
	82	"	W	0.4599	-2.418	-8.25	S
Growth of global GDP, sub-sample	64	1965-1973	NW	0.0436	0.832	1.68	NS
	62	"	W	0.0496	1.290	1.76	NS
	61	1973-1984	NW	0.0153	-0.537	-0.95	NS
	61	"	W	0.5602	-2.865	-8.66	S
Growth of Agr. GDP, total sample	68	1965-1973	NW	0.0017	0.117	0.33	NS
	66	"	W	0.0264	-0.469	-1.31	NS
	75	1973-1984	NW	0.0136	-0.276	-1.00	NS
	75	"	W	0.5216	-2.190	-8.99	S
Growth of Agr. GDP, sub-sample	52	1965-1973	NW	0.0008	-0.097	-0.19	NS
	50	"	W	0.0968	-1.078	-2.26	S
	58	1973-1984	NW	0.1440	-1.269	-3.07	S
	58	"	W	0.7134	-2.883	-11.80	S

The total sample includes all countries classified by the World Bank as having low or intermediate incomes plus high income oil exporters. The sub-sample includes only those countries where GNP per capita was lower than 1700 U.S.$ in 1984.

countries with relatively high incomes (especially oil exporters, some Latin American countries, or newly industrialized countries). The downturn is less pronounced if we restrict ourselves to the subsample of the 76 poorest countries (countries with low or low-intermediate incomes). But the negative impact of population growth on this subsample is inversely more pronounced if we consider the growth of agricultural product. Some formal tests of the significance of the shifts between the two subperiods have also been performed. They are not reported on the tables, but they show that, while being insignificant in unweighted regressions, these downturns are all highly significant when weighting is introduced. A graphical illustration of the shift between the two subperiods is given by the scattergrams of figures I and II, where countries are represented by circles whose areas are proportional to total populations. These graphs show that the shapes of the relations are not strongly influenced by any set of atypical countries. This again has been controlled more formally (we have systematically tested that regression results that are significant do not become non-significant through one-by-one exclusions of countries from the sample).

Given the long tradition of non-significant results indicated in tables 1 and 2, this emergence of a negative correlation cannot be considered without caution. There would exist, of course, a simple explanation for it, which is that it has become more difficult to cope with population growth in a context of world economic crisis than it was before, when a variety of adjustments were available, including foreign aid and growing international debt. Yet, before coming to such interpretations, it is necessary to re-ask the question of the statistical relevance of such results, and, in fact, this question can be asked when they are not significant (as was done by Malthusians up to now), as well as when they are (what anti-Malthusians could try to do in the future, if the emergence of the negative correlation happens to be confirmed).

Measurement errors

Throughout the rest of the paper, we will use the following notations. We will note $P_{i,t}$ the total population and $Y_{i,t}$ the income per capita of country i at time t (indexes being dropped as often as possible). Lower-case letters will systematically represent logarithms, so that Δp and Δy will represent the growth rates of population and income per capita. The relation we try to test through simple correlation analysis is therefore:

$$\Delta y_{i,t} = a + b\Delta p_{i,t} + u_{i,t} \tag{1}$$

It can be justified, for instance, if we assimilate the growth rate of the population and of the labour force, if we assume a Cobb-Douglas production function with constant returns to scale, with a coefficient of labour equal to $1 + b$, where the only other factor of production is a fixed one (e.g. "land") augmented with an exogenous technical progress taking place at rate a.

A first set of conditions under which least squares estimates of b in equation (1) would be either unstable or biased is the presence of measurement

Figure I. Annual growth of GDP per capita and population growth
between 1965 and 1974

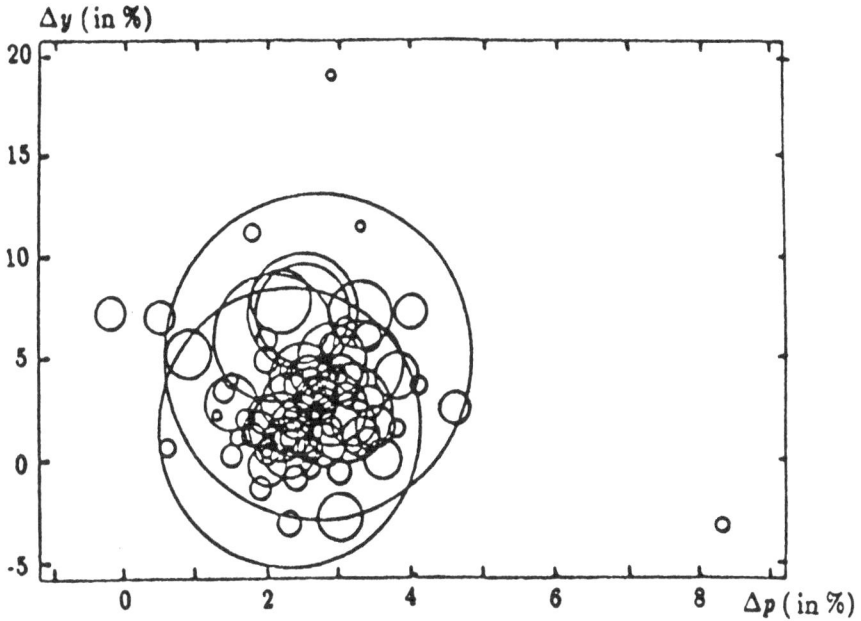

Figure II. Annual growth of GDP per capita and population growth
between 1974 and 1983

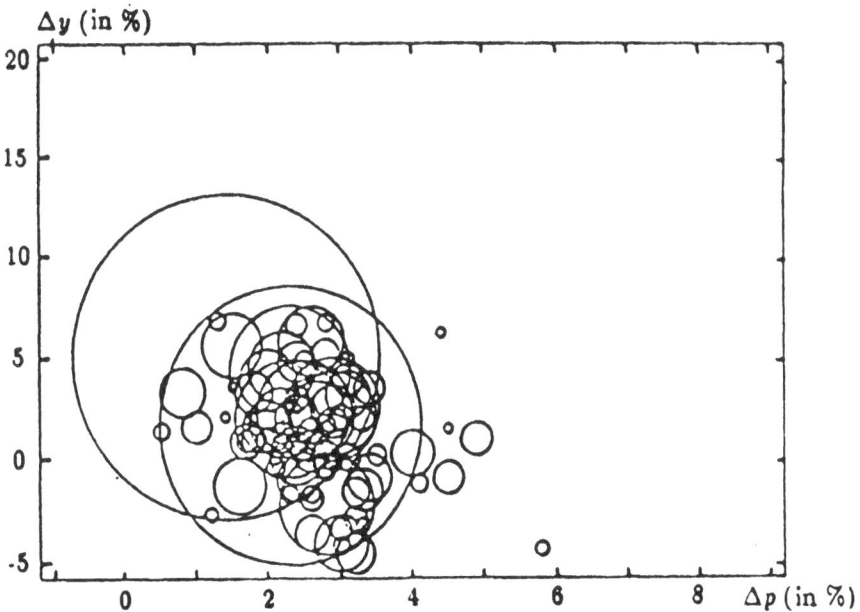

errors. That such errors exist is certain, given the imperfection of statistics for most of the countries considered. We will review their potential importance, distinguishing between random or systematic errors and between errors affecting Δp or Δy.

Random errors

A random measurement error is one that is independent from the levels of both Δy and Δp. It is generally believed that such an error will mostly affect the dependant variable Δy, given the low quality of national accounts in most developing countries. Such an error adds variability to the $u_{i,t}$ term in equation (1) and produces an estimate of b that is less stable, resulting in lower t-statistics or correlation coefficients. However, it does not introduce any systematic bias in the estimation of b so that, if b is actually negative, the estimate of b, t-statistics, and correlation coefficients should remain negative in a majority of cases. Table 1 showed that this does not seem to be the case. Of course, we could argue that the various results given in this table are not really independent because they more or less rely on the same national sources. However, it is more than likely that invoking a pure measurement error on GDPs is not the most convincing of the arguments that can be used to reject the correlation analysis.

The idea that there could be a measurement error on Δp is of more interest, since a well-known result in econometrics is the fact that random errors in the explanatory variable systematically bias regression estimates towards zero, which is the situation we would like to explain here. Demographers know very well that demographic data for developing countries are not necessarily of a better quality than economic data, at least for the earlier periods (although the situation may have improved during the 1970s). Now, as it is recalled in annex II, an underestimation of b by, say, 50 per cent, would require the measurement error on Δp to have a dispersion of the same order of magnitude as the dispersion of the true Δps. This seems quite high, so invoking measurement errors in Δp does not seem sufficient either. 4/

Systematic errors

What about systematic errors? It is difficult to see some reasons for a systematic error on Δp. What we need would be an underestimation of Δp where it is high and/or where Δy is low and vice-versa. It is difficult to see reasons why the error would go in this direction rather than the reverse. On the other hand, some suggestions have been made concerning some systematic errors on Δy. Let us consider three of them:

(a) The first is the fact that differences in GDP per capita do not exactly measure cross-national differences in standard of living. More appropriate measures of the latter can be taken from the work by Kravis and others (1982). This will not be done here. In fact, the problem is already corrected in part by the fact that we are working on variations of GDP and not on levels;

(b) The second suggestion is that GDP measures only the monetized share of the total production. Once again, since we are working on growth rates, this is important only if monetization grows at a rate that is correlated to population growth. The reasons for this are not evident. One possibility would be through urbanization, a higher population implying a higher growth of the share of total population living in towns and a more rapid increase of markets. However, this does not seem to hold empirically. Introducing the variation in the urbanization rate as a control variable in regressions does not change the regression coefficient of population and its significance. For 1960–1980, 5/ we get, without weighting (t–ratios given in parentheses):

$$\Delta y = 0.0313 + \underset{(0.051)}{0.020}\ \Delta p - \underset{(-2.448)}{0.222}\ \Delta\%URB \qquad (R^2 = 0.096)$$

and, weighting by populations in 1970:

$$\Delta y = 0.0069 + \underset{(1.541)}{0.729}\ \Delta p - \underset{(-0.460)}{0.043}\ \Delta\%URB \qquad (R^2 = 0.039)$$

As can be seen, urbanization has either no effect on economic performance or a negative one (the causality being perhaps in the opposite direction), but in any case, its introduction does not affect the significance of the coefficient of Δp.

(c) A last suggestion is made by Bairoch (1981). According to him, estimates of total product are often established by adding arbitrary values of growth rates per capita to the population growth rate. It is these arbitrary values that we get when re–subtracting population growth from growth of total GDP, and there is no reason for them to present any negative relation to population growth. According to Bairoch:

> "Population figures ... are often the only 'real' figure in an estimate. And it is much easier to postulate, say, a 5 per cent increase in any given production in a country whose population increases by 3 per cent, than to retain an increase of 4 per cent with a 2 per cent increase, and even more so 3 per cent with a 1 per cent."

Put in those terms, this hypothesis could even explain a positive relationship between Δp and Δy. It is perhaps more convincing than the two previous ones. In this case, the downturn in the relationhip between Δy and Δp could be a by–product of the improvment of statistical systems in developing countries, but it is, of course, difficult to appreciate this point without a high practical knowledge of these statistical systems.

Specification bias

We will now explore the possibility of a specification bias concerning the estimation of equation (1). Two kinds of bias will be distinguished. One is a bias due to an improper dynamic specification, i.e., the fact that we do not describe properly the various lags with which population is likely to affect income per capita. The second would be a bias due to a lack of control of other factors of economic development. This rubric includes consideration of the problem of heterogeneity among developing countries, which is generally invoked against econometric analysis of any kind of international cross-sectional data. As we have already indicated, the real problem in this respect is whether or not we are able to control for this heterogeneity, and, if we cannot, to know whether it merely introduces additional noise in the relationship or whether it can be a real source of bias.

Dynamic specification

That all the effects of population growth on economic growth are not instantaneous as postulated by relation (1) will be accepted without difficulty. The problem is to know how these effects differ between the short run and the long run and whether such differences can explain the results of simple short-run correlation.

There are two main possibilities in this respect. The simplest one would be to say that the negative impact of population growth on economic growth is only a long run one. This view can be held if we consider problems associated with natural resources. But we can also consider the opposite one, which is that it is long-run effects that are non-significant or positive and short-run effects that are negative. In this case, the impossibility of isolating these short-run effects through simple correlation analysis would be due to the high auto-correlation of population growth rates over time: If a country presently has a high population growth rate, it also had one in the past. What relation (1) measures is in fact the mix of the long- and short-run effects of this durably high demographic expansion.

Several a priori assumptions can justify this last position:

(a) First, in a model labeled "Malthusian", such as the Solow growth model, it is well known that an increase of the population growth rate has a temporary negative effect on the growth rate of income per capita but that, in equilibrium, the latter is completely independant of the former and is strictly equal to the rate of exogenous technical progress. A higher population growth rate implies a lower level of income, due to capital dilution effects, but not a lower growth rate of income (note that this result is due to the fact that this model is only weakly Malthusian, since it assumes constant returns to scale).

(b) Second, we can consider arguments à la Boserup or Simon that predict a positive long-run relationship due to positive effects of population growth on technological progress. Note that these assumptions are not in contradiction with a negative short-run impact. This negative short-run impact is even wholly imbedded in the Boserupian model (Boserup, 1965), since it is the apparition of economic difficulties that constitutes the direct stimulus to technical change (this is not the case in the various models elaborated by Simon (1986b), where technical progress is more a mechanical consequence of the increase in numbers and of production scale).

(c) Finally, we can separate short-run and long-run effects of population growth according to the way they affect the age structure of the population. A short-run increase, if it is due to a rise in fertility or a decrease of infant mortality, has only the consequence of adding young dependents to the population. It raises the denominator of income per capita without having any impact on its numerator, so its effect must be unambiguously negative. In the longer run, however, these young dependents become producers and will positively affect income per capita.

It is impossible to distinguish among all these possibilities without looking at the data. Now, if the fact that a negative relationship seems to appear after the early 1970s could be considered as supporting the idea that the negative effect is a long-run one, regressions of economic growth on current and lagged values of demographic growth (given in table 4), seem to better support the opposite idea of a positive long-run effect, since lagged values of Δp always have a positive effect on Δy. This positive effect of lagged values had been already observed by Sagnier (1979) through simple correlation analysis. We also observe that controlling lagged effects does not change anything to the sign reversal of the short-run effect documented in the first section of this paper. The coefficient is always very negative (much lower than -1) and is significant for 1970-1980, while non-significant for the first period.

A related idea, if the contrasted effect of population growth at different lags corresponds to contrasted effects on the age structure, is to distinguish between the mortality and the fertility components of the population growth rate. A high population growth rate may be due to a relatively high fertility, which will have the impact of raising the number of dependents, or to a relatively low mortality, whose effects on the age structure will be ambiguous since a rise in life expectancy can save lives at all ages. As a result, it is high fertility that should imply a low economic performance, while the impact of lower mortality could be of any sign. These predictions have been tested with some success by Coale (1986), who recalls that it was actually the consequences of high fertility, not those of low mortality, that were the concern of his seminal work with Hoover (1958).

Table 5 re-examines this point by giving multiple regressions of Δy on the birth and the death rates for 1960-1980 and for the two subperiods 1960-1970 and 1970-1980. We see that the coefficient of the death rate is indeed highly negative, which means that it is mainly when it is due to a low mortality that population growth is positively related to development. On the other hand, fertility is positively but weakly related to economic growth in the first period, contrary to expectations, and has a negative impact only during the second one.

Two points must be mentioned here. First, lower mortality implies lower morbidity, and it is well-known that the high endemicity of some diseases (e.g., malaria) has very negative effects on the productivity of labour (Barlow, 1967), so that any reduction of this endemicity has positive effects on both life expectancy and productivity of labour. This means that when economic growth is positively related to life expectancy and population growth, this may be more the effect of better health than of a higher number of producers. This point deserves particular attention, since we can have

Table 4. Multiple regressions of Δy on lagged values
of p (t-statistics in parentheses)

Period	Intercept	Δp_{50-60}	Δp_{60-70}	Δp_{70-80}	R^2
Unweighted					
1960-1970	0.001	0.943	-0.031		0.160
		(3.335)	(-0.091)		
1970-1980	0.036		0.577	-1.143	0.066
			(1.020)	(-2.162)	
1970-1980	0.028	1.026	0.135	-1.170	0.153
		(2.584)	(0.238)	(-2.305)	
Weighted					
1960-1970	0.006	0.667	0.156		0.086
		(2.385)	(0.445)		
1970-1980	0.050		0.390	-1.353	0.106
			(0.707)	(-2.680)	
1970-1980	0.028	1.928	0.931	-2.870	0.335
		(4.738)	(1.889)	(-5.285)	

Table 5. Multiple regressions of Δy on the death rate
and the birth rate (t-statistics in parentheses)

Period	Intercept	Death rate	Birth rate	R^2
Unweighted				
1960-1980	0.057	-1.591	-0.197	0.337
		(-3.339)	(-0.535)	
1960-1970	0.040	-1.721	0.316	0.245
		(-3.684)	(0.737)	
1970-1980	0.072	-1.064	-0.853	0.242
		(-1.468)	(-1.776)	
Weighted				
1960-1980	0.051	-2.265	0.252	0.440
		(-4.484)	(0.783)	
1960-1970	0.039	-2.436	0.638	0.387
		(-5.110)	(1.809)	
1970-1980	0.067	-0.920	-0.721	0.275
		(-1.141)	(-1.570)	

better health without growing numbers, if mortality reductions are exactly matched by fertility reductions.

Second, we should consider whether there are not some reverse effects with economic growth helping to reduce mortality. It is for fertility that this argument is more appealing. It is difficult to explain its positive link with Δy in the first period without considering the fact that, at the beginning of the demographic transition, it is increases in the standard of living that have a positive impact on fertility. We will reconsider this problem in the fourth section. 6/

Omitted factors of development

These remarks on the link between the health status of the population and economic growth lead us directly to the second kind of specification bias which is the omission of one or another factor of differences in economic growth between countries apart from differential population pressure.

We will not here go very deeply into this problem, which is in fact the wider problem of knowing whether there exists an adequate model accounting for differences of growth of GDP among countries. We shall only examine what is changed or not changed when we try to control regressions with some of the variables provided for the 1960s and 1970s by the World Bank reports. In doing so, we will exclude some variables for which exogeneity is not perfectly sure. For instance, although growth of exports is very intimitely connected with economic growth, we do not really know if a good performance in international markets is the source or the consequence of good economic performance inside the country. We therefore prefer an index of competitivity less susceptible to be endogenous to economic progress, which is the variation of terms of trade and which mainly corresponds to the endowment of countries with natural resources whose world prices have risen or fallen during the past 20 years.

Apart from this variable, we tested two variables describing the initial socio--economic structure of each country, the initial level of urbanization, and the initial level of schooling, given the recognized importance of education in the development process. We also added the initial density of population, since it was earlier found to have a positive impact on economic growth (see Simon and Gobin, 1980). This positive impact can be interpreted as the fact that higher density makes easier the diffusion of innovations, corresponding in fact to the systematization of the long-run positive effect of population growth, density at time t being the cumulated consequence of growth prior to t. 7/

Table 6 gives the results of these multiple regressions. We see that controlling for the variables we have chosen does not allow us to observe a significant impact of population between 1960--1980, nor does it suppress the opposition between a positive coefficient before 1970 and a strongly negative one after. We note, however, that the initial level of schooling actually has the strong positive effect that was expected, as is also the case for the index of variations for the terms of trade. Results are less clear for the urbanization rate and for density, which is significant when countries are not weighted but loses its significance after weighting, suggesting that the positive relationship might be due principally to the presence in the sample of small atypical countries with very high densities like Hong Kong or Singapore. These results are not changed when adding lagged values of Δp or when replacing Δp by the birth and the death rates (results not reported here).

Another way to control for heterogeneity in countries with regard to the development process is to work with variations of growth rates between successive periods, a procedure that controls all exogenous factors of differential growth that are stable over time. In fact, this procedure does not give better results than the more conventional correlations between growth rates. This point will be further developed in the next section, but we can note here that in any case, due to the relative stability of demographic parameters or at least of their cross-country differentials, the variations in population growth rates between two successive periods have low dispersions, which makes it difficult to assess their impact on any kind of dependent variable. Furthermore, the sign of the relation between second order differences cannot be determined accurately if there has been a shift in the relation between first order differences in successive periods.

Simultaneous determination of economic and demographic growth

The last idea that we will explore is that correlation analysis is irrelevant because it is biased by the fact that, in general, it is because there is economic development that there will be, simultaneously, demographic growth. This idea has been evoked by various authors (Cassen, 1976; McNicoll, 1984; Chesnais, 1985); we will consider that it can be operationalized in two ways:

(a) One is to write a model of feedback between demographic and economic growth. In this case, the low significance of correlation coefficients will be due to a simultaneous-equation bias, population growth being influenced by economic growth as well as influencing it. The possibility of such a simultaneity may be questioned on a priori grounds, as has been noted by a number of authors; we will try to examine it in detail.

(b) A complementary option will be to consider that computations ignore a latent variable, "development" taken in a broad sense, which simultaneously stimulates economic and demographic growth.

Simultaneity bias

Testing the value of b by simple regression or simple correlation analysis is correct only if Δp is truly exogenous, i.e., if there is no effect of economic growth on population growth. If it is not the case, i.e., if we have a reverse relation as follows:

$$\Delta p = c + d\ \Delta y + v \qquad\qquad\qquad (2)$$

then it is well known that the estimation of relation (1) will in fact produce
a mix of relations (1) and (2) whose apparent slope can be near zero if b and
d are of opposite signs and are of the same order of magnitude. The system
composed by equations (1) and (2) is in fact the simplest example of a
simultaneous equation model. It is not unuseful to develop it completely. We
have, solving (1) and (2):

$$\Delta p = \frac{1}{1 - bd} (ad + c + du + v) \qquad (3)$$

$$\Delta y = \frac{1}{1 - bd} (a + bc + u + bv) \qquad (4)$$

The regression coefficient $\hat{b}$ of Δy on Δp is the ratio of the covariance of
both variables to the variance of Δp. Assuming that residuals u and v are
uncorrelated and have dispersions $V_{\underline{u}}$ and $V_{\underline{v}}$, we get:

$$\hat{b} = \frac{dV_{\underline{u}} + bV_{\underline{v}}}{d^2 V_{\underline{u}} + V_{\underline{v}}} \qquad (5)$$

which can be near zero if d and b are of opposite signs and if $dV_{\underline{u}}$ and $bV_{\underline{v}}$
are of the same order of magnitude.

Such an approach raises two problems:

(a) First, in any case, the value of d will be much lower in absolute
value than the value we are expecting for b. The expression above shows that
this can be compensated for if the dispersion around equation (2) is much
lower than the dispersion around relation (3), i.e., if V_v is such that
V_u/V_v is approximately equal to b/d. Yet, this would imply that
demographic growth is very closely related to economic conditions, which is a
rather problematic assumption.

(b) Second, even if we admit a connection between population growth and
economic conditions, it is more usual to consider that it is the level of
income that affects population growth, not the fact that this level is
currently increasing more or less rapidly (Lee, 1983; Simon, 1986a). In fact,
it is more common to use a relation such as:

$$\Delta p = k(y - y^*) + v \qquad (6)$$

rather than relation (2). In this case we have no simultaneous
interdependency between population and income per capita, as depicted in

figure III, but only a recursive one, as depicted in figure IV, so in this context, least squares estimates of b recover all their validity.

We have developed elsewhere (1988) a model that tries to solve these difficulties. It basically consists of relations (1) and (6) but with three additional elements:

(a) First, we assume that pure recursivity is only valid on a yearly basis and we proceed to an aggregation of results over pluri-annual periods (typically 10 years), so that some interdependency is re-established. 8/

(b) Second, we introduce country-specific and time-independant error terms in equation (6), which is rewritten:

$$\Delta \, p_{i,t} \; = \; k \, (y_{i,t} - y^*) + v_{i,t} + g_t \tag{7}$$

This gives some extra variability to demographic parameters on a cross-sectional basis without having to increase the variance of $v_{i,t}$. It will also account for the empirical finding that population growth rates are very highly auto-correlated over time, the reduction of national disparities being very slow in this domain (for instance, the correlation between Δp_{70-80} and Δp_{60-70} is 0.54).

(c) Third, a country-specific error term is also added to equation (1), which is rewritten:

$$\Delta y_{i,t} \; = \; a + b\Delta p_{i,t} + u_{i,t} + f_i \tag{8}$$

The role of this last term is mainly to add another element of non-recursivity into the model, since f_i affects directly $\Delta y_{i,t}$ and indirectly $\Delta p_{i,t}$ through its effect on past values of Δy.

Under these conditions, it is possible to show analytically that, at equilibrium, realistic values of the different parameters lead to an apparent estimate of b that is very near zero. We will not reproduce these computations here. Table 7 just gives some numerical results, with a real value of b equal to -0.5, a period of temporal aggregation of 10 years, and various values of k and V_f (note that the value of V_g does not play any role in the results; it affects only the dispersions of Δy and Δp and not their relationship). We actually arrive at quite low estimates of b.

But it is much more interesting to use this model in simulation and out of equilibrium using a non-linear relationship between Δp and y, trying to reproduce the fact that the impact of income on population growth changes over the course of the demographic transition. 9/ Consider, for instance, the following relation:

Figure III.   Interdependency between economic and demographic
              growth: simultaneous case

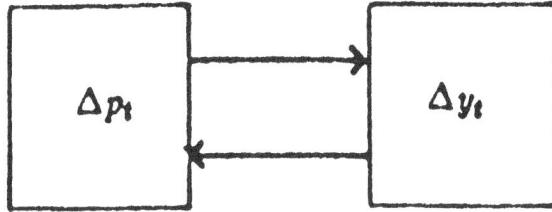

Figure IV.   Interdependency between economic and demographic
             growth: recursive case

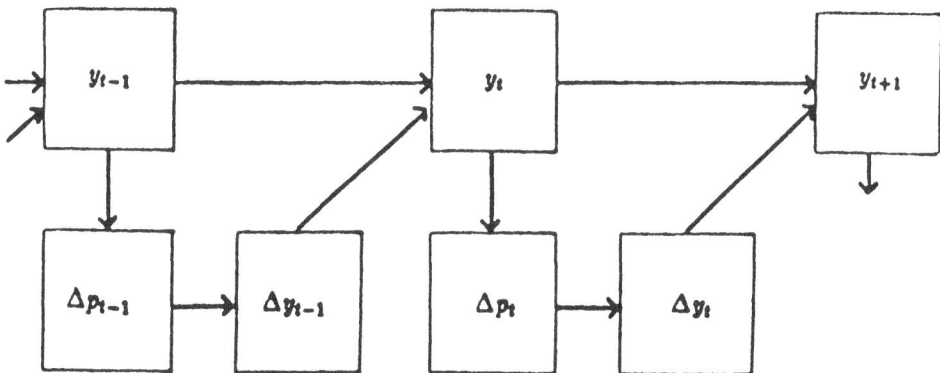

Table 6.   Multiple regressions of Δy on various indicators
(t-statistics in parentheses)

	Intercept	Δp	Initial urb. rate	Initial rate of schooling	Variation of terms of trade	Initial Density	R^2
			Unweighted				
1960-1980	0.021	0.220	-0.0002	0.0003	0.112	0.00001	0.547
		(0.123)	(-1.768)	(4.645)	(3.885)	(4.266)	
1960-1970	-0.005	0.596	-0.00007	0.00021	0.181	0.00001	0.389
		(1.869)	(-0.476)	(2.168)	(2.412)	(3.408)	
1970-1980	0.010	-0.464	-0.00015	0.00037	0.122	0.00001	0.334
		(-1.047)	(-0.761)	(2.537)	(2.483)	(2.416)	
			Weighted				
1960-1980	-0.016	0.726	-0.0001	0.00043	0.124	0.00001	0.480
		(1.959)	(-1.085)	(4.567)	(4.872)	(1.581)	
1960-1970	-0.012	1.057	0.00001	0.00012	0.362	0.00001	0.434
		(3.184)	(0.121)	(1.149)	(4.831)	(1.793)	
1970-1980	-0.004	-0.346	-0.0001	0.0005	0.087	0.00000	0.298
		(-0.585)	(-0.718)	(3.309)	(2.008)	(0.776)	

Table 7.   Ordinary least squares estimate of b in model (7,8) with
$b = -0.5$, $V_u = 0.0001$, $V_u = V_u/4$, and various values
of k and V_f

k	V_f	b	R^2
0.02	0.0	-0.2984	0.03791
	0.0001	-0.0032	0.00040
0.01	0.0	-0.3707	0.04536
	0.0001	-0.0031	0.00038
0.005	0.0	-0.4247	0.05097
	0.0001	-0.0031	0.00037

$$\Delta p = k (y-y^*) \frac{y - y^{**}}{y^* - y^{**}}^2 + v + g \tag{9}$$

which is equivalent to (6) around $y = y^*$ and has the shape given by figure V, for $k = 0.02$, $y^* = 1$, and $y^{**} = 7$. We see that we have three phases:

(a) Phase A (for y below $(2y^* + y^{**})/3$) where an increasing income implies a higher rate of population growth due to lower mortality and, eventually, to a rise in fertility;

(b) Phase B (for y between $(2y^* + y^{**})/3$ and y^{**}) where gains of life expectancy begin to be lower and where fertility begins to react negatively to income, implying a negative relationship between y and Δp.

(c) Finally, the hypothetical phase C, post-transitional, where fertility and mortality equilibrate and become independent of income.

Using this relation, we simulated the transition for 100 countries over 100 years. From an initial equilibrium with no technical progress ($a = 0$) implying, on the average, no growth of income per capita and no population growth, we shift first for ten years to a value of a equal to .025, and then for $t > 10$ to a value of a permanently equal to .05. Other parameter values are $b = -.5$, $V_u = V_f = V_g = .0001$, and $V_v = V_u/4$. Results are given in table 8. We see that, from an initial estimation of b near zero, we first go through a period where this estimate becomes positive, and which correspond to phase A of transition. Then this estimate decreases and becomes negative, and much more negative than the true value of b. This means that if the sign reversal after 1970 documented in the first section is due to such an underlying mechanism, the presently negative correlation may be an over-estimation, while previously non-significant results corresponded to an under-estimation.

Table 8 also gives the results of other estimators that could be tried to get an unbiased estimate of b. In fact, it appears that none of them yields acceptable results. Regression using second order differences (i.e., the variations of growth rates between the current period and the former one), which are theoretically designed to eliminate the effect of country-specific factors f and g, are very unstable and non-significant (t-statistics not reported); as mentioned earlier, this is due to the fact that the dispersion of $\Delta^2 p$ is very low, which makes it difficult to evaluate its impact on $\Delta^2 y$. Instrumental variable estimates, which should correct the endogeneity of Δp, also behave very unsatisfactorily, at least when y and/or y^2 are used as instruments, under- and overestimation being amplified rather than reduced. This is due to the fact that $y_{i,t}$, very highly correlated with f_i, is in fact all the contrary of a good instrument; interestingly enough, this is confirmed by regressions with actual data given in table 9, at least in the weighted case.

Table 8 gives at last the regression coefficients of Δp on y. They are always lower than k in absolute value, due to the fact that the sample always

Table 8.   Various regression results for data simulated according to model (7,9) for demographic transition

Period	Mean values		Regression coefficients				
	Δy	Δp	(1)	(2)	(3)	(4)	(5)
-10 to -1	0.0021	-0.0025	0.099	-0.737	0.135	0.094	0.0133
0 to 9	0.0257	0.0003	0.078	-0.284	0.059	0.034	0.0120
10 to 19	0.0463	0.0059	0.297	-0.868	0.593	0.552	0.0081
20 to 29	0.0441	0.0115	0.419	-0.280	1.329	0.998	0.0036
30 to 39	0.0431	0.0148	0.325	0.007	15.123	0.574	0.0003
40 to 49	0.0413	0.0163	-0.463	-0.438	-2.302	-1.750	-0.0028
50 to 59	0.0411	0.0166	-0.752	-0.659	-1.870	-1.864	-0.0046
60 to 69	0.0395	0.0159	-1.076	-0.776	-1.592	-1.590	-0.0058
70 to 79	0.0429	0.0148	-0.949	-0.298	-1.299	-1.276	-0.0063
80 to 89	0.0430	0.0127	-0.950	-0.449	-1.342	-1.233	-0.0064
90 to 99	0.0439	0.0110	-0.906	-0.874	-1.177	-1.152	-0.0061

(1) OLS regression of Δy on Δp.
(2) OLS regression of $\Delta^2 y$ on $\Delta^2 p$.
(3) 2SLS regression of Δy on Δp using y as instrument.
(4) 2SLS regression of Δy on Δp using y and y^2 as instruments.
(5) OLS regression of Δp on y.

mixes countries with low and medium income, for which the sign of the relationship is different. A sign reversal is observed when this last category of countries becomes dominant. All this, once again, is not in contradiction with actual patterns, which are shown in table 10.

Common factors affecting economic and demographic growth

Some similar results can be found if we assume that population growth and economic growth are not directly interdependent, but are under the common influence of some other unmeasured factors, as depicted in figure VI (to be compared with the diagrams of figures III and IV). Let us call z the unknown variable that summarizes these factors and that represents "development", taken in a broad sense. In such a case, we will write:

$$\Delta y = a' + b\Delta p + \alpha z + u' \tag{10}$$

$$\Delta p = \beta + \gamma z + v' \tag{11}$$

From this system, replacing z in the first equation by its value derived from the second one, we get:

$$\Delta y = a' + \left[b + \frac{\alpha}{\gamma} \right] \Delta p + u' - \frac{\beta + v'}{\gamma} \tag{12}$$

We see therefore that the regression coefficient of Δy on Δp will be equal to $b + \alpha/\gamma$. If b is negative and both α and γ are positive, as can be the case at the beginning of the demographic transition, then this regression coefficient can be near zero or even positive. We do not need to have a strong impact of z on demographic growth. On the contrary, the bias of b will be higher the lower the value of γ relative to α. Then, in the second stage of demographic transition, γ becomes negative, because "development" starts to have a negative impact on demographic growth. Then, due to a decreasing impact on death rates and an increasing negative impact on birth rates, we get an apparent impact of population growth on economic growth that is strongly negative.

As a whole, the simple model (10,11) can therefore be an alternative explanation for the sign reversal documented in the first section, without the need of any direct feedback from economic to demographic growth.

Conclusion

As mentioned in our introduction, the aim of this paper was mainly to review the various bias that can affect correlation analysis of economic and

Table 9.   Two–stage least squares regression coefficient of
           Δy on Δp (t-statistics in parentheses)

| | Un-weighted | | Weighted | |
Instruments	y	y,y^2	y	y,y^2
1960-1980 (67 obs.)	-130.642 (-0.042)	3.844 (2.013)	-11.835 (-0.575)	4.650 (2.261)
1960-1970 (74 obs.)	4.823 (1.076)	3.126 (2.273)	5.264 (1.102)	3.554 (2.559)
1970-1980 (69 obs.)	-4.519 (-1.213)	5.236 (1.119)	-4.770 (-1.570)	6.191 (1.207)

Table 10. Simple regressions of demographic variables on Y
           (t-statistics in parentheses)

| | Unweighted | | | Weighted | | |
Dep. variable	Δp	DR	BR	Δp	DR	BR
1960-1980 (78 obs.)	-0.002 (-0.450)	-0.026 (-8.924)	-0.026 (-6.532)	0.008 (2.626)	-0.022 (-8.752)	-0.016 (-4.156)
1960-1970 (78 obs.)	0.006 (1.300)	-0.028 (-9.539)	-0.021 (-5.817)	0.012 (2.957)	-0.025 (-9.843)	-0.016 (-4.727)
1970-1980 (76 obs.)	-0.007 (-1.959)	-0.018 (-8.630)	-0.024 (-7.660)	0.004 (1.434)	-0.014 (-7.459)	-0.012 (-3.632)

Figure V.   Theoretical relation between Δp and y (see relation (10))

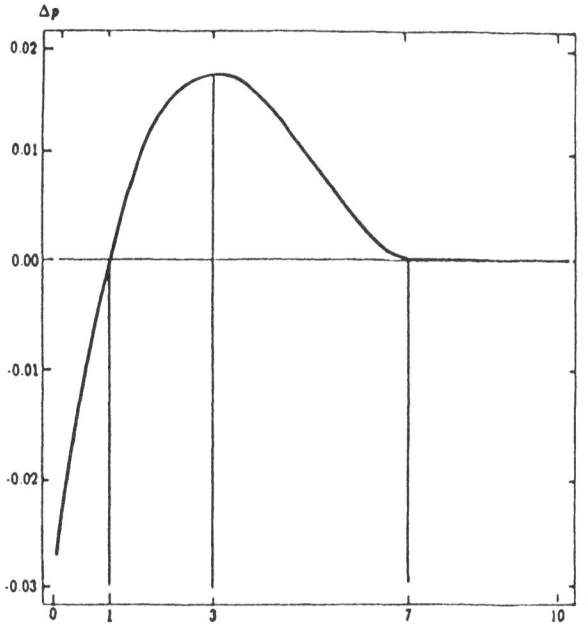

Figure VI.   Simultaneous dependency of economic and demographic growth
on a common factor

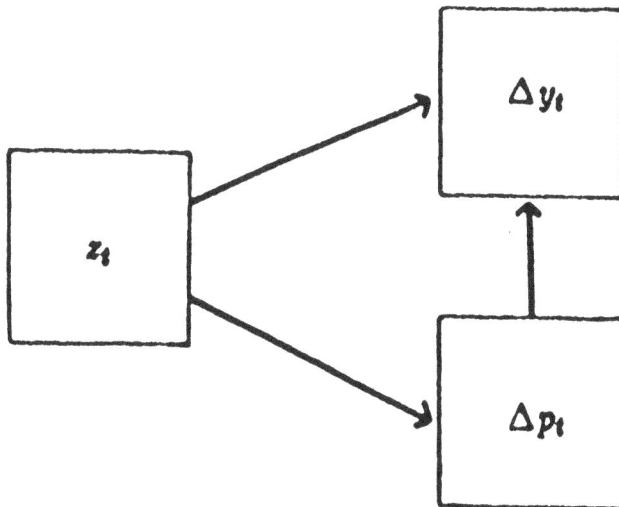

demographic growth. With these elements in hand, knowing if they actually play an important role in shaping the relations or non-relations between population and economic growth will be mainly a matter of personal appreciation. Now, a brief review of the policy implications of this discussion will be helpful. In short, we can ask what difference it makes which explanation we choose to account for the absence of correlation between economic and demographic growth. This can be done by reference to the three alternative views of demo-economic problems in developing countries suggested by Hodgson (1988):

(a) "Transition theory", i.e., the idea that demographic modernization and economic progress are phenomena that appear more or less hand in hand.

(b) The so-called "orthodoxy", that was dominant during the 1960s and 1970s, i.e., the idea that population growth has highly negative consequences, while a spontaneous reduction in fertility is by no means guaranteed, and must therefore be forced through family planning programmes.

(c) "Revisionism", or the idea that in any case demographic growth does not have the expected negative consequences, so there is no population problem.

If we consider that none of the sources of bias we have listed are really convincing, this means that correlation results actually tell us what is the true relationship between population growth and economic growth. In this case it is correct to say that population growth was not the problem in the 1960s and at the beginning of the 1970s. This is strict revisionism. But at the same time, we will have to admit that these correlations start telling another story from the 1970s and that revisionism itself needs some revision. This may be only temporary if positive consequences of population growth are to reappear in a longer run, but it nevertheless must be considered.

If we consider that correlations were irrelevant in the 1960s because of the bad quality of statistics and if we assume that the emergence of a negative relationship is due only to the fact that better statistics are available for the most recent period, this means that population growth systematically has a negative impact on economic growth and the Malthusian view is reinforced. In this case, policies aimed at reducing population growth rates are totally legitimated, provided they are not too much in conflict with individual interests; 10/ this is strict orthodoxy.

If we now consider, as in the fourth section, that we are in fact observing a mix of relationships with opposite causal directions, we get an intermediate position that bears some resemblance to the implications of transition theory. In this context, because of the presence of a negative structural relation from Δp to Δy, it remains true that any policy of exogenous reduction of population growth will have a positive impact on the growth of income per capita. But at the same time, it will be true that the existence of an equilibrating mechanism between population and resources implies that such policies are of a lower priority than is implied by strict orthodoxy. First, it is well known that if the Malthusian model of demo-economic equilibrium has the negative consequence that a population can get stuck at a low level of income, it symetrically implies that a population cannot see its level of income decrease dramatically under population pressure, since population pressure is itself the result of economic expansion. Second, and this is more important, if we believe in the stylized facts of demographic transition theory that have been used in the fourth section, we see that there is an autonomous process of escape from the Malthusian trap, as soon as exogenous technical progress is sufficient to drive countries to the point where the positive feedback from economic growth to population growth vanishes or becomes negative. In fact, as has already been recognized, a spontaneous escape from the Malthusian trap is not very difficult (Preston, 1975; Simon, 1980); although population policies may be useful in accelerating this process, they are not a sine qua non condition for it. They could become more necessary, however, in a context of international crisis where possibilities for rapid economic expansion have been largely reduced.

Notes

1/   With some nuances. See the contribution by D. Weir, this volume.

2/   Full references for the studies by Chesnais, Lefebvre, or Sauvy are not given in the references. All these studies can be found in Population.

3/   This table does not reproduce the results by Stavig (1979), whose sample includes developed as well as developing countries. However, we can note that the regression performed by Stavig on subgroups yields a significantly negative correlation for medium-income countries, while it is only for low-income countries that this correlation is non-significant. This shift could correspond at the cross-sectional level to the shift observed temporally around the early 1970s. We found a similar one with different data for the 1960-1980 period taken as a whole (Blanchet, 1985). However, we were not able to find it when considering the 1960s and the 1970s separately.

4/   Moreover, we can note that if Δy is obtained by subtracting an incorrect measure of population growth from direct measures of total output growth, then the resulting bias for the regression coefficient will be in the opposite direction, i.e., toward -1. The author is indebted to F. Bourguignon and R. Lee for pointing this out to him.

5/   For this regression as well as for all the following ones, purely demographic data (population growth, birth and death rates) are taken from United Nations (1980), and all other data from the World Bank Report, 1983.

6/   Note that these potential simultaneity biases were perhaps reinforced in the study by Coale, where rates of growth of GDP were related to demographic parameters at the end of the period rather than to their average values for the period. His more significant results are also due to the fact that he examines separate regressions of Δy on mortality and fertility, not a multiple regression using these two variables simultaneously.

7/   We also attempted to introduce the initial level of income per capita, whose effect could be a priori negative ("the advantage of backwardness") or positive (development being easier once a certain level has already been reached). This effect proved to be generally insignificant, although systematically negative. In any case, controlling for it does not change most results for the other variables.

_8/_   Note, however, that there may well be in some circumstances a direct impact of economic growth on demographic behaviour, independent of its impact on mid-period levels of income. For instance, fertility and in- or out-migration depend in part on long-term economic prospects, which are very sensitive to present growth. It has sometimes been argued that it was rapid economic growth during the 1950s or the 1960s which determined the failure of some family planning programmes, since people saw no positive reason to lower their fertility in a context of economic expansion.

_9/_   We give elsewhere another account of these potential shifts in the relationship between Δp and Δy during the demographic transition, relying on a very simple continuous-time model (Blanchet, 1989).

_10/_   This is, of course, another debate (see the contribution by Lee, this volume).

Annex I

WEIGHTING VERSUS NON-WEIGHTING

Weighting is a common practice in regression analysis when statistical units are of very different sizes, and this is the case here. On the other hand, it seems exaggerated to weight strictly by population sizes, which imply, for instance, that China will have about 100 more importance in shaping regression results than any developing country of around 10 million inhabitants. In fact, both weighted and unweighted regressions can be respectively justified with two simple and contrasting assumptions. Consider a country of population P as the reunion of n small units with populations equal to p. Then, if we have a relation at the regional level:

$$y_i = a + bx_i + u_i \qquad\qquad (13)$$

with all u_i's being independant and having the same variance σ^2, then the relationship at the country level (taking the average over all) is:

$$y = a + bx + u \qquad\qquad (14)$$

with:

$$u = \frac{1}{n} \sum_{i=1}^{n} u_i \quad \text{and} \quad Var(u) = \frac{\sigma^2}{n} \qquad\qquad (15)$$

so that the variance of u is inversely related to population size. We have therefore a justification for weighting, but this justification relies on the assumption that the u_i's are all strictly independent or, in other words, that the disparities are the same between regions of a given country than between regions of two different countries. This is certainly false because national boundaries, even arbitrary ones, have a certain meaning (uniformity of the political system, of some institutions at the intra-national level), and because of purely geographical similarities (regions of a given country are more likely to belong to the same geographical set than are regions of two different countries belonging, for instance, to two different continents).

If we now make the exactly symmetric assumption that there is perfect homogeneity within countries, then u_i is the same for all regions inside any country and the value of u for this country is equal to the common value of these u_i's, so that $Var(u) = \sigma^2$ and is independent of country size, which justifies unweighted regression.

It is clear, therefore, that weighted and unweighted regressions correspond to two equally implausible assumptions about the structure of error-terms inside and accross countries, and that the correct results lay somewhere between these two extremes.

Annex II

RANDOM MEASUREMENT ERROR ON THE EXPLANATORY VARIABLE

Consider equation (1) and assume that instead of the true value of Δp, we are using as a regressor $\Delta p'$, which is equal to Δp plus a measurement error term ε assumed to be uncorrelated to Δp. We have the relation:

$$\Delta y = a + b\Delta p' - b\varepsilon + u$$

whence the regression coefficient of Δy on Δp, which is:

$$\frac{\text{Cov}(\Delta y, \Delta p')}{\text{Var}(\Delta p')} = b \frac{\text{Var}(\Delta p)}{\text{Var}(\Delta p) + \text{Var}(\varepsilon)}$$

so that, for instance, the true value of b will be underestimated by half if the dispersion of ε is as high as the dispersion of the true value of Δp.

References

Bairoch, P. (1981). Population growth and long term economic growth. International Population Conference, Manila, vol. I. Leige: International Union for the Scientific Study of Population.

Barlow, R. (1967). The economic effect of malaria eradication. American Economic Review, vol. 57, pp. 130-148.

Blanchet, D. (1985). Croissances économique et démographique dans les pays en développement: indépendance ou interdépendance? Population, vol. 1, pp. 29-46.

_____ (1988). A stochastic version of the Malthusian trap model: consequences for the empirical relationship between economic growth and population growth in LDC's. Mathematical Population Studies, vol. 1, pp. 79-99.

_____ (1989). Croissance de la population et du produit par tête au cours de la transition démographique: un modèle malthusien peut-il rendre compte de leurs relations? Population, vol. 3.

Boserup, E. (1965). Population and Technological Change: A Study of Long-term Trends. Chicago: University of Chicago Press.

Cassen, R. H. (1976). Population and development: a survey. World Development, vol. 4, pp. 785-830.

Chesnais, J. C. (1985). Progrès économique et transition démographique dans les pays pauvres: trente ans d'expérience (1950-1980). Population, vol. 1, pp. 11-28.

_____ and A. Sauvy (1973). Progrès économique et accroissement de la population: une expérience commentée. Population, vols. 4-5, pp. 843-857.

Coale, A. J. (1986). Population trends and economic development. In World Population and U.S. Policy. The Choices Ahead, J. Menken, ed. New York: W. W. Norton and Company.

_____ and Hoover, E. G. (1958). Population Growth and Economic Development in Low Income Countries. A Case Study of India's Prospects. Princeton: Princeton University Press.

Conlisk, J. and D. Huddle (1969). Allocating foreign aid: an appraisal of a self help model. Journal of Development Studies, pp. 245-251.

Easterlin, R. A. (1967). The effects of population growth on the economic development of developing countries. Annals of the American Academy of Political and Social Sciences, vol. 369, pp. 98-108.

_____ and R. Gobin (1980). The relationship between population and economic growth in LDCs. In Research in Population Economics, vol. 2, J. Simon and J. Da Vanzo, eds. Greenwich, Connecticut: JAI Press.

Stavig, G. R. (1979). The impact of population growth on the economy of countries. Economic Development and Cultural Change, vol. 27, No. 4, pp. 737-750.

Stockwell, E. G. (1962). The relationship between population growth and economic development. American Sociological Review, vol. 27, No. 2, pp. 250-252.

_____ (1966). Some demographic correlates of economic development. Rural Sociology, vol. 37, No. 4, pp. 216-224.

_____ (1972). Some observations on the relationship between population growth and economic development during the 1960's. Rural Sociology, vol. 37, No. 4.

Thirlwall, A. P. (1972) A cross-section study of population growth and the growth of output per capita income in a production function framework. Manchester School of Economics and Social Studies, pp. 339-356.

United Nations (1988). World Population Trends and Policies: 1987 Monitoring Report. Sales No. E. 88.XIII.3.

Guillaumont, P. and M. F. Bara (1978). La croissance démographique optimale: à la recherche d'une vérification empirique. Population, vol. 6, pp. 1207–1216.

Hagen, E. (1975). The Economics of Development. Homewood, Illinois: Irwin.

Hodgson, D. (1988). Orthodoxy and revisionism in American demography. Population and Development Review, vol. 14, No. 4, pp. 541-570.

Klatzmann, J. (1975). Nourrir dix milliards d'hommes? Paris: PUF, pp. 77-79.

Kuznets. S. (1971). Population and economic growth. Proceedings of the American Philosophical Society, vol. 3, pp. 170-193.

Kravis, I., A. Heston and R. Summers (1982). World Product and Income. Baltimore: The Johns Hopkins University Press.

Lee, R. D. (1983). Economic consequences of population size, structure and growth. IUSSP Newsletter, vol. 17, pp. 43-59.

McNicoll, G. (1984). Consequences of rapid population growth: overview and assessment. Population and Development Review, vol. 10, No. 2, pp. 177-240.

Morawetz, D. (1977). Twenty-five Years of Economic Development. 1950 to 1975. Washington, D.C.: World Bank.

Preston, S. (1975). The changing relationship between mortality and the level of economic development. Population Studies, vol. 29, No. 2, pp. 231-248.

_____ (1980). Causes and consequences of mortality declines in less developed countries during the twentieth century. In Population and Economic Change in Developing Countries, R. A. Easterlin, ed. Chicago: University of Chicago Press, pp. 289-341.

Sagnier, G. (1979). Une hypothèse de décalage en démographie économique. Population, vol. 3, pp. 718-723.

Sauvy, A. (1972). Les charges et les avantages de la croissance de la population. Population, vol. 1, pp. 9-26.

Simon, J. L. (1980). There is no low-level fertility and development trap. Population Studies, vol. 34, No. 3, pp. 476-486.

_____ (1986a). Review of NAS, population growth and economic development: policy questions. Population and Development Review, vol. 12, No. 3, pp. 569-577.

_____ (1986b). Theory of Population and Economic Growth. Oxford: Basil Blackwell.

PART THREE

Adaptation to rapid population growth

Chapter 4

International economic relations and rapid demographic growth in dependent countries

J. Coussy*

Introduction

The interactions between rapid demographic growth in poor countries and their external relations have been the subject of extremely varied and even contradictory analysis, particularly when presented in the form of models. 1/ An initial identification of these interactions must be preceded by a recapitulation of the various analysis. Secondly, when these analysis differ from each other, the places and causes of these differences must be pointed out, as they are not always made very clear by their authors. It will be necessary to outline how the universalist ambitions of the models have limited their relevance.

Demographic growth and external economic relations in the principal demo–economic models

The implications of the most well–known models on the interactions between rapid demographic growth and the main external economic variables of economies have been summarized in table 1.

The main sources of the divergences between the different representations of foreign economic relations of countries with rapid demographic growth

The opposition between the conclusions of the various demo–economic models concerning the foreign economic relations of countries with rapid demographic growth is explained not by simple differences in the quantitative estimation of the parameters but by qualitative differences between the structures of the different models. These are based on hypotheses that are often both a priori and formally very simple, two characteristics that exacerbate the divergences of the conclusions beyond what simple differences in the estimation of parameters would produce.

---

*Ecole des Haute Etudes en Sciences Sociales, Paris.

Table 1

	I. Extensive growth models	II. Optimum population models
Bibliographic reference	J. E. MEADE (1955) P. T. BAUER (1981)	M. GOTTLIEB (1949) A. SAUVY (1963)
Presentation of the models	Analytical models and historical descriptions	Analytical and pedagogical models
Geographic relevance (according to the authors)	West Africa	All countries where the phase of increasing returns is followed by a phase of diminishing returns (in agriculture)
Impact of rapid demographic growth on the: Openness of economics	Rate of opening may be constant (homothetic growth)	Opening in case the diminishing returns threshold is by passed
The terms of trade	Risk of deterioration if the extensive growth goes beyond the size of the "Great nation" without modifying the export structure	Due to opposite evolution of returns in agriculture and in industry, the terms of trade tend to favour agriculture
The structure of the foreign trade	Cash crop exports Consumer goods imports Need for a transport infrastructure	Imports of agricultural products Export of Industrial products
The equilibrium of the balance of payments	Likelihood of obtaining equilibrium or even a surplus. But danger of disequilibrium is case if deterioration of the terms of trade.	Model often presented with a hypothesis of an equilibrium of the balance of payments
Capital movements	Capial inflows and outflows possible but non-essential.	Non-essential capital movements But which could favour industrialization.
Cost/advantages of external relations	Sale of goods that cannot be absorbed by the domestic market. Possibility of take off thanks the exports, But risks of specialization in the primary sector	Foreign relations enable to avoid: - a decrease in per capita income - a stoppage of growth due to the rise of differential rents
Demo-economic future	The extensive growth is ine0ly temporary. Should be replaced by another kind of growth.	Specialization increases the size of optisus population.
Special remarks	Model claiming limited relevance in time and space	Model extending the Richardian model

Table 1 (continued)

III. Macro-economic national growth models	IV. Integrated world economy models
A. J. COALE & E. M. HOOVER (1958) L. TABAH (1968) and (1969) S. ENKE (1976)	D. L. MEADOWS (1977) M. MASAROVIC & E. PESTEL (1974) BARILOCHE model (A. O. HERRERA, 1977)
Prospective and/or normative models	- MEADOWS: prospective model - MESAROVIC & PESTEL: prospective model - BARILOCHE: normative model
All developing countries suffering from shortage of capital and/or foreign currency and/or sectorial shortage	World economy
Opening made necessary in short term (due to "gaps")	The MEADOWS model disregards borders The M. & P. model takes up the logic of macro-economic models given in column III The BARILOCHE model aims at insularisation
The terms of trade are an exogenous variable influencing the external disequilibrium	The MEADOWS model disregards the international terms of trade The M. & P. model: terms of trade are exogenous to the model The BARILOCHE model: terms of trade are an exogenous factor of the model.
Structure determined by supply and demand in relation to population: likely need of importing elasticities of capital goods, food products and inputs	In prospective models: there is a growth of the needs of food, agricultural inputs and equipment. The BARILOCHE model: demand can be oriented towards the satisfaction of basic needs and imports of luxury items can be reduced.
External gap is a hypothesis (sometimes normative) of the model	The MEADOWS model: takes no interest in disequilibriums between nations. In the M. & P. model the disequilibriums are high according to the logic of macro-economic models and according to the high estimation of parameters initial disequilibriums in the BARILOCHE model but they can be corrected.
Need for foreign capital (one of the objecives of the model being to estimate it)	Do not concern the MEADOWS model Needs of Public aid are very high in the M. & P. model. Capital inflow reduction hoped in the BARILOCHE model
Opening necessary to reduce bottlenecks and to satisfy incompressable needs.	The MEADOWS model: openness only dilutes the impact of the Malthusian process by making it world-wide The M. & P. model: openness relieves regional bottlenecks. The BARILOCHE model: openness stops and distorts development.
Current deficit might be a means of obtaining future self-sufficiency in growth	Very pessimistic forecasts for the very long term about the demographic growth impact in MEADOWS as in the M. & P. models. The BARILOCHE model being more optimistic (with economic growth restroacting on the demographic growth)
The most widely used model in the 1960's	Though the three models have a common geographic field of observations and all deal with the emergence of environment problems, each one follows its own logic.

Table 1 (continued)

	V. Neo-classical model of international specialization
Bibliographic references	All neo-classical authors share this model
Presentation of the models	Theoretical model
Geographic relevance	All countries (developed and developing)
Impact of rapid demographic growth on the: Openness of economies	Openness dictated by the international disparities between the demographic growth rate and the rate of accumulation
The terms of trade	Danger of deterioration of the factorial terms of trade of labour in countries with rapid demographic growth
The structure of foreign trade	Exports of labor intensive products Imports of capital intensive products
Equilibrium of the balance of payments	- Automatic equilibrium of trade in case of no movements of capital - But possibility of imports of capital
Capital movements	Tendency to attract private capital by the disponibility of the work force Pubic aid possible, but not essential in the model
Cost/advantages of external relations	Slowing down in the deterioration of the terms of trade, due to openness The openness reduces the costs caused by the demographic growth in the case of a Malthusian situation
Demo-economic future	Tendency towards international dissemination (and dilution) of the effects of demographic growth through the international equalization of the price of factors
Special remarks	The model need not necessarily be Malthusian (despite the fact that many of the presentations sound Malthusian)

Table 1 (continued)

VI. Dependentist theories	VII. Dunlist models
S. AMIN and F. O. OKEDIJI (1971)	A. LEWIS (1954) G. RANIS and J. C. H. FEI (1961)
Criticism of the principle of of moderlization	Theoretical and sometimes econometric models Historical descriptions under the forms of models
All dependent countries, especially Sub-Saharan Africa	Developing countries with an unemployed reserve work force
Openness in an exogenous variable determined by economic dynamics of the "Centre" and not by the demographic growth	Openness does not automatically follow demographic growth, but makes its assimilation easier
(Exogenous) tendency towards deterioration fostered by international inequality and not by demographic growth	Expansion achieved mainly through competition would lead to the acceptance of lower terms of trade But the latter can raise incomes (rise in volumes)
The power given by the size of population might help dependent countries in their international negotiations on prices	At first exports of labour intensive products Diversified exports come later Imports of equipments and inputs
Exogenous disequilibriums are likely, but not inevitable	The balances of payments differ according to countries and development phases
Capital movements are determined by the economic dynamics of the "Centre" and not by the "peripheral" demographic dynamics	Attracting private foreign investors through lower labour costs (but also through internal capital formation) Public aid useful, but non-essential
Openness stops and distorts development	Openness helps to avoid multiple risks of hampering (partially and temporarily) the growth Competitivity stimulates accumulation and productivity
Demographic growth can reverse tendencies created by the international economy: - by making easier the inward looking policy - by creating scale economics based on the domestic market	Economic growth boosted by employing the reserve workforce can go on even after the reserve had been exhausted and leads to a reduced demographic growth
Some dependentist writings are less hostile to the method of models and less optimistic about the positive effects of the demogrqphic growth	Dualist models are very eclectic as well as evolutive

105

Often, however, the authors of the various models have not felt the need to make explicit the way in which their hypotheses differ from those of alternative models. It is rare that one finds detailed polemics on the basis of opposing theories (for example, between "Malthusian" models and Marxist or non-Marxist "dependentist" models) (Coussy, 1983a).

This frequent indifference to the specific hypotheses of each model has not only impoverished the debate (which is too often polarized on the basis of differences in results); it has often made it necessary to accept or reject one model and one model alone. However, this position has become more and more difficult to maintain as it has become evident that none of the models can claim to have foreseen the dynamics of poor countries with rapid demographic growth (Coussy, 1983b). Neither rates of growth of per capita income nor foreign economic and financial flows have shown simple correlations with the rates of demographic growth of the countries concerned (Chesnais and Sauvy, 1973). This failure of verification of very simple models – about which there was in itself nothing surprising – was often interpreted as a lack of reflection about the multiplicity and complexity of the economic and social-political models, as a total failure of the best-known models and sometimes even as casting doubt on modelling (Chesnais, 1981). This is an additional reason for attempting to combine hypotheses belonging to different models in order to take account of the complexity of the economic and social-political effects of demographic pressure in a real economy and to set, against the search for simple correlations, a more diversified vision of the different economies with rapid economic growth.

To prepare such combinations and weightings of the processes exhibited by the various models, it is therefore necessary to deconstruct the models, identifying their most questionable hypotheses and emphasizing those which, because they had the most influence on the results and were most specific to each of the models, were most responsible for the diversity of their results.

It seems possible to divide these strategic hypotheses into four main groups: hypotheses on the effects of external economic and financial relations; hypotheses on the form of production functions; hypotheses on capital formation; hypotheses on the incompressibility of needs.

Divergences on the effects of external economic relations

With regard to external economic relations, the demo-economic models accepted, without always saying so explicitly, different hypotheses on "gains from trade", the terms of trade, and the articulation of the internal and external dynamic.

Divergences on the reality of "gains from trade" and from factoral mobility. The assessment of "gains from trade" and factoral mobility gains created a first split among the demo-economic models: on the one side, the neo-classical specialization and growth models, the optimum population models, the extensive growth models, most of the macro-economic growth models, and some versions of the dualistic models adopted without discussion the canonical theorems of trade and factoral mobility gains; on the other side, as we have seen, the "dependentist" theories (including some macro-economic models like the Bariloche model) and some presentations of the dualistic models (including those of A. Lewis) that emphasized the costs dependent countries.

This sharp divergence, which only a few authors like A. Lewis were able to avoid, seems rather simplistic when one remembers the variety of possible perverse effects of external economic relations to which the dependentist authors have pointed over the last few decades and the increasing complexity of the debate concerning the reality of these perverse effects. Could not the opening to goods and capital flows, which was expected to make possible the absorption of demographic growth, raise the risk of increasing unemployment by encouraging the departure of labour-complementary factors (capital flight, the brain drain, and exports of unfinished raw materials). Would it slow domestic accumulation by reducing, in P. Baran's terminology, the "realized surplus" below the "potential surplus"? Would the external financing called for by the "Malthusian" macro-economic growth models in order to meet the savings deficit have the effect, as maintained by T. Weiskopf (1972), of further reducing domestic savings? (Grinols and Bhagwati, 1976; Wasow, 1979).

Would the opening to foreign consumer goods to meet the needs of the growing urban population have the effect of modifying consumer tastes thereby reducing the comparative advantages of traditional producers by contracting their markets?

Would the growth of imports permitted by external deficit financing inhibit the effects of apprenticeship and the other growth factors long emphasized by the partisans of protectionism "à la List"? Would resort to food imports in order to meet the risk of declining per capita production have the effect of discouraging potential agro-food production? Would the reduction of insecurity of food supply (climactic accident, local shortages) have the effect of increasing vulnerability to foodstuff insecurity of foreign origin (price instability, foreign payment crisis)? Does openness increase or decrease inequalities of income, wealth, and powers determine accumulation and satisfaction of essential needs?

All these questions, which it seemed possible to answer by the statement of simple converging positions when demo-economic models were constructed, must now be given answers differentiated according to the country, the period of observation, and the time-frame of the projections.

Divergences on the relations between terms of trade and demographic growth. If an attempt is made to integrate the descriptions of the evolution of terms of trade given by the various demo-economic models, it becomes evident that most of these descriptions can be articulated into a rather simple sequence.

In the first phase, assumed to take place in a closed economy, demographic growth stimulates a probable growth of traditional production, which (except in the case of closed proportional extensive growth) brings about a deterioration of the terms of trade and lowers relative labour renumeration. These tensions may stimulate two processes (alternative or simultaneous).

On the one hand, the growth of income and production may make possible the emergence of another sector (a process described by the dualistic methods), the development of which cannot be determined a priori since it will be a result of the relative rates of sectoral growth and of accumulation, relative growth of productivity, and distribution policies.

On the other hand, the economy may be open, which will suppress or delay the negative effect of demographic growth on the terms of trade, at least as long as the economy remains small in size (the process described by the neo-classical theorists). But it is clear that this negative effect will recur as soon as demographic growth increases the size of the country to the point where it influence world prices, or when the growth takes place simultaneously in several countries that together constitute a large economy. Only if the increase in external income is quickly used for the reconversion and diversification of activity will differentiated development of the terms of trade appear (as in the dynamic of closed economies).

This possible sequence of contrasting phases of the evolution of the terms of trade has had three main consequences for the place of the latter in the demo-economic models.

Firstly, in the case of many demo-economic models, their results have shown a deterioration in the terms of trade simply because, deliberately or not, they failed to introduce the possibility of the reconversion of activities; this is true for Meade's first very simple models as well as the recent models of growth in skilled-labour-exporting developing countries. 2/

Secondly, many apparently diverging statements concerning the impact of demographic growth on terms of trade result from the fact that their authors have taken into consideration only one moment of the sequence. The models fixing attention on the moment of opening see foreign trade as improving the terms of trade of overabundant products and labour, while the models dealing with an already open economy are troubled by the deterioration in terms of trade which may arise from differences in demographic growth.

Thirdly, the very exposition of the closed economy/open economy sequence seems dangerous to several authors, dependentists, who deny its historical relevance. For them the international division of labour arouse not from a gradual opening of closed economies seeking to reduce their internal tensions but from an asymmetrical act of international expansion by dominant countries, which were able politically and economically to impose unfavourable and diminishing terms of trade on the poor countries.

Divergences on the relative weight of internal and international dynamics. The debate on the reality of the closed economy/open economy sequence goes well beyond the debate on the terms of trade. For each of the parameters of foreign economic relations (balance of trade, external financing, structure of trade), differences exist concerning the historically leading variables and the relative responsibility of international and internal particular demographic dynamics.

These differences are, as we have seen, sometimes explicit. That is the case, for instance, in the debate between deficit models and dependentist models, where the explanation on the basis of the pressure of internal needs created by demographic growth is consciously criticized by partisans of the explanation on the dynamics of accumulation in the developed countries.

On the other hand, the weight attributed to the internal and the external dynamics is then the result of implicit and even unconscious choices. The pedagogical expositions (for instance, of the optimum population models and some dualistic models) usually present first the demo-economic problems of a closed economy and then the changes introduced by the opening of the economy, an opening seems essentially a means of absorbing the tensions these models have diagnosed in closed economies.

This sequence is no doubt often thought of as a pedagogical device by its authors. It nevertheless involves the risk of concealing the possibility of an opening imposed by the outside. 3/

For their part, many of the econometric measurements of external financing needs estimate those needs by a measurement of the disparity between internal financing capacity and internal financing needs (which demographic growth is assumed to increase). Accordingly, this method also leads to presenting external relations as having been induced by internal imbalances, even if those who use this method do not always intend to take sides in a theoretical debate.

Sometimes, in fact, their calculation of future deficits is arrived at only by the extrapolation of past deficits, that is to say, deficits that could only have arisen because foreign countries provided external financing. In that case, the projection of what is described as a deficit of internal origin is at the same time a hypotheses concerning the reproduction of the external dynamics that permitted such a deficit. And finally, the deficit models and the dependentist theories may reach converging forecasts, all predicting the same increase in external flows, while seeming methodologically opposed.

The differences between the macro-economic production functions

A good part of the disagreement between the conclusions of various models concerning the impact of demographic growth on the foreign relations of countries arises from the fact that these models have used very simple and very different macro-economic production functions. In particular, the identification of production factors and the measurement of their substitutability, the hypotheses concerning returns to scale and the hypotheses on productivity growth, have been greatly simplified, and what has taken place has been a succession rather than a combination of these hypotheses.

The extensive growth models, which assume the existence of unused land and consider that investment is carried out by the producers have in fact adopted a single-factor production function, with constant returns to scale and productivity invariable over time.

The optimum population models implicitly introduced the land factor by assuming that land was limited in quantity and introducing a variable labour return in order to take account of that fact.

The difference between these two models is therefore clear: it may correspond to identifiable differences of geographic situation. There would be no difficulty in constructing an integrated theory differentiating the impact of demographic growth on foreign relations according to existing densities and relationships between population and land.

The macro–economic models of the 1960s, on the other hand, introduced a clear discontinuity by adopting macro–economic functions that were also bifactoral but in which the two factors were labour and capital. It was this change in the nature of the production factors (associated with the frequent hypotheses of constant returns to scale and with the omission, in the first versions of the models, of productivity growth) that introduced a Malthusian bias into the large-scale models of the 1960s in which optimum population is always regarded as having been exceeded. It is not surprising that this Malthusian bias provoked the criticism of the authors who had presented the optimum models, particularly A. Sauvy. It is this historical discontinuity in the definition of production factors that explains the fact that the optimum population models are concerned primarily with the impact of demographic growth on the structure of trade, which is no way needs to be unbalanced, while the macro–economic models of the 1960s are concerned primarily with the effects on deficits of the balance of payments and only secondarily with the possible effects on the structure of trade.

As the neo–classical specialization models traditionally adopt the same bifactoral function (labour and capital) as the large-scale demo–economic models, their results are compatible with the latter, at least when the latter assume the substitutability of factors. Between the neo–classical growth models and the neo–classical specialization models, there are only differences of presentation with the growth models placing greater emphasis on internal disparities and the specialization models placing greater emphasis on the dynamics created by international disparities. On the other hand, the opposition between the neo–classical production functions with complementary factors is responsible for considerable divergences on the measurement of the external deficits created by demographic growth and even more on the ineluctability of these deficits which are considered incompressible by the Harrod–Domar models and compressible through the substitutability of labour for capital in the neo–classical models.

The world models constructed in the line of the Club of Rome had the merit of attempting a synthesis of the preceding models by introducing a trifactoral production function (land, labour and capital). Moreover, they introduced into the production function joint products, including a negative product: pollution. This increased complexity of the production function made it possible to reintroduce the various problems already known: the increased financial needs of poor countries with rapid demographic growth, as in the national deficit models, together with decreasing returns, as in the optimum population models. It also made it possible to introduce new causes for exceeding the demographic optimum (the exhaustion of land and pollution). However, these qualities were masked by the very marked tendency of the

Meade's model to use this greater complexity of production functions to all the possible sources of Malthusian effects (Cole and others, 1973) and of its tendency to underestimate the possibilities of substitution between resources (an underestimation emphasized by Solow as soon as the model appeared).

The dualistic models also introduced three production factors including, but not land and labour in the traditional sector and capital and labour in the modern sector. They also introduced hypotheses of decreasing returns and the complex problems of relative productivity growth in the different sectors, and stressed the need for inputs and the possibility of importing them. With regard to production functions as well as the dynamics of growth, the dualistic models showed themselves capable of introducing more complex phenomena and obtaining more generalizable results. This possibility was unfortunately restrained by the polarization of the debate around the initial definition of the two sectors and their relationships and by the temptation to present as an "obligatory itinerary" the growth process originally described as a displacement of the traditional sector towards the modern sector and a progressive opening of the domestic economy to international relations.

Lastly, the dependentist analysis paradoxically did not adopt a common attitude towards the macro-economic production functions. This explains why their common references to the need for closure of dependent economies with rapid demographic growth had different meanings.

In the first place, some Marxist authors (Samir Amin) refused to argue in terms of production functions in order to avoid making doubtful quantifications and no doubt, out of a refusal to give special status to a dynamic in terms of the additivity of production factors at the expense of dynamics in terms of conflicts between labour and capital.

Secondly, many authors (Tabah, 1968) referred to the Marxist models of Feld'man and Mahalanobis and adopted production functions with complementary factors in which demographic growth led, as in the Harrod-Domar models, to a need for investment, because of the introduction of a self-centering constraint; this investment had to be obtained not by an external deficit but through domestic savings and the national production of capital goods. The result was in fact an unlimited labour-supply model in which growth was, in the long term, a function only of the rate of internal accumulation.

Lastly, the Latin American dependentist authors who constructed the Bariloche model (Herrera, 1977) introduced a Cobb-Douglas function, which enabled them to use demographic growth for the construction of a self-centred economy employing all of its labour supply.

Although the authors of the Bariloche model were fully aware of the strategic influence of the choice of macro-economic production function, this had not always been the case. These production functions were sometimes adopted for pedagogical purposes – for instance, in the neo-classical models of international specialization or the optimum population model. Sometimes they were chosen less in order to represent reality than to meet the concerns of those who had "ordered" the models; it is apparent that the macro-economic models of the 1960s gave a special place to capital needs in order to answer the questions of the aid donors whose only means of intervention was capital.

The production functions chosen sometimes reflected particular geographic situations which would be risky to generalize (a risk did not exist for the extensive growth models, the relevance of which, as everyone was aware, was very localized).

This variety of concerns no doubt explains why the macro-economic production functions were often chosen without precise, prior econometric study and systematic comparison with the production functions utilized by the other models. This had a good deal to do with giving the literature on the external consequences of demographic growth its appearance of juxtaposing simplified analysis. It was only very gradually that econometric analysis, in particular that of Thirwall (1972), tested these functions and showed the possibility of reconciling models originally widely separated by the absence of measurement.

The paradoxical treatment of the impact of demographic growth on capital formation

The forecasts concerning the external relations of countries with rapid economic growth – in particular, the forecasts on external financing needs and the imports of capital goods – were naturally a reflection of hypotheses concerning the impact of demographic growth on internal capital formation.

Capital formation in the "large-scale", demo-economic models. The macro-economic growth models generally assumed that savings are a function of per capita income. This model is, paradoxically, adopted not only by the neo-classical growth models, in which it is responsible for the negative effect of demographic growth on the level of balance of growth and the level of optimum growth, but by the post-Keynesian models in which it is one of the causes for the creation of an external financing need by demographic growth. 4/

This savings function is often accompanied by a hypothesis on the irreversibility of per capita consumption. When, as the macro-economic models with a Malthusian bias assume, demographic growth creates a tendency toward decline of per capita income, this decline is assumed to bring about not a decline in per capita consumption but a decline of internal per capita saving, and consequently an increase in the external financial deficits needed to avoid a decline in per capita consumption over time).

These hypotheses on the formation of savings, which are so decisive for the results of the model, are the result not of statistical observation but of a desire to introduce the demographic variable by simple formulas; it seemed simple, for instance, to introduce the "demographic variable" into investment formation merely by equating it with savings and by linking the latter per capita income.

Unfortunately, this simplicity in the construction of the equations for savings and investment formation assumes, where it introduces a hypothesis of the irreversibility of per capita consumption, that one of the two following hypotheses is met: either the model becomes a normative one (as is the case with the estimated aid need models, which for the most part assume that the international community cannot allow the poor countries to experience a further decline in per capita consumption), or it is assumed that this irreversibility of the level of per capita consumption is an observable fact resulting from the fact that population growth sooner or later imposes a redistribution of income such that the minimum needs of every individual belonging to that population (which are often assumed to be equal, by commodity, to average prior consumption) are met.

Demographic pressure and the incompressibility of per capita consumption in the other demo-economic models. This capacity of the "newcomers" to obtain a level of consumption equal to that of the population of the prior period is not confined to the deficit models.

A similar hypotheses can be found in the dualistic models, which assume an institutional income equal to per capita production in the traditional sector. In that sector, the "hidden unemployed" are assumed to have an extra-economic power to obtain the satisfaction of their essential needs. And it is this extra-economic power which in the end determines the level of renumeration in the modern sector and internal capital formation.

In a much more indirect fashion, similar hypotheses can be found in the dependentist models, where these assume dialectically that after a temporary worsening of inequalities in the open economies (inequalities which, according to these theories, create luxury consumption rather than investment), demographic growth has the power to accelerate the social changes and possibly political revolutions to create a more egolitarian society which in the Feldman and Mahalanobis models would accelerate both expenditures for mass consumption and increased investment while making possible capital savings in the Bariloche model. For the dependentists, these would even be accompanied by a change in external economic relations through a disconnection between North and South, which could accelerate the equalizing dynamics set in motion by rapid demographic growth.

The opposition between the demo-economic models and the traditional theories of distribution and accumulation. Is there any need to emphasize that such a capacity of demographic growth to reduce inequalities and consequently reduce the level of savings and investment is only exceptionally verified? Any world comparison of savings rates shows that the Keynasian savings function is not verified at the international level and that, except where the extremes of the international income hierarchy are compared, there is little correlation between the level of resources and the rate of savings. There is no automatic reduction of the latter when a decline in per capita income occurs. Moreover, the hypotheses of the demo-economic models on this point seem very paradoxical if they are compared with traditional economic theories.

On the one hand, these theories, which traditionally link income distribution with the economic bargaining power of social groups, have mostly emphasized that demographic pressure weakens the bargaining power of labour. In that case demographic pressure risks creating inequality. If it is added that this inequality may create savings, and would be in conformity with a theoretical tradition adopted by the initial Keynesian function of domestic savings, demographic growth becomes a factor of accumulation. On this point, the large-scale demo-economic models, without always being aware of it, adopted hypotheses that are diametrically opposed to the traditional theories.

These models are also opposed to the theoretical tradition which links the rate of accumulation to the level of profit through both stimulation and financing of investment. It would have been possible, with the help of these theories, to construct a dynamic in which demographic growth, because it raises the relative marginal productivity of capital, would have raised the rate of profit and accelerated investment. Evidently, these demo-economic models departed from the traditional analysis of accumulation because they thought it possible, unlike traditional analysis, to introduce an irreversible needs pressure.

The hypotheses on the active role of needs pressure and the challenge dialectic.

The adoption by the demo-economic models of paradoxical hypotheses on capital formation is in fact only a special case of their propensity to assume that demographic growth leads to incompressible needs proportional or more than proportional to such growth and that society will sooner or latter be obliged to satisfy those needs. The rise in the latter would be a process sufficiently irresistible to the society to proceed (by socio-political adjustments, if the economic adjustments proved inadequate) to a redistribution of income, a reallocation of resources, technical or social innovations, or any other form of productivity growth or, in the absence of a spontaneous process, to resort to foreign aid.

The multiple hypotheses of incompressibility of needs. This tendency to suppose that the growth of needs is sufficiently irresistible to predict that the needs will, in the end, be satisfied (or should be satisfied by the decision-makers for whom the model is intended) is in fact very frequent in the demo-economic models. In particular one finds in these models:

(a) An assumed incompressibility of global per capita consumption (already referred to), which generates external financing needs;

(b) An assumed incompressibility of food consumption, which generates food imports or, where there is elasticity of domestic supply, orientation of domestic production towards domestic market;

(c) An assumed incompressibility of other consumption needs corresponding to "essential needs", which generates sectoral trade deficits (medicines), also a demand for services which make for closing the economy or create a demand for technical assistance in health and education;

(d) An assumed incompressibility of "demographic investment" needs in particular in education, health and housing - investments that tend to reduce immediately productive investment and consequently aggravate "saving deficits". They tend also to unbalance public finances, demands for external State financing, and to create an internal demand in sectors like housing which increases the effects of internal population increase;

(e) An assumed incompressibility of rates of per capita income growth generating, in many macro-economic models, increasing internal financing needs and the growth of capital goods import needs;

(f) An assumed incompressibility of capital needs in relation to production growth in the complementary-factor models and in the models where substitution among factors takes place only after a long lag;

(g) An assumed incompressibility of import needs created by the rigidity of production and consumption in the "structuralist" models and the Leontieff model (1987).

The justifications for the incompressibility hypotheses. The number and frequency of the hypotheses on the incompressibility of needs are without doubt symptomatic of a common tendency in the various demo-economic models. Consciously or unconsciously, these have a propensity to emphasize the need to introduce the demographic dynamics into the economic models by presenting demographic growth as generating incompressible tensions which impose themselves on societies, by forcing them to adapt or disappear, whatever the original economic mechanisms of those activities. In particular those societies cannot, in contradiction to what is assumed by the strictly economic models, neglect the rise of needs, even if those needs are not originally solvent and would, therefore, be neglected by the usual macro-economic models, and even if those needs do not express themselves initially in the preferences of their carriers and would, therefore, be neglected by the usual micro-economic models.

What is involved is in fact a questioning, in the name of the "weight" of demographic phenomena, of the long effort made by economists to free themselves of the notion of "needs" because of its normative, tutelary, or "materialist" connotations. But this common tendency to assume an incompressible rise of needs is expressed by different and even conflicting hypotheses corresponding to different legitimations of this incompressibility.

On the one hand, many models describing the external impact of rapid demographic growth are explicity normative: many deficit models establish as a norm that the level of life in poor countries should be non-decreasing, and their conscious objective is to evoke, particularly in rich countries, the behaviour which will make possible this incompressibility. The latter is, therefore, explicity a goal to be pursued, not an observation of spontaneous tendencies. This normative orientation should not be forgotten today when the history of the last decades is compared with the projections made by these models: the latter did not propose to predict reality, but to set goals for aid flows or, internally to demonstrate the need for demographic regulation.

Other models, particularly the structuralist, reach similar assessments of the incompressibility of needs without intending to be normative, for example, Harrod has always emphasized that the rigidities of his model, which is the source of the highest estimates of external deficits created by demographic growth derive only from a (Keynesian) observation of the constraints created by the limits on income flexibility.

The opposition between normative and structuralist models should not, however, be exaggerated. There are in fact constant slippages between the structuralist observation of economic rigidities, the observation of social resistance to adjustments, the complicity of the foreign observer with these resistances, and the normative affirmation that the costs of adjustment are too high.

At the opposite pole to these positions are the demo-economic analyses, which, while also believing in the incompressibility of needs created by demographic growth, consider that such growth creates a "challenge" dialectic capable of bringing about the social transformations needed for their satisfaction. This challenge dialectic, which is not specific to the demo-economic models (it is indeed the key to development strategy in A. O. Hirschman), has nevertheless been taken up by them, particularly under the stimulus of E. Boserup (1970). It did, in fact, fit very well with the tendency of the demo-economic models to introduce dynamics that are not exclusively economic and make it possible to meet the needs created by demographic pressure. Here, again the demo-economic models introduce processes very far removed from the logic of macro-economic production functions since it is not resource endowments, but resource scarcities, that are the driving force.

This dynamic may, of course, create economic incentives such as modification in the self-consumption sector of the established work-leisure ratio (the example of the intensification of agricultural work in the case of land scarcity) and the creation, in the commercial sector, of a solvent demand (the example of the stimulation of food demand by urban growth). But the challenge dynamic may also lead to all the processes (state intervention, pressure group action, social conflicts, information, and raising levels of aspiration) by which a society may be led to modify its land ownership system, cultural techniques, income distribution, a collective solidarities.

This process, it is often assumed, would be facilitated by the strength of numbers: not only would demographic growth create the essential needs to be satisfied, but it would increase the number of actors exerting pressure for the satisfaction of these needs. 5/ Is there any need to recall that this hypotheses of strength in numbers is contrary to the macro-economic logic by which the number of suppliers or demanders leads to the weakening of their bargaining power?

The consequences of the hypotheses of need incompressibility. The hypotheses concerning the incompressibility of the needs generated by demographic growth and the effectiveness of the responses to the challenges created by this growth have had important consequences for the differentiation and the relevance of demo-economic models.

In the first place, the different demo-economic models, because they have generally been simple in structure, have presented the phenomena of need incompressibility and the dialectics of challenges by the adjustment of a single variable. For example, the deficit models have assumed incompressibilities and rigidities such that all the adjustments arise through external relations, and have thus obtained sizeable external financing and import figures. Theories assuming that the demographic challenge will stimulate an internal social dynamic adequate to meet the challenge have sometimes reached the contrary conclusion that no external financing is necessary and that it could even have the perverse effect of reducing the internal challenge. The simplicity of the techniques used to represent processes as complex as the logic of needs and the dialectic of challenges has thus greatly increased the differences between the conclusions of the models. 6/

This same desire for simplicity in the models has led them to represent the responses to the demographic challenges by simple variables (constancy of per capita aggregates and proportionality of growth; productivity increases adequate to compensate for the lag in capital growth; intensification of labour at a rate adequate to compensate for the decline in the people-to-land ratio), while the historic responses to demographic challenges have always been complex phenomena combining many adjustments. The same desire for simplicity has led to presenting as automatic some processes which are only possible eventualities; history has multiplied the counter-examples of failures by societies incapable of meeting the demographic challenge.

There has likewise been a tendency to emphasize the cases in which the response to the challenges was sufficiently effective to avoid any decline in per capita aggregates and the level of satisfaction of essential needs. Finally, many models, by incorporating the hypotheses of incompressibility into short-term projections, have neglected the fact that even when the challenges have been net, it was often at the end of long delays in response and lags and inequalities in the rate of growth of the different variables.

This overestimation of the simplicity, automaticity, effectiveness, and rapidity of the responses to the demographic challenge has therefore considerably reduced the relevance of the models. It is evident that these difficulties arise because in introducing, often under the cover of extremely simple formal relationships, very complex and very uncertain political, social and anthropological processes, the demo-economic models have introduced undeniable but as yet inadequately measured phenomena.

Moreover, there are few a priori reasons for supposing that these processes take place in a similar manner in all countries with rapid demographic growth. All the national or regional specificities that influence the mode of accumulation, the mode of distribution, and the mode of regulation cannot fail to differentiate geographically the internal and external effects of the same rate of demographic growth.

The possible orientations for an empirical research

As the different models of interactions between rapid demographic growth and international economic relations have hardly been confronted among themselves, they have seldom been confronted with reality in order to compare their respective relevance.

This is certainly no place to carry out such a confrontation, especially since an earlier attempt to decide between only two groups of these models -

the Malthusian macro-economic models and the dependentist theories revealed the complexity of the task (Coussy, 1988b). No model can be considered as either relevant or irrelevant on all scores; even confirmation or invalidation backed by figures can turn out to be only apparent. Finally, every model is flexible enough to integrate, either in reality or in words, facts that it would not be able to anticipate.

Consequently, only the general orientations of a possible empirical research on the relevance of different models will be obtained here.

The dangers of universalist ambitions

Nearly all the models and theories analysed above have sought to offer conclusions that would be relevant to all developing countries. Hence, all of them are put forward as models (or theories) that are incompatible with each other, making it not only possible but necessary to choose one. By means of a world transversal analysis, it would be enough to identify the correlations between the demographic growth rate and the different economic variables mentioned above as having possible interactions with this growth rate.

It seem that this method has led to several deceptions. None of variables of the international economy enumerated above seem to react univocally in different countries with a rapid demographic growth. This is also true of terms of trade, degree of openness, net commercial balance, inflow of private capital, and public financing and product inflows, food product imports, agricultural and industrial exports, equipment and inputs imports. The ambition of these models to be universalist as well as the simplicity of the relations assumed between demography and external flows seem unlikely to succeed.

The same is true and, in this case it is even more significant, of the quest for simple correlations between the population growth rate and the variables that, in different models, play the role of intermediate variables between this growth rate and the international economic parameters: saving rate, desired investment, growth in agricultural productivity, relations between distribution and accumulation, capital intensity, risks taken to meet basic needs. None of these factors reveal the simple relationships (on the one hand, with demographic variables and, on the other hand, with external variables) that would be necessary to give to the interactions between these variables the forms anticipated by the different models.

Conversely, in the particular cases where the flows seem to correspond to the forecasts of a given model (e.g., the increase in imports of food products by the rapid growth countries forecast by several macro-economic gap models), we observe that they can, in fact, be explained by several models that were thought to be antagonistic at the beginning. If increases in imports of food products can indeed be explained by several "gap" models as well as by optimum population and dualist models, what is more significant is that the same is true of dependentist theories contrary to the first three models, disregard the demographic dynamics as a source of these imports and attribute them to the economic dynamics of rich countries exporting their surplus. The choice or the updating of the complementarities between the antagonistic explanations can only result from a finer analysis that gives very differentiated results for continents, nations, and even regions.

Finally, it should be kept in mind that for the last two decades, some of the factors not anticipated by any of the models proved to be decisive for the external economic movements of the dependent countries and have made their relations with the rapid economic growth vague or more complex: the rise (fall) in oil income has scarcely populated oil-producing countries and increased (lowered) the costs of demographic growth while making them more (less) acceptable; they have also created qualitatively differentiated growth dynamics between densely and scarcely populated countries. The rise and the subsequent crisis in the international credit economy have made the relations between purchasing power and population still more complex; climactic accidents, especially in the Sahel region, have accentuated the cost of population growth while giving birth to crises that were partially independent of short-term demographic growth but dependent, of course, on long-term rates.

The diversity of the national dynamics created by a similar economic growth rate

Even if these disturbing phenomena could be eliminated, it would probably be better to give up the ambitious idea of building a model to explain international relations through disparities in demographic growth. The same population growth rate causes a wide range of clearly diversified political as well as socio-economic dynamics; the opportunities and constraints of the international relations structuring the world economy are generated as much by the diversity of reactions to the growth rate as by disparities in the same growth rate.

Moreover, the diversity of local reactions to the same growth rate can already be perceived in different models which, despite their universalist ambitions, reflect the place where they were created. It is obvious that the extensive growth models (outdated by now) represent some sub-Saharan forest areas; the optimum population models originated from commentaries on English and Japanese development; the macro-economic Malthusian models originated from observations made in India and were applied to sub-Saharan African countries in the Sahel region; and the dualist model fits the descriptions of the newly-industrialized Asian countries remarkably well. 7/ International relations (e.g., between Asia and Africa) can be explained both through the disparities between the Asian and African economic dynamics as well as through the disparities in their demographic growth.

The lessening influence of demographic growth rate disparities on the structure of international relations is due to at least four more sources of national differences.

First, it is obvious that the differences between nations and the international relations affected by these differences, are due to demographic variables other than population growth. The density, dimension, and homogeneity of the populations and their age structure are the decisive factors for potential growth. The intra-family and intergenerational circulation of capital and the commercial and non-commercial goods movements vary greatly according to different civilizations; these differences are decisive in the formation of savings as well as for the intensity of domestic urban–rural relations (and therefore, inversely, they affect foreign relations). The domestic and international mobility of populations is rather a variable phenomenon at the very heart of a nation; it introduces cultural specificity in relations with the outside world.

Second, the "challenges" are met, as we have seen, with very uncertain "answers"; hence, they can vary greatly from country to country and from one region to another. To illustrate but one example, the "food challenge" caused by population growth has been met in different ways. In some places, there has been rise in productivity thanks to endogenerous innovations (a rise in the intensity of local labour), a rise in productivity thanks to imported innovations applied locally (the green revolution), or a rise in productivity due to innovations abroad (progress made by the United Nations and (the European Economic Community agricultural productivity in anticipating world demand). In other places the challenge met by domestic and international migrations (exempting countries from increasing productivity) or by food product imports paid for either through local production or by food aid. The diversity of answers is at least as great as the relative importance of food needs affecting the structure of the food product trade network.

Third, this network is also structured by differences in economic policies and in social regulations. In the preceding example, the answers to the food challenge varied according to differences in prices paid to the food producers (that is to say, in accordance with the real exchange rates, taxes, and domestic subsidies), import (export) policies, decisions made in allotting resources to agriculture, and public investment policies in the food sectors.

There are deeper reasons behind the differences in decision–making which are not always explicit. The differences came from social regulations (land reforms, domestic migrations, types of urbanization, satisfaction of basic needs). Just as plain refusal to implement agrarian reforms can turn some countries into food–exporters despite their declining food situation (as illustrated by some Latin American countries), so other countries can become food importers even though their agricultural potential is not fully exploited (as can be seen from the example of sub–Saharan Africa).

Finally, differences arising out of the retroaction of development methods and of external relations on the demographic growth rate cannot be ignored. Outward expansion of the South-East Asian countries resulted from demographic pressure but later became a factor in slowing demographic growth; after a while, continuing outward–looking economic growth could no longer be imputed to demographic pressure but to a rise in qualifications. This succession of different causes of outward–looking economic growth does not permit one to find a correlation with the demographic growth rate over a long period. Conversely, the growth of food product imports in sub–Saharan Africa, (which, at the beginning was not, in the coastal areas, the inevitable results of demographic pressure) has allowed Africa to maintain a high rate of demographic growth.

Conclusions

To conclude, it is perhaps less the disparities in demographic growth than the differences between the reactions of the various societies to the same demographic growth that are decisive in the structuring of the international division of labour and the movements of capital.

Would not, for instance, the present positions of the various continents in this structure be more the result of these differences in reaction to demographic growth than of disparities in growth?

It is only if the growth of the constraint on international competition, which we are now witnessing in developing countries, becomes sufficiently powerful to bring the national politico-economic dynamics closer to each other and to weaken regional socio-anthropological specificities that we might witness a growing similarity – although with discontinuities – in the external effects of rapid demographic growth and possibly a similar feedback from latter to the former.

Notes

1/ In what follows we shall have to present theories which do not accept the analysis of poor countries in terms of dependence. We shall therefore try to use the term "dependent economies" only when we are dealing with them within the framework of theories accepting that terminology.

2/ Inversely, many demo-economic models of the 1960s were fixed-price models and paid but scant attention to the problem of terms of trade.

3/ That this pedagogical trick does not always express a theoretical choice is attested to by the fact that dualist models have at times used this presentation (Ranis and Fei, 1961) and at times, inversely underlined the role of external factors in the growth and exploitation of developing countries (Lewis, 1954).

4/ This adoption of the Keynesian function of saving by the neo-classical balanced-growth model can be explained historically by the fact that Solow built it as an answer to the Harrod Domar model. This answer was all the more efficient as it accepted most of the latter's hypotheses. It is nevertheless a paradox in so far as it introduces, in a neo-classical model, an investment function that is linked neither to investment opportunities nor to capital renumeration.

5/ The hypotheses, as has been seen, underlies the hypotheses of internal redistribution generating a need for external savings. It can be used to assume an international redistribution by a rise in the terms of trade or an increase in aid. It is also used to support the theses of the ineluctable rise of power of large countries, the ineluctable migration from South to North etc.

6/   By pushing the method to its limits, one might construct an international challenge dialectic that would make it possible to hope that the needs of poor countries would inevitably bring about the necessary world transformations (the innovations in agricultural inputs of the Green Revolution, an international redistribution etc.).   Inversely, one could, by adopting a "structuralist" view of the international economy, consider any international action impossible and affirm that only internal actions can contribute to solving the problems.

7/   Other models originated from the analysis or observations of all the countries (integrated world economy models, neo-classical models of specialization, dependentist theories).   But it would not be difficult to show how they have underlined constraints and opportunities that have unevenly affected different regions.

References

Amin, S. and F. O. Okediji (1971). Land use, agriculture and industrialization. Population in African Development, P. Cantrelle, ed. Liege: VISP.

Bauer, P. (1981). Equality, the Third World and Economic Debate. London: Weidenfeld and Nicholson.

Boserup, E. (1970). Evolution agraire et prévision démographique (Agrarian development and demographic forecasting). Paris: Flamarion.

_____ (1981). Population and Technology. Oxford: Basil Blackwell.

Chesnais, J. C. and A. Sauvy (1973). Progrès économique et accroissement de la population: une expérience commentée (Economic progress and population increase: an annotated experiment). Population (Paris), Nos. 4 and 5.

_____ (1981). Prévision et projection. L'imaginaire des grands modèles démo-économiques (forecasting and projection. The imaginary in the large-scale demo-economic models). Le Débat (Paris), No. 8.

Coale, A. J. and E. M. Hoover (1958). Population and Economic Development in Low Income Countries. Princeton, New Jersey: Princeton University Press.

Cole, H. S. O. and others (1973). Thinking About the Future. London: Chatto and Windus.

Coussy, J. (1983a). Croissance démographique et dynamique de la spécialisation du Tiers Monde (Demographic growth and the dynamic of specialization in the Third World), Tiers Monde (April-June).

_____ (1983b). Pression démographique et structure des échanges Nord-Sud: quelques observations empiriques (Demographic pressure and the structure of North-South trade; some empirical observations). Mondes en Developpement (Brussels), Nos. 43 and 44.

Enke, S. (1972) International economic and financial implications of the population explosion. In International Aspects of Overpopulation, J. Barnett and M. Louw, eds. London: Macmillan.

_____ (1976). Economic consequences of rapid demographic growth. In Population, Public and Economy Development, M. Keeley, ed. New York: Praeger.

_____ and G. Ranis (1979). Agriculture in two types of open economies. In Agriculture in Development Theory, L. G. Reynolds, ed. New Haven: Yale University Press.

Gottlieb, M. (1949). Optimum population, foreign trade and world economy. _Population Studies_ (September).

Grinols, E. and J. Bhagwati (1976). Foreign capital, savings and dependence. _Review of Economics and Statistics_, vol. 58. No. 4.

Herrera, A. O. (1977). _Un monde pour tous._ (A world for all). Paris: P.U.F.

Klatzmann, J. (1975). _Nourrir dix millards d'hommes (To feed ten billion people)._ Paris: P.U.F.

Leeson, P. T. (1979). The Lewis model and development theory. _The Manchester School_, vol. 47.

Leontieff, W., A. P. Carter and P. Petri (1977). _1999, L'expertise de Wassily Leontieff_ (1999, The Expertise of Wassily Leontieff).   Paris: Dunod.

Lewis, A. (1979). The dual economy revisited. _The Manchester School_, vol. 47.

_____ (1954). Development with unlimited supply labour. _The Manchester School_, vol. 22, pp. 139–191.

Meade, J. (1955). _Trade and Welfare_. New York: Oxford University Press.

Meadows, D. L. and others (1977). _Dynamique de la croissance dans un monde fini_ (Dynamique of growth in a finished world). Paris: _Economica_.

Mesarovic M. and E. Pestel (1974). _Stratégie pour demain. Deuxième rapport du Club de Rome_ (Strategy for tomorrow. Second report of the Club of Rome). Paris: Editions du Seuil.

Mueller, E. (1977). The impact of demographic factors in economic development in Taiwan. _Population and Development Review_, vol. 3, No. 1/2, pp. 1–22.

Oshima, H. T. (1963). The Ranis Fei model of economic development: comment. _American Economic Review_, vol. 53, No. 3.

Ranis, G. and J. C. H. Fei (1961). The theory of economic development. _American Economic Review_, vol. 51, No. 4.

Roca, Z. (1987). Endogenous and exogenous factors in population development: towards the theory of dependent demographic transition. 5th Conference E.A.D.I, Amsterdam. Mimeographed.

Rybczynski, T. M. (1955). _Factor Endowments and Relative Commodity Prices_. Paris: _Economica_.

Sauvy, A. (1963). _Théorie générale de la population_ (General theory of population). Paris: P.U.F.

Tabah, L. (1968). Démographique et aide au Tiers Monde, I. Les modèles (Demography and aid in the Third World. I. The models). <u>Population</u>, vol. XXIII, No. 3.

_____ (1969). Démographie et aide au Tiers Monde, II. Calcul du dificit au cours de période 1960-1980 (Demography and aid in the Third World II. Calculation of deficit during the period 1960-1980). <u>Population</u>, vol. XXIV, No. 3.

Thirwal, A. P. (1972). A cross-section study of population growth and the growth of per capita income in a production function framework. <u>The Manchester School</u>, vol. 40.

Vasow, B. (1979). Savings and dependence with externally financed growth. <u>Review of Economics and Statistics</u>, vol. 61, No. 1, pp. 150-154.

Weisskopf, T. (1972). The impact of foreign capital inflow on domestic savings in underdeveloped countries. <u>Journal of International Economics</u>, vol. 2.

Chapter 5

Rapid population growth and technical and institutional change

● V. W. Ruttan* and Y. Hayami**

Within the fields of population policy and population research, there has been a continuing argument over whether changes in population growth rates are induced primarily by factors that act to reduce the demand for children or by supply-side factors that act to reduce the costs of fertility control. Some scholars have maintained that changes in the rate of population growth have been primarily a response to changes in the opportunity costs, values, and motivations associated with economic development. Others have insisted that the combination of insufficient birth control technology and inadequate knowledge about family planning has limited the ability of poor families in developing countries to control family size.

The theory of induced innovation provides a framework that incorporates both demand- and supply-side perspectives. In the theory of induced innovation, changes in relative resource endowments, such as shifts in the ratio of agricultural labour to land, are viewed as directing technical change along a path that permits the substitution of relatively more abundant factors for the relatively scarce factors of production. Institutional changes are also viewed as being induced by changes in relative resource endowments, by changes in cultural endowments, and technology.

In this paper we draw on our own and related work, carried out within the framework of the induced innovation paradigm, to examine the relationship between rapid population growth and technical and institutional change. 1/

*Department of Agricultural and Applied Economics and Department of Economics, Hubert H. Humphrey Institute of Public Affairs, University of Minnesota, Minneapolis, Minnesota, United States of America.

**School of International Politics, Economics and Business, Aoyama-Gakuin University, Tokyo.

The authors are grateful to Georges Tapinos for comments on an earlier draft of this paper.

Induced technical change

A first step in an attempt to understand the relationship between population growth and technical change is to abandon the view that either technology or institutions in pre-modern societies were or are essentially static. Sustained rates of growth in agricultural output in the 0.5–1.0 per cent per year range were feasible over long periods of time in many preindustrial societies. With the advent of industrialization, potentials for the growth of agricultural output shifted upward to the range of 1.5–2.5 per cent per year. Since the middle of the twentieth century, the growth potential of agricultural production has again shifted upward to annual growth rates of over 4.0 per cent. Sustained growth rates of agricultural production in this range have been observed primarily in a number of newly industrializing countries such as Brazil, China (Taiwan Province), and Mexico, rather than in the older industrialized economies. Any theory that attempts to provide insights into the dynamic relationships between population growth and agricultural development should be sufficiently general to encompass economies that include both modern and pre-modern growth rates of population and agricultural production.

The theory of induced technical change

The process by which technical change is generated has traditionally been treated as exogenous to the economic system, the product of autonomous advances in scientific and technical knowledge. Over the last several decades, advances in economic theory and the accumulation of empirical evidence have tended to confirm that the rate and direction of technical change can be interpreted as being largely endogenous to the economic system, induced by differences or changes in the conditions of factor supply and product demand.

Theories of induced innovation have been developed mainly within the framework of the theory of the firm. There have been two traditions in the attempt to incorporate into economic theory the innovative behaviour of profit-maximizing firms. One is the Hicks tradition, which focuses on the factor-saving bias induced by changes in relative factor prices resulting from changes in relative resource scarcities (Hicks, 1932). [2] The other is the Schmookler–Griliches tradition, which focuses on the influence of the growth of product demand on the rate of technical change (Griliches, 1957; Schmookler, 1962, 1966; Mowery and Rosenberg, 1979; Scherer, 1982).

In the dynamic process of economic development, changes in product demand and relative factor prices are inseparably related. For example, when food demand rises because of growth in population or per capita income, or both, the demand for factor inputs in food production increases more or less proportionately. When increases in factor demands are confronted with different elasticities in the supply of production factors, the result is change in relative factor prices. The different rates of change in factor prices result, in turn, in changes in the level and distribution of income among factor owners, thereby affecting the aggregate product demand. A fully developed general-equilibrium induced innovation model capable of explaining the dynamic process of agricultural development should incorporate the mechanisms by which changes in both product demand and factor endowments interact to influence the rate and direction of technological change. 3/

We do not, of course, regard technical change as wholly induced by economic forces. In addition to the effects of changes (or differences) in resource endowments and growth in demand, technical change may occur in response to autonomous advances in scientific knowledge. Progress in general science that lowers the "cost" of technical and institutional innovations may have influences on technical change that are unrelated to changes in factor proportions and product demand. Even so, the rate of adoption and the impact on productivity of such autonomous or exogenous changes in technology will be strongly influenced by conditions of resource supply and product demand.

The significance of the induced technical change hypothesis for economic development is that there are multiple paths of technical change available to society. The constraints imposed upon agricultural development by an inelastic supply of land may be offset by advances in biological technology. The constraints imposed by an inelastic supply of labour may be offset by advances in mechanical technology. The ability of a society to achieve rapid growth in agricultural productivity and output seems to hinge on its ability to make efficient choices among alternative paths. There is substantial evidence that the direction of technical change has been responsive to relative resource endowments in both the agricultural and non-agricultural sectors, in both traditional and modern societies (Thirtle and Ruttan, 1987). In the next section, we illustrate some of the results of efforts to test the induced technical change hypothesis during the process of agricultural development in both preindustrial and industrial societies.

Induced technical change in preindustrial society

Interest in the relationship between population growth and technical change in both historical and contemporary preindustrial societies has been stimulated by the seminal work of Ester Boserup (1965, 1981). In Boserup's analysis, changes in land use in preindustrial societies in both temperate and tropical regions suggest a continuous development from extensive to intensive systems of cultivation in response to rising population density (table 1). The sharp distinction between cultivated and uncultivated land, implied by the concepts of intensive and extensive margin, is replaced in her work by the concept of increasing frequency of cropping and by changes ranging from forest and bush fallow to multicropping systems in which the same plot bears two or more crops per year. In the Boserup perspective, soil fertility becomes a dependent variable, responding positively to the intensity of land use, rather than a determinant of the intensity of land use.

The most rigorous attempt to test the Boserup hypothesis under contemporary preindustrial systems of agriculture has been a series of studies by Hans P. Binswanger and several colleagues at the World Bank (Pingali, Bigot and Binswanger, 1987). 4/ The objective that Binswanger and his colleagues set for themselves was to explain the persistence of hand-hoe husbandry and the conditions leading from primary reliance on hand tools to the use of animal and mechanical traction. In the Binswanger model, the demand for agricultural intensification may arise out of both population growth and increased market demand. The response to this demand includes "a transition from the hand hoe to the plow; an increase in investment for destumping, drainage, and terracing; an increase in the maintenance of fertility through manuring; and the movement from general use rights to specific land rights" (Pingali, Bigot and Binswanger, 1987). The sequence of farming systems and technologies that occurs during the process of intensification is illustrated in table 1.

The stylized model presented by Binswanger and his colleagues for interpretation of the transition from hand husbandry to animal traction captures, in a more analytical form, the changes in fixed and variable costs associated with the process of technological succession (figure I).

The cost of training the animals is independent of the intensity of farming (line AB). The cost of destumping is extremely high when the forest-fallow and early bush-fallow systems are used because of the high density of stumps and the highly developed network of roots. As the length of fallow decreases, the costs of destumping decline because the density of trees and roots has been reduced. Destumping requirements disappear at the grass-fallow stage (level CB). The costs of feeding and taking care of draft animals – the difference between lines EF and CB – is also high during the forest-fallow and early bush-fallow stages.... Beyond the annual cultivation stage, however, grazing land becomes a limiting factor that necessitates the production of fodder crops, which in turn leads to an increase in the cost of feeding and maintaining draft animals.... Animal-drawn plows are the dominant technology at the point at which the cost of hand cultivation exceeds the cost of transition to animal power (Pingali, Bigot and Binswanger, 1987).

Binswanger and his colleagues also note that tractor-drawn plowing was not successfully introduced into Sub-Saharan Africa earlier than the grass-fallow stage. There are both technical and institutional constraints that make it difficult to bypass the animal-traction stage and move directly to tractor.

Induced technical change in industrial society

There are now, as mentioned above, a large number of tests of the induced technical change hypothesis based on recent historical experiences in both developed and developing countries. In this section, we summarize some results from our work on induced innovation in agriculture.

One implication of the induced innovation model is that alternative paths of technical change can be expected to emerge in response to differences or changes in relative resource endowments. Figure II shows the changes in partial productivity ratios, output per worker, and output per hectare for a large number of developed and developing countries for 1960-1980. Three distinct, long-term growth paths are apparent: (a) a new-continent growth path; (b) a European growth path; and (c) an Asian path. The new-continent path includes countries with relatively high land-labour ratios, while the Asian path includes countries with relatively low land-labour ratios. The long-term historical growth paths for selected countries are plotted in figure III. The historical path for the United States passes through the scatter of points for the new-continent countries; the path for Japan passes through the

Table 1.   Proportion of population in 0–19 age group in
           selected cities

Operation or situation	Farming system				
	Forest fallow	Bush fallow	Short fallow	Annual cultivation	Multiple cropping
Land Clearing	Fire	Fire	None	None	None
Land preparation and planting	No land preparation. Use of digging stick to plant roots and sow seeds	Use of hoe and digging stick to loosen soil	Plow	Animal-drawn plow and tractor	Animal-drawn plow and tractor
Fertilization	Ash; Perhaps household refuse for garden plots	Ash; Sometimes chitimene techniques[a]; household refuse for garden plots	Animal dung or manure; sometimes composting	Manure; sometimes human waste; composting; cultivation of green manure crops; chemical fertilizers	Manure; sometimes human waste; composting; cultivation of green manure crops; chemical fertilizers
Weeding	Minimal	Required as the length of fallow decreases	Intensive weeding required	Intensive weeding required	Intensive weeding required
Use of animals	None	Animal-drawn plow begins to appear as length of fallow decreases	Plowing, transport, inter-culture	Plowing, transport, inter-culture, posthar-vest tasks and ir-rigation	Plowing, transport, inter-culture, posthar-vest tasks and irrigation
Seasonality of demand for labor	Minimal	Weeding	Land preparation, weeding and harvesting	Land preparation, weeding and harvesting	Acute peak in demand around land preparation, harvest, and postharvest tasks
Supply of fodder	None	Emergence of grazing land	Abundant open grazing	Open grazing restricted to marginal lands and stubble grazing	Intensive fodder management and production of fodder crops

Source: Prabhu Pingali, Yves Bigot and Hans P. Binswanger, _Agricultural Mechanization and the Evolution of Farming Systems in Sub-Saharan Africa_, (Baltimore, The Johns Hopkins University Press, 1987).

a/   To augment the ashes from the bush cover, branches are cut from surrounding trees, carried to the plot of land to be cultivated, and burned to provide extra nutrients for the soil.

Figure I. A comparison of labour costs with the practice of hand
          cultivation and animal-powered cultivation

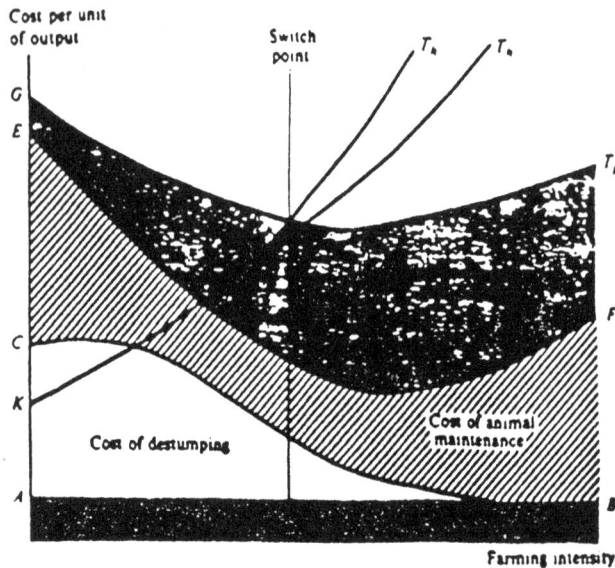

     Source: Prabhu Pingali, Yves Bigot and Hans P. Binswanger,
Agricultural Mechanization and the Evolution of Farming Systems in
Sub-Saharan Africa (Baltimore, The Johns Hopkins University Press,
1987), p. 34.

Notes:

     T_p = Total labour costs for land preparation, early season
weeding and manuring, using animal traction.

     T_h = Labour costs for land preparation and early season weeding,
using the hand hoe.

     T_h = T_h plus labour costs for maintaining soil fertility
without manure from draft animals.

     Switch point = Farming intensity at which animal traction becomes
the dominant technology.

Figure II. International comparison of labour and land productivities in agriculture

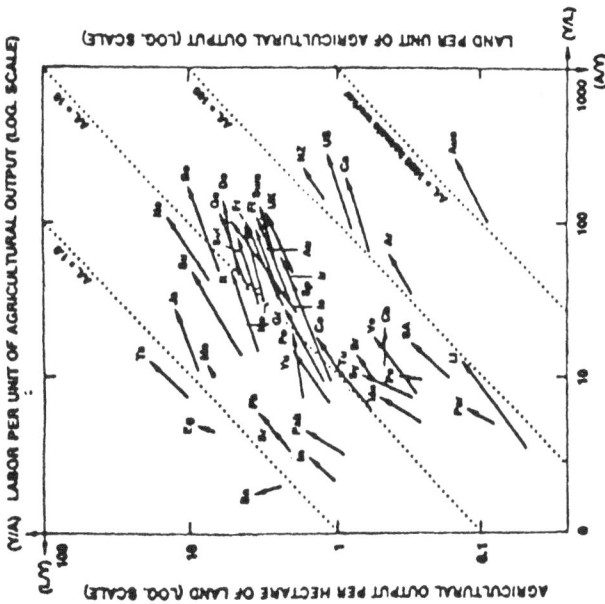

Source: Y. Hayami and V. W. Ruttan, Agricultural Development: An International Perspective, rev. ed. (Baltimore, The Johns Hopkins University Press, 1985), chap. 5.

Figure III. Historical growth paths of agricultural productivity of Denmark, France, Japan, the United Kingdom, and the United States for 1960-1980 compared with intercountry cross-section observations of selected countries in 1980

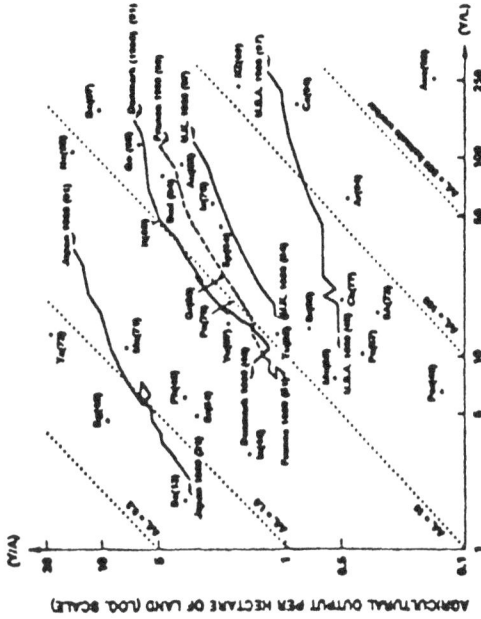

Source: Y. Hayami and V. W. Ruttan, Agricultural Development: An International Perspective, rev. ed. (Baltimore, The Johns Hopkins University Press, 1985), chap. 5.

Symbol key for figures II and III

Ar	:	Argentina	Ma	:	Mauritius
Aust	:	Australia	Me	:	Mexico
Au	:	Austria	Ne	:	Netherlands
Ba	:	Bangladesh	NZ	:	New Zealand
Be	:	Belgium	No	:	Norway
Br	:	Brazil	Pak	:	Pakistan
Ca	:	Canada	Par	:	Paraguay
Ch	:	Chile	Pe	:	Peru
Co	:	Colombia	Ph	:	Philippines
De	:	Denmark	Po	:	Portugal
Eg	:	Egypt	SA	:	South Africa
Fi	:	Finland	Sp	:	Spain
Fr	:	France	Sr	:	Sri Lanka
Ge	:	Germany, Fed. Rep. of	Su	:	Suriname
Gr	:	Greece	Sw	:	Sweden
In	:	India	Sy	:	Syria
Ir	:	Ireland	Ta	:	Taiwan (Province of China)
Is	:	Israel	Tu	:	Turkey
It	:	Italy	Uk	:	United Kingdom
Ja	:	Japan	USA	:	United States of America
Li	:	Libyan Arab Jamahiriya	Ve	:	Venezuela
			Yu	:	Yugoslavia

scatter of points for the African and Asian countries; and the historical paths for Denmark, France, and the United Kingdom pass through the scatter of points for the European countries.

Our initial tests of the induced innovation hypothesis were against the experience of the United States and Japan for the period 1880–1960. Additional tests have been conducted against the experience of other developed and developing countries. In a recent publication, we extended the Japan–United States tests from 1880–1960 to 1880–1980 (Hayami and Ruttan, 1985). Japan and the United States are characterized by extreme differences in relative endowments of land and labour. In 1880, total agricultural land area per male worker was more than 60 times as large in the United States as in Japan, and arable land area per worker was about 20 times as large. These differences have widened over time. By 1980, total agricultural land area per male worker was more than 100 times as large and arable land area per male worker about 50 times as large in the United States as in Japan.

The relative prices of land and labour also differed sharply in the two countries. In 1880, in order to buy a hectare of arable land, a Japanese hired farm worker would have had to work eight times as many days as a United States farm worker. In the United States, the price of labour rose relative to the price of land, particularly between 1880 and 1920; in Japan, the price of land rose sharply relative to the price of labour, particularly between 1880 and 1900. By 1960, a Japanese farm worker would have had to work 30 times as many days as a United States farm worker to buy one hectare of arable land. This gap was reduced after 1960, partly because of extremely rapid increases in wage rates in Japan. Land prices in the United States rose sharply in the post–war period, yet in 1980 a Japanese farm worker still would have had to work 11 times as many days as a United States worker to buy one hectare of land.

Agricultural growth in the United States and Japan during the period 1880–1980 can best be understood when viewed as a dynamic factor substitution process. Factors have been substituted for each other along a "metaproduction function" in response to long–run trends in relative factor prices. Each point on the metaproduction surface is characterized by an available technology that can be described in terms of a specific activity or factor combination. The movements along the metaproduction function may be inferred from figures IV and V, in which United States and Japanese data are plotted to show the relationship between farm draft power (from both tractors and draft animals) per male worker and the machinery–labour price ratio, and the relationship between fertilizer input per hectare of arable land and the fertilizer–land price ratio. Despite the enormous differences in climate and other environmental conditions, the relationship between these variables is almost identical in both countries.

The relationships between relative factor prices and factor use portrayed in figures IV and V are clearly consistent with the hypothesis that the alternative paths of technical change followed by Japan and the United States have been induced by relative resource endowments interpreted through relative factor prices. When simple relationships emerge as powerfully as in figures IV and V, one is tempted to forego more formal tests. The intuitive implications of the data presented in these two figures have, however, been confirmed by more formal tests. 5/

Figure IV.   Relation between farm draft power per male
              worker and power-labour price ration, the
              United States and Japan quinquennial
              observations for 1880-1980.

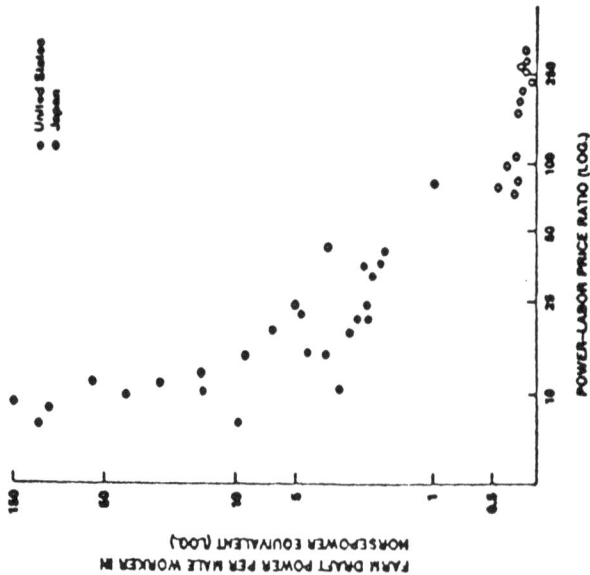

Source: Y. Hayami and V. W. Ruttan, Agricultural
Development: An International Perspective, rev. ed.
(Baltimore. The Johns Hopkins University Press, 1985),
chap. 7.

Note: Equals hectares of work days that can be
purchased by one horsepower of tractor or draft animal.

Figure V.   Relation between fertilizer input per
             hectare of arable and and fertilizer-arable
             land price ratio, the United States and Japan,
             quinquennial observations for 1880-1980

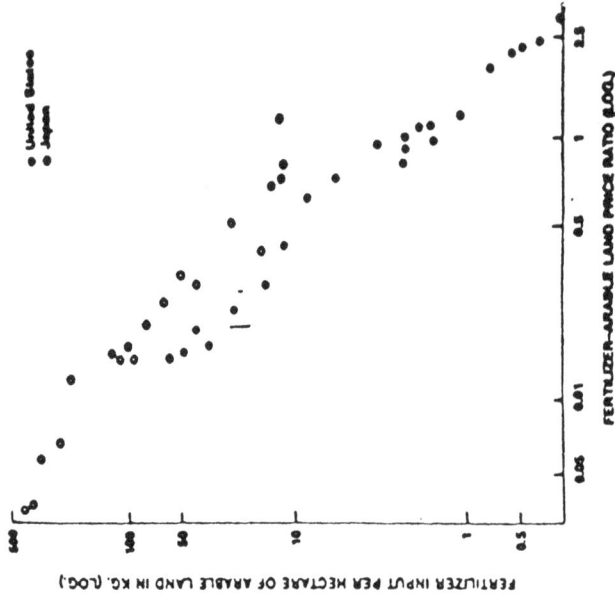

Source: Y. Hayami and V. W. Ruttan Agricultural
Development: An International Perspective, rev. ed.
(Baltimore. The Johns Hopkins University Press, 1985),
chap. 7.

Note: Equals hectares of arable land that can be
purchased by one ton of N + P_2O_t + K_2O contained
in commercial fertilizers.

Some conclusions and inferences

In this section, we have interpreted technical change as being largely endogenous to the economic system. It should be clear, however, that we do not presume the existence of a "hidden hand" that automatically guides technical change along an efficient path.

The question is frequently raised as to whether advances in indigenous technology induced by population density, along the lines outlined by Boserup and by Binswanger and his colleagues, would be sufficient to sustain rising levels of per capita income and consumption (Robinson and Schutjer, 1984). A positive response would be excessively romantic. We agree with Boserup that in pre-industrial societies, agricultural production often responded "far more generously to additional inputs of labour than assumed by neo-Malthusian authors" (1965). But Boserup herself argued that the transition to more intensive cultivation would be accompanied by a rise in days worked per year and a decline in output per hour worked (1965). And we should not ignore the findings of Ronald Lee that in preindustrial England, annual population growth rates beyond 0.4 per cent had "dramatic consequences." The effect of more rapid population growth rates was to raise rents and turn the domestic terms of trade against the agricultural sector (Lee, 1980). 6/

Under pre-industrial conditions, growth in output per hectare was typically accompanied by reductions in output per unit of labour input. However, a decline in labour productivity, measured in terms of output per hour or per day, if accompanied by an increase in the number of hours or days worked per year, is not incompatible with a rise in annual output or income per worker. This is the classic pattern followed in the wet rice cultivation areas of East Asia during the shift from upland to rainfed rice production and then from rainfed to irrigated rice production. It is the pattern described by Binswanger and his colleagues in the transition in farming systems and technology from forest fallow to multiple cropping. In the long run, however, even with relatively slow growth in population or labour force, output per worker per year tends to stagnate or decline as the response of indigenous technical change to growth of population declines.

Higher rates of growth in agricultural production and in output per hectare and per worker have required institutionalization of the capacity to supplement indigenous knowledge with science-based knowledge and craft-generated technology with industrial inputs that embody advances in scientific and technical knowledge. It is also necessary to institutionalize the delivery of this new knowledge and technology to farm people and to maintain higher levels of investment in human capital in rural areas if the new technical opportunities are to be effectively exploited. In our own work, therefore, we were forced to turn to an attempt to acquire a more adequate understanding of the process of institutional change, which is described in the following section.

Induced institutional change

In the previous section, we outlined a model in which technical change was treated as largely endogenous to the economic system. But the success of the theory of induced technical change gives rise to the need for a more adequate understanding of the sources of institutional change. This is in part because the disequilibrium resulting from technical change represents a major source of demand for institutional change. But it also reflects the fact that technical change is itself often the consequence of prior institutional change. Furthermore, the institutional changes that give rise to and facilitate the technical changes are often induced by the same changes in resource endowments that induce the changes in technology.

In this section, we elaborate a theory of institutional change in which shifts in the demand for institutional innovation are induced by changes in relative resource endowments and by technical change. We then present a case drawn from recent Philippine experience in which changes in technology and rising population pressure become the source of institutional changes in land tenure and labour relationships.

What is institutional innovation?

Institutions are the rules of a society or of organizations that facilitate co-ordination among people by helping them form expectations that each person can reasonably hold in dealing with others. They reflect the conventions that have evolved in different societies regarding the behaviour of individuals and groups relative to their own behaviour and that of others. In the area of economic relations, they have a crucial role in establishing expectations about the rights to use resources in economic activities and about the partitioning of the income streams resulting from economic activity. Runge has noted that "institutions provide <u>assurance</u> respecting the actions of others, and give order and stability to expectations in the complex and uncertain world of economic relations" (Runge, 1981a; also Runge, 1981b and Sen, 1967). <u>7/</u>

Towards a theory of induced institutional innovation

The sources of <u>demand</u> for technical and institutional change can be viewed as essentially similar. A rise in the price of land (or natural resources) in relation to the price of labour induces technical changes that release the constraints on production from an inelastic supply of land and, at the same time, induces institutional changes that lead to greater precision in the definition and allocation of property rights in land. A rise in the price of labour relative to land (or natural resources) induces technical changes that permit the substitution of capital for labour; at the same time, it induces institutional changes that enhance the productivity of the human agent and increase workers' control over the conditions of employment. The new income streams generated by technical change and by institutional efficiency induce changes in the relative demand for products and open up new and more profitable opportunities for product innovations. And the new income streams generated by either technical or institutional change induce further institutional changes designed to modify the way the new income streams are partitioned among factor owners and to alter the distribution of income among individuals and classes.

Marx considered technological change as a primary source of institutional change. 8/ Our view is somewhat more complex in that we consider changes in factor endowments and product demand to be equally important sources of institutional change. Nor is our definition of institutional change limited to the dramatic or revolutionary changes of the type anticipated by Marx. Rather, we share with Davis and North (1971) the view that basic institutions such as property rights and markets are more typically altered through the culmination of "secondary" or incremental institutional changes, such as modifications in contractual relations or shifts in the boundaries between market and non-market activities.

Shifts in the supply of technical and institutional change may also be generated by similar forces. Advances in knowledge in science and technology reduce the cost of the new income streams generated by technical change. Advances in knowledge in the social sciences and related professions reduce the cost of the new income streams generated by gains in institutional innovation and improvements in institutional performance.

Collective action leading to changes in the supply of institutional innovations often involves severe stress among the interest groups and communities that stand to gain or lose from the changes. The supply of institutional innovations is strongly influenced by the cost of achieving social consensus (or of suppressing opposition). The rate and direction of institutional change depend critically on the cultural traditions and ideology that influence the cost or acceptability of changes in institutional arrangements and on the power balance among interest groups. Education, both general and technical, that facilitates people's understanding of their common interests can reduce the cost of institutional innovation.

We illustrate, in figure VI, the elements of a model that maps the general equilibrium relationships among resource endowments, cultural endowments, technology, and institutions. 9/ The model goes beyond the conventional general equilibrium model in which resource endowments, technologies, institutions, and culture (conventionally designated as tastes) are given. 10/ In the study of long-term social and economic change, the relationships among the several variables must be treated as recursive. The formal micro-economic models that are employed to analyse the supply and demand for technical and institutional change can be thought of as "nested" within the general equilibrium framework of figure VI.

One advantage of the "pattern model" outlined in figure VI is that it helps to identify areas of ignorance. Our capacity to model and test the relationships between resource endowments and technical change is relatively strong. Our capacity to model and test the relationships between cultural endowments and either technical or institutional change is relatively weak. A second advantage of the model is that it is useful in identifying the components that enter into other attempts to account for secular economic and social change. Failure to analise historical change in a general equilibrium context tends to result in a unidimensional perspective of the relationships bearing on technical and institutional change.

Figure VI.   Interrelationships between changes in resource endowments,
             cultural endowments, technology and institutions

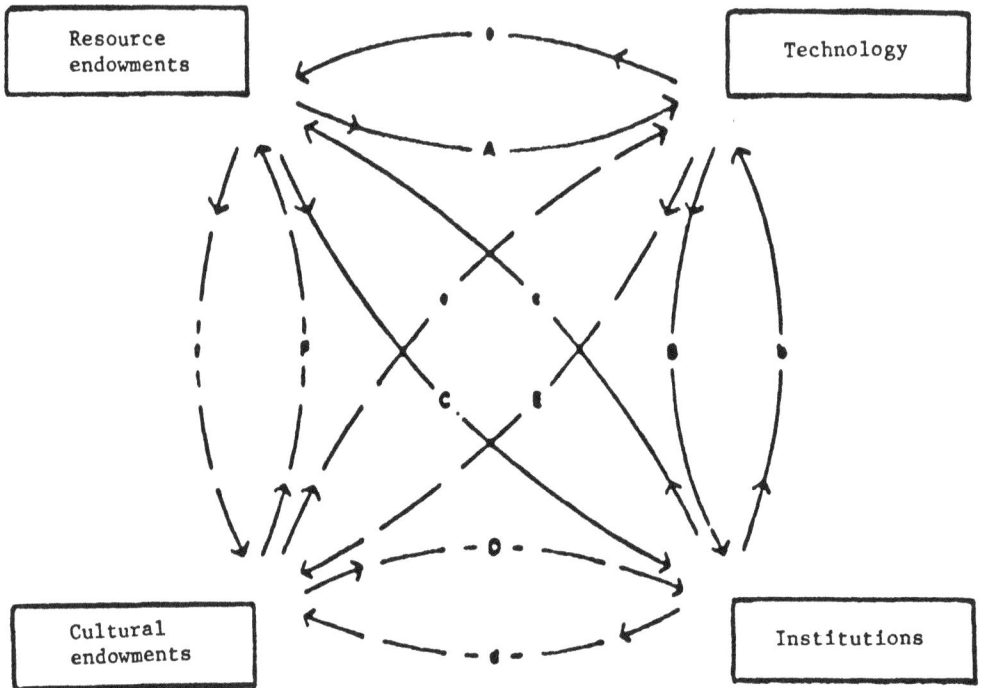

For example, historians working within the Marxist tradition often tend to view technical change as dominating both institutional and cultural change. In his book Oriental Despotism, Karl Wittfogel views the irrigation technology used in wet rice cultivation in East Asia as determining political organization (Wittfogel, 1957). As applied to figure VI, his primary concern was the impact of resources and technology on institutions (B) and (C).

A serious misunderstanding can be observed in contemporary neo-Marxian critiques of the green revolution. These criticisms have focused attention almost entirely on the impact of technical change on labour and land tenure relations. Both radical and populist critics have emphasized relation (B), but they have tended to ignore relationships (A) and (C). This bias has led to repeated failure to identify effectively the separate effects of population growth and technical change on the growth and distribution of income (Cleaver, 1972; Griffin, 1974).

Armen Alchian and Harold Demsetz identify a primary function of property rights as the development of incentives to achieve greater internalization of externalities (Alchian and Demsetz, 1973; Demsetz, 1967). They consider that the clear specification of property rights reduces transaction costs in the face of growing competition for the use of scarce resources as a result of population growth and/or growth in production demand. North and Thomas (1970), building on the Alchian-Demsetz paradigm, attempted to explain the economic growth of Western Europe between 900 and 1700 primarily in terms of changes in property institutions. 11/ During the eleventh and thirteenth centuries, the pressure of population against increasingly scarce land resources induced innovations in property rights that in turn created profitable opportunities for the generation and adoption of labour-intensive technical changes in agriculture (line C).

In a more recent work, Mancur Olson has emphasized the proliferation of institutions as a source of economic decline (Olson, 1982). 12/ He also regards broad-based encompassing organizations as having incentives to generate growth and redistribute incomes to their members with little excess burden. For example, a broadly based coalition that encompasses the majority of agricultural producers is more likely to exert political pressure for growth-oriented policies that will enable its members to obtain a larger share of a larger national product than is a smaller organization that represents the interests of the producers of a single commodity. Small organizations representing narrow interest groups are more likely to pursue the interests of their members at the expense of the welfare of other producers and the general public. In contrast, an even more broadly based farmer-labour coalition would be more concerned with promoting economic growth than would an organization representing a single sector. But large groups, in Olson's view, are inherently unstable because rational individuals will not incur the costs of contributing to the realization of a large group programme; they have strong incentives to act as free riders. As a result, organizational "space" in a stable society will be increasingly occupied by special-interest "distributional coalitions." These distributional coalitions make political life divisive. They slow down the adoption of new technologies (line b) and limit the capacity to reallocate resources (line c). The effect is to slow economic growth or in some cases to initiate a period of economic decline.

Population growth and the demand for institutional innovation:
a Philippine village case

In some cases the demand for institutional innovation can be satisfied by
the development of new forms of property rights, more efficient market
institutions, or evolutionary changes arising out of direct contracting by
individuals at the level of the community or the firm. In other cases, in
which externalities are involved, substantial political resources may have to
be brought to bear to organize non-market institutions to provide for the
supply of public goods.

The agricultural revolution that occurred in the United Kingdom between
the fifteenth and nineteenth centuries involved a substantial increase in the
productivity of land and labour. It was accompanied by the enclosure of open
fields and the replacement of small peasant cultivators, who held their land
from manorial lords, by a system in which large farmers used hired labour to
farm the land they leased from the landlords. The First Enclosure Movement,
in the fifteenth and sixteenth centuries, resulted in the conversion of open,
arable fields and commons to private pasture in areas suitable for grazing.
It was induced by an expansion in the export demand for wool. The Second
Enclosure Movement, in the eighteenth century, involved the conversion of
communally managed arable land into privately operated units. It is now
agreed that this change was largely induced by the growing disequilibrium
between the fixed institutional rent received by landlords under copyhold
tenures (with lifetime contracts) and the higher economic rents expected from
the adoption of new technology, which became more profitable as a consequence
of higher grain prices and population growth leading to lower wages. When the
land was enclosed, there was a redistribution of income from farmers to
landowners, and the disequilibrium was reduced or eliminated. 13/

There are limits, however, to the rigour that can be brought to bear on
even carefully studied historical cases. Research conducted in the
Philippines in the late 1970s (Kikuchi and Hayami, 1978; Hayami and Kikuchi,
1981) has enabled us to examine a contemporary example of the interrelated
effects of technical change and population growth on the demand for
institutional change in land tenure and labour relations. The case is
particularly interesting because the institutional innovations occurred as a
result of private contracting among individuals. The study is unique in that
it is based on a rigourous analysis of micro-economic data for one village
over a period of about 20 years.

Changes in technology and resource endowments

Between 1956 and 1976, rice production per hectare in the study village
rose dramatically, from 2.5 to 6.7 metric tons per hectare per year. This
increase resulted from two technical innovations. In 1958, the national
irrigation system was extended to the village, which permitted double cropping
to replace single cropping, thereby doubling the annual production per
hectare. The second major technical change was the introduction in the late
1960s of the modern, high-yield rice varieties. The diffusion of modern
varieties was accompanied by the increased use of fertilizer and pesticides

and by the adoption of improved cultural practices such as straight-row planting and intensive weeding.

Population growth in the village was rapid. Between 1966 and 1976 the number of households rose from 66 to 109 and the population rose from 383 to 464, while cultivated areas remained virtually constant. The number of landless labour households increased from 20 to 54. In 1976, half of the households in the village had no land to cultivate or to rent. The average farm size declined from 2.3 to 2.0 hectares.

The land is farmed primarily by tenants. In 1976, only 1.7 of the 108 hectares of cropland in the village were owned by village residents. Traditionally, share tenancy was the most common form of tenure. In both 1956 and 1966, 70 per cent of the land was farmed under share tenure arrangements. In 1963, a new agricultural land reform code was passed that was designed to break the political power of the traditional landed elite and to provide greater incentives to peasant producers of basic food crops. A major feature of the new legislation was an arrangement that permitted tenants to initiate a shift from share tenure to leasehold, with rent under the leasehold set at 25 per cent of the average yield for the previous three years. Implementation of the code between the mid-1960s and the mid-1970s resulted in a 30 per cent decline in the amount of land farmed under share tenure.

Institution innovation

The shift from share tenure to lease tenure was not, however, the only change in tenure relationships that occurred between 1966 and 1976. There was also a sharp increase in the number of plots farmed under subtenancy arrangements, from 1 in 1956 to 5 in 1966, and to 16 in 1976. Subtenancy was illegal under the land reform code, so the subtenancy arrangements were usually made without the formal consent of the landowner. All cases of subtenancy were on land farmed under a leasehold arrangement; the most common form was a 50-50 sharing of costs and output.

It was hypothesized that an incentive for the emergence of the subtenancy institution was the fact that the rent paid to landlords under the leasehold arrangement was below the equilibrium rent, the level that would reflect both the higher yields of rice obtained with the new technology and the lower wage rates implied by the increase in population pressure against the land. To test this hypothesis, market prices have been used to compute the value of the unpaid factor inputs (family labour and capital) for different tenure arrangements during the 1976 wet season. The results indicate that the share-to-land was lowest and the operators' surplus wage was highest for the land under leasehold tenancy. In contrast, the share-to-land was highest and no surplus was left for the operator who cultivated the land under the subtenancy arrangement (table 2). Indeed, the share-to-land when the land was farmed under subtenancy was very close to the sum of the share-to-land plus the operators' surplus under the other tenure arrangement.

The results are consistent with the hypothesis. A substantial portion of the economic rent was captured by the leasehold tenants in the form of operators surplus. On the land farmed under a subtenancy arrangement, the

Table 2. Factor shares of rice output per hectare, 1976 wet season

	Number of plots	Area (ha)	Rice output	Current inputs	Land Landowner	Land Sublessor	Land Total	Labor	Capital[b]	Operators' surplus
				.... kg/ha						
Leasehold land	44	66.7	2.889	657	567	0	567	918	337	410
			(100.0)	(22.7)	(19.6)	(0)	(19.6)	(31.8)	(11.7)	(14.2)
Share tenancy land	30	29.7	2.749	697	698	0	698	850	288	216
			(100.0)	(25.3)	(25.4)	(0)	(25.4)	(30.9)	(10.5)	(7.9)
Subtenancy land	16	9.1	3.447	801[c]	504	801	1.305	1.008	346	-13
			(100.0)	(23.2)	(14.6)	(23.2)	(37.8)	(29.3)	(10.1)	(-0.4)

Source: Yujiro Hayami and Masao Kikuchi, Asian Village Economy at the Crossroads: An Economic Approach to Institutional Change (Tokyo, University of Tokyo Press, 1981; and Baltimore, The Johns Hopkins University Press, 1982), pp. 111–113.

Notes:

a/   Percentage shares are shown in parentheses

b/   Sum of irrigation fee and paid and/or imputed rentals of carabao, tractor and other machines.

c/   Rents to subleasors in the case of pledged plots are imputed by applying the interest rate of 40 per cent crop season (a mode in the interest reate distribution in the village) rent was shared between the leaseholder and the landlord. An important point is that subtenancy was practised despite the fact that it was illegal. Under the laws, if a sublessee appealed to the agrarian reform office and proved himself to be the actual tiller of the land, he could obtain a formal title of leasehold tenancy by forfeiting his lessor's title. However, the sublessee was constrained in taking such opportunistic action for fear of social opprobrium and perhaps ostracism, since at the time subtenancy was considered a legitimate institution in terms of the traditional moral principles of work-sharing within the village community. The common cultural endowments among contracting parties thus reduced the transaction costs involved in this otherwise hazardous arrangement.

A second institutional change, induced by higher yields and the increase in population pressure, has been the emergence of a new pattern of employer-labour relationship between farm operators and landless workers. According to the traditional system called _hunusan_, labourers who participated in the harvesting and threshing activity received a one-sixth share of the paddy (rough rice) harvest. By 1976, most of the farmers (83 per cent) had adopted a system called _gamma_, in which participation in the harvesting operation was limited to workers who had performed the weeding operation without receiving wages.

The emergence of the _gamma_ system can be interpreted as an institutional innovation designed to reduce the wage rate for harvesting to a level equal to the marginal productivity of labour. In the 1950s, when the rice yield per hectare was low and labour was less abundant, the one-sixth share may have approximated an equilibrium wage level. The shift to double cropping and the adoption of high-yielding varieties had the effect of increasing the institutional wage rate under traditional sharing arrangements. But at the same time, the growing pressure of population against the land was exerting downward pressure on market wage rates. The result was a widening disequilibrium between institutional and market wage rates. 14/

To test the hypothesis that the _gamma_ system was rapidly adopted primarily because it represented an institutional innovation permitting farm operators to equate the harvesters' share of output to the marginal productivity of labour, imputed wage costs were compared with the actual harvesters' shares (table 3). The results indicate that a substantial gap existed between the imputed wage for the harvesters' labour alone and the actual harvesters' shares. This gap was eliminated when the imputed wages for harvesting and weeding labour were added.

These results are consistent with the hypothesis that changes in institutional arrangements governing the use of production factors were induced when disequilibrium occurred between the marginal returns and the marginal costs of factor inputs as a result of changes in factor endowments and technical change. Institution change was therefore directed towards the establishment of a new equilibrium in factor markets.

Why, then, was _gamma_ chosen over alternative methods of re-establishing equilibrium? The labour cost of harvesting can be reduced by reducing the share rate under the _hunusan_ system or by replacing _hunusan_ with the labour of daily wage workers (_upahan_). A number of advantages can be counted for the

Table 3. Comparison between the imputed value of harvesters,
share and the inputed cost of _gamma_ labour

	Based on employers' data	Based on employees' data
Number of working days of _gamma_ labor (days/ha)[a]		
Weeding	20.9	18.3
Harvesting/threshing	33.6	33.6
Imputed cost of _gamma_ labor (P/ha)[b]		
Weeding	167.2	146.4
Harvesting/threshing	369.6	369.6
(1) Total	536.8	516.0
Actual share of harvesters:		
In kind (Kg/ha) [c]	504.0	549.0
(2) Imputed value (P/ha)[d]	504.0	549.0
(2)-(1)	-32.8	33.0

Source: Yujiro Hayami and Masao Kikuchi, Asian Village Economy at the
Crossroads: An Economic Approach to Institutional Change (Tokyo, University
of Tokyo Press, 1981; and Baltimore, The Johns Hopkins University Press,
1982), p. 121

Notes:

a/   Includes labour of family members who worked as _gamma_ labourers.

b/   Imputation using market wage rates (daily wage = P8.0 for weeding;
P11.0 for harvesting.

c/   One sixth of output per hectare

d/   Imputation using market prices (1 Kg = P1).

gamma system. First, it incorporates a mechanism to reduce labourers'
shirking, since an incentive for employees to do more conscientious work in
weeding is provided in the form of output sharing. Second, even though labour
is normally abundant, it can be difficult for an individual farmer to find a
sufficient number of daily wage workers at the right time for his harvesting.
Under the gamma system, the availability of labour at harvest time is
guaranteed by contract.   From the employee's side, gamma is more secure,
involving less risk in finding employment in the narrow labour market.

However, the most critical consideration in the choice of the gamma
system appears to be the fact that gamma is more congruent with traditional
moral   principles   in   village   communities,   such   as   mutual   help   and
income--sharing, and thereby involves less social friction.   Farmer employers
could have lowered the real wage rates of harvesting labour by reducing the
output share of harvesters or by employing labourers from the market with a
fixed daily wage contract. However, the cost arising from resistance to a
change in a long-established village custom, such as the one-sixth share for
harvesting workers, would not have been small.   In fact, when a farmer in a
neighbouring village tried to reduce the harvesters' share under the hunusan
system, his action was met by the indignation of labourers and his rice crop
in the field was destroyed during the night.

Efficiency and equity implications

It is important to recognize that subtenancy and gamma contracts were the
institutional innovations that facilitated more efficient resource allocations
through   voluntary   agreements   by   assigning   more   complete   private   property
rights. The land reform laws gave tenants enhanced protection of their tenancy
rights with the result that a part of the land property right (the right to
continue tilling the soil at a rent lower than the marginal product of land)
was assigned to tenant operators.   But the laws prohibited tenants from
renting their land to someone else who might use it more efficiently when, for
example, they became elderly or found more profitable off-farm employment.
Subtenancy   was   developed   to   reduce   inefficiency   resulting   from   the
institutional rigidity in the land rental market based on the land reform
programmes.   Likewise, the gamma system was developed to counteract the
institutional rigidity in the labour market based on the traditional rural
community custom of a fixed harvesters' share.

It might appear that these institutional innovations increased efficiency
at the expense of equity.   But if the subtenancy system had not been
developed, the route would have been closed for some of the landless labourers
to become farm operators and use their entrepreneurial abilities more
profitably. If the implicit wage rate for harvesting work had been raised in
the absence of the gamma contract, it might have encouraged mechanization in
threshing and thereby reduced employment and labour earnings.   It must be
recognized that the institutional innovations used to develop more efficient
markets   by   assigning   more   complete   private   property   rights   did   not
necessarily impair equity, as is often argued by Marxist and populist
critiques against private market institutions.

In the case reviewed here, the induced innovation process leading towards the establishment of equilibrium in factor markets occurred rather rapidly even though many of the transactions among landlords, tenants, and labourers were less than fully monetized. Informal contractual arrangements or agreements were used. The subleasing and the _gamma_ labour contract evolved without the mobilization of substantial political activity or bureaucratic effort because the contracting parties shared common cultural endowments.

The development and introduction of new institutions in larger populations characterized by considerable cultural heterogeneity would require the mobilization of many bureaucratic and political resources. A richer model is needed in environments where institutional change involves the redistribution of existing resources or income shares rather than the partitioning of growth dividends, or where inequities in the distribution of economic and political resources preclude the kind of simple recontracting that characterized the Philippine village case presented in this section. 15/ The value of this case is that it exhibits so clearly the interaction of population pressure, change in agricultural technology, and change in agrarian institutions.

Perspective

In this paper we have illustrated the power of the theory of induced innovation to advance our understanding of technical and institutional change in both industrial and pre-industrial societies. The Boserup model, which interprets land-use intensification as a response to growing pressure of population against land reserves, is fully consistent with the more general induced innovation model. The Boserup model assumes a self-contained agriculture in a pre-industrial society in which indigenous efforts to maintain subsistence under decreasing land resources per capita induced the development of more land-saving and labour-using farming systems. Advances in agricultural practice proceed through a process of trial and error. In the West advances in tillage equipment and in crop and animal husbandry during the Middle Ages and well into the nineteenth century evolved almost entirely from husbandry practice and mechanical insight. Associated change in agrarian institutions, such as more exact specification of property rights consistent with intensification in land use, is not explicitly modeled. The required institutional innovations are assumed to occur relatively smoothly over time through agreements among community members sharing common cultural endowments, as in the Philippine village case reported here.

This type of technical and institutional development was, in pre-industrial societies, capable of sustaining growth of agricultural output in the range of 0.5-1.0 per cent per year, a level fully consistent with pre-industrial rates of population growth. With the advent of industrialization both population and income growth have accelerated. The resulting increases in food demand have exceeded the rates of supply increases expected from indigenous technology development. One response has been the institutionalization of capacity for research in agricultural science and technology. The capacity to advance biological technology has involved the establishment of publicly supported agricultural experiment stations.

This institutional innovation was initially developed in Germany in the late nineteenth century and diffused to the United States and Japan (Hayami and Ruttan, 1985). Biological and chemical technologies capable of increasing yields per hectare of arable land were adopted relatively rapidly in the Western world and in Japan in institutional environments characterized by well-defined private property rights to arable land. The development and sustainability of modern arable farming systems were supported by public investments in land infrastructure such as drainage and irrigation.

The dramatic advances in rice and wheat production technology in the tropics, especially in South and South-East Asia, since the mid-1960s can be interpreted as a diffusion of the institutional innovation of public sector agricultural research to developing countries. Fertilizer inputs and rice and wheat yields had remained very low before the mid-1960s in spite of substantial declines in the fertilizer-land and fertilizer-crop price ratios. This situation represented a major disequilibrium between economic incentives and technological opportunities. The movement to a new equilibrium was delayed until the needed investments were made in public experiment station capacity so that the prototype technology available in advanced countries in the temperate zone could be adapted to the agro-climatic and socio-economic environments of developing countries.

A major current concern is why the development of new seed-fertilizer technology, so successful in South and South-East Asia, has had much less impact in Africa, where there has been a gross underinvestment in the human capital needed to invent, diffuse, and effectively utilize new agricultural technology. Institutionalization of capacity for agricultural research was neglected while both donor agencies and national governments focused their efforts on rural development projects and technology transfer. Unlike traditionally land-scarce Asia, the concepts of private land property rights and state/communal control of natural resources for conservation have been less well established.

The lag in institutional development represents a serious constraint against the development and diffusion of new seed-fertilizer technology in Africa. The lag in both technical and institutional development appears to reflect the misperception, common even as recently as a decade ago, that Africa is a land-abundant region. The result is the emergence of a disequilibrium between economic incentives and technological innovation that is ever more massive than the disequilibrium in South and South-East Asia a quarter century ago.

The existence of heterogeneous cultural endowments among different ethnic groups and tribes that make consensus on new rules and institutions extremely difficult. This presents a major obstacle to the mobilization of the political resources needed to bring about the institutional innovations that could move African agriculture to a new equilibrium on the metaproduction function. The evolution of political institutions capable of implementing and sustaining the institutional innovations that will allow African countries to effectively respond to the growth of population and food demand will represent a major challenge over the next several decades.

Notes

1/   In this paper, we have been unable to avoid drawing on our earlier research on technical and institutional change. Our work on induced technical change was first outlined in Hayami and Ruttan (1970). It was elaborated and the concept of induced institutional innovation was introduced in Hayami and Ruttan (1971). The concept of induced institutional innovation was developed more fully in Binswanger and Ruttan (1978), Hayami and Kikuchi (1981), Ruttan and Hayami (1984), and Hayami and Ruttan (1985). We have used the induced innovation framework to examine the relationships between population growth and technical change in Hayami and Ruttan (1987) and Ruttan (1984).

2/   The history of thought and the current state of knowledge in the field of induced technical change is reviewed in Thirtle and Ruttan (1987).

3/   Hans P. Binswanger (1974a, 1978c) has developed an induced technical change model incorporating a research production function. By assuming decreasing marginal productivity of research resources in applied research and development, he was able to construct a model of induced factor-saving bias in technical change based on the profit-maximizing behaviour of the firm. Binswanger also incorporates into the model the effect of product demand on research resource allocation. In his model, the growth in product demand increases the marginal value product of resources devoted to research, thereby increasing the optimal level of research expenditure for the profit-maximizing firm. The larger research budget implies a shift of the innovation possibility curve (IPC), defined as an envelope of unit isoquants corresponding to the alternative technologies that can potentially be developed for a given research budget at a given state of the art, towards the origin. In the Binswanger model, technical change is guided along the IPC by changes in relative factor prices, while the IPC itself is induced to shift inward towards the origin by the growth in product demand. He was thus able to incorporate both the Hicks approach, which focused on the effect of relative factor prices on factor-saving bias, and the Schmookler-Griliches approach, which focused on the effect of product demand on the rate of technological change, into a single model of induced technical change.

4/   The work of Binswanger and colleagues also draws very heavily on Ruthenberg's (1980) careful classification of tropical farming systems.

5/   A method for measuring biases of technical change with many factors of production was originally developed by Hans Binswanger (1974b, 1978b) using the transcendental logarithmic (translog) function. In our 1985 study, we employed a two-level constant elasticity of substitution (CES) production function (Hayami and Ruttan, 1985 and 1987). The results of the 1985 study were confirmed by Kawagoe, Otsuka, and Hayami (1986) using a more general model. The Binswanger method was applied to Japanese agriculture by Kako (1978) and Nghiep (1979).

6/   There is not, however, complete consensus on the Lee results (see the paper by D. Weir in this volume).

7/   There is considerable disagreement regarding the meaning of the term
institution. A distinction is often made between the concepts of institution
and organization. The broad view, which includes both concepts, is most
useful for our purpose and is consistent with the view expressed by both
Commons (1950) and Knight (1952). Our definition also encompasses the
classification employed by Davis and North (1971). We employ the more
inclusive definition so as to be able to consider changes in the rules or
conventions that govern behaviour: (a) within economic units such as
families, firms, and bureaucracies; (b) among economic units, as in the case
of the rules that govern market relationships; and (c) between economic units,
as in the case of the relationship between a firm and a regulatory agency.

8/   "At a certain stage of their development, the material forces of
production in society come in conflict with the existing relations of
production, or--what is but a legal expression from the same thing--with the
property relations within which they have been at work before. From forms of
development of the forces of production, these relations turn into their
fetters. Then comes the period of social revolution. With the change of the
economic foundation the entire immense superstructure is more or less rapidly
transformed" (Marx, 1913). For a discussion of the role of technology in
Marxian thought, see Rosenberg (1982). The relationship between the theory of
induced innovation and Marxian thought has been discussed by Palladino (1987).

9/   Fusfeld (1980) uses the term "pattern" or "Gestalt" model to
describe a form of analysis that links the elements of a general pattern
together by logical connections. The recursive multicausal relationships of
the pattern model imply that the model is always "open"--"it can never include
all of the relevant variables and relationships necessary for a full
understanding of the phenomena under investigation." For an attempt to use
more formal modelling of general equilibrium relationships to understand the
sources of institutional innovation in medieval society, see Townsend (1988).
Townsend argues that "market structure should be endogenous to the class of
general equilibrium models at hand. That is, the theory should explain why
markets sometimes exist and sometimes do not, so that economic organization
falls out in the solution to the mechanism design problem."

10/   In economics, the concept of cultural endowments is usually subsumed
under the concept of tastes, which are regarded as given, that is, not subject
to economic analysis. Our use of the term culture is consistent with the
definition suggested by White: "When things and events are considered in the
context of their relation to the human organism, they constitute behaviour,
when they are considered ... in their relationship to one another, they become
culture" (1974). We use the term cultural endowments to capture those
dimensions of culture that have been transmitted from the past. Contemporary
changes in resource endowments, technology, and institutions can be expected
to result in changes in cultural endowments. For a discussion of attempts to
employ the concept of culture by development economists, see Ruttan (1988).

11/   For a critical review of the North-Thomas model, see Field (1981).
Field is critical of attempts by North and Thomas to treat institutional
change as endogenous. For criticism of the Hayami-Ruttan approach to induced
institutional change, see Koppel and Oasa (1987), Burmeister (1987), and
Bromley (1989).

12/   For a critical review of the Olson work, see North (1983).

13/   There has been a continuing debate among students of English agricultural history about whether the higher rents that landowners received after enclosure was because (a) enclosed farming was more efficient than open–field farming, or (b) enclosures redistributed income from farmers to landowners (see Allen, 1982).

14/   Real wages for agricultural labour declined significantly between the mid–1950s and the mid–1960s in the Philippines (Kahn, 1977).   Thus, although we cannot be certain that the labour market was in equilibrium in the 1950s, it is clear that the degree of disequilibrium widened as a result of both higher yields and lower wage rates before the introduction and diffusion of the *gamma* system.

15/   Boyce (1987) finds that in Bangladesh, where the institutional environment is severely biased by market imperfections and unequal distribution of economic and political resources, that differences in population density and population growth rates influence the rate and direction of technical change in a manner consistent with the induced technical change hypothesis.   He also finds that these imperfections in economic and political markets have represented a serious constraint on the development and reform of irrigation and other water control institutions. The induced innovation framework outlined and employed in this paper has been referred to by Boyce as the "pure" theory of institutional innovation.   In other work, we have drawn on cases, such as those described in the work of de Janvry (1973), Sanders (1978), and Feeny (1982), in which biases in political resources acted to prevent or delay the process of induced institutional innovation and where substantial political and bureaucratic resources had to be mobilized to transform the latent demand into effective demand for institutional change.

References

Alchian, A. A. and H. Demsetz (1973). The property rights paradigm. _Journal of Economic History_, vol. 33, pp. 16–77.

Allen, R. C. (1982). The efficiency and distributional consequences of eighteenth century enclosures. _Economic Journal_, vol. 92, pp. 937–953.

Binswanger, H. P. (1974a). A microeconomic apoproach to induced innovation. _Economic Journal_, vol. 84, pp. 940–958.

_____ (1974b). The measurement of technical change biases with many factors of production. _American Economic Review_, vol. 64, pp. 964–976.

_____ (1978a). Induced technical change: evolution of thought. In _Induced Innovation: Technology, Institutions and Development_, H. P. Binswanger and others, eds. Baltimore: The Johns Hopkins University Press.

_____ (1978b). Measured biases of technical change: the United States. In _Induced Innovation: Technology, Institutions and Development_, H. P. Binswanger and others, eds. Baltimore: The Johns Hopkins University Press.

_____ (1978c). The microeconomics of induced technical change. In _Induced Innovation: Technology, Institutions and Development_, H. P. Binswanger and others, eds. Baltimore: The Johns Hopkins University Press.

_____ and V. W. Ruttan, eds. (1978). _Induced Innovation: Technology, Institutions and Development_. Baltimore: The Johns Hopkins University Press.

Boserup, E. (1965). _The Conditions of Agricultural Growth: The Economics of Agrarian Change and Population Press_. Chicago: Aldine.

_____ (1981). _Population and Technical Change: A Study of Long-Term Trends_. Chicago: University of Chicago Press.

Boyce, J. K. (1987). _Agrarian Impasse in Bengal: Institutional Constraints to Technological Change_. Oxford: Oxford University Press.

Bromley, D. M. (1989). _Economic Interests and Institutions: The Conceptual Foundation of Public Policy_. New York: Basil Blackwell.

Burmeister, L. L. (1987). The South Korean green revolution: induced or directed innovation. _Economic Development and Cultural Change_, vol. 34, pp. 767–790.

Cleaver, H. M., Jr. (1972). The contradiction of the green revolution. _American Economic Review_, vol. 62, pp. 177–186.

Commons, J. R. (1950). The Economics of Collective Action. New York: Macmillan.

Davis, L. E. and D. C. North (1971). Institutional Change and American Economic Growth. New York: Cambridge University Press.

de Janvry, A. (1973). A socioeconomic model of induced innovations for Argentine agricultural development. Quarterly Journal of Economics, vol. 87, pp. 410-435.

Demsetz, H. (1967). Toward a theory of property rights. American Economic Review, vol. 57, pp. 347-359.

Feeny, D. (1982). The Political Economy of Productivity: Thai Agricultural Development, 1880-1975. Vancouver: University of British Columbia Press.

Field, A. J. (1981). The problem with neoclassical institutional economics: a critique with special reference to the North/Thomas model of pre-1500 Europe. Explorations in Economic History, vol. 18, pp. 174-198.

Fusfeld, D. R. (1980). The conceptual framework of modern economics. Journal of Economic Issues, vol. 14, pp. 1-52.

Griffin, K. (1974). The Political Economy of Agrarian Change: An Essay on the Green Revolution. Cambridge, Massachusetts: Harvard University Press.

Griliches, Z. (1957). Hybrid corn: an exploration in the economics of technical change. Econometrica, vol. 25, pp. 501-522.

Hayami, Yujiro and Masao Kikuchi (1981). Asian Village Economy at the Crossroads: An Economic Approach to Institutional Change. Baltimore: The Johns Hopkins University Press; and Tokyo: University of Tokyo Press.

_____ and V. W. Ruttan (1970). Factor prices and technical change in agricultural development: the United States and Japan, 1880-1960. Journal of Political Economy, vol. 78, pp. 1,115-1,141.

_____ and V. W. Ruttan (1971). Agricultural Development: An International Perspective. Baltimore: The Johns Hopkins University Press.

_____ and V. W. Ruttan (1985). Agricultural Development: An International Perspective, rev. ed. Baltimore: The Johns Hopkins University Press.

_____ and V. W. Ruttan (1987). Population growth and agricultural productivity. In Technological Prospects and Population Trends, J. P. Espenshade and G. J. Stolnitz, eds., Boulder, Colorado: Westview Press. Also in Population Growth and Economic Development: Issues and Evidence, D. G. Johnson and R. D. Lee, eds. Madison, Wisconsin: University of Wisconsin Press.

_____ and others (1975). A Century of Agricultural Growth in Japan. Minneapolis, Minnesota: University of Minnesota Press; and Tokyo: University of Tokyo Press.

_____ and others (1976). Agricultural growth against a land resource constraint: the Philippine experience. Australian Journal of Agricultural Economics, vol. 20, pp. 144-159.

Hicks, J. R. (1983). The Theory of Wages. London: MacMillan and Co.

Kahn, A. R. (1977). Poverty and Landlessness in Rural Asia. Geneva: International Labour Office.

Kako, T. (1978). Decomposition analysis of derived demand for factor inputs: the case of rice production in Japan. American Journal of Agricultural Economics, vol. 60, pp. 628-635.

Kawagoe, T., K. Otsuka, and Y. Hayami (1986). Induced bias of technical change in agriculture: the United States and Japan, 1880-1980. Journal of Political Economy, vol. 94, pp. 523-544.

Kikuchi, M. and Y. Hayami (1978). Agricultural growth against a land resource constraint: a comparative history of Japan, Taiwan, Korea and the Philippines. Journal of Economic History, vol. 38, pp. 839-864.

Knight, F. H. (1952). Institutionalism and empiricism in economics. American Economic Review, vol. 42, p. 51.

Koppel, B. and E. Oasa (1987). Induced innovation theory and Asia's green revolution: a case study of ideology and neutrality. Development and Change, vol. 18, pp. 29-67.

Lee, R. D. (1980). A historical perspective on economic aspects of population explosion: the case of pre-industrial England. In Population and Economic Change in Developing Countries, R. H. Easterlin, ed. Chicago: University of Chicago Press.

Marx, K. (1913). A Contribution to the Critique of Political Economy. Chicago: Charles H. Kem and Co.

Mowery, D. and N. Rosenberg (1979). The influence of market demand upon innovation: a critical review of some recent empirical studies. Research Policy , vol. 8, pp. 102-153.

Nghiep, L. T. (1979). The structure and changes of technology in prewar Japanese agriculture. American Journal of Agricultural Economics, vol. 61, pp. 687-693.

North, D. C. (1983). A theory of economic change. Science, vol. 219, pp. 163-164.

_____ and R. P. Thomas (1970). An economic theory of the rise of the western world. Economic History Review, vol. 23, pp. 1-17.

Olson, M. (1982). The Rise and Decline of Nations: Economic Growth, Stagflation, and Social Rigidities. New Haven: Yale University Press.

Palladino, P. (1987). Science for whom? Agricultural development and the theory of induced innovation. Agriculture and Human Values, vol. 4, pp. 53-64.

Pingali, Prabhu, Y. Bigot and H. P. Binswanger (1987). Agricultural Mechanization and the Evolution of Farming Systems in Sub-Saharan Africa. Baltimore: The Johns Hopkins University Press.

Robinson, Warren C. and Wayne Schutjer (1984). Agricultural development and demographic change: a generalization of the Boserup model. Economic Development and Cultural Change, vol. 32, pp. 355-366.

Rosenberg, N. (1982). Inside the Block Box: Technology and Economics. New York: Cambridge University Press.

Runge, C. F. (1981a). Institutions and Common Property Externalities: The Assurance Problem in Economic Development. Ph.D. Dissertation, University of Wisconsin, Madison, Wisconsin.

_____ (1981b). Common property externalities: isolation assurance and resource depletion in a traditional grazing context. American Journal of Agricultural Economics, vol. 63, pp. 595-606.

Ruthenberg, H. (1980). Farming Systems in the Tropics, 3rd ed. Oxford: Clarendon Press.

Ruttan, V. W. (1984). Perspectives on population and development. Indian Journal of Agricultural Economics, vol. 39, pp. 631-638.

_____ (1988). Cultural endowments and economic development: what can we learn from anthropology?. Economic Development and Cultural Change, vol. 36 (April, Supplement), pp. S247-272.

_____ and Y. Hayami (1984). Toward a theory of induced institutional innovation. Journal of Development Studies, vol. 20, pp. 203-223.

_____ and others (1978). Factor productivity and growth. In Induced Innovation: Technology, Institutions and Development, H. P. Binswanger and others, eds. Baltimore: The Johns Hopkins University Press.

Sanders, J. H. and V. W. Ruttan (1978). Biased choice of technology in Brazilian agriculture. In Induced Innovation: Technology, Institutions and Development, H. P. Binswanger and others, eds. Baltimore: The Johns Hopkins University Press.

Scherer, F. M. (1982). Demand pull and technological invention: Schmookler revisited. Journal of Industrial Economics, vol. 30, pp. 225-238.

Schmookler, J. (1962). Changes in industry and in the state of knowledge as determinants of industrial invention. In Rate and Direction of Inventive Activity, R. R. Nelson, ed. Princeton, New Jersey: Princeton University Press.

_____ (1966). Invention and Economic Growth. Cambridge, Massachusetts: Harvard University Press.

Sen, A. K. (1967). Isolation, assurance and the social rate of discount. Quarterly Journal of Economics, vol. 81, pp. 112–124.

Thirtle, C. G. and V. W. Ruttan (1987). The Role of Demand and Supply in the Generation and Diffusion of Technical Change. London: Harwood Academic Publishers.

Townsend, R. M. (1988). Models as economies. The Economic Journal, vol. 98, pp. 1–24.

White, L. A. (1974). Human culture. Encyclopedia Britannica, vol. 8, 15th ed. Chicago: Benton.

Wittfogel, K. A. (1957). Oriental Despotism: A Comparative Study of Total Power. New Haven: Yale University Press.

PART FOUR

Some specific aspects of rapid population growth

Chapter 6

Rapid population growth and environmental stress

● B. Commoner*

Introduction

It is useful to begin this paper by considering the purpose of analysing the relationship between rapid population growth and environmental quality. One purpose is self-evident: rapid population growth is characteristic of most developing countries and, as a guide to national policy, it is important to determine whether this growth creates a distinctive impact on the quality of the environment. Another aspect of the issue is more general and is the subject of a considerably wider range of discussion. It is concerned with the origin of the environmental crisis; the sharp decline in environmental quality world-wide in the past 40-50 years.

Some observers have concluded that population growth is the dominant cause of the environmental crisis. The classic statement of this position is Ehrlich's:

> "The causal chain of the deterioration [of the environment] is easily followed to its source. Too many cars, too many factories, too much detergent, too much pesticide, multiplying contrails, inadequate sewage treatment plants, too little water, too much carbon dioxide – all can be traced easily to too many people." (Ehrlich, 1968)

For a more recent expression of the same position, which relates it to ecological principles, we can turn to Russell W. Peterson, the former president of the Audubon Society:

* Center for the Biology of Natural Systems, Queens College, City University of New York, Flushing, New York. The author acknowledges with thanks the contribution of his colleagues, Michael Frisch and Tom Webster, to the analyses described in this paper.

"Almost every environmental problem, almost every social and
political problem as well, either stems from or is exacerbated
by the growth of human population.... As any wildlife
biologist knows, once a species reproduces itself beyond the
carrying capacity of its habitat, natural checks and balances
come into play.... The human species is governed by the same
natural law. And there are signs in many parts of the world
today – Ethiopia is only one of many places, a tip of the
iceberg – that we Homo sapiens are beginning to exceed the
carrying capacity of the planet." (Peterson, 1985)

If this proposition – that environmental degradation is chiefly a
consequence of population growth – were true, the issue under discussion here
could be resolved and the operational solution identified; rapid population
growth correspondingly intensifies environmental degradation, which must
therefore be mitigated by reducing the rate of population growth.

Such statements are generally supported by anecdotal data about
environmental changes that appear to occur distinctively in countries with
high rates of population growth. Thus, intensive urbanization in Mexico, a
country with a 2.6 per cent annual rate of population growth in 1980–1985
(United Nations, 1986a), has been accompanied by very high levels of
photochemical smog in Mexico City. Similarly, forests are rapidly being
destroyed for firewood in countries such as Kenya that have high rates of
population growth. However, such anecdotal data are not definitive, for they
do not establish a necessary relationship between environmental quality and
rapid population growth. For example, despite the rapid increase in the
population of Mexico City, its photochemical smog level would be much lower if
the City had developed an adequate system of electrified mass transit – a
well–established technology – as it grew. Similarly, deforestation in Kenya
could be greatly diminished despite the rapid growth if the rural population
were provided with cookstoves fired by methane (perhaps produced from sewage
and manure) instead of using firewood for that purpose. In both of these
cases, the concurrence of rapid population growth and environmental
degradation does not necessarily reflect a direct, causal connection between
them. Moreover, counter examples can readily be cited; for example, both Los
Angeles and Tokyo, located in countries with low rates of population growth,
have experienced photochemical smog levels approximating those of Mexico City.

Analysis of the factors influencing environmental impact

These examples suggest that population is only one of several factors
that can influence environmental quality and that the degree of its influence
cannot be assessed without comparing it with the effects of other relevant
factors.

For this purpose, environmental stress is defined here as the amount of
pollutant emitted into the environment annually, where the term pollutant is
in turn defined as a substance that contributes to the deterioration of
environmental quality. An analysis has been developed for the purpose of

assessing the origin of the environmental crisis in developed, industrialized countries (Commoner, 1972). It is based on a simple algebraic identity that relates environmental impact (for example, the amount of pollutant introduced into the environment) to the three chief factors that can influence it: population, "affluence" (the amount of goods or resources consumed per capita), and "technology" (the relationship between the pollutant and the production technology that generates it, expressed as pollutant generated per unit of goods produced). Thus:

$$\text{Pollutant} = \text{Population} \times \frac{\text{good}}{\text{population}} \times \frac{\text{population}}{\text{good}} \qquad (1)$$

In this equation, "good" represents an economic good, the production of which generates the pollutant. For example, automotive travel (expressed as vehicle miles) is a good that, as it is produced, generates the pollutant carbon monoxide. By evaluating each of the three factors we can determine the degree to which each of them contributes to environmental impact and in that way assess the relative importance of population growth. Generally this can be done in terms of rates of change over time, so that equation (1) takes the form:

$$1 + \Delta \text{Pol} = 1 + \Delta \text{Pop} \times \frac{1 + \Delta \text{Good}}{1 + \Delta \text{Pop}} \times \frac{1 + \Delta \text{Pol}}{1 + \Delta \text{Good}} \qquad (2)$$

where ΔPop, ΔGood, and ΔPol are, respectively, the rates of change in the size of the population, in the amount of a given good, and in the amount of the pollutant generated when that good is produced.

When this analysis was applied to the sharp increase in pollutant emissions that occurred in the United States between 1950 and 1970, results of the type shown in table 1 were obtained, showing that the dominant contribution to the sharply rising pollution levels during that period was the technology factor rather than increasing population or affluence. The rate of increase in the amount of pollutant generated by the production of a unit amount of goods was considerably greater than the concurrent increase in goods produced per capita or in population.

To my knowledge, this type of analysis has not yet been applied to countries characterized by rapid rates of population growth, i.e., developing countries. One reason is that the necessary environmental data – yearly values of pollutant levels – are generally lacking. It is possible, however, to approach the problem indirectly, based on what is now known about the operational relationship between a number of pollutants and the production processes that generate them. For example, it has been established that the rising levels of nitrate, a pollutant that contributes to eutrophication and to health problems in drinking-water supplies, in United States and European surface waters is largely due to the application of nitrogen fertilizer to crops, which represent the economic good. Some of the nitrogen is not taken up by crops, but leaches into rivers and lakes (the amount depending on the

Table 1. Relations between the rates of change in pollutant
          output and the rates of change of environmental
          impact factors, United States

Pollutant	Good	Period	Pollutant (Rate of change) [a]	Environmental impact factors (rate of change)		
				Population	$\frac{Good}{Population}$	$\frac{Pollutant}{Good}$
Nitrogen oxides	Vehicle-miles	1946–67	7.28	1.41	2.00	2.58
Phosphate	Détergent	1946–68	19.45	1.42	1.00	13.78
Synthetic pesticides	Crops	1950–67	3.66	1.30	1.05	2.68
Beer Bottles	Beer	1950–67	6.93	1.30	1.05	5.08

Source: Barry Commoner "The environmental costs of economic growth",
Chemistry of Britain, vol. 8 (February 1972), pp. 52–65.

a/ Rate expressed as the increment ratio over the indicated period
of time – i. e., value in final year/value in initial year.

rate of application, soil conditions, and rainfall). In temperate areas where such data have been obtained, about 20–25 per cent of the applied nitrogen reaches surface waters (Vollenweider, 1968). Subject to this range of uncertainty, the amount of nitrogen fertilizer applied to crops can serve as a proxy for the resultant level of nitrate in surface waters – i.e., for environmental impact. Hence, the relative effects of the population, affluence, and technology factors can be estimated if, for a given country or area, changes over time can be computed in the following parameters: population, agricultural production per capita, and nitrogen fertilizer used per unit of agricultural production.

In the same way, the number of automotive vehicles (passenger cars and trucks) operating in a country can be used as an approximation of the pollutants that the vehicles emit, e. g., carbon monoxide, nitrogen oxides, and, in the case of diesel engines, carcinogen–containing carbon particles. In this case, we are compelled to use a very general measure, gross domestic product (GDP), to represent the economic good produced by operating the vehicles. Similarly, the amount of electricity produced can be used as an approximation of the amount of pollution generated by typical power plants. Depending on the fuel used, pollutants may include airborne dust, carbon monoxide, nitrogen oxides, and sulfur dioxide, as well as various toxic chemicals. Here, too, GDP must be used to represent the economic good yielded by the use of electricity.

Since equation (2) is based on changes in the relevant values over a given period of time, the computed values of the three determinant factors can be compared among countries that differ in absolute values of population size, GDP, number of vehicles, electricity production, or nitrogen fertilizer utilization. Naturally, the results of such computations will be affected by the influence on the pollutant level of factors not considered in equation (2), which are likely to differ among countries. Thus, agricultural production is influenced not only by nitrogen fertilizer but also by additional factors such as the use of pesticides. Similarly, GDP is certain to be influenced by many factors in addition to motor vehicles or electricity production. These extrinsic factors will, of course, blur the relations among the three components of the environmental impact equation. Nevertheless, as shown below, the computations do permit, at least as a first approximation, an estimate of the relationship between rapid population growth and environmental impact.

In recent years the necessary data have become available for a number of developing countries, enabling the type of computation outlined above. Such analyses have been carried out for three cases of environmental degradation: vehicular pollutants (e. g., carbon monoxide and nitrogen oxides), in which the number of motor vehicles serves as an approximation of emitted pollutants; power plant pollutants (e. g., nitrogen oxides and sulfur dioxide), in which the amount of electricity produced serves to approximate the resultant pollutants; and nitrate pollution, in which the amount of nitrogen fertilizer used serves as an approximation of the resultant concentration of nitrate in ground and surface waters.

The results of the first of these analyses, regarding the environmental impact of operating motor vehicles in 65 developing countries over the period 1970-1980, are summarized in table 2. The histograms shown in figure I describe the variation in the values of the three factors among the different countries. The mean value of the technology factor (vehicles/GDP), 1.054, is significantly greater than that of the other factors (1.025 for population and 1.002 for GDP per capita). These data can also be used to examine quite directly the influence of variation in the rate of population growth on the inferred environmental impact. This relationship is shown in figure II, which is a plot of the rate of increase in motor vehicles versus the concurrent rate of population growth for the 65 developing countries. Regression analysis shows that there is no statistically significant relationship between the two parameters ($R^2 = 0.18$). These results are in sharp contrast to the relationships expected according to the view that population growth is the determinant of environmental degradation. This theory can be stated in the framework of equation (2) in the following way: assume that population growth wholly determines environmental impact, which in the preceding example is expressed as the concurrent increase in motor vehicles. This implies that in equation (2) the product of the affluence factor (1 + ΔGDP/ΔPop) and the technology factor (1 + Δvehicles/ΔGDP) is 1. This means that the environmental impact, as represented by a positive rate of change in the number of vehicles, is exerted only by the increase in population. Any departure from this condition means that the affluence and/or technology factors do influence environmental impact, to a degree represented by their size relative to that of the population factor. Thus, from the mean values of the results shown in table 2, we can conclude that the relative impacts of the three factors are given by their respective annual rates of change; population, +2.5 per cent; affluence, +0.2 per cent; technology, +5.4 per cent. In this instance, therefore, the influence of the technology factor on environmental impact is more than twice the influence of the population factor.

This conclusion is also evident in the results shown in figure II. If population growth were the sole source of environmental impact, the rate of increase in motor vehicles would be equal to the rate of population growth, and the points representative of the different developing countries should lie on a line with a 45-degree slope (the broken line in figure II; note the different scales of the axes). Figure II shows that this is true of only 6 countries. In the remaining 59 countries, the rate of increase in motor vehicles is independent of the rate of population growth, indicating that factors other than population growth contribute to the increase in motor vehicles and, by inference, to environmental impact. Since the influence of GDP/capita is very small, it is clear that most of the nearly universal departure from the total influence of population growth is due to the rapid increase in the number of motor vehicles -- the technology factor.

Table 3 summarizes the results obtained from an analysis of the environmental impact represented by the production of electricity in 65 developing countries over the period 1970-1980. The average annual population growth is 2.7 per cent; the average annual change in GDP/capita is -0.7 per cent; the average annual increase in electricity/GDP is 8.1 per cent. Thus, the impact of the echnology factor is three times that of population growth.

Table 2. Relation between the rate of change of motor vehicles used and the rates of change of environmental impact factors, 1970–1980

Country	Motor vehicles in use (rate of change 1970–1980)	Environmental impact factors (rate of change 1970–1980)		
		Population	$\frac{GDP}{Population}$	$\frac{Vehicles}{GDP}$
Algeria	1.127	1.030	1.007	1.086
Botswana	1.173	1.044	1.047	1.073
Burundi	1.050	1.016	0.995	1.039
Central African Republic	1.055	1.022	0.970	1.065
Egypt	1.130	1.023	1.031	1.071
Ethiopia	1.009	1.022	0.983	1.004
Ghana	1.055	1.021	0.995	1.082
Ivory Coast	1.084	1.042	0.998	1.052
Kenya	1.057	1.039	0.976	1.042
Libya	1.159	1.044	0.994	1.117
Madagascar	1.015	1.025	0.960	1.032
Malawi	1.036	1.030	0.987	1.019
Mauritius	1.086	1.015	0.984	1.087
Morocco	1.075	1.026	0.994	1.054
Nigeria	1.099	1.030	0.977	1.092
Rwanda	1.106	1.031	1.019	1.052
Seychelles	1.123	1.017	1.061	1.041
Sierra Leone	1.022	1.017	0.985	1.021
South Africa	1.053	1.026	0.984	1.043
Swaziland	1.132	1.028	0.992	1.110
Tanzania	1.034	1.029	0.983	1.022
Zambia	1.002	1.028	0.953	1.023
Zimbabwe	1.030	1.028	0.983	1.020
Bahreïn	1.172	1.046	0.994	1.127
Bangladesh	1.076	1.027	1.005	1.042
Brunei	1.149	1.037	1.040	1.066
Burma	1.056	1.020	0.998	1.037
Cyprus	1.055	1.002	1.024	1.029
India	1.070	1.022	0.987	1.060
Indonesia	1.126	1.023	1.033	1.065
Iran	0.996	1.030	0.963	1.004
Iraq	1.133	1.034	0.963	1.138
Kuwait	1.137	1.061	0.906	1.183
Pakistan	1.029	1.026	1.000	1.003
Philippines	1.065	1.027	1.006	1.030
Singapore	1.030	1.015	1.060	0.957
South Korea	1.153	1.017	1.051	1.079
Sri Lanka	1.041	1.017	1.010	1.013
Syria	1.153	1.033	1.016	1.098
Thailand	1.045	1.024	1.019	1.002
Turkey	1.134	1.023	1.001	1.107
Costa Rica	1.088	1.028	1.005	1.053
Dominican Republic	1.090	1.029	1.009	1.050
El Salvador	1.105	1.027	0.981	1.096
Guatemala	1.145	1.030	0.996	1.117
Haïti	1.098	1.017	1.011	1.068
Honduras	1.096	1.034	0.980	1.082
Mexico	1.123	1.028	1.006	1.086
Nicaragua	1.068	1.031	0.977	1.060
Panama	1.073	1.025	1.000	1.047
Saint Lucia	1.080	1.012	1.044	1.022
Saint Vincent and the Grenadines	1.057	1.011	1.024	1.021
St. Christopher and Nevis	1.061	0.996	1.127	0.946
Trinidad et Tobago	1.081	1.010	1.030	1.040
Fidji	1.095	1.019	1.015	1.059
Tonga	1.084	1.011	1.032	1.039
Argentina	1.071	1.016	0.994	1.060
Bolivia	1.056	1.024	0.994	1.038
Chile	1.074	1.017	0.992	1.064
Columbia	1.098	1.021	1.008	1.067
Ecuador	1.108	1.028	1.030	1.047
Guyana	1.056	1.006	1.008	1.041
Peru	1.034	1.027	0.977	1.030
Uruguay	1.023	1.002	1.023	0.998
Venezuela	1.113	1.035	0.971	1.107
Average	1.082	1.025	1.002	1.054

Source: Statistical Yearbook, 1983/84 (United Nations publication, Sales No. EF, 86.XVII.I).

Figure I.   Rates of increase in population, GDP per capita
            and vehicles/GDP

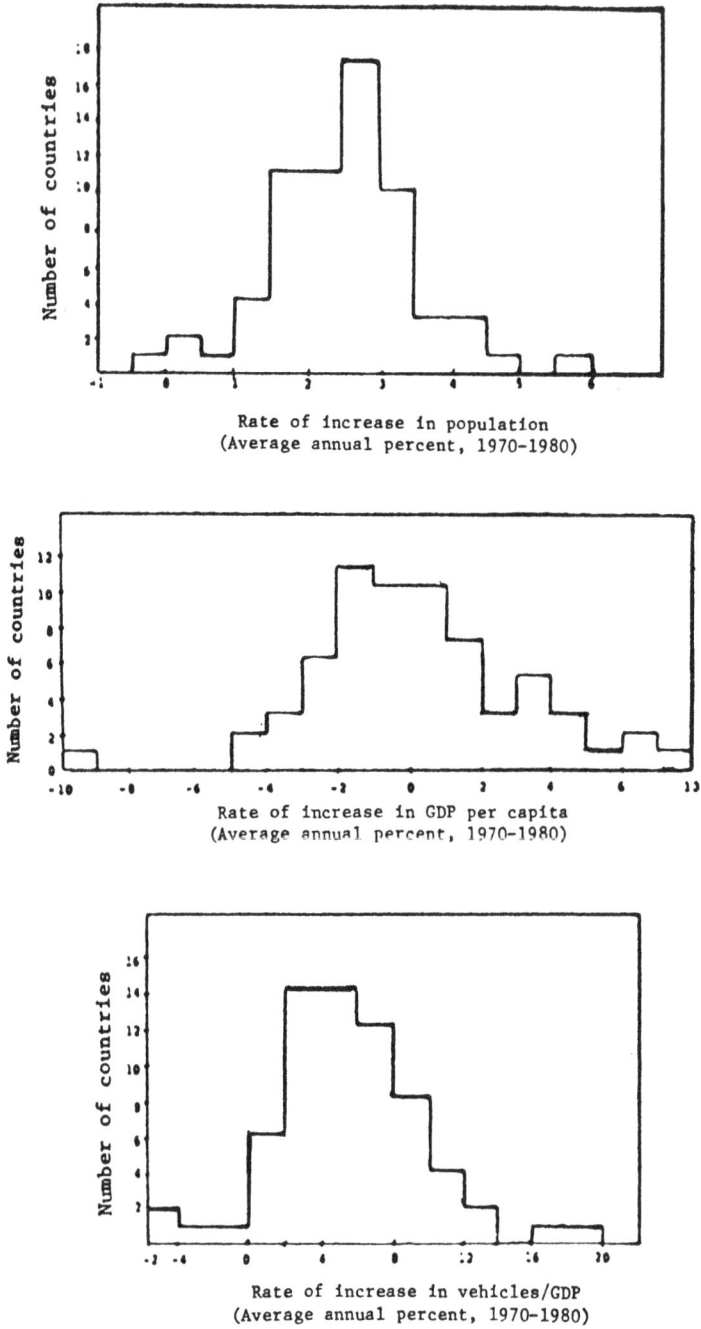

Rate of increase in population
(Average annual percent, 1970-1980)

Rate of increase in GDP per capita
(Average annual percent, 1970-1980)

Rate of increase in vehicles/GDP
(Average annual percent, 1970-1980)

Table 3. Relation between the rate of change of electricity production and the rates of environmental impact factors, 1970-1980

Country	Electricity production (rate of change 1970–1980)	Environmental impact factors (rate of change 1970–1980)		
		Population	$\frac{GDP}{Population}$	$\frac{Electricity}{GDP}$
Algeria	1.137	1.030	1.007	1.096
Benin	0.871	1.027	0.987	0.859
Burundi	1.000	1.016	0.995	0.990
Central African Republic	1.029	1.022	0.970	1.038
Egypt	1.096	1.023	1.031	1.039
Ethiopia	1.026	1.022	0.983	1.021
Ghana	1.062	1.021	0.955	1.089
Ivory Coast	1.129	1.042	0.988	1.096
Kenya	1.098	1.039	0.976	1.082
Liberia	1.061	1.031	0.957	1.075
Libya	1.256	1.044	0.994	1.210
Madagascar	1.057	1.025	0.960	1.074
Malawi	1.114	1.030	0.987	1.095
Morocco	1.098	1.026	0.994	1.076
Nigeria	1.165	1.030	0.977	1.157
Rwanda	1.034	1.031	1.019	0.984
Senegal	1.053	1.028	0.959	1.068
Sierra Leone	1.012	1.017	0.985	1.011
Somalia	1.116	1.051	0.927	1.146
South Africa	1.059	1.026	0.984	1.049
Tanzania	1.048	1.029	0.983	1.036
Tunisia	1.334	1.024	1.031	1.263
Uganda	0.977	1.026	0.926	1.028
Zaïre	1.033	1.027	0.970	1.037
Zambia	1.255	1.028	0.953	1.281
Zimbabwe	0.966	1.028	0.983	0.956
Afganistan	1.093	1.019	0.967	1.109
Bahrein	1.146	1.046	0.994	1.102
Brunei	1.131	1.037	1.040	1.049
Burma	1.095	1.020	0.998	1.075
Cyprus	1.054	1.002	1.024	1.028
India	1.069	1.022	0.987	1.059
Indonesia	1.118	1.023	1.033	1.058
Iran	1.127	1.030	0.963	1.136
Iraq	1.147	1.034	0.963	1.152
Kuwait	1.135	1.061	0.906	1.181
Malaisia	1.111	1.023	1.038	1.046
Nepal	1.124	1.023	0.976	1.126
Philippines	1.076	1.027	1.006	1.041
Saudi Arabia	1.334	1.051	0.999	1.270
Singapore	1.122	1.015	1.060	1.043
South Koread	1.154	1.017	1.051	1.080
Sri Lanka	1.074	1.017	1.010	1.045
Syria	1.151	1.033	1.016	1.096
Thailand	1.128	1.024	1.019	1.082
Turkey	1.104	1.023	1.001	1.078
United Arabe Emirates	1.693	1.139	0.888	1.673
Antigua and Barbuda	1.058	1.004	1.012	1.041
Costa Rica	1.081	1.028	1.005	1.046
Dominican Republic	1.127	1.029	1.109	1.086
El Salvador	1.086	1.027	0.981	1.078
Guatemala	1.079	1.030	0.996	1.052
Haïti	1.100	1.017	1.011	1.070
Honduras	1.113	1.034	0.980	1.098
Jamaïca	1.036	1.014	0.968	1.056
Mexico	1.088	1.028	1.006	1.052
Nicaragua	1.055	1.031	0.977	1.047
Trinidad and Tobago	1.055	1.010	1.030	1.015
Fidji	1.072	1.019	1.015	1.037
Argentina	1.062	1.016	0.994	1.052
Bolivia	1.071	1.024	0.994	1.053
Chile	1.045	1.017	0.992	1.035
Colombia	1.102	1.021	1.008	1.071
Ecuador	1.134	1.028	1.030	1.071
Paraguay	1.134	1.031	1.021	1.077
Peru	1.059	1.027	0.977	1.055
Surinam	1.018	0.995	1.071	0.955
Uruguay	1.043	1.002	1.023	1.018
Venezuela	1.110	1.035	0.971	1.104
Average	1.101	1.027	0.993	1.081

Source: Statistical Yearbook, 1983/84 (United Nations publication, Sales No. EF.86.XVII.I).

Figure III is a plot of the relationship between the environmental impact (as represented by the rate of increase in electricity production) and population growth. Regression analysis shows that the relationship is not statistically significant ($R^2 = 0.54$). Again, in only a few (5) of the countries does the rate of increase in electricity production match the concurrent rate of population growth, indicative of an effect entirely due to population growth. In the remaining 64 countries, it is the technology factor that exerts the greatest effect on environmental impact.

Analysis of a third class of environmental impact – nitrate pollution, as represented by the amount of nitrogen fertilizer used – for 90 developing countries over the period 1980–1984 is summarized in table 4. The relative effect of the different factors on the rate of change in nitrogen fertilizer utilization is expressed by the annual rate of change in population (2.5 per cent), of agricultural production per capita (–0.6 per cent), and nitrogen use per unit agricultural production (6.6 per cent). The influence of the technology factor is more than twice the influence of population growth. From figure IV it can be seen that there is no statistically significant relationship between the rate of increase in nitrogen use and the rate of population growth ($R^2 = 0.04$). Figure IV also shows that relatively few countries exhibit rates of increase in nitrogen use equal to the concurrent rate of population growth. Here, too, it is evident that the dominant effect on environmental impact is exerted by the technology factor. The effect of population growth is on the average less than half the effect of the technology factor, and the effect of the affluence factor is very small.

These analyses of the relative roles of the factors that are expected to influence environmental impact, as represented by the levels of several pollutants in developing countries, conform to the generalization reached earlier with respect to industrialized countries. The nature of production technology has a much greater influence on environmental impact than either population growth or increased affluence. Environmental impact is not correlated with the rate of population growth. In sum, the theory that environmental degradation is largely due to population growth is not supported by the data.

The origin of the environmental crises

The preceding discussion was directed towards the specific question of how rapid population growth is related to environmental impact. However, as noted earlier, this question is a subsidiary part of a more general consideration, namely, the origin of the environmental crisis that for nearly 20 years has been the target of widespread remedial efforts. Indeed, as the quotations cited earlier indicate, the (erroneous) expectation that environmental degradation is largely determined by population growth derives from an effort to explain this more general issue. It is useful, therefore, to examine the broader issue, especially because a more substantial collection of data than that available for countries characterized by rapid population growth can then be applied to resolving it.

Table 4. Relation between the rate of change in nitrogen fertilizer consumption and the rates of change of environmental impact factors, 1970–1980

Country	Nitrogen fertilizer consumption (rate of change 1980–1984)	Environmental impact factors (rate of change 1980–1984)		
		Population	$\frac{Agric.Prod.}{Population}$	$\frac{Nitrogen}{Agric.Prod.}$
Algeria	0.996	1.033	0.968	0.996
Angola	0.797	1.025	0.981	0.792
Benin	1.351	1.028	1.011	1.300
Botswana	1.000	1.031	1.011	0.960
Burkina	1.197	1.024	0.979	1.195
Burundi	1.158	1.024	0.979	1.156
Cameroun	0.974	1.027	0.981	0.967
Central African Republic	1.899	1.018	0.991	1.882
Congo	1.682	1.026	0.981	1.882
Egypt	1.096	1.019	0.988	1.088
Ethiopia	1.030	1.033	0.962	1.036
Gabon	1.565	1.016	1.002	1.537
Ghana	1.070	1.031	0.991	1.047
Guinea	0.821	1.023	1.012	0.793
Guinea-Bissau	1.316	1.020	1.070	1.206
Ivory Coast	0.881	1.035	0.960	0.886
Kenya	1.114	1.041	0.984	1.088
Lesotho	1.057	1.026	0.967	1.066
Liberia	0.680	1.034	0.976	0.674
Libya	1.108	1.045	0.975	1.087
Madagascar	1.215	1.028	0.993	1.190
Malawi	1.151	1.031	0.998	1.119
Mali	1.211	1.025	0.985	1.199
Mauritius	1.022	1.014	1.023	0.986
Morocco	1.026	1.033	0.972	1.022
Mozambique	0.968	1.032	0.956	0.981
Niger	1.150	1.028	0.944	1.186
Nigeria	1.186	1.034	0.985	1.165
Rwanda	1.000	1.034	0.985	1.165
Senegal	0.953	1.027	1.032	0.899
Sierra Leone	0.964	1.018	0.971	0.976
Somalia	2.060	1.041	0.961	2.060
Sudan	1.251	1.029	0.993	1.224
Swaziland	1.282	1.043	0.988	1.243
Tanzania	0.906	1.032	0.961	0.913
Gambia	0.925	1.012	1.036	0.883
Togo	0.931	1.029	0.970	0.933
Tunisia	1.055	1.024	0.975	1.057
Zambia	1.035	1.025	0.988	1.022
Zimbabwe	1.083	1.028	1.028	1.072
Afganistan	1.026	1.026	0.981	1.019
Bangladesh	1.072	1.022	0.990	1.059
Burma	1.133	1.028	1.028	1.072
China	1.065	1.012	1.060	0.993
Cyprus	1.039	1.012	0.992	1.035
Indonesia	1.140	1.022	1.013	1.101
Iran	1.260	1.032	0.990	1.233
Iraq	0.953	1.035	0.964	0.955
Israël	1.055	1.020	1.028	1.006
Jordanie	1.091	1.037	0.981	1.073
Laos	1.495	1.026	1.038	1.404
Lebanon	1.030	0.998	1.000	1.032
Malaisia	1.048	1.023	1.004	1.020
Mongolia	1.263	1.027	1.013	1.214
North Korea	1.019	1.024	1.010	0.985
Pakistan	1.042	1.031	1.005	1.006
Philippines	1.015	1.026	0.982	1.007
Saudi Arabia	1.585	1.041	1.096	1.389
Singapore	1.027	1.012	0.983	1.032

171

Table 4 (continued)

Country	Nitrogen fertilizer consumption (rate of change 1980-84)	Environmental impact factors (rate of change 1980–1984)		
		Population	$\frac{\text{Agric.Prod.}}{\text{Population}}$	$\frac{\text{Nitrogen}}{\text{Agric.Prod.}}$
South Korea	0.954	1.016	1.031	0.911
Sri Lanka	0.184	1.014	0.966	0.188
Syria	1.086	1.034	0.969	1.084
Thaïland	1.124	1.021	1.018	1.082
Turkey	1.068	1.021	1.000	1.046
Vietnam	1.317	1.021	1.025	1.258
Malta	1.000	1.011	0.980	1.009
Barbados	1.041	1.003	0.961	1.080
Costa Rica	1.082	1.031	0.966	1.086
Cuba	1.000	1.007	1.042	0.953
République Dominicaine	0.924	1.029	0.992	0.905
El Salvador	1.041	1.032	0.953	1.058
Guatemala	1.012	1.024	0.953	1.037
Haïti	0.913	1.009	1.008	0.898
Honduras	1.163	1.035	0.994	1.130
Jamaïca	1.086	1.015	0.992	1.078
Mexico	1.052	1.026	0.990	1.035
Nicaragua	1.239	1.037	1.001	1.194
Panama	0.981	1.022	0.991	0.968
Trinidad and Tobago	0.954	1.002	0.980	0.971
Fidji	0.887	1.015	1.024	0.854
Papouasia New Guinea	1.023	1.047	0.982	0.995
Argentina	1.023	1.016	1.012	0.995
Bolivia	1.170	1.028	0.973	1.170
Brazil	0.923	1.023	1.010	0.894
Chile	1.064	1.017	1.014	1.032
Ecuador	1.037	1.029	0.981	1.028
Guyana	1.102	1.020	0.998	1.083
Péru	0.880	1.026	1.016	0.845
Uruguay	0.994	1.007	1.030	0.959
Venezuela	0.936	1.029	0.974	0.934
Average	1.086	1.025	0.994	1.066

Source: Statistical Yearbook, 1983/84 (United Nations publication, Sales No. EF.86.XVII.I).

Figure II.   Relation between rate of increase in number of
motor vehicles and population growth, 1970–1980

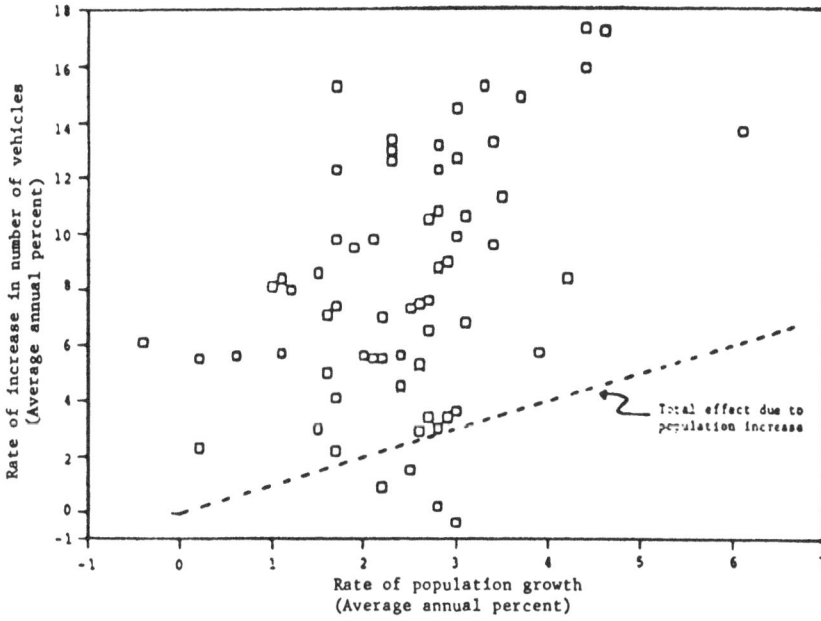

Figure III.   Relation between rate of increase in electricity
production and population growth, 1970–1980

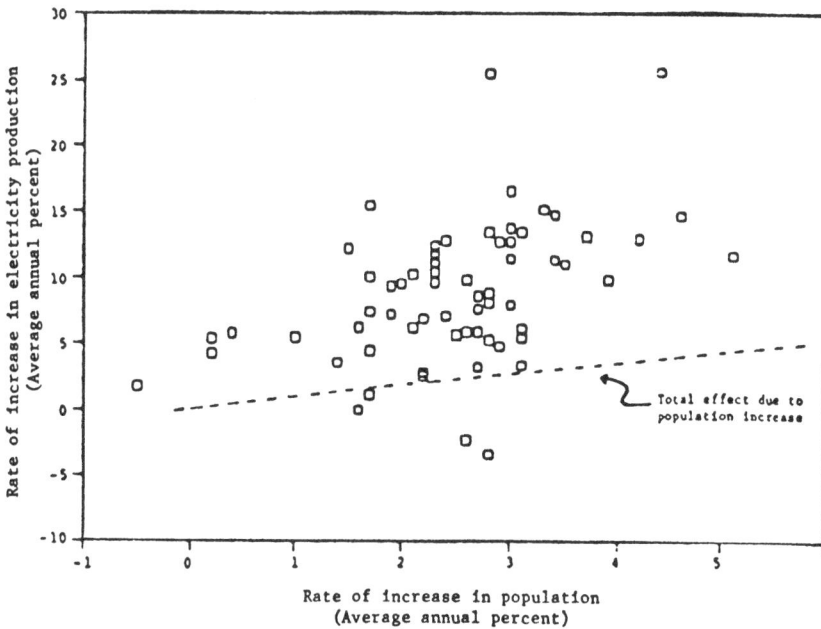

Figure IV.   Relation between rate of increase in nitrogen fertilizer consumption and population growth, 1980–1984

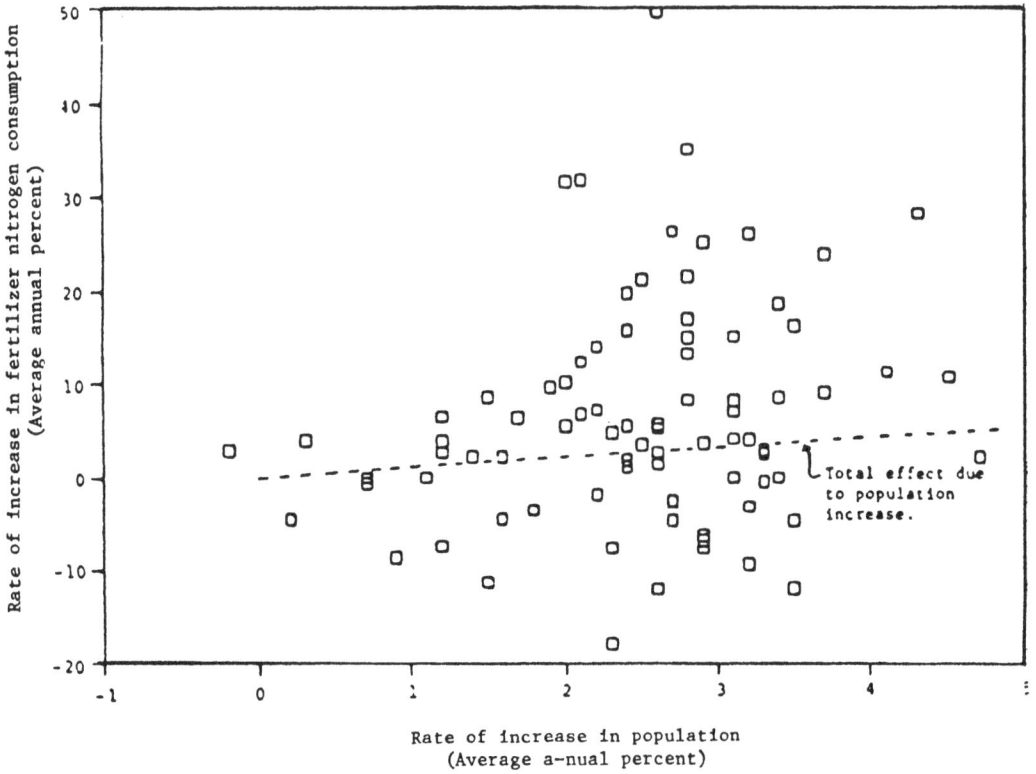

In an industrialized country such as the United States, data on environmental quality and the factors related to it are available for both 1950–1970 – a period of decreasing environmental quality – and a period beginning in the early 1970s, when a massive effort was made to improve environmental quality. Analysis of the earlier period of environmental degradation has led to the conclusion that the dominant causal factor was the change in the technologies of industrial and agricultural production and transportation. (For a summary, see Commoner, 1971.) Thus, United States automobile engines initially produced much more nitrogen oxide per mile – and therefore smog – because they were redesigned after the Second World War to run at high compression and temperature. This caused oxygen and nitrogen in the cylinder air to react and form nitrogen oxides, which triggered the photochemical smog reaction. Similarly, the ongoing increase in nitrate levels in ground and surface waters can be traced to the introduction after the Second World War of increasing amounts of inorganic nitrogen fertilizer. In the same way, the sharp increase in glass trash from bottles resulted from the replacement of returnable bottles, which were used about 40 times before being discarded, with non-returnable ones, which are discarded after only one use.

These changes are part of the dramatic transformation in production technology that has occurred in every industrialized country since the Second World War. Many natural products, including soap, cotton, wool, wood, paper, and leather, have been displaced by synthetic petrochemical products, such as detergents, synthetic fibers, and plastics. In agriculture, natural fertilizers have been displaced by chemical ones, and natural methods of pest control, such as crop rotation, have been displaced by synthetic pesticides. In transportation, rail freight has been displaced by truck freight. In manufacturing, the amount of energy, especially in the form of electricity, used per unit of goods produced has increased sharply. In commerce, reusable goods have been replaced by throwaways.

In nearly every case the new, rapidly growing production technologies have intensified environmental degradation. The toxic pollution generated by the petrochemical industry – the inevitable accompaniment of the production and use of its new synthetic products – is notorious. In return for the benefits that farmers gain from the heavy use of nitrogen fertilizer, we pay the price exacted by eutrophication of rivers, lakes and estuaries and by toxic levels of nitrate in drinking water. Since truck freight uses four times more fuel than rail freight per ton-mile of freight, more fuel is burned, worsening air pollution.

With the increased use of electricity comes acid rain from coal-burning plants and radioactive hazards from nuclear plants. Throwaway goods have sharply increased the burden of trash. These technological changes far outweigh the influence of increasing population or affluence on the rising levels of pollution.

With the introduction of corrective measures since the early 1970s, we have a new source of data. We can now ask: which ameliorative methods have effectively reduced pollution and which have not? Such a comparison can help explain the failures, define the principles of success, and provide new insights into the origin of the environmental crisis.

In the United States, data are available that provide a fairly detailed picture of trends in pollution levels since the enactment in the 1970s of extensive remedial legislation. Since 1975 the United States Environmental Protection Agency has published consistent sets of data regarding the annual emissions and ambient concentrations of a series of standard air pollutants; particulates, sulfur dioxide, nitrogen oxides, carbon monoxide, ozone, volatile organic compounds and lead. Data on water pollution are less comprehensive but nevertheless describe time trends in the concentrations of basic water pollutants such as fecal coliform bacteria, phosphate, and nitrate. From these and various other reports, it is possible to determine what changes in the levels of a number of environmental pollutants in the United States have been brought about by the considerable effort to reduce them.

Perhaps the most striking aspect of these data is their very wide range. At one extreme are a few clear-cut successes – the few environmental pollutants that have decreased by 70 per cent or more in the past 10–15 years. On the other hand, most pollutant levels decreased by only 10–20 per cent in that period, and some have actually increased. Given this range of effects, it is possible to relate the magnitude of changes in pollution levels to the types of corrective measures employed and thereby to identify reasons for the successes and the failures.

The changes in air pollution in the United States can be summed up fairly simply (see table 5). For all the standard air pollutants except lead, the average annual rate of emission has declined only moderately – by 14.1 per cent between 1975 (when consistent measurements began) and 1985. In that period, the annual emission of nitrogen oxides actually increased by about 4 per cent. This is hardly the sort of accomplishment envisioned in the environmental legislation adopted in the early 1970s, which called for a 90 per cent reduction in air pollution levels by 1977. On the other hand, lead emissions decreased by 86 per cent (and the level of lead in blood declined about 40 per cent) in that period, an accomplishment that does approximate the goal of solving the environmental crisis.

The situation with regard to water pollution is similar. A recent survey of water pollution trends at some 300 sites in United States rivers shows that between 1974 and 1983 there was no improvement in water quality at 90 per cent of the test locations (see table 6). Concentrations of fecal coliform bacteria, dissolved oxygen, suspended sediments, and phosphorus improved at only 13–17 per cent of the test sites. The nitrate pollution problem has become progressively worse: nitrate concentration increased at 30 per cent of the river sites and decreased at only 7 per cent of them. For the five standard water pollutants, sites with improving levels averaged 13.2 per cent of the tested locations; sites with deteriorating levels averaged 14.7 per cent of the total; 72.1 per cent were unchanged.

If a reduction of 70 per cent or more in national pollution levels is taken as evidence of a qualitative solution to the problem, a search through the available data reveals that only a very short list of pollutants can meet this criterion; lead, DDT (and related insecticides), PCB, mercury in fresh waters, radioactive fallout from nuclear bomb tests, and in some local situations, phosphate. Of course, in certain localities a river or a lake has

Table 5. Changes in emissions of standard air pollutants, 1975–1985, United States

Pollutant	Emissions		
	(Million metric tons/year)		Percent
	1975	1985	change
Particulates	10.4	7.3	-29.8
Sulfur dioxide	25.6	20.7	-19.1
Carbon monoxide	81.2	67.5	-19.1
Nitrogen oxides	19.2	20.0	4.2
Volatil organic compounds	22.8	21.3	-6.6
Average			-14.1
Lead	147.0	21.0	-85.7

Source: United States Environmental Protection Agency, National Air Quality and Emissions Trends Report, 1984 and 1985, (Research Triangle Park, North Carolina, Office of Air Quality Planning and Standards).

Table 6.   Water quality trends in United States rivers, 1974–1983

Pollutant	Trends in concentration (Percent of sites)		
	Improving	Deteriorating	No change
Fecal coliforms	14.8	5.2	80.0
Dissolved oxygen	17.1	11.1	71.8
Nitrate	7.0	30.3	62.7
Phosphorus	13.1	11.3	75.6
Suspended sediments	14.1	14.7	71.2
Average	13.2	14.7	72.1

Source: R. A. Smith and others, "Water–quality trends in the nations rivers", Science, vol. 235, pp. 1,607–1,615.

been greatly improved by halting the dumping of specific pollutants into it. But as the trend data show, there has been little or no overall national improvement.

What can we learn from these observations? Table 7 lists the few environmental successes and the measures used to achieve them. There is a common theme in the successful remedial measures. In each case the pollutant was prevented from entering the environment not by recapturing it after it was produced, but by simply <u>stopping its production or use</u>. Thus, the sharp drop in lead emissions is the result of removing lead from gasoline; the environment is less polluted with lead because less of it is now being used. In the same way, the decline in environmental levels of DDT has been achieved because the insecticide has been banned from United States agriculture, and the decline in environmental PCB followed legislation that banned its production and use. There has been a sharp decline in strontium 90 levels since 1963 because atmospheric nuclear bomb tests that produce it have nearly ceased. In certain rivers, phosphate concentrations have been sharply reduced by banning the use of phosphate-containing detergents; as a result, that much less phosphate is sent down drains into the aquatic ecosystem.

In contrast to these successes, control measures designed to recapture the pollutant after it is produced, rather than to halt its production or use, are relatively ineffective. Devices designed to recapture or destroy air pollutants, such as the power plant scrubbers that trap sulfur dioxide or the catalytic converters that destroy carbon monoxide in automobile exhaust gases, have had little overall impact on emissions. In these instances, the basic production technology is unchanged and the control device is simply appended to it. The sulfur dioxide scrubber is attached to the power plant without changing the power-producing technology; the catalytic converter is attached to the gasoline engine's exhaust without significantly changing the engine itself.

Thus, a decade or more of efforts to improve the quality of the environment teaches us a fairly simple lesson: pollution levels can be reduced enough to at least approach the goal of elimination only if the production or use of the offending substance is halted; the control device strategy is ineffective. Environmental pollution is an essentially incurable disease; it can only be prevented by replacing the production technology that generates it.

The sharply reduced level of mercury in fresh water sediments is a particularly informative example of what prevention means. This improvement came about when it was discovered that the major source of environmental mercury in the Great Lakes was plants that produce chlorine by electrolysing a brine solution (mercury is used to conduct the electric current). Required to give up this practice, the plant operators substituted a semi-permeable diaphragm for mercury in the production process. The plants no longer dump mercury into nearby rivers for the simple reason that they are no longer using it. The plant output is chlorine, which is largely consumed by the chemical industry, and chlorine consumption has not decreased. On the contrary, as shown in table 8, during the period 1970-1979, when mercury pollution declined sharply, the total national production of chlorine increased by 26 per cent.

Table 7. Improvements in pollution levels, United States

Pollutant	Time period	Percent change	Control measure	Reference
Lead emissions[a]	1975-1985	-86	Removed from gasoline	U.S. EPA, 1986.1987
D.D.T. in body fat[b]	1970-1983	-79	Agricultural use banned	U.S. EPA, 1984a
P.C.B. in body fat[b]	1970-1980	-75[c]	Production banned	U.S. EPA, 1984a
Mercury in lake sediments[b]	1970-1979	-80	Replaced in chlorine production	U.S. EPA, 1984b
Strontium 90 in milk[b]	1964-1984	-92	Cessation of atmospheric nuclear tests	U.S. EPA, 1984a
Phosphate in Detroit river water[b]	1971-1981	-70	Replaced in detergent formulation	U.S. EPA, 1984b

Notes:

a/ Measured as amount emitted per year.
b/ Measured as concentration.
c/ Change in percentage of people with PCB body fat levels greater than 3 parts per million.

The pollution due to mercury was eliminated by preventing its entry into the environment; this was achieved by changing the means of producing chlorine, rather than by consuming less of it.

The same pattern is evident in lead pollution. In this case, the production process is automobile travel, and what is "consumed" is passenger miles traveled. As shown in table 8, between 1975 and 1984, while vehicular lead emissions declined by 86 per cent, passenger-miles travelled increased by 26 per cent. Clearly, this considerable environmental improvement was not achieved by limiting consumption of the good, but rather by changing the technological means of producing it.

DDT provides a similar example. Here the good produced for consumption is the crop protected from insects (in the United States this is primarily cotton). Between 1970 and 1984, environmental levels of DDT decreased by 70-80 per cent; yet the production of cotton increased by 31 per cent. Again, what was changed was not the amount of goods produced or consumed, but the technological means of producing it. And certainly none of these changes was brought about by reducing the United States population.

Although they are less complete, European environmental data follow the pattern evident in the United States. For example, between 1978 and 1982, sulfur dioxide emissions decreased by an average of 26 per cent in European countries, while average nitrogen oxide emissions declined by only 1.7 per cent (excluding a 358 per cent increase in Poland). Environmental changes in the Baltic Sea closely resemble those in Lake Erie where, because of continued phosphate and nitrate pollution, eutrophication has persisted and oxygen levels have declined. In the Baltic Sea between 1979 and 1984, average oxygen levels decreased by 11 per cent, phosphate concentrations increased by 101 per cent, and nitrate concentrations increased by 37 per cent. And as in Lake Erie, for apparently the same reasons, the levels of DDT and PCB in fish improved considerably, by 80 and 45 per cent, respectively (United Nations Economic Commission for Europe, 1987).

Recent reports by Weidner (1986, 1987) provide data comparable to the United States trends in air pollutant emissions as shown in table 5. As in the United States, the data are based on annual compilations of emissions from different sources, made by the relevant government agencies. As shown in table 9, trends in emission levels in the Federal Republic of Germany and the United Kingdom of Great Britain since the institution of modern regulatory efforts are comparable to the very modest improvements in the United States, but in the United Kingdom of Great Britain there is almost no overall improvement.

These examples help to define the meaning of the factors that have brought about the few sharp declines in environmental pollution. Clearly, what has been changed is not population pressure or affluence (as measured by the level of consumption), but the technology of production. The improvements were not achieved by reducing levels of production or consumption of goods, nor by reducing the population, but by changing the technology of production.

Table 8. Changes in output of production processes with significantly reduced pollution levels, United States

Pollutant	Relevant goods produced	Time period	Change in amount of goods produced (%)	Reference
Lead emissions	Automobile passenger-miles	1975-1985	+26	U.S. Dept of Commerce, 1986
D.D.T. in body fat	Cotton	1970-1985	+31	U.S. Dept of, Commerce, 1986
P.C.B. in body fat	Electrical transformers	1970-1985	-12	U.S. Dept of Commerce, 1986
Mercury in lake sediments	Chlorine	1970-1979	+26	U.S. Dept of Commerce, 1985

Table 9. The effect of controls on emission of standard air pollutants

Pollutant	West Germany (percent change in emissions, 1970-1982)	Great Britain (percent change in emissions, 1970-1982)
Sulfur dioxide	-17	-30
Nitrogen oxides	+29	+0.3
Carbon monoxide	-37	+15
Volatile organic compounds	-6	+12
Dust	-46	–
Average	-15.4	-0.75

Source: Helmut Weidner, Clear Air Policy in Great Britain. Problem Shifting as Best Practicable Means (Berlin, Ed. Sigma Bohn, 1987).

In sum, three classes of data have been analysed. We have examined data for industrialized countries concerning the origin of both the sharp increase in environmental degradation in the period before the early 1970s and the few significant improvements since then, as well as the less direct evidence from developing countries. The results for each category lead to the same conclusion: the most powerful factor determining environmental quality is the technology chosen to produce goods and services.

The relationship between economic development and environmental quality

The foregoing provides a useful link between the issue of environmental quality and that of economic development, which rightfully dominates the concerns of developing countries. Production technology is clearly a major determinant of economic development. If, as we have seen, it also largely determines environmental quality, a crucial question arises: are technologies that are more economically productive always more hazardous to the environment? If so, developing countries must make a cruel choice between environmental quality and economic development. Or, on the contrary, are some production technologies both economically productive and environmentally benign, and therefore a means of solving the environment/development dilemma?

The conventional approach, which is based on the experience of industrialized countries, is that those technologies that are highly productive economically generally have a serious impact on the environment. This leads to the view that developing countries must use such technologies as the means of economic development and that environmental quality can then be achieved, or at least approached, only by using control devices to minimize their untoward effects. It is this view that has largely governed the introduction of new production technologies in developing countries. In the absence of contrary evidence, it is assumed that the economic strength of industrialized countries is largely derived from the economic merits of their production technologies and that these technologies will yield the same benefit when transferred to a developing country. In theory, the means of dealing with the technology's environmental impact – "controlling" emissions rather than preventing them – is imported along with the technologies themselves. In practice, however, developing countries are likely to make a much greater effort to introduce economically productive technologies than to control their environmental impact. Thus, as the recent Brundtland report points out:

> "The industries most heavily reliant on environmental resources
> and most heavily polluting are growing most rapidly in the
> developing world, where there is more urgency for growth and
> less capacity to minimize damaging side effects." (Brundtland,
> 1987)

Unfortunately, as we have seen, the strategy of appending control devices to the polluting technologies has already failed in developed countries and therefore offers no hope of solving the problem in developing ones. Clearly a new approach is needed, which must be based on technologies that are both economically productive and environmentally benign. But this appears to be a vain hope; it is contradicted by the belief that the new technologies were introduced after the Second World War <u>because</u> they were more economically productive than the older, more environmentally benign technologies that they displaced. And given the huge economic expansion that accompanied these changes in industrialized countries and their uniformly harmful effects on the environment, it might be argued as well that the linkage between economic merit and environmental malevolence is unbreakable. On these grounds, the environmental crisis is often viewed as an inevitable consequence of the technological choices that were made in order to enhance economic development after the Second World War. It is this view that often leads to the impression that economic development is necessarily accompanied by environmental pollution and that developing countries must accept this burden as an unavoidable cost of development.

But this impression is misleading. There is reason to question both the economic merit of the post-war production technologies and the notion that all highly productive technologies are inherently polluting. Nuclear power provides a sobering example. When nuclear power - the major post-war innovation in generating electricity – was introduced, it was hailed as an economic panacea. The head of the United States atomic energy programme declared at one point that nuclear power would be so cheap that no one would bother to meter it. But the reality is very different. Nearly everywhere, the initial rapid expansion of nuclear power has slowed and in a number of countries has come to a halt. In the United States, no new plants have been ordered in the past 10 years; many orders have been cancelled; nearly completed plants have been abandoned, and even some completed ones are not allowed to operate; and a power company heavily dependent on nuclear power has gone bankrupt, the first such failure since the Great Depression.

Nuclear power is an economic failure <u>because of its environmental faults</u>; the need to protect against accidents and routine radiation hazards has so severely increased the capital cost of nuclear power that it has become the most expensive large-scale source of electricity. In effect, the high costs generated by its environmental hazards have been <u>internalized</u> economically and are therefore directly reflected in its low level of economic productivity.

There are more general examples that appear to be less dramatic only because, unlike nuclear power, the technology's environmental defects, although serious, have thus far remained economic <u>externalities</u> and do not yet appear in the industry's profit-and-loss columns. The petrochemical industry is an instructive example. The enormous and increasing environmental hazards generated by this industry are only too well known. But the petrochemical industry is equally famous for its economic success, having grown in the United States to a $100 billion industry (in value of output) in less than 40 years. What is less well known, however, is that a serious effort to rectify the industry's environmental defects would severely damage its economic viability.

The United States petrochemical industry generates about 300 million tons of toxic waste annually, 99 per cent of which is introduced into the environment, primarily through deep-well injections, surface lagoons, or temporary storage tanks. The only way to ensure that these often long-lasting and highly dangerous substances do not accumulate and eventually threaten living things is to destroy them; but only 1 per cent of the waste is now treated in this way. If incineration, the present (and still environmentally unsatisfactory) method of destruction, were applied to the active agents in the annual hazardous waste stream (about 1 per cent of the total mass), the cost would be so high as to more than wipe out the industry's annual profit (Commoner, 1987a). In sum, the petrochemical industry has been in a favourable economic position only because it has thus far managed to avoid paying its environmental bill. If the industry were required to meet the full cost of its environmental impact, at the very least its ability to compete with the production of alternative products – e.g., natural fibers, paper, glass, metal, and wood – would deteriorate.

The environmental costs of other industries are more difficult to evaluate, but many of them may also be large enough to drastically unbalance the industries' books. How viable would the power industry be if it were required to pay the cost of acid rain, not to mention the many other pollutants that it produces? What would remain of the auto industry's already shaky profits if they were diminished by the cost of eliminating smog? And how can we reckon the net economic gain of modern industry after we confront the immeasurable cost of the flooding and climatic disruption that will ensue when the rising levels of carbon dioxide become critical, as they surely will if the numerous technologies based on fossil fuel consumption are not replaced?

Apart from these unmet costs, there are more general economic defects in the highly polluting post-war technologies. Most of them are large-scale, highly centralized capital- and energy-intensive enterprises. As a result, they are economically encumbered by low capital productivity (i.e., output per unit capital) and low energy productivity (i.e., output per unit energy). These economically burdensome factors are closely related to the industries' harmful environmental effects. For example, conventional power plants not only have a much lower capital productivity than cogenerators but, since they use more fuel per unit energy output, they are also a more serious source of pollution.

Thus, it can be argued that not only are the post-war technologies environmentally unsound, but this very failing also limits their continued ability to contribute to economic development. It appears, in sum, that the developed nations have been relying on production technologies that are severely limited in their ability to support further economic development because they have harmful effects on the environment.

It is significant in this connection that the effort to internalize environmental costs in developed countries by enforcing controls on heavily polluting industries has been accompanied by a reduction in their relative contribution to the gross domestic product. Thus, Janicke and others (1987) have shown that in most industrialized countries, between 1973 and 1983 the contributions of especially polluting industries such as energy production, steel, cement, and transport to the gross domestic product have decreased significantly. As indicated earlier, in developing countries the opposite is true, as for example with respect to motor transport. Such shifts may reflect the financial benefits to multinational corporations of moving a polluting operation from a highly regulated country to a developing country that may be willing to tolerate the environmental burden for the sake of the immediate economic benefit. This trend is probably responsible for the increasing appearance of petrochemical plants and insecticide factories such as the notorious one in Bhopal, India, in developing countries. And more recently, as environmental constraints have sharply raised the cost of toxic waste and urban trash disposal in the United States, these pollutants are being shipped with increasing frequency to developing countries.

In sum, instead of being changed, the polluting technologies are being relocated; instead of being eliminated, the environmental crisis is being spread. These are the global consequences of reliance on production technologies that are inherently dangerous to the environment.

It is possible, however, to construct an approach that enhances development without intensifying environmental degradation. The basic precept can be stated quite simply, albeit negatively: Developing countries should avoid the production technologies that have characterized the post-war production system in developed countries. These include centralized power systems, particularly nuclear power; transportation based on high-compression internal combustion engines; agriculture based on the intensive use of synthetic chemicals; and the petrochemical industry, almost in its entirety (excepting necessary and irreplaceable products such as medicinal drugs). Stated positively, the precept calls for the introduction in developing countries of those new technologies that correct both the environmental and economic defects - which, as we have seen, are closely linked - of the major production technologies that have caused so much trouble in the developed countries.

Energy production, which is such a crucial component of economic development, is a useful example of this approach. In those developing countries that have already introduced them, modern energy systems are at present almost entirely based on the consumption of non-renewable fuels (chiefly coal, oil, and natural gas); they are also highly centralized, involving large capital-intensive facilities such as power plants and refineries. These features have generated environmental and economic difficulties that could be avoided by adopting policies favouring renewable fuels and decentralized systems.

This could be accomplished by a series of linked steps. To begin with, the need for electric power, in the past necessarily based on non-renewable fuels, can now be met by means of decentralized power plants based on cogeneration. Such plants recover both heat and electricity from the fuel; they are therefore more economical and less polluting than conventional power plants, which waste two thirds of the fuel's energy in the form of rejected heat. For the sake of efficiency, co-generators must be sized according to the local demand, avoiding huge investments in a central power plant and its attendant large-scale transmission network.

Once such a decentralized, energetically and economically efficient energy system is in place, its energy supply can be gradually shifted from non-renewable to renewable sources. The co-generator's conventional fuel can be replaced by solar fuels, such as ethanol produced from crops or vegetation,

Figure V.   Annual growth rates of production or consumption,
            United States

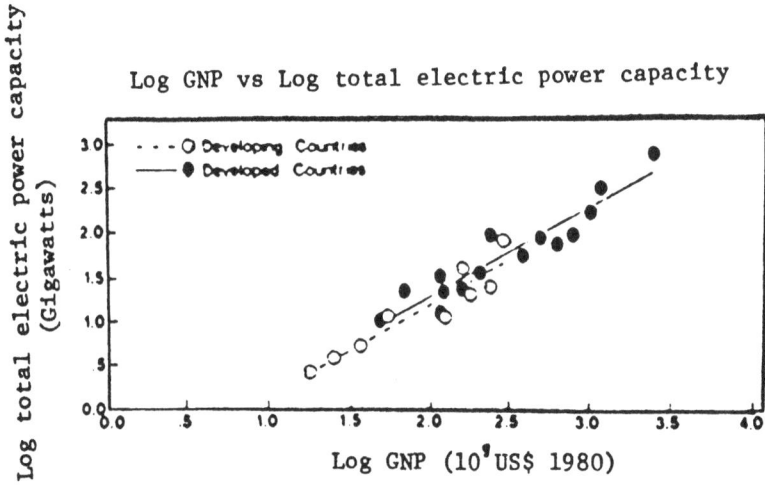

Log GNP vs Log total electric power capacity

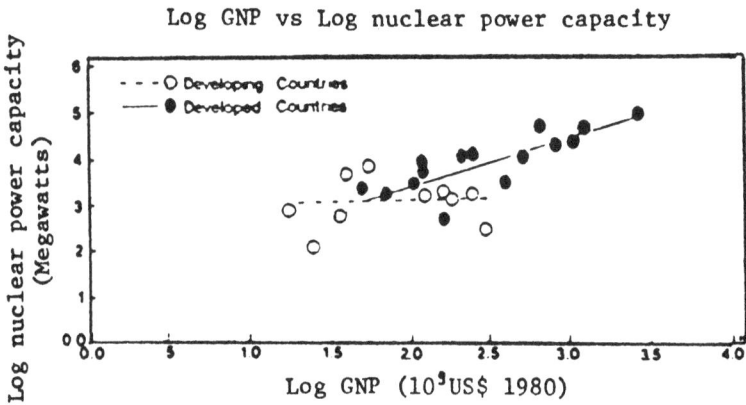

Log GNP vs Log nuclear power capacity

Source: Barry Commoner, "The environmental cost of economic
growth", Chemistry in Britain, vol. 8 (February 1972), pp. 52-65

or methane produced from sewage and manure or from marine algae. Similarly, ethanol and methane can gradually replace non-renewable motor fuels and photovoltaic cells can be used to produce electricity, augmented by solar collectors for heat. In each case, these technologies sharply reduce environmental impact as compared with the conventional ones. They also cut energy costs and eventually free the economy from the self-destructive effect of the ever-increasing cost of non-renewable fuels.

The importance of this approach to economic development in developing countries is emphasized by the consequences of perhaps the most spectacular example of its inverse – the introduction of nuclear power in a number of developing countries. As shown in a recent study (Commoner, 1987b), in developing countries nuclear power does not make the contribution to economic development that is expected of a source of electricity. Figure V indicates that although there is a close correlation between total electric power capacity and GDP among both developed and developing countries (regression analysis shows that 90 per cent of the variations in GDP are accounted for by its relation to total electric power capacity), this is not true of nuclear power. The close correlation between GDP and electric power capacity breaks down in developing countries when nuclear power capacity is considered, although the correlation is maintained in developed countries.

An explanation can be gleaned from the disparities between nuclear technology and the technical needs of the rest of the production system in developing countries. The remaining productive uses of nuclear energy are limited to gamma-ray testing of metal structures, radiation-induced mutations of agricultural plants, radiation sterilization, and tracer experiments in research. Alternative energy sources, by contrast, have very considerable secondary implications. Production of solar collectors, for example, will enhance a country's facilities for glass, metal, and plastics fabrication; photovoltaic cell production is a point of entry into the semi-conductor industry. Similarly, the production of plant material, or biomass, for energy – sugar crops, for instance, can be used to produce ethyl alcohol, an effective automotive fuel – stimulates agriculture, forestry, and marine enterprises.

From almost every point of view, then, nuclear power is a very unsuitable source of electricity for developing countries. It is uneconomical; it often requires a plant size incompatible with developing countries' small power systems; it poses environmental hazards that developing countries are woefully unprepared to cope with; and, unlike electricity, it generally appears to make no contribution to the economic development of developing countries.

Conclusion

The chief conclusion of this analysis of the relationship between rapid population growth and environmental quality is that the latter is largely governed not by population growth but by the nature of the technologies of production. As already noted, this conclusion links environmental quality directly to the issue that quite properly dominates the concerns of developing countries – economic development. And indeed, because of that linkage, these issues are themselves closely related to the problem of population growth.

I refer here to the analysis that offers the best explanation of historic and current population trends: the demographic transition. Briefly stated, this analysis shows that rapid population growth is the natural response to a partial improvement in living standards that reduces the death rate without creating the level of economic security that motivates the next stage of the demographic transition. In this second stage, the birth rate begins to fall, through social effects such as increased education and delayed marriage and cultural effects such as the influence of reduced infant mortality on fertility. But this has occurred only where standards have advanced enough to encourage these effects – i.e., in developed, industrialized countries. As has been pointed out in more detail elsewhere (see, for example, Commoner, 1977), in many developing countries rapid population growth is largely the unresolved residue of their economic exploitation during the period of colonialism. Deprived of the economic resources needed to raise living standards to levels that enable the second, population–stabilizing phase of the demographic transition, the former colonies suffer through a prolonged period in which their economic development is insufficient to reduce their high rates of population growth. In sum:

"Hunger and overpopulation are not ecological manifestations; they are signs of economic and political problems that can be solved, humanely, by economic and political means." (Commoner, 1987a)

Thus, the resolution of the major problems confronted by developing countries – economic development, stabilization of population growth, and environmental quality – all hinge on the proper choice of production technologies, which can improve both economic development and environmental quality. Since such choices will enhance the demographic transition by stimulating economic development, they will also contribute to the stabilization of the population. This choice is, therefore, a supreme requirement of national policy.

The chemical disaster at Bhopal, India, is only the most dramatic evidence that many of the new industrial technologies are particularly unsuited to developing countries. Trouble arises because modern technological developments are often accepted uncritically as "objectively good", despite the fact that they have been designed with the total well–being of neither industrialized societies nor developing countries in mind. "Appropriate technology" is a concept that ought to be applied everywhere. However, developed countries have a special obligation, for the technological transformation that they must undertake for the sake of environmental quality and long–term economic development is itself well adapted to the needs of developing countries. By initiating this transformation and providing the material resources needed to carry it out in developing countries, industrialized countries can properly repay their debt to their former colonies.

References

Brundtland, Gro Harlem (1987). World Commission on Environment and
    Development. Our Common Future. Oxford: Oxford University Press.

Commoner, Barry (1971). The Closing Circle. New York: Alfred A. Knopf, Inc.

_____ (1972). The environmental cost of economic growth. Chemistry in
    Britain, vol. 8 (Feb), pp. 52–65.

_____ (1987a). A reporter at large: the environment. New Yorker
    (15 June). See also Il cerchio da chiudere, 2nd ed. (1986). Milan:
    Garzanti Editore.

_____ (1987b). Nuclear power for the third world: bane or blessing?
    World Policy Journal (Spring).   (This is a condensed version of
    Environmental impacts of expanded utilization of nuclear energy, prepared
    for the United Nations Environment Programme, 19 April 1985).

Economic Commission for Europe (1987). Environment Statistics
    in Europe and North America.   Conference of European Statisticians.
    Statistical Standards and Studies, No. 39.   United Nations publication,
    Sales No. 87.II.E.28.

Ehrlich, Paul (1968). The Population Bomb. New York: Ballantine Press.

Janicke, Martin and others (1987). Economic structure and environmental
    Impact: A Survey of 31 Countries. Berlin: University of Berlin, Research
    Unit Environmental Policy.

Peterson, Russell W. (1985). Our stake in global issues. Interaction,
    vol. 5, No. 2.

Smith, R. A. and others (1987). Water–quality trends in the nation's rivers.
    Science, vol. 235, pp. 1,607–1,615.

United Nations (1986a). World Population Prospects. Estimates and
    Projections as Assessed in 1984. Sales No. E.87.II.E.28.

_____ (1986b). Statistical Yearbook 1983/84. Sales No. EF.86.XVII.1.

United States. Department of Commerce (1985). Business Statistics 1984,
    24th ed. Washington, D.C.: Bureau of Economic Analysis.

_____ (1986). Statistical Abstract of the United States, 1987,
    107th ed. Washington, D.C.: Bureau of the Census.

United States. Environmental Protection Agency (1984a). Environmental
    Qualilty. 15th Annual Report of the Council on Environmental Quality.
    Washington, D.C.

_____ (1984b) Lake Erie Intensive Study 1978–1979. Final Report
(EPA–905/4–84–001), prepared by D. E. Rathke. Columbus:
Ohio State University.

_____ (1986). National Air Quality and Emissions Trends Report 1984.
Research Triangle Park: Office of Air Quality Planning and Standards.

_____ (1987). National Air Quality and Emissions Trends Report 1985.
Research Triangle Park: Office of Air Quality Planning and Standards.

Vollenweider, R. A. (1968). Scientific Fundamentals of the Eutrophication of
    Lakes and Flowing Waters, with Particular Reference to Phosphorus and
    Nitrogen as Factors in Eutrophication. OECD Technical Report,
    (DAS/CSI/68.27). Paris: Organisation for Economic Co-operation and
    Development.

Weidner, Helmut (1986). Air Pollution Control Strategies and Policies in the
    Federal Republic of Germany. Berlin: Ed. Sigma Bohn.

_____ (1987). Clean Air Policy in Great Britain. Problem–Shifting as
    Best Practicable Means. Berlin: Ed. Sigma Bohn.

Chapter 7

Urban population growth, employment and poverty in developing countries : A conceptual framework for policy analysis

● A. S. Oberai*

Introduction

Rapid urbanization and the attendant problems of urban squalor, poverty and un- and under-employment have emerged as major socio-economic issues having potentially important political implications in many developing countries. By the year 2000, almost half of the world's population will be living in urban areas; in less than 40 years more than half the population in developing countries will be urban. By the year 2000, the urban population in developing countries will be double that of the industrialized countries, and there will be almost 50 cities in developing countries with populations of over 4 million (United Nations, 1987).

Most population distribution policies designed to moderate the rate of rural-urban migration in developing countries appear to have had only a marginal impact so far. But even if such policies succeed in the future, large cities in the third world are likely to grow larger because of high natural population increase in urban areas. In 1985, of the 20 largest cities in the world, 13 were in less developed regions. By the year 2000, 17 of the 20 largest cities will be in less developed countries (see annex I).

The rapidity and scale of these demographic changes pose a major challenge to developing countries. Of particular concern is the fact that urbanization has been, and is likely to continue to be, accompanied by massive growth in the numbers of urban poor. In most large cities in the developing world, at least one fourth of the population is estimated to be living in absolute poverty. The manifestations of this poverty are low and insecure incomes due to low productivity and unprotected employment, and poor health and limited access to housing and basic social services. Some sections of the city populations, such as recent migrants and women, are particularly underprivileged in terms of job access and incomes. Public investment often misses the urban poor, with expenditures biased towards higher-income groups.

* Employment Planning and Population Branch, International Labour Office, Geneva.

Relatively little attention is paid to water, sanitation, hygiene, nutrition, maternal and child care, and family planning and health needs of the poor, since new roads, hospitals, and other infrastructure developments tend to bypass the slums. The lack of these services leads to higher fertility accompanied by high infant mortality among the urban poor, particularly among slum dwellers. Any serious effort to alleviate global poverty and improve working and employment conditions would thus have to face these problems, particularly in large cities in developing countries.

The enormous problems facing the third world's large cities have been made much worse by the economic crisis of the 1980s. Blair (1984) sums up the central issues very well when he says the Dynamic City of developmental dreams is a Problem City in search of solutions to a range of critical and interrelated factors:

(a) Unbalanced population, spatial and economic growth;

(b) Large-scale deprivation and unmet provision of land, housing, employment and transportation needs;

(c) Deteriorating environments and inadequate basic services;

(d) Shortages of public fiscal resources and qualified manpower for effective plan implementation and management;

(e) Unco-ordinated national and municipal urban policies and inadequate organizational structures;

(f) Costly imported finance and inappropriate planning ideas and technology; and

(g) The absence of meaningful public participation in the planning and development process.

Taken together, these problems constitute a measure of "city poverty," the gap that remains between the reality of underdevelopment and the goal of balanced social, economic and physical development. But how well have these problems been dealt with by policy-makers, planners, and city administrators? And what are the prospects for the future? These central questions should constitute the essential focus of future research efforts. The purpose of this paper is to provide a conceptual framework for the analysis of the main policy issues in the context of available theoretical and empirical studies on urbanization, employment, and poverty in developing countries.

The paper is divided into five sections. After a brief introduction, second section discusses the structural features of urbanization in relation to economic development. It also examines the major sources of urban growth and spatial concentration and analyses the conflict between economic efficiency and decentralization. The third section assesses the implications of rapid urban growth for employment generation and poverty alleviation. In particular, it examines the effects of labour force growth on labour market structure and assesses the role of the informal sector in employment promotion. The fourth section discusses the relationship between urban low productivity and poverty. And finally, the last section summarizes the main conclusions and suggests priority areas for further policy research.

Urbanization and spatial concentration

Urbanization, industrialization, and economic development

Urban centres play a strategic role in development. Historically, the process of industrialization and economic development has been associated with considerable migration to the growing urban centres of labour demand. To make the best use of scarce public sector resources by exploiting economies of scale, facilities for power generation and water treatment, transportation systems, and other items of public infrastructure tend to be located in urban areas. Access to urban infrastructure confers a cost advantage to industrial firms located in those areas, as do the economies of scale associated with access to larger and more diversified markets for labour and other input factors. In the development scenario usually postulated by economists, the increase in industrial output leads to relatively more high-wage industrial employment. Savings tend to increase as a result of the consequent improvement in incomes, providing funds for investment in industrial capital. As incomes increase, the composition of domestic demand also tends to shift from food to non-food goods, including modern health care and housing services, as well as to manufactured goods, further stimulating modern-sector growth. With continued changes in the composition of output and patterns of consumption, the agricultural share of employment declines and the share of industry and services increases (Oberai, 1978).

In response to expanding modern-sector employment, migration from rural areas in search of higher incomes continues. As urban population densities increase, however, the price of urban land rises, driving up the cost of housing and other urban amenities. This narrows the real rural-urban income gap, thus slowing migration and the pace of urbanization. As development proceeds, modern-sector economic activity diversifies and the urban sector diffuses into an integrated system of cities, each tending towards specialization in some set of economic activities. In this highly stylized description, urbanization contributes to overall development by attracting human resources to activities with greater economic returns. The movement of labour from relatively low-income rural activity to higher-income industrial and modern service sectors contributes to higher overall average income levels, further stimulating economic growth.

Real world conditions, however, do not always conform to the hypothetical framework of the economists' development scenario. Although contemporary rates of urbanization in developing countries are comparable with those in the now-developed countries at the end of the nineteenth century, there are significant differences in the urbanization process, both in its antecedents and in its consequences. The proportion of the non-agricultural labour force engaged in manufacturing, for example, is significantly lower in today's developing countries than in their historical counterparts – approximately 40 per cent in 1981 (World Bank, 1983) compared with 55 per cent in 1900 (Squire,

1981). One reason cited for the lower proportion of industrial employment in developing countries relative to the comparable period in the history of the now–developed countries is the labour–saving bias in the former, in spite of abundant labour. Moreover, in the now–developed countries, urbanization was initially the product of increases in agricultural productivity, which on the one hand provided capital accumulation and on the other created a rural labour surplus. Capital inputs were therefore available for urban development, including capital goods for increased productivity of urban labour and expanded industrialization. The higher incomes that followed operated to pull surplus agricultural labour to urban areas where the growing manufacturing sector provided job opportunities. The increase in the size of the urban population and workforce led to a greater division of labour, increased specialization, easier application of technology, economies of scale, and mass production. Significant results of these developments included increased productivity, higher wages, and higher standards of living in urban areas, which encouraged rural–urban migration. Urbanization in the experience of now–developed countries was thus both a cause and a consequence of higher standards of living.

In contrast, urbanization in developing countries has taken place largely as a result of the movement of rural inhabitants to urban areas. In the post–Second World War period, mortality declined at unprecedented rates in developing countries in both urban and rural areas. This decline was largely due to the use of modern public health measures and imported medicines such as antibiotics. As a consequence, death rates plummeted while fertility rates remained high. The resulting increase in natural growth had a double–barreled effect, increasing both the growth of cities and the rate of urbanization. The more rapid natural increase in rural areas led to population and labour force growth that could not be absorbed in the agricultural sector. Population pressure resulting in reduced agricultural holdings in many parts of the third world (particularly in Asia), increasing poverty; a much–reduced scope for international migration therefore contributed to the acceleration of rural–urban migration. Thus urban growth, rather than being a response to increased productivity and higher standards of living, aggravated problems of labour absorption and its effective utilization, contributing to the slums and urban squalor that are among the most visible problems associated with poverty.

In addition to the differences in the nature of the urbanization process experienced by the third world and the developed countries, there are significant structural differences in the large cities of these two groups of countries. The essential difference lies in the fact that third world cities are subject to what may be called "expanding" urbanization, while those in the developed countries are experiencing "mature" urbanization (World Bank, 1979). In the latter case, instead of increasing in size, large cities are often losing population to smaller cities. One important reason for this trend is that unlike developing countries, the smaller cities in advanced countries already possess the necessary infrastructure for modern business activity. When the diseconomies due to congestion, higher rents, or transportation inconveniences become too large in the big cities, there is a movement of people and businesses to small cities or suburbs. Thus in mature urbanization, city-to-city migration is the main factor affecting the system of cities. The determinants of city-to-city migration are rather different from those of rural–urban migration experienced by the third world cities. This is because city–to–city migrants are fully urbanized and are much more sensitive to differences in amenities between cities.

Determinants of urban growth and spatial concentration

Because of their different relationship to the development process, city growth rates and increases in urbanization must be carefully distinguished. While city growth rates are defined as the percentage change in the absolute number of people living in a given city or a group of cities, increases in urbanization refer to a growing proportion of the national population living in urban areas. It is also useful to differentiate between urbanization patterns exhibiting a high degree of primacy, in which a large proportion of all urban residents live in the largest city (such as in Mexico and Bangkok), and more diffused patterns, such as in India and Malaysia.

In general, there are three major sources of urban growth: net migration, natural increase, and reclassification. The first two contribute the most to urban population growth. However, the urban population in developing countries grows more through natural increase than through migration. Of course, the relative contributions of migration and natural increase to city growth vary in different parts of the third world. In general, at an early stage of development, when levels of urbanization are low and rates of both urban and rural natural increase are moderately high, net migration generally contributes more to urban population growth than does natural increase. At an intermediate stage of urbanization, natural increase predominates. At a late stage, with high levels of urbanization and low rates of natural increase, the relationship is more likely to be reversed again in favour of net migration. A large number of developing countries, particularly in Latin America, are now in the intermediate stage. The most recent evidence indicates that in general about two thirds of the increase in the population of large cities in developing countries comes from natural increase (United Nations, 1985).

Although migration is not the major source of urban growth in many developing countries, the relatively young age of rural migrants to cities means a greater contribution to natural population increase through more births and fewer deaths. This effect tends to offset the declines in fertility rates typically associated with urban residence (Stolnitz, 1984), so that urban rates of natural population increase (the difference between birth and death rates) often approximate national population growth rates. The age selectivity of the migration process and the relatively higher fertility among migrants than among urban natives thus also lead to young age distributions in urban areas. In most cities of developed countries, population within the 0–19 age group as a proportion of the total city population is less than 30 per cent (table 1). For many cities in developing countries it is over 40 per cent. This has enormous implications, particularly for the provision of social services such as education in urban areas.

Migrants move to urban areas mainly in response to better employment and income opportunities. The true determinants of urbanization and spatial countries it is over 40 per cent. This has enormous implications, particularly for the provision of social services such as education in urban areas.

Migrants move to urban areas mainly in response to better employment and income opportunities. The true determinants of urbanization and spatial concentration in developing countries are therefore to be found in the forces that determine the location of employment opportunities such as the nature and pattern of industrialization, the pace of agricultural development, and the growth of transportation and communications networks.

As noted, however, the pace and pattern of industrial development is the most important of these determinants of urbanization and spatial concentration. Industries locate themselves in urban areas, especially in larger cities, because there they can benefit from ready access to capital and labour as well as to specialized needs such as financial, legal, and technical support services. Cities offer markets for industrial products and provide convenient access to other domestic and international markets through established transportation systems. The spatial concentration of economic activity and the emergence of large cities is therefore a necessary adjunct of a development process that relies predominantly on the growth of modern industry rather than on agriculture. However, public policies commonly bias this basic spatial development pattern towards more rapid urbanization and more extreme spatial concentration.

Foreign exchange policies, tariffs, and industrial incentives often support activities of the type located in the major urban centres more than those located in economically less progressive regions, as has happened, for example, in Brazil and Nigeria. Governmental regulation of transport tariffs and energy prices often favours large cities, as do public investment and subsidies for other urban services that influence the location of industries. Urbanization is also influenced by the pace of rural development. The ability of the agricultural sector to absorb a growing rural labour force depends on such factors as climate, availability and distribution of land, choice of agricultural technology, demand for agricultural products, and availability of credit, fertilizers, and technical assistance. Climate and land availability are usually immutable constraints. The Sahel region of Africa, where recurrent droughts in recent years have spurred migration and urbanization, provides an extreme example of the effect of climate. In some developing countries, particularly in Latin America and Africa, new land can still be brought into agricultural use, but in most countries there is little room for increased agricultural employment and earnings based on newly cultivated land. Other factors impeding the expansion of agricultural employment can more readily be influenced by policy. Highly unequal distribution of landownership (especially in Latin America), slow growth and premature mechanization of agricultural production, and market barriers in industrialized nations have made it difficult for the agricultural sector to absorb the growing rural labour force. This in turn has increased the rate of rural–urban migration.

Policies that protect domestic industries from foreign competition, and give more favourable incentives to industry than to agriculture, agricultural credit that is biased towards machinery instead of labour, and neglect of potential for rural-urban migration. Urban-rural income differentials are unlikely to narrow until rural output per capita rises faster than urban output per capita. It has, however, proven difficult to raise agricultural output growth to levels high enough to reduce the income differential. This is unlikely to change because extension of cultivated areas, a major contributor to past agricultural output growth, is becoming increasingly costly in many developing countries or involves using progressively less fertile soils. Moreover, if agricultural growth depends increasingly on intensification, demands for urban-based inputs are likely to increase disproportionately. Rising rural per capita incomes will also produce disproportionate increases in demand for goods and services primarily produced in urban areas. This will not only affect the structure of urban output but will also stimulate urban expenditures and incomes overall. Raising average rural per capita income relative to urban income levels is thus critically dependent on lowering rural population growth, which is itself a function of natural population growth and rural-to-urban migration. Overall population growth rates are now moderating in many developing regions, except in sub-Saharan Africa and some Middle Eastern countries; migration to urban areas speeds up the resulting reduction in rural population growth. Seen in this light, some observers argue that what is often considered "excessive" migration that multiplies problems of urban management becomes a necessary and desirable contributor to raising relative rural per capita incomes.

Spatial concentration, economic efficiency, and growth

As discussed above, urban growth often gives rise to economies of scale. Industries benefit from concentrations of suppliers and consumers, which allow savings in communications and transport costs. Large cities also provide big, differentiated labour markets and often help to accelerate the pace of technological innovation. They also allow the exploitation of economies of scale for such services as water supply and electric power. Against these benefits, unemployment is generally considered to be higher in urban than in rural areas. Air pollution, congestion, social disturbances, crime, and similar problems are also thought to increase with growth in city size.

The judgment that major cities have become too large normally rests on the assumption that urban diseconomies - for example, pollution or traffic congestion - have become so severe that the only answer is to deconcentrate both population and economic activity. Such an argument has several failings. First, it does not recognize that diseconomies are only one side of the argument; if urban agglomerations generate still greater urban economies, then the balance of economic advantage rests with spatial concentration. Second, even if diseconomies exceed economies, the best policy may be to improve urban management rather than to deconcentrate population and employment. To reduce traffic congestion, for example, the best policy may be to improve public transport, to reduce the use of private cars, or to introduce parking meters. Air pollution can be reduced by the physical removal of polluting industries, but it can also be cut by fining errant companies. With regard to unemployment, as we shall discuss later, Governments are sometimes themselves responsible for reducing the absorptive capacity of cities by intervening in labour markets (for instance, through minimum wage legislation and by imposing licensing requirements and restrictions on small businesses) and by pursuing inappropriate pricing policies for public services. National economic policies, which provide fiscal incentives and low-interest loans to promote capital-intensive industry, may also exacerbate urban problems by encouraging rural-urban migration without creating enough new urban jobs.

Moreover, the view that the geographical dispersal of population and economic activity is both possible and without negative consequences is highly misleading. Many economists believe that government intervention in the distribution of economic activity is likely to waste scarce capital resources and thereby slow the rate of economic growth. Thus, in the longer term the country will be less able to redistribute income and remedy the problems of poverty. Regional balance and urban deconcentration should, therefore, be postponed until a nation has achieved a higher level of development. If a high rate of economic growth is to be achieved, further concentration of population into a few large metropolitan areas cannot be avoided.

This view is supported by the finding that large cities are often more efficient and innovative than other urban centres. "In brief, there is no basis for the belief that primacy or over-urbanization per se is detrimental to the efficiency goal of economic development. There are good grounds for believing in increasing returns to urban size" (Alonso, 1969). Several observers have sought to demonstrate that there is no "optimum" city size beyond which further growth is undesirable and that, in general, large cities are more efficient and even more equitable than smaller urban centres. A number of studies indicate that industrial productivity is relatively high in the largest cities even when allowance is made for differences in capital per worker and size of enterprise (Rocca, 1970; Richardson, 1973). The evidence also suggests that the per capita costs of social overhead capital tend to fall with increasing city size, or at least fail to rise (Richardson, 1973). These findings therefore support the view that urban economies exceed urban diseconomies even in today's largest cities and that there is no prima-facie case in favour of deconcentration.

Such a recommendation is not uncontroversial, however, and the evidence on which it is based has been criticized on numerous grounds. The efficiency of the largest cities has also recently been called into question. Gilbert (1976) argues that evidence of higher productivity in large cities should not be attributed only to agglomeration economies, for such "economies" may derive from better urban infrastructure or higher-quality labour. In the latter case, it may be argued that higher productivity in large cities is to some degree achieved at the cost of lower productivity in smaller cities; if equivalent infrastructure or labour were available in small and medium-sized cities, then the productivity of those cities might well rise. In addition, high productivity among private firms in large cities may be apparent because private companies are often subsidized indirectly by the state. If firms had to bear the full externality costs they impose, the higher productivity of large cities might well be less pronounced. Moreover, if the firms were forced to pay some share of the diseconomies they create, they might find the large city less attractive and many might decide to move to the intermediate cities. This process would reduce the apparent differential in industrial productivity between small and large cities.

Even if urban economies outweigh the diseconomies in large cities in developing countries, are the overall benefits equitably distributed? It can be argued that urban diseconomies most affect the lower-income groups, who are least able to escape them. Middle- and upper-income groups often have the resources and knowledge to change their residential areas, command better public services, and influence political decisions. Industrial zones are designated to keep pollution and truck traffic out of high-income areas. Urban renewal schemes rarely displace the rich but often dislocate low-income communities. Public roads, telephone, water, and electricity services in the high-income areas are often superior, and where the public sector cannot provide adequate services, as in health and education, wealthy groups can resort to the private sector. The operation of the land and housing markets guarantees that the wealthy gain most from uncontrolled speculation.

Thus, those who support decentralization argue that in the short run we may achieve the objectives of growth and efficiency by encouraging population concentration in a few urban centres, but in the longer term the expected results are more likely to be mass starvation, greater economic and regional inequalities, urban discontent, and social unrest. The state must therefore redistribute income and wealth among regions and income classes not only because extreme income inequality is morally wrong but also because it is impossible to achieve national unity and to prevent social unrest in the face of glaring regional and family income disparities.

Urban growth, employment and poverty

Labour force growth, labour market structure, and labour absorption

The size and distribution of a city's labour supply are determined by the natural population growth in the city, net migration to (or from) the city, the participation rate of the labour force, and the human capital embodied in the labour force (that is, the availability of skills and the health of the labour force, both of which affect the composition and quality of the urban labour force).

The unprecedented growth of cities and the urban labour force in developing countries and the prospect that this will continue have aroused great concern about the ensuing economic and social consequences particularly since many urban areas, especially large cities, have serious employment and poverty problems. A widely noted characteristic of urban labour markets in developing countries is the degree of segmentation. One segment (the formal sector) is characterized by protected wage work, advanced technology, and high labour productivity, while the other segment (the informal sector) retains the features of a low capital-labour ratio, lack of protection, dominance of self-employment, easy entry, and low productivity. According to Squire (1981), a key distinction between the two sectors is that the rate of return to labour in informal activities is determined primarily by supply and demand conditions, whereas market imperfections tend to limit modern sector wage flexibility, generating unemployment and supply spill-overs to the informal sector. Perhaps because of these rigidities, rapid population growth is associated in cross-national results with a slower absorption of the labour force into industrial and modern sector activities (Oberai, 1978; Squire, 1981).

There are several possible sources of labour market imperfections in the modern sector, including wage inflexibility in government employment and union pressure. The large-scale production firms might be motivated to pay a wage premium to encourage worker productivity and ensure stability, given the relative scarcity of skilled workers and the costs of training. Another imperfection might arise from discrimination based on race, ethnicity, or sex, which may restrict access to high-wage employment (Knight and Sabot, 1982). It is also important to highlight the role of rural-to-urban migration among the factors behind the progressive growth of the informal sector and which contribute towards widening the gap in intersectoral productivity, thereby generating the dualistic economic structure.

In the Lewis model with unlimited labour supply, migrant workers from low-productivity rural jobs are absorbed into high-productivity urban industrial jobs, which implies a one-stage process of labour transfer. However, Todaro (1969) emphasizes a two-stage migration process: at the first stage, the migrants enter the "urban traditional sector" (informal sector) due to their limited access to the "modern sector" (formal sector). With the duration of stay increasing, workers in the urban traditional sector are likely to acquire skills and graduate to the formal sector, or what Todaro calls "eventual attainment of a more permanent modern sector job," implying the second stage of the migration process. But his model is essentially based on the assumption of free entry of labour from the urban traditional sector into the urban modern sector, which seems to be unrealistic. Alternatively, what one might find in actual labour market conditions is that many of the unskilled rural labourers are not in a position to meet the skill requirements of the urban modern sector, nor can they afford to remain unemployed for long. Even if they possess the requisite skills, their absorption into the industrial sector might not take place on a large scale either because of the limited spread of this sector or because of the sluggish growth of employment resulting from the sluggish growth of output and/or the adoption of capital-intensive technology. Consequently, they might continue to work in the unorganized segment of the urban labour market permanently or for a long time. Thus, when the employment-generating capacity of the formal sector lags behind the growth of the urban labour force, the informal sector is overburdened with the excess labour supply. The concentration of employment in low-productivity activities or marginal jobs leads to increased dualism, as has occurred in several Latin American countries during the recent economic crisis (see table 2).

But while there is evidence of labour market imperfections, it would be a mistake to conclude that supply factors have no impact on modern-sector wage levels. Indeed, there is evidence that, as theory would predict, rapid increases in labour supply result in slower wage growth both in manufacturing and in non-manufacturing modern-sector activities (Squire, 1981).

How does the labour market adjust to the substantial and growing imbalances in labour demand and supply? The adjustment can take five principal forms:

Table 1. Proportion of population in 0-19 age group in selected cities

Developed Countries		Developing Countries	
Paris 1982	18.7	São Paolo 1980	40.0
Frankfurt 1981	24.8	Santiago 1982	41.7
London 1981	27.6	Seoul 1980	42.5
New York 1980	28.1	Bangkok 1981	44.1
Tokyo 1981	28.2	Cairo 1976	47.7
Los Angeles 1980	28.8	Mexico City 1980	48.5
Rome 1981	29.6	Delhi 1980	48.9
Madrid 1980	33.5	Jakarta 1981	52.9

Source: Adapted from J. T. Martin, I. Ness and S. T. Collins, Book of World City Rankings (New York, Collier Macmillan; London, The Free Press (Macmillan), 1986).

Table 2. Informal sector employment as a percentage of non-agricultural labour force in selected Latin American countries

	1980	1985
All	26.1	30.7
Argentina	26.3	28.9
Brazil	24.1	30.1
Colombia	32.0	35.4
Mexico	24.2	29.5
Venezuela	25.6	26.2

Source: Adapted from ILO/PREALC: Creation of productive employment: a task that cannot be postponed (Santiago, 1986).

increases in labour supply result in slower wage growth both in manufacturing and in non-manufacturing modern-sector activities (Squire, 1981).

How does the labour market adjust to the substantial and growing imbalances in labour demand and supply? The adjustment can take five principal forms:

(a)   A reduction in rural-urban migration;

(b)   A rise in open unemployment;

(c)   A decline or stagnation in formal sector employment;

(d)   A fall in formal sector wages; and

(e)   An expansion of informal sector employment accompanied by a decline in wages and earnings.

A recent study of several African countries based on data on growth in the non-agricultural labour force during the periods 1970-1980 and 1980-1985 concludes:

"There has been a steady deterioration in the employment situation in most sub-Saharan African countries in the seventies with a marked accentuation in the eighties. This is the result of a continuing deceleration in economic growth accompanied by a rise in the growth of labour supply.

"The brunt of the crisis had to be borne by the urban sector. Reduction in rural-urban migration and rise in open unemployment have been of limited importance in most countries as means of adjustment to the pressures in the urban labour markets. The predominant way in which the labour markets have adjusted to the economic crisis of the past decade has been through sharp reductions in real wages which have helped sustain employment in the formal sector and a rapid expansion of the informal sector with falling real wages and earnings, resulting in work-sharing and increasing under-employment." (Ghai, 1987) [see table 3]

In the informal sector, the relatively free play of supply and demand means that labour force growth does influence wage levels. Because informal sector output is generally not traded internationally, prices of output tend to decline with increases in supply, so that rapid labour force growth in this sector tends to depress the wages of people employed in it. Indeed, Portes and Benton (1984) emphasize that low wages in the informal sector are the prime cause of income inequalities and poverty among the urban populations of developing countries.

Table 3.   Growth of enumerated non-agricultural employment and
real wages in selected African countries
(percentage per annum)

	Enumerated employment		Real wage	
	Period	Growth	Period	Growth
Burundi	1972-79	4.7	1977-82	-4.9
	1981-85	0.7	1980-85	3.8
Cameroon	1969-81	8.5	1976-81	0.0
Ghana	1979-79	1.7	1975-80	-24.2
Kenya	1972-85	5.1	1976-85	-3.3
Malawi	1969-84	4.4	1969-83	-2.1
	1977-84	2.7	1980-84	-6.4
Mauritius	1969-85	5.2	1982-85	-0.8
Nigeria			1975-80	-7.5
Sierra Leone	1974-81	2.2	1969-81	-4.2
Tanzania	1970-81	5.4	1971-81	-6.5
Zambia	1969-84	0.3	1972-84	-3.9

Source: Adapted from D. Ghai, "Economic growth, structural change and
labour absorption in Africa: 1960-85". Paper prepared for a meeting
organized by the Organisation for Economic Co-operation and Development, on
evaluation of urban employment research and policies in developing countries,
Paris, 2-4 November 1987.

Family size and structure, employment, and poverty

Urban poverty is usually associated with two principal sets of employment and household characteristics. One type of urban poor household is characterized by low (and often irregular) earnings of the principal income earner and by a high dependency ratio because of the large household size relative to the number of earners (Sant'Anna and others, 1976). The other kind of urban poor household is represented by what may be called the "floating migrants", usually young, who still have close ties with their rural homes and who "float" into and out of the city in response to urban labour availability and seasonal labour surplus in the countryside. This floating migration has been observed, for instance, in the Sahelian countries of Africa (Cohen, 1978) and in Bombay (Mazumdar, 1979). In general, it is probably the first household that accounts for the overwhelming majority of the urban poor.

Several recent studies suggest that the following are generally more likely to be poor than others:

(a) Those with little or no education;

(b) Households headed by the very young, the very old, and those in the age group 35-44; and

(c) Large households with relatively more women and children.

The well-known positive association among education, skill, experience and earnings level explains why those with little or no education and households headed by the very young are overrepresented among the poor. At the same time, the income of many workers, especially those with little or no education, often does not rise much with age. Thus, when they get married and children arrive, the household sinks into poverty. Family size often peaks when the household head is between 35 and 44 years old, at a time when children are still too young to work and the mother's ability to work is also limited because of child-care responsibilities. Hence, the overrepresentation among the poor of households headed by people in this age group. The larger the family, the more likely this will happen, even if the earnings of the head of the household are otherwise "reasonable".

Thus at the household level, an urban household may be poor for any of the following reasons: (a) too many of its adult members cannot find work; (b) the jobs available to its members pay poorly; (c) there are too many children or other members who must necessarily be dependents even if total income is relatively high.

These alternative explanations of poverty are related, but they are not identical; different explanations give rise to different ways of identifying the poor and of designing ways to help them. A recent study attempts to separate the effects of household size, family composition, and employment status of household members on relative poverty in 10 cities in five Andean countries (Musgrove, 1980).

Two results of this study are worth noting. First, family composition alone is at least as strongly related to poverty as are variables involving employment rates. Second, there is a weak association between poverty and the adult employment rate, Nw/Na. This is the variable that the household presumably adjusts in the short run in relation to its composition, its consumption needs, and its employment opportunities. Three effects can be distinguished here. As Nw/Na rises, other things being equal, income rises and poverty should be less likely. However, as there is an increase in the income that a family could earn if all the adults were employed, part of the potential income will be taken as leisure, leading to a negative relation between Nw/Na and C/N. Finally, the presence of children not only increases N, making poverty more likely, but it may reduce adult employment by requiring at least one adult to stay home and care for the children, again leading to a negative relation between adult participation and welfare. The positive effect of income appears, for these cities, to outweigh the negative effects, but only slightly.

The finding that large households are more likely to be relatively poor than small households and that poverty is associated more with family composition than with employment rates suggests that much relative poverty might be simply a life–cycle effect. As children are added to a family, consumption per person almost necessarily declines, so a family may pass through a period of relative poverty at one stage of the life cycle, although it would not have seemed poor before the children were born or once they are old enough either to begin earning income or to leave home and reduce the family size.

Several points deserve attention here. First, such a life–cycle effect is still sensitive to the number of children; many families will show a decline in C/N as they add children, but how far C/N declines obviously depends on the maximum household size reached. Second, whether the life–cycle decline in consumption per person leads to relative poverty also depends on the income of the working members and on whether that income tends to rise significantly with age. Some families would never become poor because their incomes start high or grow rapidly, unless they had an implausibly large number of children. Third, although income is positively associated with total family size, it may not be positively related to the number of children. If parents with low incomes tend to have more children than higher–income parents, their poverty is not a life–cycle phenomenon: although C/N will decline as they add children, such parents may be poor all their lives. Finally, the fact that poverty may be "temporary" for many families does not mean it is transitory or of no importance for welfare, since temporary poverty may last for a decade or two. This kind of life–cycle effect would be relatively unimportant only if families could save in anticipation of the trough or borrow during the years of low C/N and repay later, so as to maintain satisfactory levels of consumption per person. When they cannot do that, temporary poverty requires sacrifices that may fall particularly heavily on children; they may, for example, have to leave school early and take poorly paid jobs, thus perpetuating poverty.

By estimating life–cycle effects, Musgrove shows that if the household head has some secondary education, relative poverty will occur only if there are six or more children, and families with post-secondary education will never appear poor (table 4). When the head is uneducated, relative poverty may occur as soon as there is one child in the family and will always occur once there are two children; for this group a definite life-cycle effect can be identified. Families whose heads have some primary education are also likely to pass through a stage of relative poverty in the life cycle, but only with a relatively larger number of children.

The two most striking findings to emerge from this study are negative: poverty, defined as low levels of consumption per person, is not strongly associated with low average income, and it is hardly associated at all with low employment rates among adults. Both low wages and unemployment bear some relation to poverty, but neither relation is as strong as might be expected. In contrast, poverty is quite markedly associated with large household size and low overall employment rates, both of which reflect a large number of children per adult member. Low wages and high dependency levels together, of course, virtually guarantee that a family will be poor; but dependency alone can explain much of poverty.

An important implication that appears to follow is that it matters, for the distribution of welfare and the reduction of poverty, how employment is created. If families are poor because their adult members cannot find work, the important step is to create more jobs, even if they pay little. However, this strategy is of no help to poor households with no unemployed members; what they need is not more jobs but better paid work. The evidence presented above suggests that the second situation may be more typical of families in poverty, despite the high rates of open unemployment characteristic of large Latin American cities. Open unemployment can be considered a luxury out of the reach of really poor families, who suffer from low productivity in the jobs they are forced to take. These two factors are not entirely separable, since low wages by themselves are a poor indicator of poverty; but low wages per family member (whether working or not) mean poverty almost by definition. Of course, this kind of evidence in favour of (possibly) fewer jobs but better pay runs counter to two pressures in favour of rapid expansion of employment even with low wages: that such expansion is needed both to absorb increases in the labour force and to minimize capital requirements. The first of these pressures links the question of employment to that of population growth, since slower demographic growth could improve welfare directly and also make it easier to concentrate on raising labour productivity.

Nature and the role of the informal sector in employment generation and poverty alleviation 1/

It is often alleged, as noted earlier, that informal-sector activities are relatively easy to enter, requiring little skill or capital, and are only marginally productive. Additional entrants add little to the total output of this sector and share the same business. Income per worker is therefore low and close to subsistence level. The popular impression is that the informal sector is composed primarily of "marginal activities" such as hawking, shoe-shining, or domestic service.

This somewhat negative view of the informal sector has been challenged in recent years. Many informal sector activities, far from being marginally

Table 4. Predicted permanent income per person (Y*/N) as a function of
          life–cycle stage, household size and education of the head,
          in Bogota, Quito and Lima (1968, US dollars per year)

| | Age 12-34 No children | Age 35-49 Oldest child aged 8-18 years | | | | |
	$N^*=2$	$N=3$	$N=4$	$N=5$	$N=6$	$N=8$
Bogota[1]						
Head uneducated	658	557	418	335	278	209
Primary education	809	685	514	411	342	257
Secondary education	1379	1280	961	769	640	480
Quito[2]						
Head uneducated	424	313	235	188	156	117
Primary education	570	421	315	252	210	158
Secondary education	923	935	701	560	467	350
Lima[3]						
Head uneducated	655	454	341	273	227	170
Primary education	733	558	419	335	279	209
Secondary education	1108	1031	773	618	515	387

Source: Adapted from P. Musgrove, "Household size and composition,
employment and poverty in urban Latin America". Economic Development and
Cultural Change, vol. 2, No. 2 (1980), table 9.

Notes:

a/ Poverty line = 40th percentile of C/N at $421 per year
b/ Poverty line = 40th percentile of C/N at $355 per year
c/ Poverty line = 40th percentile of C/N at $416 per year

productive, are now considered economically efficient. Although low incomes are common in the informal sector, all informal sector workers are not necessarily poor.

For analytical purposes it is now considered more useful to divide the informal sector into two broad subsectors based on organizational structure, behavioural pattern, and related characteristics: (a) the individual enterprise, or irregular, sector, and (b) the family enterprise sector. The irregular sector corresponds to the popular image of informal sector activities described above. The family enterprise sector involves a higher degree of organization and is more productive. The enterprises in this sector generally have a fixed place of work and use a larger amount of capital per worker. The enterprise may be operated individually or with the help of family members or hired workers. Thus, this sector includes both non-wage earners – consisting of own–account workers, employers, and unpaid family workers – and wage earners. Because capital is required to set up and operate an enterprise and it cannot generally be obtained from formal credit institutions, entry into the family enterprise sector as an own–account worker or employer is more difficult than entry into the irregular sector and is restricted to those who have the necessary financial resources or can afford to borrow from private moneylenders. Lack of skill can also be a barrier to entry into certain activities, particularly manufacturing, as an own–account worker.

The tendency to regard the informal sector as synonymous with self–employment, and the controversy over whether this sector is unproductive or a potential dynamic growth point for employment–led development, have resulted in relative neglect in the development literature of wage employees in the family enterprise sector. Jobs within this sector often require few specific skills. Employers therefore have little incentive to provide on–the–job training, or to be selective in their recruitment. This reduces the fixed costs of hiring new workers and, consequently, the concern over labour turnover. Employers are therefore not motivated to pay premium wages, develop internal labour markets, or enter into long contractual relationships with their workers. The limited possibilities for career advancement and the other limitations in turn reduce the incentive of workers to remain on the job or to perform exceptionally well. Hence, it is argued that wage employment in the informal sector is characterized by high rates of labour turnover, which favours ease of entry.

Tokman (1987) thus observes that even when there are support programmes for family enterprises, the first impact will be to increase the incomes of entrepreneurs without necessarily transferring it to the wages of their employees, given the abundance of labour, job instability, low skill requirements, and lack of labour contracts or organization. A second-round effect will be an increased demand for labour, which could mean either new jobs or longer periods of work for the already employed, in both cases with a progressive effect on equity.

There has indeed been a noticeable revival of interest in the role of the informal sector in labour absorption in many developing countries in recent years, particularly in Latin America. Tokman (1987) suggests that the main or to perform exceptionally well. Hence, it is argued that wage employment in the informal sector is characterized by high rates of labour turnover, which favours ease of entry.

Tokman (1987) thus observes that even when there are support programmes for family enterprises, the first impact will be to increase the incomes of entrepreneurs without necessarily transferring it to the wages of their employees, given the abundance of labour, job instability, low skill requirements, and lack of labour contracts or organization. A second-round effect will be an increased demand for labour, which could mean either new jobs or longer periods of work for the already employed, in both cases with a progressive effect on equity.

There has indeed been a noticeable revival of interest in the role of the informal sector in labour absorption in many developing countries in recent years, particularly in Latin America. Tokman (1987) suggests that the main economic reasons for the increased appeal of policies for the informal sector have been:

(a) The failure of the trickle-down strategy to reduce significantly the share of the informal sector in urban employment;

(b) The over-expansion of the informal sector as a result of the crisis of the 1980s;

(c) The   strong   correlation   between   poverty   and   informal-sector employment;

(d) The gloomy prospects for rapid growth in the next decade; and

(e) Increased evidence as to the low resource requirements for the implementation of informal-sector policies.

Urban poverty and access to housing and basic social services

Urban growth process and slum formation

As discussed earlier, the urban labour market in most developing countries is marked by structural dualism. The above analysis also suggests that the existence of the informal sector has to be seen not simply as a short-run transitory phenomenon but as a persistent one.

The persistence of trade and service dominated informal sector activities and of the slums must not be seen merely as two unrelated phenomena that happen to exist simultaneously; rather the former is to be causally linked to the latter. The low levels of income accruing to workers in the informal sector do not enable them to face the challenges of urban life in general and the high cost of living in particular. In large cities where there is not enough scope for geographical expansion in the face of high population density, land scarcity leads to high land prices and speculation. In such

In many third-world cities, more than half of the population lives in slums and squatter settlements; between one fourth and one third of the urban population in these countries has no access to safe water supply and no facilities for the disposal of human waste. Rapid urban population growth puts great stress on the existing stock of shelter and service infrastructure and frequently has deleterious effects on health and environmental conditions.

The policy problems of housing are not only related to meeting the basic needs of the people for shelter; they also have an important bearing on a host of other issues such as the informal sector, employment generation, resource mobilization, and zoning laws. Most government agencies count only new units as progress in housing supply, whereas the vast majority of informal sector housing investment is channelled into the upgrading or expansion of existing units. But there is an even broader misconception in this regard that has to do with the way Governments view investment in housing (as a durable consumer good) as opposed to investment in industry, which they see as generative of economic development. Janice Perlman notes that as we come to understand the workings of the informal sector, the standard view of housing as a durable consumer good is wide of the mark in relation to third-world cities where houses are often used for the making, storing, and selling of goods. Yet, because this is part of the conventional wisdom in the official circles, it has led to "misguided investments in 'finished product' homes and self-defeating codes, standards, and zoning regulations" (Perlman, 1986).

The construction of housing is clearly a source of both employment creation and income generation. It can, however, also be a source of substantial resource mobilization to the extent that with the aid of the "self-help" and "user-participation" schemes, it leads to informal-sector dwellers using their own labour to improve and extend existing homes or to build new ones. Despite the many limitations of such schemes, they do have significant multiplier effects on the urban economy.

More unused urban land could be made available for residential use if it were not for institutional constraints. The subdivision of urban land and the conversion of land for different uses are often impeded by restrictive zoning regulations, cumbersome land registration requirements, high land transfer taxes, and disputed land titles. The poor are least able to overcome these institutional barriers. If they are not willing to accept overcrowded living conditions, they must engage in various forms of illegal land deals. If they do so, they suffer from insecure tenure, which in turn limits their ability and willingness to improve their shelter. Where land and services are available, lack of finance probably is the primary reason for the difficulties poor households encounter in their efforts to build or improve shelter.

Financial markets are underdeveloped, particularly for housing finance, and are hampered by government regulations concerning interest rates and the conditions under which funds may be lent. The poor are the first to be excluded from such a capital market, especially where disputed land titles make it impossible to use land as collateral in borrowing.

Urban poverty and provision of social services

Public involvement in the provision of social services, especially those relating to education, health, nutrition and family planning, is a well-established practice in all developing countries. Serious policy issues arise in the delivery of urban social services because of their important effects on the labour productivity and welfare of the urban poor.

One area in which city authorities can make a direct and important contribution to alleviating urban poverty is in the development of policies to improve the quality and productivity of the labour force by increasing the access of the urban poor to social services. In principle, cities and towns should be able to deliver social services more efficiently than the scattered rural areas. On average, urban households are in fact usually more educated, healthier, and better served by public and private education and health facilities than are their rural counterparts. The urban poor, however, are often considerably worse off than the average statistics suggest. The main reason for this is usually the lopsided distribution of urban social services towards the more well-to-do sections of the urban society.

Schools are often scarce in squatter and slum areas, attendance rates are low, and dropout rates are high. Many children of school age in poor neighbourhoods perform a range of economic tasks such as helping with the family business or even baby-sitting at home, which permits the mother to work. The parents of these children may not be able to afford to send them to school unless such schooling is available in the evenings near the place of residence. Also, the urban poor usually have limited access to private or public health care, due to the high costs of medical attention and drugs, lack of information, and the physical as well as cultural inaccessibility of modern curative care. Infant malnutrition and mortality in urban slums are aggravated by the fact that mothers are increasingly switching from breast-feeding to commercial baby foods, frequently diluted with unsafe water.

Regarding nutrition, there is convincing evidence that the urban poor are frequently worse off than the rural population. As long as the urban poor live in overcrowded housing with no access to safe water or disposal of human and solid waste and with only limited availability of preventive health care, they are likely to be seriously affected by ill health. This problem is compounded by the fact that their nutritional intake in general tends to be lower and less well-balanced than that of the rural poor.

Thus, the urban poor are trapped in a vicious circle in which low incomes ensure poor education, nutrition, and health, which in turn leads to low productivity and income. The main policy question is therefore how to help the poor to break this cycle in which they are trapped. Even within existing budgets, redirection of city services towards the poor should help to increase their productivity and income. The rationale behind such a policy is not only an ethical one – that is, the alleviation of poverty – but also one of efficiency.

The synergistic interactions of education, health, nutrition and family planning, however, imply that private and public resources – educational, health, and sanitation services, as well as family planning efforts - are more likely to be wasted unless a comprehensive and co-ordinated effort is made to assist the urban poor (Austin, 1980). Beginning with education and its relation to other social services, it is well established that higher levels of education tend to be associated with lower fertility and that family planning programmes, in order to be fully effective, must be complemented by specific educational programmes. At the same time, reduced fertility lowers the demand on the educational system because of the consequent decline in the school-age population. At the household level, some studies have found a negative correlation between family size and the intelligence quotient (IQ) of each additional child (Boulier, 1977). Education and training programmes are also essential in improving nutritional practices, especially in instructing low-income women on the value of breast-feeding and on the preparation of balanced and uncontaminated food for infants and children. Poor nutrition is known to interfere with the ability of children to benefit from educational programmes.

The links between health, nutrition,and family planning are particularly close. On the one hand, improved health, as measured by reduction in morbidity or increase in life expectancy, is known to lead to a reduction in fertility, albeit with a variable time lag (World Bank, 1980). On the other hand, a reduction in household size tends to increase overall family health (Boulier, 1977); more specifically, the reduction in the number of births and an increased spacing of children contribute to improved maternal and infant health and nutrition (Boulier, 1977). Poor nutrition is a major cause in increasing susceptibility to illness, and malnutrition is itself a major cause of morbidity and death (Austin, 1980).

Besides the internal links within the system of education, health, nutrition and family planning, there is an important connection between individual social services and other factors. For instance, improved sanitation (water supply, sewerage, and solid waste disposal) has important effects on the health of the urban population, but these health benefits can be reaped in full only if improved sanitation is combined with educational measures aimed at improving the personal hygiene of urban dwellers. The quality of housing, in particular the extent of crowding, is closely related to health, since with high density the likelihood of contamination and disease transmission is considerably increased (Linn, 1983).

Finally, probably the most important external linkage of the education–health–nutrition–family planning complex is its relation to the level of income. Higher incomes - at the household, city, and national levels - are associated with significantly improved levels of education, health, nutrition, and family planning in a pattern of two-way causation. Better education, health, nutrition, and family planning increase productivity and reduce the drain on household resources associated with poor health and large household size; in contrast, higher incomes permit greater household, municipal and national expenditures to achieve and maintain good educational, health, and nutritional levels and may directly affect parental decisions regarding reproduction. Indeed, what for a poor family is a vicious cycle - low income induces poor education, health, nutrition, and family planning and leads again to low income - is for a high-income family a self-reinforcing cycle where high income yields good education, health, nutrition, and family planning and perpetuates high income.

Concluding remarks

This paper has outlined the main policy problems requiring urgent attention in large cities in developing countries. The analytical issues discussed and the analysis of trends in urbanization, employment, and poverty provide an essential part of the policy framework within which specific policy issues need to be examined.

Rapid urbanization and concentration of economic activity in a few locations, particularly in large cities, are an inevitable outcome of economic and industrial development. However, in the absence of information on the relative costs and benefits of urban versus rural development and of the growth of large versus small cities, it is difficult to determine the optimal rate of urbanization and the best spatial distribution of economic activity in any given country. It is also difficult to judge the optimum size of a city. None of the studies reviewed has been able to pinpoint at what city size the losses created by congestion and environmental deterioration equal or exceed the benefits of agglomeration. In any case, economic efficiency is not the only aspect of urbanization with which Governments are concerned. In most developing countries, particularly those with distinct regional or ethnic interests, it is extremely important to maintain a balance among regions and between rural and urban development; hence, some attempt to slow down the urbanization process and to spread economic development more evenly across regions may be politically necessary, even if its economic desirability is less obvious.

The range of policy instruments available for controlling migration is, however, quite limited. Governments should, instead of directly intervening in population distribution policies, try to correct the biases of national development policies that have implications not only for industrial location patterns but also for regional income inequalities. Removal of urban bias in national policies and regional development efforts are, however, unlikely to have much impact on deconcentration of population in large cities, at least in the short term. Policies designed to improve the internal efficiency in large cities must therefore be vigorously pursued. This should include implementation of programmes that would improve the conditions of the urban poor.

A common argument against actions to alleviate poverty in urban areas is based on the fear that this will accentuate "urban bias", increase rural-urban inequalities, and exacerbate rural-urban migration. Until recently, city authorities in many developing countries had even justified reduced investments in urban services by arguing that the more houses, schools, hospitals, and jobs that are provided in the cities, the more migrants would be attracted to them. Such arguments are not entirely persuasive. First, the focus of poverty is rapidly shifting to urban areas in many countries and concern for overall poverty alleviation must increasingly deal with its manifestation in cities. Second, although average incomes in urban areas are almost everywhere higher than in rural areas, the urban poor are as poor as their rural counterparts. In spite of their location in urban areas they are as badly off as the rural poor in terms of access to social services such as health and education. In some respects, for example, the overcrowded and unsanitary living conditions in urban slums, they are arguably worse off. Moreover, the withholding of urban infrastructure or social services, the bulldozing of slums or squatter settlements, and employment have all been shown not to affect migration flows significantly. They do, however, seriously impede the efficiency of urban markets, destroy valuable capital stock, and wreak havoc with the lives and welfare of the majority of the urban population. In fact, measures designed to improve the efficiency of the urban economy, in particular the pricing of public services at marginal social cost and the elimination of subsidies for private investors, are more likely to have much more important, albeit indirect, effects on migration.

Greater emphasis also needs to be placed on the importance of bringing down birth rates in order to slow population growth in general and urban natural growth in particular. In sub-Saharan Africa and low-income Asia, family planning efforts in rural areas are needed to reduce migration to urban areas. In Latin America, slowing the natural growth rate of the urban population holds the most direct hope for reducing the explosive growth of cities. An important reason for the high fertility among the urban poor, particularly among slum dwellers, is their limited access to education, health, and family planning services due to their low productivity and incomes. Thus, improving the access of urban poor to employment opportunities and social services and raising their productivity and incomes are more likely to relieve population pressure in large cities.

Coping with employment and poverty problems in large cities is thus the major challenge facing the developing countries. There is an urgent need to examine the scope and adequacy of current policies relating to employment promotion particularly in the informal sector; promote small-scale industry; generate employment through investments in housing and community infrastructure for the poor; and improve productivity and working conditions of vulnerable groups in the urban labour market. Particular attention will need to be paid to the question of the adequacy of the existing institutional structure for dealing with employment and poverty problems at the city level. In most developing countries, city authorities are primarily oriented towards the provision and maintenance of urban infrastructure and services. They have little interest in, and no capacity to deal with, social and economic issues such as the promotion of employment and the alleviation of poverty. Unless this situation is changed it will be virtually impossible to think of any viable way of initiating and implementing comprehensive anti-poverty programmes in third-world cities. The solution to the problems of employment and urban poverty cannot be found in an institutional vacuum.

Note

1/ For a more detailed discussion on these issues, see especially Lee (1987) and Sethuraman (1981).

References

Alonso, W. (1969). Urban and regional imbalances in economic development. Economic Development and Cultural Change, vol. 17, pp. 1-14.

Austin, J. (1980). Confronting Urban Malnutrition. Baltimore: The Johns Hopkins University Press.

Blair, T. L. (1984). Urban Innovation Abroad: Problem Cities in Search of Solutions. New York: Plenum Press.

Boulier, B. L. (1977). Population policy and income distribution. In Income Distribution and Growth in the Less Developed Countries, C. R. Frank and R. C. Webb, eds. Washington, D.C.: Brookings Institution.

Chenery, H. and M. Syrquin. (1975). Patterns of Development 1950-1970. New York: Oxford University Press.

Cohen, M. (1978). Urban Growth and Economic Development in the Sahel: Prospects and Priorities. World Bank Staff Working Paper, No. 315. Washington, D.C.: World Bank.

Fields, G. (1975). Rural-urban migration, urban unemployment and underemployment and job search activity in LDCs. Journal of Development Economics, vol. 3, pp. 165-187.

Ghai, D. (1987). Economic growth, structural change and labour absorption in Africa: 1960-85. Paper prepared for the meeting organised by OECD on Evaluation of Urban Employment Research and Policies in Developing Countries, Paris, 2-4 November.

Gilbert, A. G. (1976). The arguments for very large cities reconsidered. Urban Studies, vol. 13, pp. 27-34.

Harris, R. and R. Sabot (1982). Urban unemployment in LDCs: toward a more general search model. In Migration and Labor Market in Developing Countries, R. Sabot, ed. Boulder, Colorado: Westview Press.

India (1987). National Commission on Urbanization. Interim Report. New Delhi.

International Labour Office (1987). World Recession and Global Interdependence. Geneva.

Knight, J. B. and R. Sabot. (1982). Labour market discrimination in a poor urban economy. Journal of Development Studies, vol. 19, No. 1, pp. 67-87.

Lee, E. (1987). The informal sector and aid policy. Paper prepared for a
     meeting organized by DANIDA on The Informal Sector as an Integral Part of
     the National Economy: Research Needs and Aid Requirements, Copenhagen,
     28–29 September.

Linn, J. (1983). Cities in the Developing World. New York: Oxford University
     Press.

Mitra, A. (1987). Duality, employment problem and poverty incidence: slum
     perspective. Delhi: Delhi School of Economics. Mimeographed.

Musgrove, P. (1980). Household size and composition, employment and poverty
     in urban Latin America. Economic Development and Cultural Change,
     vol. 28, No. 2, pp. 249–260.

Oberai, A. S. (1978). Changes in the Structure of Employment with Economic
     Development. Geneva: International Labour Office.

_____ (1987). Migration, Urbanization and Development. Geneva:
     International Labour Office.

Perlman, J. (1986). Six misconceptions about squatter settlements.
     Development, vol. 14.

Portes, A. and L. Benton (1984). Industrial development and labour force
     absorption. Population and Development Review, vol. 10, No. 4,
     pp. 589–612.

Richardson, H. W. (1973). Economics of Urban Size. Farnborugh: Saxon House.

Rocca, C. A. (1970). Productivity in Brazilian manufacturing. In Brazil:
     Industrialization and Trade Policies, Joel Bergsmann, ed. Oxford:
     Oxford University Press. pp. 22–41.

Rodgers, G., ed. (forthcoming). Trends in Urban Poverty and Labour Market
     Access. Geneva: International Labour Office.

Sethuraman, S. V. (1981). The Urban Informal Sector in Developing Countries:
     Employment, Poverty and Environment. Geneva: International Labour
     Office.

Squire, L. (1981). Employment Policy in Developing Countries. New York:
     Oxford University Press.

Stolnitz, G. J. (1984). Urbanization and Rural–to–Urban Migration in Relation
     to LDC Fertility. Bloomington: Indiana University.

Todaro, M. P. (1969). A model of labour migration and urban unemployment in
     less developed countries. American Economic Review, vol. 59,
     pp. 393–423.

Tokman, V. (1987). Evaluation of research and policies on employment problems in Latin America. Paper prepared for the OECD Meeting on Evaluation of Urban Employment Research and Policies in Developing Countries, Paris, 2-4 November.

United Nations (1985). Migration, Population Growth and Employment in Metropolitan Areas of Selected Developing Countries. (ST/ESA/SER.R/57).

_____ (1987). The Prospects of World Urbanization: Revised as of 1984-1985. Sales No. E.87 XIII.3.

World Bank (1979). National Urbanization Policies in Developing Countries. Working Paper, No. 347. Washington, D.C.: World Bank.

_____ (1983). World Tables, Social Data, vol. II. Baltimore: The Johns Hopkins University Press.

Annex Table. Largest urban agglomerations by population size
(millions)

Agglomeration/ country	Popul. in 1970	Agglomeration/ country	Popul. in 1985	Agglomeration/ country	Popul. in 2000
New York/North-eastern		Tokyo/Yokohama, Japan	18.8	MexicoCity, Mexico	25.8
New Jersey, USA	16.3	Mexico City, Mexico	17.3	SaoPaulo, Brazil	24.0
Tokyo/Yokohama, Japan	14.9	Sao Paulo, Brazil	15.9	Tokyo/Yokohama, Japan	20.2
London, United Kingdom	11.6	New York/North-eastern		Calcutta, India	16.5
Shanghai, China	11.4	New Jersey, USA	15.7	Greater Bombay, India	16.0
Mexico City, Mexico	9.1	Shanghai, China	12.0	NewYork/North-eastern	
Greater Buenos Aires,		Calcutta, India	11.0	NewJersey, USA	15.8
Argentina	8.6	Greater Buenos Aires,		Shanghai, China	14.3
Los Angeles/Long Beach	8.4	Argentina	10.9	Seoul,Republic of Korea	13.8
USA		Rio de Janeiro, Brazil	10.4	Teheran, Iran	13.6
Paris, France	8.3	London, United Kingdom	10.4	Riode Janeiro, Brazil	13.3
Beijing, China	8.3	Seoul, Republic of Korea	10.3	Delhi,India	13.2
Sao Paolo, Brazil	8.2	Greater Bombay, India	10.1	Greater Buenos Aires,	
Osaka, Kobe, Japan	7.6	Los Angeles/Long Beach		Argentina	13.2
Rio de Janeiro, Brazil	7.2	USA	10.0	Jakarta, Indonesia	13.2
Moscow, USSR	7.1	Osaka/Kobe, Japan	9.5	Karachi, Pakistan	12.0
Calcutta, India	7.1	Beijing, China	9.3	Dhaka,Bangladesh	11.2
Tianjin, China	6.9	Moscow, USSR	9.0	Beijing, China	11.2
Chicago/North-western		Paris, France	8.7	Cairo/Giza/Imbaba, Egypt	11.1
Indiana, USA	6.8	Jakarta, Indonesia	7.9	Manila, Philippines	11.1
Greater Bombay, India	6.0	Tianjin, China	7.9	LosAngeles/Long Beach	
Cairo/Giza/Imbaba, Egypt	5.7	Cairo/Giza/Imbaba, Egypt	7.7	USA	11.0
Milan, Italy	5.5	Teheran, Iran	7.5	Bangkok, Thailand	10.7
Seoul, Republic of Korea	5.4				

Source: Adapted from The Prospects of World Urbanization:
Revised as of 1984-1985 (United Nations publication, Sales
No. E.87.XIII.3.

Chapter 8

Rapid population growth, the quality of health, and the quality of health care in developing countries

● J. E. Potter*

Introduction

The interrelations between rapid population growth and health, particularly between high fertility and health, seem to warrant fresh attention in the debate over development policies. Arguably, what happens in one of these "sectors" has a substantial influence on what happens in the other. On the one hand, the negative health consequences of rapid population growth and high fertility constitute a principal justification for government interventions designed to alter fertility patterns and levels. On the other, the implications of developments in the health care system for fertility trends, and for the capacity to affect fertility trends, may warrant increased allocation of resources to health, particularly maternal and child health.

The evidence, at least at the international level, of concern for improving the health of the populations of the less developed countries is plentiful. The World Health Organization (WHO) has received widespread support for its campaign to achieve "health for all by the year 2000" by way of primary health care. The United Nations Children's Fund (UNICEF) has been remarkably successful in attracting the attention of world leaders concerning the plight of infants and children and in mobilizing resources for the implementation of a "child survival revolution". The World Bank's attempt to call attention to and direct resources towards the problem of maternal mortality was well received. So, too, was the effort by the Population Council and other agencies to increase awareness of the possibility of achieving better health for mothers and children through family planning.

This concern with health seems to derive from recognition of (a) the seriousness of the health problems in many parts of the world, (b) the extent of popular demand for better health care services, and (c) the potential to achieve better health without enormous expenditures of scarce financial resources. Optimism concerning the prospects for achieving "good health at low

---

*University of Texas at Austin, Austin, Texas, USA.

cost" -- yet another of the current slogans -- seems to be based on a favourable assessment of the potential of a number of available, low-cost technologies, as well as on the discovery that the health transition that has taken place in countries such as Costa Rica, Sri Lanka, and China is largely behavioural in nature. The temptation is to believe that a reallocation of resources to preventive and/or primary health care, together with a certain amount of social engineering and mass communication, could have a major impact on the quality of health in developing countries.

As enthusiasm for meeting the challenge of improving health has grown during the past decade, concern for the problems posed by rapid population growth has languished. In the face of an emerging disparity in the political and technical resources for the two sectors, the population community has frequently jumped at the chance to show that family planning has a beneficial impact on the health of mothers and children. Somewhat surprisingly, there has not been a parallel effort to highlight the macro-level strains and constraints that rapid population growth places upon the health sector. Nor is there evidence of a major new focus on the influence of health on fertility.

The objective of this paper is to evaluate some of the principal linkages between rapid population growth, the quality of health (as measured by mortality), and the quality of health care. The review begins with an examination of the increasingly close cross-country association between the level of fertility and the level of mortality, together with a discussion of the various "common causes" of these two phenomena. The second part of the paper assesses the evidence for causal connections between health and reproduction at the level of individual behaviour and outcomes. The third and final part touches briefly on the macro-level or sectoral linkages between health and population.

Fertility and mortality in the international cross-section

Two decades ago the cross-national association between the level of fertility and the infant mortality rate or life expectancy was an object of study and debate (e.g., Heer, 1966). As quantitative investigations have become more sophisticated and there has been a vast increase in the amount of data from surveys and other sources available for analysis, less notice has been paid to this highly aggregate relationship. It is not without interest, however, that in the course of the past 20 years the association has become noticeably closer.

Data for both 1965 and 1985 from developing countries with relatively reliable data have been reexamined to provide a crude demonstration of this point. The 41 countries selected for this exercise are shown, together with their respective demographic rates, in table 1. The sample includes nations from all regions of the third world, although those from sub-Saharan Africa are underrepresented. Figure I shows a scatter plot of the estimated total fertility rate (TFR) in 1965 and the estimated infant mortality rate (IMR) in 1960-1965, while figure II shows a scatter plot of 1965 estimates of the TFR and life expectancy. These plots may be compared with those corresponding to 1985 as shown in figures III and IV. There is considerably less scatter in the plots corresponding to the later time period.

Figure I .   Estimated values of the TFR in 1965 and the
             IMR in 1960-1965 for 38 countries

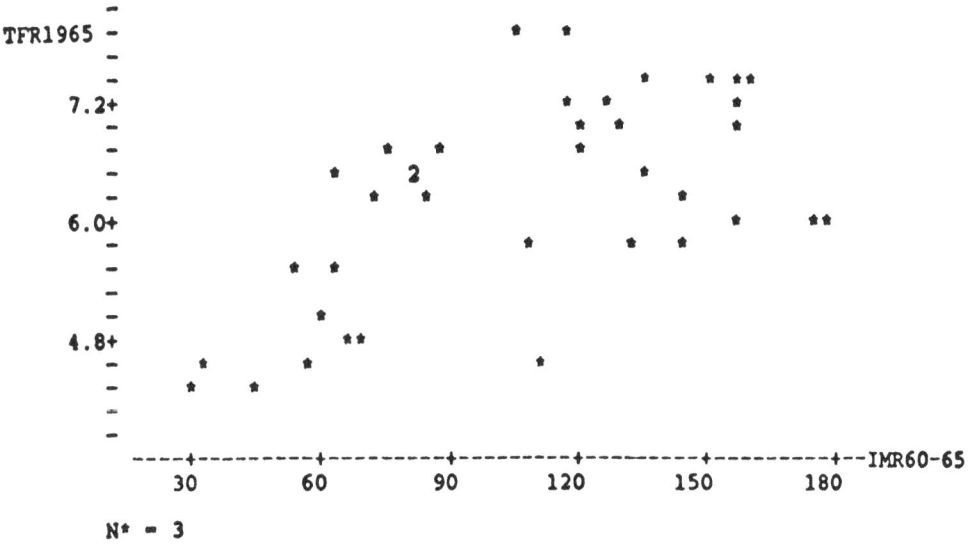

Figure II.   Estimated values of the TFR in 1965 and life
             expectancy in 1965 for 38 countries

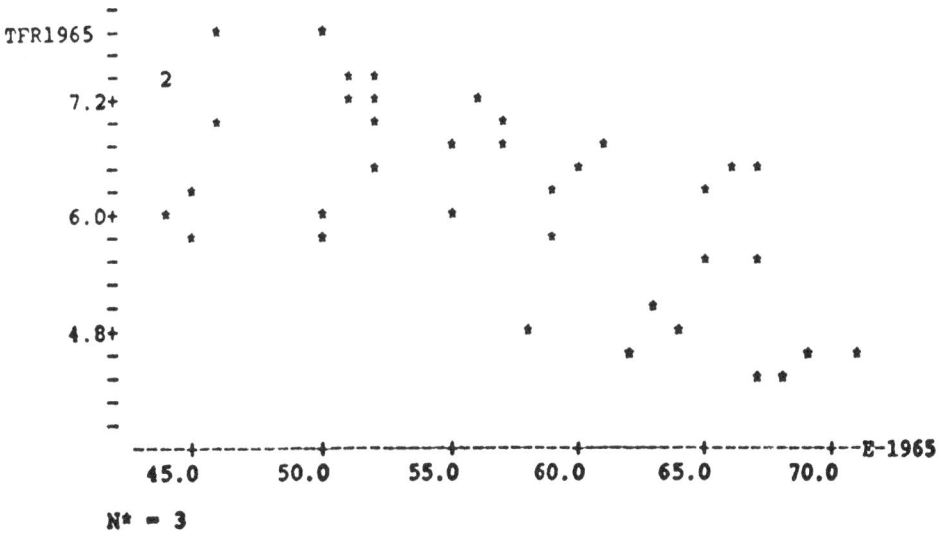

Figure III.   Estimated values of the TFR in 1985 and the
              IMR in 1980-1985 for 41 countries

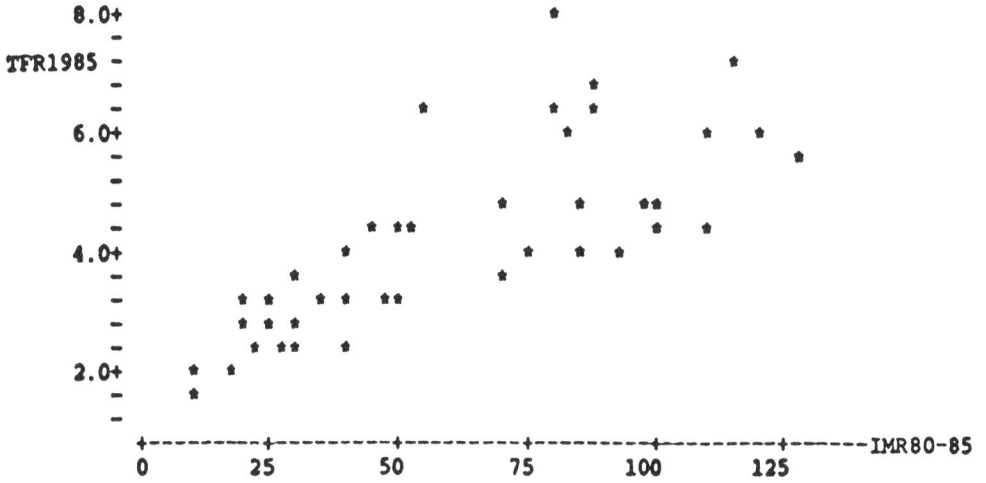

Figure IV.   Estimated values of the TFR in 1985 and life
             expectancy in 1985 for 41 countries

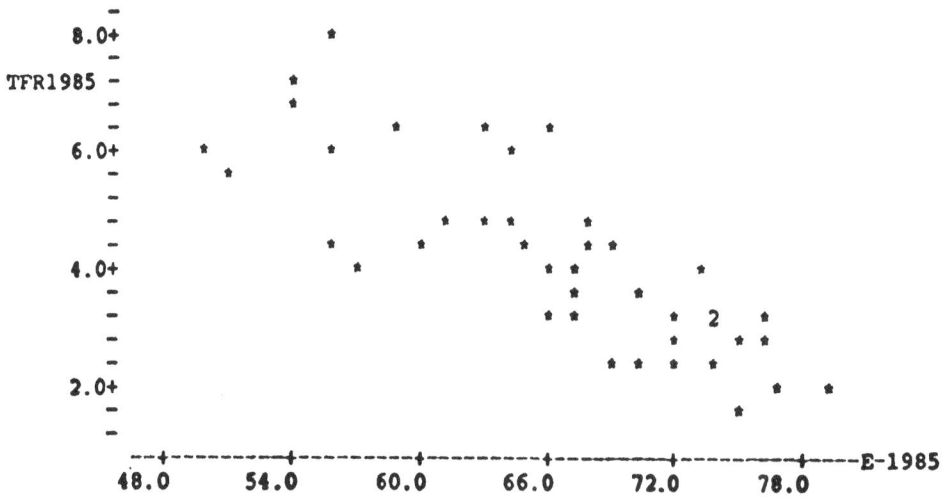

Table 1. Total fertility rate, international mortality rate
and female life expectancy in 41 countries

No	Countries	TFR 1965[1]	TFR 1985[2]	IMR 60-65[3]	IMR 80-85[3]	Female life expectancy 1965[2]	Female life expectancy 1985[2]
1	Bangladesh	7.4	5.7	150	128	44	51
2	India	5.9	4.5	157	110	44	56
3	Kenya	8.0	7.8	118	80	46	56
4	Tanzania	6.3	7.0	143	115	45	54
5	China	6.6	2.3	121	39	55	70
6	Pakistan	7.5	6.1	155	120	44	50
7	Sri Lanka	4.9	3.2	65	39	64	72
8	Zambia	6.9	6.8	130	88	46	54
9	Lesotho	5.8	5.8	145	111	50	56
10	Indonesia	5.8	4.1	133	84	45	57
11	Morocco	7.1	4.9	155	97	51	61
12	Philippines	6.8	4.3	76	51	57	65
13	Egypt, Arab Rep.	5.9	4.7	175	100	50	63
14	Zimbabwe	8.0	6.2	106	80	50	59
15	Honduras	7.4	6.0	136	82	52	64
16	Dominican Rep.	7.3	4.0	117	75	56	66
17	Thailand	(-)	3.2	95	48	58	66
18	Paraguay	6.5	4.4	81	45	67	68
19	Jamaica	5.4	2.8	54	21	67	76
20	Peru	6.5	4.3	136	99	52	60
21	Turkey	5.9	3.9	176	92	55	67
22	Mauritius	5.0	2.5	61	28	63	69
23	Ecuador	6.9	4.7	119	70	57	68
24	Tunisia	7.0	4.6	155	85	52	64
25	Costa Rica	6.4	3.3	81	20	66	76
26	Colombia	6.3	3.3	84	50	59	67
27	Chile	4.5	2.5	111	23	62	74
28	Jordan	7.2	6.2	125	54	52	66
29	Brazil	5.7	3.6	109	71	59	67
30	Uruguay	(-)	2.6	48	30	72	75
31	Malaysia	6.5	3.7	63	30	60	70
32	Mexico	6.7	4.3	86	53	61	69
33	Panama	5.6	3.2	63	26	65	74
34	Argentina	(-)	3.3	60	36	69	74
35	Korea, Rep. of	4.8	2.4	70	30	58	72
36	Algeria	7.4	6.3	160	88	51	63
37	Venezuela	6.3	3.9	73	39	65	73
38	Trinidad and Tobago	4.3	2.8	44	24	67	72
39	Hong Kong	4.6	1.8	33	10	71	79
40	Singapore	4.2	1.7	30	10	68	75
41	Cuba	4.5	2.0	56	17	69	77

Source: For 1965 TFR: R. J. Lapham and W. P. Mauldin, "Conditions of fertility decline in developing countries, 1965-1980". Paper presented at the 1984 Annual Meeting of the Population Association of America. For 1985 TFR and 1965 life expectancy (female): World Development Report, 1987 (Washington, D. C., World Bank, 1988). For IMR: Mortality of Children under Age 5 (United Nations publication, Sales No. E.88.X.III.4).

Another observation about statistical associations in the international cross-section that is as valid today as it was 20 years ago is that mortality is a better predictor of the level of fertility (and vice versa) than any other indicator of development, health, or national well-being. For example, when the estimates of the per capita daily calorie supply and estimates of the population per physician shown in table 2 are included along with life expectancy in a multiple regression having the TFR as the dependent variable, neither proves to be a significant predictor. Conducting this analysis with both the 1965 and the 1985 data, the relative predictive power of these ancillary indicators seems to have changed little during the last two decades. Last but perhaps not least, there remains a remarkable lack of correspondence in the international cross-section between the estimated level of GNP per capita and either mortality or fertility.

What, in this day and age, is to be made of the strong cross-national correlation between fertility and mortality? It would seem that there are three possible, and complementary rather than competing, interpretations. The first, and for our purposes the least provocative, is the familiar and widely accepted view that the transitions of both fertility and mortality from high to low levels are determined by the "development" or "modernization" taking place in a society, and that there are few reliable indicators of this underlying process. A slightly different interpretation with, it could be alleged, more interesting and less well-explored implications is that there is only one transition. It is not that the fertility transition and the mortality transition both have modernization as a "common cause"; rather, changes in both of these dimensions are part and parcel of a transformation less comprehensive than modernization that involves the adoption of new technology for personal purposes and a dramatic change in family relationships.

The third possible interpretation of the cross-national association between fertility and mortality is that there are causal connections between these two variables at the level of individual or family behaviour and in terms of macro-level or sectoral linkages. That this is just one of three possible interpretations of the aggregate relationship, and that it encompasses the possibility that causation flows in both directions, speaks for the difficulty of arriving at solid conclusions regarding the nature and magnitude of the relevant relationships.

Micro-level connections between health and reproduction

Family building patterns and child survival

It has frequently been observed that death rates for infants vary according to the mother's age and parity (Nortman, 1974). The relationship in both cases appears to be U-shaped. Mortality is high at the extremes of the reproductive age range and lower in the middle of this span; it is high for both first and higher order births and lower for second, third, and fourth births.

Table 2. Indexes of health care, life quality
and economy in 41 countries

No	Countries	Population Per Physician		Daily Calorie Supply per capita		GNP ($) per capita
		1965	1981	1965	1985	1985
1	Bangladesh	8400	9700	1964	1899	150
2	India	4880	3700	2100	2189	270
3	Kenya	12820	10140	2287	2151	290
4	Tanzania	21700	(-)	1970	2335	290
5	China	3780	1730	2034	2602	310
6	Pakistan	(-)	2910	1747	2159	380
7	Sri Lanka	5800	7460	2155	2385	380
8	Zambia	11400	7800	2073	2137	390
9	Lesotho	19800	(-)	2065	2385	470
10	Indonesia	31740	12300	1792	2533	530
11	Morocco	12120	18600	2182	2678	560
12	Philippines	(-)	6710	1936	2341	580
13	Egypt, Arab Rep.	2300	760	2435	3263	610
14	Zimbabwe	8000	7100	2089	2954	680
15	Honduras	5400	3120	1963	2211	720
16	Dominican Rep.	1700	1400	1870	2461	790
17	Thailand	7230	6870	2200	2462	800
18	Paraguay	1850	1750	2627	2796	860
19	Jamaica	1980	2700	2232	2585	940
20	Peru	1620	(-)	2324	2171	1010
21	Turkey	2900	1530	2636	3167	1080
22	Mauritius	3860	1800	2272	2740	1090
23	Ecuador	3000	(-)	1942	2054	1160
24	Tunisia	8000	3900	2296	2836	1190
25	Costa Rica	2000	(-)	2366	2803	1300
26	Colombia	2500	(-)	2174	2574	1320
27	Chile	2100	(-)	2591	2602	1430
28	Jordan	4700	1200	2282	2947	1560
29	Brazil	2500	1300	2405	2633	1640
30	Uruguay	880	500	2811	2695	1650
31	Malaysia	6220	3920	2249	2684	2000
32	Mexico	2020	1200	2643	3177	2080
33	Panama	2130	1010	2255	2419	2100
34	Argentina	600	(-)	3209	3221	2130
35	Korea, Rep. of	2700	1390	2255	2841	2150
36	Algeria	8590	(-)	1682	2677	2550
37	Venezuela	1210	1000	2321	2583	3080
38	Trinidad and Tobago	3820	1500	2497	3006	6020
39	Hong Kong	2460	1300	2502	2698	6230
40	Singapore	1900	1100	2214	2771	7420
41	Cuba	1150	720	2371	3122	(-)

Source: World Development Report, 1987 (Washington, D. C., World Bank, 1988).

A number of studies conducted through the years have also reached the conclusion that birth spacing influences child survival (Wolfers and Scrimshaw, 1975; Winikoff, 1983); that is to say that a child born after a long inter-birth interval is less likely to die than one born closely following an earlier pregnancy.

The amount of information concerning these relations in developing countries was greatly expanded when Hobcraft, McDonald, and Rutstein (1983), using data collected by the World Fertility Survey, published impressive results for 26 countries. Employing Poisson regression and a classification of the spacing patterns that both preceded and followed children born in the period extending from 5 to 15 years before the date of the survey, the authors found significantly higher mortality for closely spaced births. For example, the risk of dying in the first month of life for a child born within two years following the birth of his elder sibling was greater by 50 per cent or more in all but two of the 26 countries, and twice as high in 14 of them, as compared with children who were born after an interbirth interval of more than two years. They found similar effects on the risk of dying in the next 11 months of life, and discernible but progressively weaker effects for the second year of life, and mortality at ages three through five. In addition, they found that intensive child-bearing 2-6 years before the birth of a child elevated the risk of neonatal and post-neonatal mortality and that the length of the following interval was inversely associated with toddler and child mortality.

Two studies of individual surveys have given additional credence to the notion that birth spacing influences child survival. An analysis of the Sri Lanka World Fertility Survey (WFS) by Trussell and Hammerslough (1983) found that the length of the preceding interval was associated with infant and child mortality. And Cleland and Sathar (1984) came to a similar conclusion in their study of the Pakistan WFS after taking the precaution of controlling for the survival status of the preceding child so as to avoid the potential confounding effect of a child death on the length of a subsequent interval. 1/

In a second, expanded cross-national study of the demographic determinants of infant and early child mortality, Hobcraft, McDonald, and Rutstein (1985) introduced controls for the age of the mother at the time of the birth, birth order, the sex of the child, and the survival status of preceding and following births. Again, closely spaced births were found to be subject to higher risks of mortality, but the estimated effects were smaller than those obtained in the earlier analysis. The authors did, however, find that the probability that a child would die in the first year of life was strongly influenced by having an elder sibling who died before the child was born. When the deceased elder sibling was born within two years of the birth of the child, the risk of mortality was more than doubled in 34 out of 35 countries and more than trebled in 26 of them. Surprisingly, the impact of this "indication of the level of mortality within the family" was less strongly related to mortality in the second year of life and, on average, had no influence on mortality in the third, fourth, and fifth years of life.

These results have drawn considerable attention. Major efforts have been undertaken to estimate the potential impact of changes in fertility on infant and child mortality (Trussell and Pebley, 1984) and to disseminate the agreeable finding that longer birth intervals lead to an increase in child survival (Maine and McNamara, 1983; Black, 1987). Trussell and Pebley used the Hobcraft and others (1983) results along with some other studies to simulate the effects of changing spacing patterns, as well as those that would result from changing the distribution of births according to maternal age and birth order. They note that there is little that family planning programmes can expect to do to "improve" the age pattern of births and that the estimated elevation in risk for high-parity births may be spacing effects in disguise. Overall, after listing numerous caveats, they conclude that "there is a definite potential for reducing infant, child, and maternal mortality through increased use of contraception" and that although these effects are modest, they are certainly important.

Is there any basis for skepticism? To date, three main reservations have been voiced concerning these results and their interpretation. The first is that the two studies by Hobcraft and others (1983, 1985) place large demands on the accuracy of retrospective pregnancy histories. Although the evaluations of World Fertility Surveys were reassuring (Chidambaram, Cleland, and Verma, 1983), it was never expected that the questionnaires would result in accurate enumeration and dating of the births and deaths of children of poor, illiterate women in all parts of the world. There are two ways that pregnancy histories can be in error: events can be omitted from the record or, if recorded, they can be dated incorrectly. Omissions of deceased children and misdating of the births of deceased children, it has been argued (Potter, 1988a), accounts for at least some of the estimated effect of spacing patterns, and for a larger fraction of the estimated effect of the death of a preceding child.

An unpublished work with an obviously deficient set of pregnancy histories collected in Jordan has confirmed the notion that errors in the data are something to worry about. The 1983 Jordan Fertility and Family Health Survey (JFFHS) showed a level of mortality only about one half as great as that recorded for an overlapping time frame by the earlier WFS. In this survey, it was also possible to establish that births of deceased children were dated less accurately than live births. 2/ When models similar to those estimated by Hobcraft and others (1985) were estimated with the JFFHS data, they showed that short inter-birth intervals were associated with even greater relative risks of mortality than was the case in the WFS.

The second reservation concerning the Hobcraft and others results is that the models are incomplete and possibly misspecified. There is nothing in the equations that reveals how longer birth intervals are related to decreased risks of mortality. Trussell and Pebley (1984) conjectured that at least some of the observed association was due to breast-feeding, which would lead to both longer intervals and improved prospects of survival. Palloni and Millman (1986) sought to measure the mediating role of breast-feeding with WFS data from 12 Latin American countries. Their main findings were that taking account of breast-feeding does not weaken the association between birth-spacing and child survival; the effect of breast-feeding on survival declines as the age of the child increases (breast-feeding was important to survival only in the first six months of life); and both breast-feeding and the length of the following birth interval were more strongly associated with survival among those groups (e.g., the less educated) where mortality is highest.

Since breast-feeding does not seem to mediate the effect of birth spacing on child survival in the models estimated by Palloni and Millman, one might conclude that only relatively prolonged breast-feeding affects interval length and that this phenomenon has no influence on survival in the pertinent age segments. But what if the women who curtailed breast-feeding in these countries were those who had the best access to medical care? The observed diminution in the effect of breast-feeding on survival that occurred as the focus shifted from earlier to later age segments may well have been the product of such positive selection. 3/

Experience with a fertility survey conducted in Mexico has suggested that a mother's use of modern maternal health care is correlated with both breast-feeding and contraceptive use, that contraceptive use is inversely associated with both the initiation and the continuation of breast-feeding, and that contraception rather than breast-feeding is the dominant influence on the length of birth intervals (Potter, Mojarro, and Nunez, 1987a, 1987b). To provide an illustration of these problematic relationships, the data were used to estimate models of use of pre-natal care, a hospital-based delivery, a medical examination of the newborn child, and inoculation of the newborn child with polio, DPT, and measles vaccines (Potter, 1988a). The predictor variables were, alternately, whether the mother had breast-fed her most recently born child to the age of six months, whether she had breast-fed this child to the age of 12 months, and whether she had ever used an efficient modern method of contraception.

The estimated probability that a child's mother had received each one of these services, after adjusting for selected values of the same controls used by Palloni and Millman, was as follows. The probability that a mother who breast-fed her last child for less than six months had pre-natal care is 1.63 times that of a mother who breast-fed for at least six months. The relative risk of either a hospital delivery or an infant checkup is slightly over two for the same breast-feeding categories. A very similar pattern of differential use of these three services is found between children who were breast-fed for at least 12 months and those who were weaned before their first birthday. The children in the latter group were also slightly more likely to have been inoculated with polio, DPT, and measles vaccines. Finally, ever-use of at least one of the four major modern methods of contraception was strongly associated with greater use of all four services.

These results suggest that according to Palloni and Millman's WFS data, any legitimate relation between prolonged breast-feeding and survival beyond the age of six months was masked by the empirical association that exists between breast-feeding and use of health care. The other suggestion is that in both the Palloni and Millman models and those estimated by Hobcraft and others, the association between use of modern contraception and use of other types of health services produced a spurious association between birth interval length and infant and child mortality.

A further problem with the specification of the models estimated by Hobcraft, McDonald, and Rutstein (1983 and 1985) is that they do not control for prematurity. Using data from Sweden, Hungary, and the United States, Miller (1989) has shown that prematurity accounts for a large part of the association between the length of the preceding birth interval and perinatal mortality. In this analysis, controlling for the length of gestation dramatically reduced the excess risk associated with a birth interval of less than one year in length. While the study is not based on data from developing countries, and instruments such as the WFS did not collect data on the length of gestation, the results provide yet another reason for supposing that the Hobcraft and others estimates of the effect of birth-spacing on child survival are biased upwards.

The third and last reservation that has been raised regarding the influence of family-building patterns on infant mortality concerns whether the postulated mechanisms actually operate in practice. Bongaarts (1987) has recently taken the Hobcraft and others (1985) estimates of excess risk, adjusted some of them, and then investigated whether the distribution of births by age, parity, and spacing status improves in the contemporary cross-section of developing countries as contraceptive prevalence increases. He assumes that births to teenagers are subject to 24 per cent excess risk in the first year of life, first births to 62 per cent excess risk, births of order seven or higher to 21 per cent excess risk, and births following an interval of less than two years to 30 per cent excess risk.

After piecing together evidence concerning the composition of births in countries with varying contraceptive prevalence rates, Bongaarts then calculates how much the infant mortality rate of countries at various stages of the fertility transition is raised by the occurrence of births in high-risk groups. The somewhat surprising result is that excess infant mortality is 30.4 per cent in countries where the contraceptive prevalence rate is less than 10, 32.0 per cent in countries where prevalence is between 10 and 40, and 37.5 per cent where prevalence is between 40 and 65. The anomaly results from the fact that while high-parity births represent a substantially smaller percentage of all births where prevalence is greatest, first births represent a much higher fraction of the average cohort in these countries. The total effect of the changing composition of births by spacing status is relatively small, but it, too, goes in the "wrong" direction, since average birth intervals seem to shrink slightly as prevalence increases.

Some controversy has arisen in the wake of these findings, and several reactions to Bongaarts's paper have since appeared. Trussell (1988) has called Bongaarts to task for accepting cross-sectional results at face value, and has suggested that the calculus used is inappropriate. He argues that the infant mortality rate is a misleading measure of mortality when examining the effect of family planning because an increase in the incidence of first-order births is an inevitable result of the successful use of contraception. The other point he makes is that the abandonment of traditional spacing practices that is concomitant with modernization is being attributed (unfairly) in Bongaarts's analysis to the change in contraceptive prevalence.

Another reaction to the Bongaarts piece alleges that too much attention has been focused on the influence of the composition of age, parity, and spacing status of births on infant and child mortality, and that attention should be directed towards a number of other possible mediating mechanisms

(Potter, 1988b). The neglected effects highlighted are those that family planning may have on the social composition of birth cohorts, on the avoidance of high-risk pregnancies, and on the affective relationships between mothers and children. The reasons for taking the social composition of births into account are that mortality varies greatly according to the occupation of the head of the household, education, and other indicators of social class in most developing countries; and that this composition is apt to change substantially over the course of the fertility transition. Other things being equal, fertility will decline first among the rich and well-educated, and only well into the transition will this tendency towards a less-favourable social composition reverse itself. The incremental effect of government-sponsored family planning programmes is presumably to minimize this effect by increasing access to services and helping the poor to catch up with the rich.

A second way that family planning may influence infant (and maternal) mortality is by bringing about a reduction in the proportion of children born to mothers whose health status is poor or impaired. The idea is similar to that underlying the usual focus on age, parity, and spacing, but the mechanism is a direct behavioural one. There are a number of potentially recognizable indicators of excess maternal and foetal risk, such as a history of difficulties with pregnancy or labour, previous complications of delivery, diabetes, hypertension, jaundice, malaria, chronic infections, iron-deficiency anaemia, and malnutrition (Haaga, 1987). Whether women who have experienced such symptoms, conditions, or events are disproportionately represented among family planning acceptors depends on the ability of both mothers and medical practitioners to recognize excess risk and on the salience of risk as a motivation to avoid becoming pregnant. Since there is ample evidence of the latter and since the prevention of high-risk pregnancies is a high priority of medical practitioners, it may frequently be the case that an increasing level of contraceptive prevalence leads to a reduction in the proportion of high-risk pregnancies.

The final mediating mechanism identified in this comment is a change in parenting practices and in the affective relationships between a mother and her children. Caldwell has repeatedly emphasized the importance of family relationships to child survival and has often argued that family planning programmes are likely to undermine the nature of the traditional family (Caldwell, Reddy, and Caldwell, 1983; Caldwell, 1986). To illustrate these effects, the author points to the experience of China, where it is frequently observed that national fertility policy has increased parental demand for child health care and has led to an increase in the amount of care that parents lavish on their children.

Health care and contraceptive acceptance

The possibility that the "quality of health" exerts an influence on the fertility ideals and reproductive behaviour of individual couples has long been recognized. A considerable effort has been made over the past 20 years to investigate both the sequential responses to actual child deaths and the effects of the perceived level of child survival (Heer, 1983). It has been hypothesized that both types of relationships will depend on the perceived psychic and monetary costs of birth control and on the difference between the "number of surviving children demanded and their maximal supply."

Perhaps the most appealing notion advanced in this literature concerns the connection between the level of mortality in a community or family and the amount of emotional energy that parents are willing to invest in their children. The supposition is that where mortality levels are high one might expect parents, in the interest of self-protection, to place relatively little emotional involvement in any one child. On the other hand, low rates of mortality promote low fertility by encouraging intensive emotional investment with each child (Heer and Smith, 1968). The difficulty in finding strong empirical support for this proposition is, of course, that this very same emotional investment is probably an extremely important determinant of child survival (Sagan, 1987).

Rather than attempt an updated review of the mixed evidence for replacement effects and other influences of mortality level on demand for children, the focus here is on a less obvious influence that the "quality of health," particularly the "quality of health care," exerts on reproductive behaviour. By far the most important proximate determinant of the variation in the fertility rates shown in table 1 is the utilization of contraception, particularly modern methods such as the pill, the intra-uterine device (IUD) and surgical sterilization. There are both theoretical and empirical grounds for thinking that exposure to modern medical ideas and contacts with modern medical institutions and practitioners are important determinants of the practice of such methods.

A recurrent finding in the family planning literature is that women frequently are afraid of what modern contraceptives will do to them. Many of the sociologists who had close personal involvement in the early efforts to promote family planning in third-world settings were very much aware of the fear and distrust with which women in these settings regarded most modern family planning methods and of the pernicious role of rumours concerning their health consequences and ineffectiveness (e. g., Stycos, 1955) In a book on communication strategies for family planning, Rogers (1973) took up the topic of rumours in detail, commenting on the nature of rumours, the type of people who start them, and strategies for their control. Finally, Bogue (1975), trying to encapsulate the major problems of family planning in a few categories, listed "fears of permanent damage to health from prolonged use of the pill, IUD, or other contraceptives" as the number one obstacle to success in this realm.

Anthropologists have frequently come to the same conclusion. In a study of the obstacles to family planning practice among the urban poor in Morocco, Mernissi (1975) concluded that "failures to control fertility appear much less at the level of motivation than at the level of practice," later noting that "the principal impediment to the adoption of modern methods appeared in the interviews to be the prevalence in the community of negative opinion about modern methods – terrifying rumours detailing the disasters awaiting the woman daring to take the pill or use an IUD", Shedlin and Hollerbach (1981) provided detailed information concerning the perceptions that women in a rural Mexican community had concerning modern methods and the cultural beliefs that led them to perceive these methods as potential threats to their health and even to life itself. More recently, Tucker (1986) observed that in rural Peru, "the fear of being incapacitated and unable to perform daily chores becomes a major obstacle to the use of modern contraception."

What factors are most likely to determine the perceived riskiness of modern methods, and how much of an obstacle are they to the adoption of contraception? The degree and type of medicalization that prevails at the societal, community, and individual levels may be among the most important factors. It seems reasonable to suppose that perceptions of the safety and moral acceptability of modern contraceptive methods will be affected by the consumption of pills, injections, and surgical procedures for ailments of all kinds; the number of medical consultations; and the prestige and authority that is accorded to the modern medical profession. At one remove would be the accessibility of pharmacies, private practitioners, government clinics, and hospitals, as well as social insurance schemes that make these services available at little or no monetary cost to a segment of the population.

The argument is that the presence of modern medicine per se will reduce fear of contraception by legitimating body care, the use of medicines, surgery, and the self-control of organic functions. And while family planning programmes will often motivate medical practitioners in public institutions to deliver information and services, doctors in both private and public institutions may be willing to take on this responsibility even in the absence of such stimulae. What is more, as the medical profession grows in stature, there is apt to be a nearly universal tendency for other agents, such as those of religious institutions, to cede their authority to advise and arbitrate on matters related to human reproduction. 4/

The mechanisms and processes postulated in the preceding section meld well with the evidence advanced by those who argue that ideas and their diffusion are the essential determinants of fertility decline. In a recent review, Cleland and Wilson (1987) dispute the importance of "the changing balance between costs and benefits of childbearing" and argue that there is a widening gap between "demand theories" of fertility and the rapidly accumulating evidence concerning the fertility transitions taking place throughout the developing world. They note that these transitions have been too large and too sudden to have been accounted for by structural change.

The ideas that Cleland and Wilson suspect are critical concern the means of fertility control, and they emphasize the "danger of underestimating the fundamental nature of the change from reproduction without conscious control to a regime of deliberate regulation of births within marriage", On the basis of the evidence referred to earlier, part of that sentence could be rewritten to read "from a reproductive regime in which only dangerous and/or ineffective traditional methods were at hand to one in which modern methods were the dominant means of fertility regulation".

The proposition that medicalization promotes the spread of new ideas concerning birth control and has a causal influence on the acceptance of modern contraceptive methods is, like some other interrelations between health and fertility, difficult to document empirically. A fairly large number of single-round retrospective fertility or contraceptive prevalence surveys conducted in the last 15 years have collected information on both the respondent's use of maternal and child health services and her use of different family planning methods. But while it is a simple matter to assess the statistical association that exists between one type of variable and another -- for example, between use of pre-natal care during the last completed pregnancy and current use of pills, injectables, IUDs, or sterilization -- such an association does not lend itself to a causal interpretation. It might well be spurious, resulting only from the fact that both types of behaviour have a large number of determinants in common. 5/

A recent attempt to grapple with these difficulties relied on data from a single-round retrospective survey carried out in rural Mexico in 1981, supplemented with information from detailed information collected from medical practitioners who served the population in the survey sampling frame (Potter and others, 1987a; Potter, Gribble, and Wong, 1989). It was a context in which fertility had recently begun to decline from a very high level. The decline was driven by an increase in contraceptive prevalence and took place while there was a substantial expansion in the coverage of the two major public health institutions and a major effort to implement a national family planning programme. At the time of the survey, the main source of maternal care in Mexican villages was still the partera empirica or traditional birth attendant, but an increasing number of women were making use of clinics and hospitals for pre-natal care and delivery.

In estimating the relationship between use of health care and contraceptive acceptance among respondents to the individual survey, two different strategies were used to circumvent the difficulties posed by using an endogenous variable as a covariate. The primary predictor variable of interest in these models was use of pre-natal care or, alternatively, place of delivery. 6/ In one analysis, the use of these services was simply aggregated at the level of the community in which the respondent lived, creating variables referring to the proportion of women making use of particular types of care. For both pre-natal check-ups and attention at delivery, a distinction was drawn between care provided by (a) public institutions, (b) private doctors, and (c) traditional practitioners or relatives. In the second analysis, simultaneous equation methods were used to estimate the influence of these same community-level predictors. Here the exogenous variables referred to various aspects of the community, including the presence and/or proximity of health clinics and hospitals. The main result of both analyses was that the coverage of public care in the community (whether pre-natal or at delivery) was closely associated with an individual respondent's practice of a modern contraceptive method. The estimated effect of private care, although often significant, was much smaller than that of public care. Public care had a particularly strong influence on acceptance of both the IUD and female surgical sterilization, the two methods that practitioners reported were especially feared by women in this population.

What about the associations and relationships that are to be found in other countries and other parts of the world? Two other surveys that have been examined in a preliminary way were carried out in Jordan and in the Brazilian Northeast. In each case there is a close association between the use of maternal and child health (MCH) services and use of contraception after adjusting for the various other available indicators of social and economic status. Where each of these surveys differs from the rural Mexican data is with respect to the differential effect of private as compared with public care on contraceptive choice. In both Jordan and Brazil, respondents who made use of private care were more likely to be using a more medical, higher-technology method than were respondents who obtained MCH services from public institutions. In Jordan the predominant higher-technology method was the IUD, while in Brazil it was female sterilization. This is exactly the reverse of the pattern found in Mexico. The disparity most likely stems at least in part from the difference in the strength of the role that the public sector plays in promoting contraception in the respective countries.

Macro-level connections between health and population growth

The health sector and family planning programmes

The individual-level relationships between the use of health care and contraceptive acceptance discussed in the preceding section have a direct analogue at higher levels of aggregation. The experience of particular countries supports the notion that modernizing maternal health care leads to contraceptive practice. In such diverse contexts as China, Thailand, and Costa Rica, a rapid transformation of maternity services predated an unusually rapid adoption of modern methods. Even in Kenya, high utilization of maternal and child health services offered by Protestant missionary hospitals seems to have been the critical antecedent of the surprising acceptance of contraception in the Chogoria region (Goldberg and others, 1987). Lower levels of contraceptive prevalence in other regions of Kenya where Catholic missionaries have provided extensive maternal and child health services serve to underscore the role of the orientation of medical personnel towards family planning.

From a sectoral perspective, a strong health care system is an important asset to programmatic attempts to promote family planning and reduce population growth. Hospitals, clinics, pharmacies, and community health posts all constitute potential delivery points for contraceptive methods, and the staff of such installations have the potential to educate and motivate their patients or clients regarding the practice of birth control. Those who provide maternity services have been said to be particularly strategic. They are in regular contact with the target population of fertile women, and at a time -- during the pregnancy, labour, and puerperium -- when these mothers may be especially receptive to messages regarding the importance of health and other benefits that could be obtained by postponing the next pregnancy or putting it off completely (Taylor, 1966).

The longstanding discussion of whether family planning activities should be organized into an autonomous, "vertical" programme or incorporated into existing public health infrastructures has centred on determining the appropriate course of action when the health care system is either weak or non-responsive. In that case, the options have been either to build up the health sector so that it can deliver services effectively or to go outside the sector and establish stand-alone services (Simmons and Phillips, 1987). That the easier and more economical course of establishing a vertical programme has sometimes been chosen in no way negates the advantages of integration in situations where the health care system is both strong and responsive.

Rapid population growth and the health sector

Studies of the impact of alternative population trajectories on the health sector in developing countries have been few in number. Several of the better-known analyses were conducted in the early 1970s and referred to Sri Lanka and Thailand (Jones, 1975; Jones and Selvaratnam, 1972; Jones and Boonpratuang, 1973). They arrived at several seemingly robust conclusions. First, there are savings in health sector expenditures to be realized from reduced population growth. Simply maintaining a constant level of coverage and service takes fewer resources in the "low" population projections than in the "high" or "medium" projections. Moreover, if the goal is to improve the ratio of health services and personnel to population, the task is easier with reduced fertility. But these savings are not astronomical. In one of the studies, the expenditures required over a 30-year period with a low population trajectory were 83 per cent of those required in the high trajectory (Jones, 1975).

The second conclusion is that the change in the age distribution occasioned by fertility decline is approximately neutral in its effect on the demand for health services. There are fewer infants and small children and fewer deliveries, both proportionately and absolutely. But the proportion of the population over age 50 or 60, after which there is a marked increase in the demand for services, increases. Moreover, although the average health care needs per capita will not change greatly, the kind of health care needed will alter considerably. The diseases that affect the young, such as diarrhoeal diseases, respiratory infections, and tetanus, require very different preventive and curative health care than the chronic ailments that afflict the aged, such as heart disease, cancer, poor eyesight, and rheumatism (Jones, 1990).

Models of the health sector often involve disaggregation of the population by region as well as by age and sex. Since service ratios are usually many times higher in the cities than in the countryside, urbanization implies a sharp increase in health expenditures. To achieve improvements in coverage when a population is both growing rapidly and becoming more urban requires vast increases in the number of nurses, doctors, and auxiliaries being trained. It follows that the proportion of gross domestic product (GDP) devoted to health also has to increase. Primary health care approaches that stress the use of paramedical personnel and greater community involvement may be seen as an attempt to increase coverage and improve the quality of health in a population without generating such increases in expenditures (Bender and Pitkin, 1987).

Effective primary health care policies oriented towards the infectious diseases of infancy and childhood offer some promise of increasing the quality of health in populations with high fertility and mortality. They will not, however, be sufficient in the many developing countries where fertility has declined and an epidemiological transition is well under way. In Latin America and East and South-East Asia, the legacy of high rates of growth and fertility in earlier decades --- a very rapid absolute and proportionate increase in the elderly population --- poses an enormous challenge to the health sector.

In Brazil, for example, the proportion of the population over age 60 is expected to increase from 6 per cent in 1980 to 13 per cent by the year 2020. 7/ This shift in the age distribution will exacerbate a pronounced change in the proportion of mortality attributable to chronic diseases, a trend that has been under way for some time. As life expectancy in Brazil increased from 41 years in 1940 to 51 years in 1960 and to 59 years in 1980, deaths due to infectious and parasitic diseases fell from 80 per cent to 30 per cent to 8 per cent of all deaths in those respective years. From 1980 to 2020, the absolute number of deaths due to chronic diseases should increase by 60 per cent due to the expected change in the age distribution.

Death rates due to heart disease, stroke, and cancers have not fallen over the past 40 years, and they may well increase in the future. There will almost certainly be a rise in lung cancer as result of the large increase in the consumption of tobacco. And there is reason to think that other risk factors for the chronic diseases, such as poor diet, lack of exercise, and pollution, are also increasing. At the same time, the Brazilian population is still beleaguered by childhood malnutrition, infectious diseases, and a rate of infant mortality that is much higher than that of most other countries at a comparable level of industrialization. Moreover, the strain placed on the health care system by the increase in the elderly population will be compounded by the increases in the demand for medical services that are associated with urbanization, expansion of social security coverage, and increased exposure to physicians, hospitals, clinics, and pharmacies.

In contrast to the optimism regarding the prospects for improving child health in poor countries with high mortality, there is far less hope regarding the health of the elderly in countries that have already begun to progress through the demographic and epidemiological transitions. The prospects of being able to provide the needed curative care seem dim, at least without radical reforms in the ways that services are provided and financed. And conviction is lacking that, even in China, policies aimed at changing the prevalence of risk factors such as smoking are politically and economically viable.

Conclusion

By and large, the relations between health and population reviewed in this paper offer the promise that effective health and population policies can be mutually reinforcing. Policies that promote increased use of contraception should, partly but not exclusively through lengthening birth intervals, improve the health of mothers and children. And smaller numbers of births will make it easier to improve the coverage of maternal and child health services. On the other hand, it has been argued here that improving maternal health services should make it easier to promote family planning and reduce fertility. This prospect, which is in accord with the close association between fertility and mortality in the international cross-section noted at the outset, stands in marked contrast to the recurrent but often unspoken apprehension that health policies only serve to increase population growth and impede economic development.

Notes

1/   These authors were concerned that short preceding intervals were selectively initiated by deceased children who, in turn, could be expected to have siblings subject to elevated risks of death.

2/   As in the WFS, if a respondent was unable to supply even the calendar year in which a birth occurred, she was asked to date the birth in terms of how long ago the child was born. The vast majority of the birth dates of children who died were reported in this manner, while calendar month and year were supplied for most living children.

3/   Selection may also account for some of the observed positive impact of breast-feeding on survival in the first six months. Mothers who stopped breast-feeding at very early durations may have done so because their children were sick and thus at higher risk of mortality.

4/   There has been a definite shift of authority in this area from the Catholic priesthood towards the medical profession in Latin America, as has been documented for Brazil (Loyola and Quinteiro, 1982).

5/   Incorporating a large number of plausible "common causes" in a multivariate analysis would not solve this difficulty if some determinants were either left out or imperfectly measured.

6/   Other predictors included in the models as controls were the duration of the open interval; the mother's age, parity, and education; the husband's education and occupation; the floor and electrification of the dwelling; the proximity of the market town; the daily wage for agricultural labour in the community; and, in some models, the current breast-feeding status of the mother.

7/   The information on adult health in Brazil was kindly supplied by John Briscoe of the World Bank.

References

Bender, D. E. and K. Pitkin (1987). Bridging the gap: the village health
   worker as the cornerstone of the primary health care model. Social
   Science and Medicine, vol. 13A.

Black, M. (1987). Family planning: an essential ingredient of family health.
   Paper prepared for the International Conference on Better Health for
   Women and Children through Family Planning, Nairobi, Kenya, 5-9 October.

Bogue, D. (1975). Twenty-Five Communication Obstacles to the Success of
   Family Planning Programs. Chicago: University of Chicago Community and
   Family Study Center.

Bongaarts, J. (1987). Does family planning reduce infant mortality rates?
   Population and Development Review, vol. 13, No. 2, pp. 323-334.

Caldwell, J. (1986). Routes to low mortality in poor countries. Population
   and Development Review, vol. 12, No. 2, pp. 171-220.

_____, P. H. Reddy and Pat Caldwell (1983). The social component of
   mortality decline: an investigation in South India employing alternative
   methodologies. Population Studies, vol. 37, No. 2, pp. 185-205.

Chidambaram, V. C., J. G. Cleland and V. Verma (1983). Some aspects of WFS
   data quality: a preliminary assessment. World Fertility Survey
   Comparative Studies, No. 16. Voorburg: International Statistical
   Institute.

Cleland, J. G. and Z. A. Sathar (1984). The effect of birth spacing on
   childhood mortality in Pakistan. Population Studies, vol. 38,
   pp. 401-418.

_____ and C. Wilson (1987). Demand theories of the fertility
   transition: an iconoclastic view. Population Studies, vol. 41, pp. 5-30.

Goldberg, H. and others (1987). 1985 Chogoria Community Health Survey:
   report of principal findings, Chogoria Hospital and Centers for Disease
   Control. Mimeographed.

Haaga, J. G. (1987). Mechanisms for the association of maternal age, parity,
   and birthspacing with infant health. Unpublished background paper
   prepared for the NAS Working Group on the Health Consequences of
   Contraceptive Use and Controlled Fertility.

Heer, D. M. (1966). Economic development and fertility. Demography, vol. 3,
   pp. 423-444.

_____ D. M. (1983). Infant and child mortality and the demand for children. In <u>Determinants of Fertility in Developing Countries</u>, Rodolfo A. Bulatao and Ronald Lee, eds. New York: Academic Press.

_____, D. M. and D. O. Smith (1968). Mortality level, desired family size, and population increase. <u>Demography</u>, vol. 5, pp. 104--121.

Hobcraft, J. N., J. W. McDonald and S. O. Rutstein (1983). Child--spacing effects on infant and early child mortality. <u>Population Index</u>, vol. 49, pp. 585--618.

_____, J. W. McDonald and S. O. Rutstein (1985). Demographic determinants of infant and early child mortality: a comparative analysis. <u>Population Studies</u>, vol. 39, pp. 363--385.

Jones, G. W. (1975). Population growth and health and family planning. In <u>Population Growth and Development Planning</u>, W. C. Robinson, ed. New York: The Population Council, pp. 69--94.

_____ (1990). <u>Population Dynamics and Educational and Health Planning</u>. Paper prepared for the International Labour Office, Geneva.

_____ and C. Boonpratuang (1973). <u>The Effect of Population Growth and Urbanization on the Attainment of Public Health Goals in Thailand</u>. Bangkok: Manpower Planning Division, National Economic Development Board.

_____ and S. Selvaratnam (1972). <u>Population Growth and Economic Development in Ceylon</u>. Colombo: Hansa Publishers.

Lapham, R. J. and W. P. Mauldin (1984). Conditions of fertility decline in developing countries, 1965-1980.   Paper presented at the 1984 Annual Meeting of the Population Association of America.

Loyola, M. A. and M. Quinteiro. (1982) <u>Estudos de Populacao-VIII-Instituicoes e Reproducao</u>. Sao Paulo: CEBRAP.

Maine, D. and R. McNamara (1983). <u>Birth Spacing and Child Survival</u>. New York: Columbia University, Center for Population and Family Health.

Mernissi, F. (1975). Obstacles to family planning practice in urban Morocco. <u>Studies in Family Planning</u>, vol. 6, pp. 418--425.

Miller, Jane E. (1989) Is the relationship between birth interval and infant mortality real?   Evidence from three developed countries.   Paper presented at the 1989 Annual Meeting of the Population Association of America.

Nortman, D. (1974). Parental age as a factor in pregnancy outcome and child development. <u>Reports on Population/Family Planning</u>, No. 16. New York: The Population Council.

Palloni, A. and S. Millman (1986). Effects of inter-birth intervals and breast-feeding on infant and early childhood mortality. Population Studies, vol. 40, pp. 215-236.

Potter, J. E. (1988a). Birth spacing and child survival: a cautionary note regarding the evidence from the WFS. Population Studies, vol. 42, No. 3, pp. 443-450.

_____ (1988b). Does family planning reduce child mortality? An exchange. Population and Development Review, vol. 14, No. 1, pp. 179-187.

_____, J. Gribble and R. Wong (1989). Contraceptive choice and use of health care in rural Mexico. Paper presented at the 1989 Annual Meeting of the Population Association of America.

_____, O. Mojarro and L. Nunez (1987a). The influence of health care on contraceptive acceptance in rural Mexico. Studies in Family Planning, vol. 18, pp. 144-156.

_____ O. Mojarro, and L. Nunez (1987b) The influence of maternal health care on the prevalence and duration of breast-feeding in rural Mexico. Studies in Family Planning, vol. 18, No. 6, Part 1, pp. 309-319.

Rogers, E. M. (1973). Communication Strategies for Family Planning. New York: The Free Press.

Sagan, L. A. (1987). The Health of Nations: True Causes of Sickness and Well- being. New York: Basic Books.

Simmons, R. and J. Phillips (1987). The integration of family planning with health and development. In Organizing for Effective Family Planning Programs, R. J. Lapham and G. B. Simmons, eds. Washington, D.C.: National Academy Press.

Stycos, J. N. (1955). Birth control clinics in crowded Puerto Rico. In Health, Culture, and Community, B. D. Paul, ed. Chicago: University of Chicago Press.

Taylor, H. C. (1966). A family planning program related to maternity service. In Family Planning and Population Programs, B. Berelson and others, eds. Chicago: University of Chicago Press.

Trussell, J. (1988). Does family planning reduce infant mortality? An exchange. Population and Development Review, vol. 14, No. 1, pp. 171-178.

_____ and C. Hammerslough (1983). A hazards-model analysis of the covariates of infant and child mortality. Demography, vol. 20, pp. 1-26.

_____ and A. R. Pebley (1984) The potential impact of changes in fertility on infant, child, and maternal mortality. Studies in Family Planning, vol. 15, No. 6, Part 1. pp. 267-280.

Tucker, G. (1986). Barriers to modern contraceptive use in rural Peru. _Studies in Family Planning_, vol. 17, pp. 308-316.

United Nations (1988). _Mortality of Children Under Age 5_. Sales No. E.88.XIII.4.

Winikoff, B. (1983). The effects of birth spacing on child and maternal health. _Studies in Family Planning_, vol. 11, pp. 231-245.

Wolfers, D. and S. Scrimshaw (1975). Child survival and intervals between pregnancies in Guayaquil, Ecuador. _Population Studies_, vol. 29, No. 3. pp. 479-496.

World Bank (1988). _World Development Report, 1987_. Washington, DC: World Bank.

Chapter 9

Rapid population change and kinship : the effects of unstable demographic changes on Chinese kinship networks, 1750-2250

● E.A. Hammel, C. Mason, K. Wachter, F. Wang & H. Yang*

Introduction 1/

Socio–demographic micro–interactions

There are few interesting theories of human social behaviour that do not have implications for demographic conditions, and there are no interesting theories of demographic behaviour that do not reflect social and cultural considerations. Yet the interactions of these two analytically separate but empirically intertwined spheres are more often assumed, or modelled only at the macro level, than they are explored at the level of individual actors or those primary social units within which, most would agree, fundamental decision processes are carried out. Our interest is particularly attracted here to the way in which demographic regimes conspire to shape the availability pool of "relatives" (kin and affines) from which may be drawn those social actors who have mutual expectations of support under culture–specific conditions. We know, of course, that mutually supporting persons are not always genealogically related and that genealogically related persons are not always mutually supporting. Nevertheless, most people in the world (perhaps other than social scientists) entertain the notion that some subset of genealogically related persons is the recourse of first resort when support is sought. Therefore we ask here how demographic conditions might

*Graduate Group in Demography, University of California, Berkeley, California, United States of America. The authors are indebted to Jiang Lin and Christophe LeFranc for assistance in checking simulation results. Support for this research was provided by the Graduate Group in Demography at the University of California at Berkeley, the Quantitative Anthropology Laboratory at Berkeley, and the Office of Information Systems and Technology at Berkeley in disbursing funds from a grant from Cray Research, Inc. Support for original development of the SOCSIM programmes was provided by the National Science Foundation. None of these persons or institutions is responsible for errors of fact or interpretation. The results are presented cautiously, conscious of a proverb from the author's favorite source: "There is no point in picking up a stone only to drop it on your own feet."

influence social action by providing more or less of such genealogical kin. In this paper we continue a line of research earlier directed at household composition in historical England (Hammel and Wachter, 1977; Wachter and others, 1978); kinship networks for the aged in the United States (Hammel and others, 1981); the effect of incest taboos on population viability (Hammel and Hutchinson, 1974; Hammel and others, 1979, 1981); the effect of interspousal differences in age or other characteristics on rates of consanguineal marriage (Hammel, Hutchinson, and Wachter, 1976); and the effect of propinquity on types of consanguineal marriage (Gilbert and Hammel, 1963, 1966).

Here we explore, through examination of one historical and realistic example, the effects of rapid population change on kinship networks. Although the subject of the symposium is rapid population growth, we regard rapid growth as only one aspect of rapid change. Furthermore, we consider the effects on kinship networks to be the outcome of changes in mortality or fertility, or of both, so that the direction and rate of growth itself are best regarded as epiphenomena of these more basic, underlying causes. While the direction and rate of growth as such may be useful variables for the understanding of exogenous macro-effects (for example, on the economy or the natural environment), we find concentration on the underlying changes in mortality and fertility preferable when considering micro-effects endogenous to population composition itself.

Aspects of the modelling of demographic phenomena

There are two ways to model phenomena. One is to describe relationships in a fashion we will here call <u>analytic</u> or <u>macrosimulation</u>, sometimes with natural language but most frequently with mathematical expressions of the relationships of quantities with respect to time or space. Such modelling is usually deterministic; that is, it takes no account of chance variation. The unit of analysis is the population itself, even though it may be obvious that the underlying processes are at a lower level. Examples in our own area of concern would be any model life table, or Richard Easterlin's largely verbal formulation of the implications for fertility behaviour of the relative sizes of adjacent cohorts. Another would be the Club of Rome or Global 2000 graphical modelling of the relationships between population and resources, or any of the more explicitly mathematical models of similar relationships. Of particular importance is the recent development of family status life tables, since these target the same phenomena we address here in a different way. Such models are almost always at the aggregate level, addressing central tendencies and seldom paying heed to intrapopulation variability, because the unit of analysis is the population itself. We do not here distinguish purely analytic modelling, for example with the use of integral calculus, from macro-simulation with the use of computers, because the latter is often only the numerical working out of the former.

The second method is micro-simulation. In micro-simulation the unit of analysis is smaller than the population under consideration; it can consist of regions, communities, families, or individuals. The technique is to posit relationships at a very detailed level and to step through the execution of those relationships in discrete units of time, often allowing independently determined events to interact, observing and recording the results.

Micro-simulation is a tool increasingly used in complex sciences and engineering, such as theoretical chemistry or aerodynamics or the design of electronic circuits. It can be deterministic, but in the application here it is stochastic, taking account of chance variation. It requires the use of computing machinery, often of an advanced kind.

Micro-simulation has several advantages and drawbacks. First, it is indispensable when the relationships between simulated objects are complexly multidimensional, so that the use of natural language or of ordinary mathematics is too difficult or involves too many simplifying assumptions. Second, micro-simulation is invaluable when interest lies not only in central tendencies but also in variability, for aggregate models cannot yield information on variability, and the study of variance with analytical models is often intractable or involves unwarranted assumptions. Third, at every step of model construction this method forces clear decisions about the nature of the posited relationships, because computer programmes are intolerant of inspecificity. The superiority of the technique over ordinary social science prose or its pseudo-mathematized forms in the prevention of self-deception is remarkable. But it has a cost. It is expensive in the time required to specify the models. It requires expert programming effort. So much information can be generated that either much thought must be given to what to discard or more time must be allowed for data reduction. If models are stochastic, observations must be taken a sufficient number of times to achieve some desired level of sampling reliability. It can be expensive due to the purchase of machinery or the costs of machine time. It is also, and this is perhaps the greatest danger, so seductively simple at the level of detailed specification that the researcher can easily become lost chasing phantom realities or lose sight of the major theoretical problems that should be informing the research.

Stochastic micro-simulation is a form of experimental method intended to test ideas about relationships between kinds of entities. It is not a simulacrum designed to discover what actual events will occur or would have occurred if something had been different. Consider, for example, a micro-simulation of the stock market, operating according to some theory of such markets as are propounded in textbooks or voiced over cocktails. It would be foolish to expect the price established by a single execution of the micro-simulation for some stock in tomorrow's trading actually to be realized. There could be two reasons for the "failure". The theory specifying the relations might be wrong. The theory might be correct but the operation of chance so important that a single execution might give results very wide of the mark. We can attempt to correct the last condition in two ways: We can execute the simulation many times and examine both average behaviour and variability for particular stocks, or we can aggregate results for classes of stocks. But in any case, what we are testing with the simulation is not the stock market but a theory about the stock market. The simulation results can lead us to describe what the market would look like if the theory were correct; it cannot tell us what the market did look like or will look like. If we were traders, the more money we made by relying on the theory, the more we would believe it; most traders use some theory, believing or correcting from experience. We simulators can test market theories without risk. If traders want to test our theories in actuality, they may do so, but then they are no longer simulating.

The SOCSIM programs

History of the SOCSIM programs

The SOCSIM ("social simulation") programmes are based on early work by Gilbert and Hammel (1963, 1966) that paralleled similar efforts by Kunstadter and others (1963). Concretely, they were an adaptation of earlier work growing out of efforts by Orcutt and others (1961), conducted by Horvitz and others (MS), Giesbrecht and Ranney (1968), and Lachenbruch and others (1968). The SOCSIM programmes were fully documented and made publicly available in Hammel and others (1976). Similar models have been used and their results reported, but apart from Howell and Lehotay's AMBUSH (1978), and in some degree the recent work of Watkins and others (1987) and Zeng (1986, 1988), their mechanics have seldom been presented in sufficient detail to permit methodological evaluation (Ruggles, 1987; Menken, 1985; MacCluer, 1967, 1968, 1973; MacCluer and others, 1971). It is uncommonly easy to produce results that are an unintended artifact of a programmer's tricks rather than of the interaction of intended assumptions; only a detailed description of the programmes and public availability of the computer code allow the necessary evaluation.

General structure of SOCSIM 2/

SOCSIM works by accepting an initial population of notional individuals having some desired age/sex structure--for example, a stable population structure from any standard model life table. The individuals have no necessary characteristics other than age and sex. Using tables of demographic rates specified by the user, SOCSIM assigns a demographic event and date thereof to each individual through an event competition in which each individual has computed all possible events, and the earliest of these is the one that is scheduled to occur. The "losing" or later events are ignored. SOCSIM then begins to step through time, month by month, executing the scheduled event for each individual and then scheduling that individual's next event in the same manner. In any month, individuals are selected in random order from those who have an event scheduled in that month. Men and women can be scheduled for death, marriage, or (if married) divorce. Women can also be scheduled for giving birth. Whenever any event other than death occurs to an individual, a new event competition is held for that person and the next event to occur is scheduled for that individual. Some events occurring to one person also have implications for another. For example, when a married person dies, the marital status of the spouse changes; since birth and death rates are marital-status specific, a new event competition must be held for the surviving spouse (according to sex) under the newly prevailing rates.

SOCSIM simulates the events of birth, marriage, divorce, and death. It does not simulate the more detailed events of the reproductive cycle such as ovulation, lactation, or other components of the model set forth by Bongaarts and Potter (1983), although in principle these could be prepended to the birth simulation routines. Similarly, it does not simulate migration other than that involved in marital migration between subpopulations. Our choice of events to simulate has been conditioned by the level of the problems we were attacking and by the availability of plausible rates for these events in the context of those problems. Some critics of our earlier procedures (Fitch, 1980; Willigan and Lynch, 1982; Ruggles, 1987) have stressed the invention of rates for unknowable events in their pursuit of an elusive reality, a pursuit we declined to join. We cannot reiterate too often the most important lesson of simulation research: the pursuit of reality by the construction of a simulacrum must not be permitted to lead to specifications that are accepted as realistic even though they are based on unknowables, and it cannot be permitted to lead to the construction of hidden or obscure logical paths. No result is acceptable if it cannot be tracked by hand through the recorded life histories of the notional individuals. It is better to have a clearly delineated artificial path that tests a theory than an obscure one that pretends to mirror reality. Clarity, in this instance, is more important than vague truth, because only clarity can be falsified.

When an individual is born, it is recorded into the population, as are the identities of its parents. When it marries, its spouse's identity is recorded. If it is a member of a specific social group (according to some user-defined criterion), that too is recorded; demographic rates can be made specific to social groups if they are interpreted as subpopulations with different demographic regimes. Expectations of intermarriage between such subpopulations can be specified and relations of endogamy/exogamy and marital alliance thus tested. The potential for migration (other than by marriage) between subpopulations exists but is not implemented here. If the social group of choice for the simulation is something like a household, the membership of households can be maintained and later analysed. At the end of the simulation or at any intermediate point or points, the records of these procedures can be examined to recover the demographic structure of the population, the genealogical connections of individuals, the constitution of the social groupings, and the like.

There are two points of interest for the problems here addressed. The first is that SOCSIM is a "closed" simulation model. In a closed simulation model, all of the individuals entering into population processes are recorded as notional individuals who are either in the initial population or born into the population. By contrast, in an "open" model like the original POPSIM of Horvitz and others, individuals can be created when required. But for the reckoning of kinship or the investigation of marriage markets, all interpersonal links must be known, the population must be bounded, and a closed model is dictated. (There are alternatives, but they are complex and have undesirable consequences; compare Smith, 1987.) The second point is that the only event retained for individuals in SOCSIM is the next event to occur. Some other simulation models generate all of the events that might occur and execute them in order, with death of course constituting a definitive exit. For example, a woman might be scheduled for marriage, the births of all of her children, a divorce, a remarriage, and death, and all of these would occur when scheduled. This kind of advance scheduling is most appropriate in one-sex models, but it is cumbersome when there is any interaction between demographic events or between demographic events and the sociological characteristics or milieu of the individuals. Finally, if demographic events are contingent on characteristics like the kinship constitution of a household (e.g., the eldest daughter must marry first), we have no choice but to fall back on the simplest of procedures, a month–by–month simulation of the events for the population. The cost we pay for renewed event competitions every time an event occurs is small, given the great speed of floating point computation in modern computers, and it pales beside the danger of more complex algorithms that cannot simply plod ahead, month by month.

Kinship networks: an example from China

Introduction

The SOCSIM programmes are employed here in an exploration of the consequences of irregular population change for the structure of Chinese kinship networks, circa 1750–2150. Kinship networks, in the sense of genealogical sets, have as their proximate cause the age structure of a population, since it is the distribution of persons by age and sex, linked by relations of consanguinity and affinity, that constitutes the kinship network structure. Underlying this age distribution are the demographic rates that give rise to it. Under conditions of demographic stability and therefore of unchanging age structures, kinship networks must themselves also remain unchanging on average. Given knowledge of these rates, expected numbers of kin of particular types, by age, for persons of particular sex, by age, can be calculated analytically (Goodman and others, 1974, 1975; Pullum, 1987). The problem of how to calculate the variances of these numbers has not been solved analytically. Furthermore, the estimation of even the expected numbers of kin under conditions of instability seems approachable at the moment only through micro–simulation. The simulation must be capable of reckoning kinship relationships (and thus is most conveniently a closed model simulation), and it must be capable of introducing any desired number of age–, status–, and sex–specific rate changes over time. There are alternatives in successive stable–state estimates from family status life tables, but these methods seem to us more constraining and less flexible. We believe that it would be virtually impossible to obtain useful cross–sections of kinship relationships in a population with a history of population instability except through micro–simulation methods.

For many purposes, the ideal unit of analysis is the household, as it provides the best estimate of the social unit with minimal boundaries and maximal corporacy (Hammel, 1984; Wachter and others, 1978; Zeng, 1986, 1988); but for others it is the kinship network, as it is the sampling universe from which support personnel are ordinarily drawn (Hammel and others, 1981; Menken, 1985; Watkins and others, 1987). We focus here on kinship networks in order to give a simpler example than would be possible if household formation rules also had to be constructed and simulated.

Some general expectations of the effects of changes in demographic rates on kinship structures may be easily imagined. Higher levels of fertility should generate larger sibling sets, _ceteris paribus_. Under these circumstances, individuals will have more kin of all kinds except for lineal ascendants; that is, they will have more descendants and more collateral relatives at all generational levels. Lower levels of mortality will preserve such relationships and will in particular extend the coexistence of persons, so that the lifetime experience of living with kin will be prolonged. Combinations of these conditions will lead to different outcomes. If fertility and mortality are both high, many kin will be born but few will survive, so both the expectation of having kin and the duration of coexistence with them will be depressed. The paucity of kin will be exacerbated if fertility is low and mortality is high. We would also expect that those combinations of rates leading to rapid rates of growth would generate rather more descending lineal and descending or co-equal collateral linkages than ascending collateral linkages, while population decline would generate the reverse. But these expectations from stable population theory are hard to extend to realistic historical situations in which the underlying rates, subject to different causes, fluctuate rapidly. We therefore approach this exploration as a problem in the detection of results under conditions of instability, but still within a general context of population growth.

China affords an ideal testing ground for such an exploration. First, the instability of Chinese rates and especially the marked fluctuations in fertility in recent decades make any arguments based on stable population theory difficult. Second, data collection in China since the Revolution has been intensive and excellent, especially in recent years, and age misstatement is lower for cultural reasons in Chinese populations than in any others. In this exploration we use empirically observed rates as inputs to the simulation up to the present and compare the resulting simulated age structures with those empirically observed at selected census dates (1953, 1964, and 1982) to confirm the reasonableness of the simulation results, grosso modo. We then select a plausible future path for Chinese rates and project the population forward to 2250. We next calculate exemplary expected frequencies of some of those relationship types that seem particularly relevant to traditional and developing Chinese patterns of kinship structure at the years 1950, 1972, 2020, 2060, and 2150. We use 1950 to depict traditional kinship structure under traditional rates in a stable population, the next three dates to show kinship structure at the end of intermediate rate periods, and 2150 to depict kinship structures under modern conditions of presumed stability. (We do not take a kinship census in 2250 but instead in 2150 because one of our aims is to display expectations of coexistence, and we need substantial time after the last census date to do that.) We inquire into the number of brothers, sons, spouses, parents, and grandparents for men of varying ages. For each of these we also examine the distribution by age of those men having none of the relatives named, since there is a qualitative difference between having some such relatives and having none at all. All these measures are period measures in the sense that they are taken at points in time, but they are age-specific and thus reflect cohort experience for the index person and the relative in question. We also measure empirically the average years of coexistence between index persons of specific ages and certain relatives. This is a cohort measure that is taken across time, but it is reported for persons alive at a given point in time.

We draw particular attention to the outstanding analyses by Zeng (1986, 1988) that use Bongaarts's multi-state family life-table simulation approach (Watkins and others, 1987) and come to similar conclusions where our foci of interest overlap. Zeng's concern was family structure rather than kinship structure, but his conclusions about nuclear versus three–generational families are mirrored in our own on expected numbers of children and grandparents. We caution again that what we produce is not a simulacrum of reality but a simulacrum of what reality might be like for a population under the rates described. Where we use historical rates and produce kinship structures for times already past, those kinship structures constitute a model of what Chinese kinship structures would likely have been under the conditions of the model. We cannot know what other conditions might have obtained, nor can we know what cultural adjustments and redefinitions of genealogical types for purposes of social interaction and exchange might have occurred. Where we extrapolate into the future by making what seem to us reasonable assumptions, we cannot know nor do we predict what Chinese kinship structure will actually be like. In addition to the difficulties just named, we have the additional one of not knowing what the rates will really be. Nevertheless, we will know more after the exercise than before it.

For statistical stability we ran 12 large simulations with final population sizes averaging about 8,000 and aggregated the results. We began each simulation with an arbitrary population of 1,080 persons. This starting population, identical for each of the 12 simulations, was then subjected to a set of mortality, fertility, and nuptiality rates we call Rate Set I. These are reasonable average rates for the period 1750–1949. The starting population was simulated at these rates 12 times for a period of 200 years ending in 1950 in order to yield 12 different populations of stable age structure under Rate Set I. We call these populations Period I populations.

We then continued each such simulation from Period I through five successive periods, II–VI, ending in 1988, each characterized by empirical rates called Rate Set II–VI, with rate changes in 1950, 1959, 1962, 1972, and 1977. We then used the 1977 rates until 2020, when we shifted to rate set VII, and continued at these new rates until 2060, when we shifted to rate set VIII, under which we ran to 2250. At selected times we took a population or a kinship census. The general outlines of Rate Sets I–VIII are shown in table 1. Greater detail on the input rates, as well as on the output censuses, is provided in a more technical exposition found in Hammel and others (1989).

Rates for 1750–1949 are taken from Notestein and Chiao and other data in Buck (1937) as amended by Barclay and others (1976). We use these rates as the only currently convenient source, with the knowledge that there has been some dispute about the accuracy of fertility data from the Buck survey (cf. Wolf, 1984; Coale, 1984). The age–specific marital fertility rates are taken from the Barclay readjustments, the mortality rates from Coale-Demeny Model East, Level 3, as suggested by the Barclay reassessment, and the rates for first marriage from the Notestein and Chiao chapter.

China experienced unprecedented social, political, economic, and demographic changes between 1950 and 1982. One example is the rapid fertility decline that occurred during the 1970s, in which the total fertility rate dropped from above 5 to below 3. In urban areas, the total fertility rate dropped to below replacement level. This period was divided into five different segments (II–VI) for convenience on an intuitive basis, periodizing rate changes that were in some cases available annually.

Table 1. General input rates

| Simulation Time period | Rate set | Empirical rates from time period | | |
		Fertility	Mortality	Marriage
1750-1949	I	1929-31	1929-31	1929-31
1950-1958	II	1950-58	1953-64	1963
1959-1961	III	1959-61	1953-64	1963
1962-1971	IV	1964	1964-82	1963
1972-1976	V	1974	1964-82	1979
1977-1988	VI	1981	1982	1979
1989-2020	VI	1981	1982	1979
2021-2060	VII	1982 (urban)	1982 (urban)	1979
2061-2250	VIII	1982 (urban, TFR=2.1)	Model West, level 23	1979

During the first such period, 1950–1958, fertility stayed at the previous high level, but mortality started to decline. During the second period, 1959–1961, China suffered its worst economic and demographic catastrophe in recent history. Mortality rose sharply and fertility dropped drastically within that short–time period. The third period, 1962–1971, witnessed continuing high fertility and further declines in mortality. The fourth period, 1972–1976, saw declining fertility in most parts of China as a result of the Later–Longer–Fewer campaign. In the fifth period, 1977–1988, fertility in China was further reduced with the varying implementation of the one–child–per–couple policy.

Fertility data for all five time periods after 1949 are from Coale and Chen's (1987) calculations from a large–scale fertility survey conducted in 1982. We assume a minimum birth–spacing interval of 10 months and implement it as a single–server queue with loss. Although data on parity–specific fertility rates are not available directly, after 1950 we "parify" the Coale and Chen rate sets by reference to the 1–in–1,000 survey results for Shansi in 1946–1985, maintaining the same overall levels as indicated in the Coale and Chen rate sets. Both birth–spacing and parity–specific rates are introduced in order not to depress variances in age between siblings, since such variability can be expected to influence kinship networks importantly.

Two sets of mortality rates (1953–1964 and 1964–1982) are from Coale's (1984) calculation based on the same fertility survey and other population statistics from China. Mortality rates for 1982 are from results of the 1982 Chinese census.

First marriage rates are calculated from the age–specific first marriage rates reported in a Chinese source (Population and Economy, 1982) and from the proportion ever married by age group presented in Coale (1984). We implement only two different sets of marriage rates after Period I, based on a simple classification of an early marriage regime before 1972 (average age at first marriage for females about 19) and a higher age at first marriage regime after 1972 (average age at first marriage for females about 22).

We then assume that the demographic patterns of 1977 (Rate Set VI) will continue to 2020. A variety of other assumptions are possible, and the number of potential paths is very large. We strive for a simple, exemplary path focusing on rural China. We assume no change in current nuptiality patterns through 2250. In 2020 we assume a national shift to urban fertility and mortality patterns of 1982, and in 2060 we assume a further mortality shift to the pattern of Coale–Demeny Model West, Level 23, where expectation of life at birth is about 71 for males and 75 for females.

Results of the Chinese simulations

Space limitations do not permit full exposition of the results, and we here concentrate on the most striking and informative patterns. Fuller detail is given in Hammel and others (1989). The text of this paper sometimes refers to patterns for which there are no graphical illustrations presented here; we have restricted the illustrations to the most informative ones.

Since available survey data from China provide no information on the actual composition of kinship networks (other than kin within households), the reasonableness of the simulations can be checked only by comparing simulation results to census age distributions. In 1953 the simulated age distribution for persons over 3 years is determined largely by the inputs from the Barclay reassessment of the Buck survey, and for younger persons by the introduction of Rate Set II. The number of persons under age 10 is a bit high and that over 40 is a bit low, yielding a relatively constant small error in the cumulative distribution. The fit in 1964 shows a small deficit of persons under 10 balanced by an excess aged 10–20. In 1982 the simulated distribution matches the irregular peaks of the empirical distribution very well in shape, but with about a 3 percentage point deficit in the youngest age group and a 1 percentage point excess at age 30. In fact, the worst fit of the simulated age distribution to the empirical one is in 1982, and we display it in figure I. The fit of the cumulative distributions (not shown here) is very good. We conclude that the simulations have matched the empirical age distributions quite reasonably.

Figure II shows the proportional age distributions for the kinship census dates of 1950, 1972, 2020, 2060, and 2150 to illustrate the simulated age structures at the precise points of the kinship counts. Examination of these distributions assists in the interpretation of the kinship structures as functions of the age distributions. We are not able to compare these age distributions with the work of Zeng (1986), since he does not provide output age distributions or compare them with empirical census age distributions in this way.

We now move to examination of kinship networks at the five kinship census dates. We follow a graphical convention – the density of the lines increases with time, so that 1950 is represented by a dotted line, successive censuses by longer and longer dashes, and 2150 by a solid line. For parents and grandparents, fertility rates have no effect, since only persons ever born enter the sample and the effects of improvements in mortality for the generations preceding the index survivors are clear. The improvement in the survivorship of parents between census dates is greatest between 1950 and 2020 and greatest for index persons aged between 30 and 40. To encapsulate this information, we point out that a man aged about 45 in 2150 would have on average 1.1 surviving parents, while that level of parental survivorship would have been enjoyed in 1950 only by a man aged about 25. At age 40 the difference between 1950 and 2150 accounts for about 0.85 surviving parents, on average. For grandparents the same general relationships hold, with the most change occurring between 1950 and 2020. However, most of the improvement in survivorship of grandparents is enjoyed by children aged 5–15. A child in the earliest age groups in 1950 would have fewer than 2 living grandparents, while a child of that age in 2150 would have 3.4 on average. In 2150 a man aged 20 would have about the same number of living grandparents as an infant in 1950. However, the mean number of living grandparents enjoyed by males in 2150 exceeds that in 1950 by only 0.02. It is interesting and important to note this convergence between patterns in 1950 and 2150.

The expectation of having living sons at the index person's age x is more complex (figure III). Survivorship is irrelevant for the index person, but both fertility and mortality are involved in the number of surviving sons.

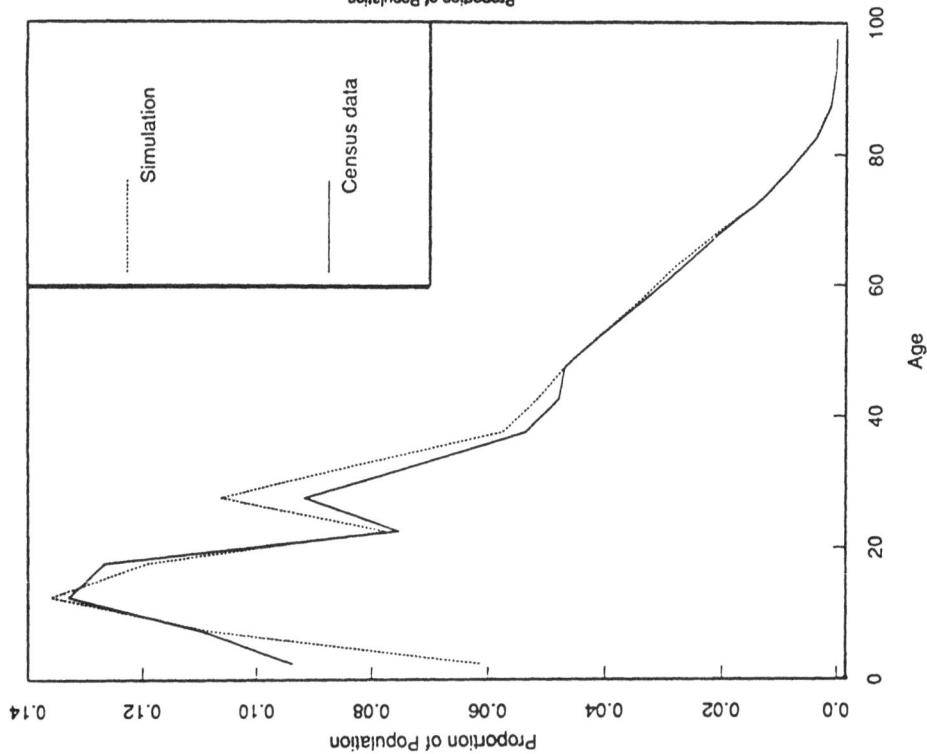

Figure I. Proportional age distribution, 1982

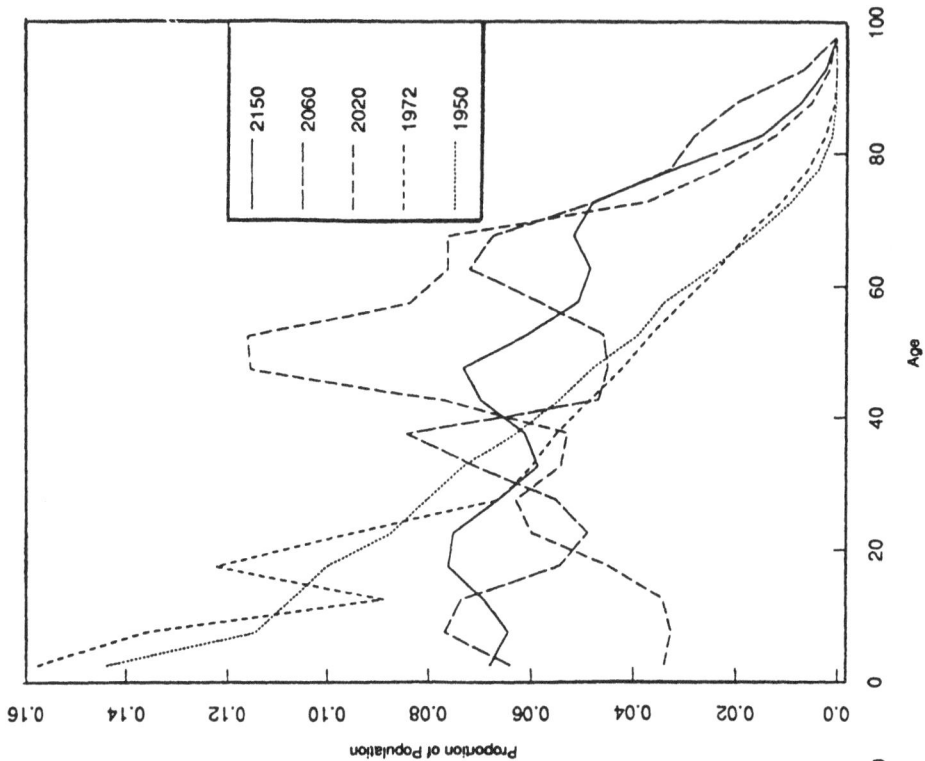

Figure II. Proportional age distributions, 1950, 1972, 2020, 2060, 2150

254

Both of these are dependent on the age of the index person, since this age establishes the cohort fertility rates of the index person and the period effects in those rates, as well as the cohort mortality rates and period fluctuations therein for the sons. In brief, we see that the peak number of surviving sons is usually reached at about age 40–45. The peak is highest for 1950 and 1972, but survivorship of sons falls off rapidly; in this we see the effect of high fertility rates for the cohorts reaching middle age into the 1970s. The peak is higher for 1972 than for 1950 because of the improved survivorship of sons. In 2020 the peak is about as high as in 1972 but is shifted far to the right, falling at about age 90. Men aged 90 in 2020 married in about 1950 and had high fertility except for the crisis of 1958–1961. The cohorts coming after them had successively lower fertility. Thus, even though the survivorship of sons increased through time, the curve for expected surviving sons increases with age of index person in 2020 because of rapidly declining fertility to about 2000, when some of the 20–year-olds in 2020 would have married. By 2020 the peak has fallen to 1.1 sons from 2.3 in 1972. The graphs for later periods tend to fall off more gently because of the improved mortality of sons relative to earlier years. By 2150 there emerges a different pattern, in which the peak level is about the same but is maintained with no diminution until the index person is about 90. In this we see the effect of enhanced survivorship of sons. The key point is that a man aged about 80 in 2150 could expect to have the same number of surviving sons as one in 1950 (about one), but would not have had to have so many to begin with. Indeed, the 80–year-old in 2150 could expect as many surviving sons as the 30–year-old in 1972, but would have had to raise only half as many or fewer.

The expectation of living brothers is not as difficult to determine, because the rates producing the patterns are in the same cohort for the index person as for the relative (figure IV). In 1950, 2060, and 2150 the peak expectation is about 1.2, falling off more rapidly for persons alive in 1950 and 2060 and less rapidly in 2150 because of differences in mortality. A man of 55 in 2150 would have about as many surviving brothers as a man of 35 in 1950. The picture is different in 1972, when the expectation reaches a peak of over two brothers for men aged in their late teens, but the curve drops off rapidly, since the older men in 1972 lost more brothers to heavier mortality further back in time. The distribution for 2020 has a somewhat lower peak but a similar shape and is shifted to the right, reflecting the successively higher fertility of the parents of the successively older surviving men.

The expectations of having living wives are also interesting but are not illustrated here. The peaks in all time periods are slightly under one, reflecting near-universal marriage, but they shift to the right to reflect advancing age at marriage. The decline in surviving wives with increasing age of the index male is ameliorated in the later periods, reflecting the improvements in adult mortality. By 2150 the distribution of surviving wives has a plateau rather than a peak, indicating longer coexistence, a pattern that we will see for other kinship relationships as well.

By contrast we may examine briefly the expectations having no relatives of particular types at all. These data are of interest because of the great qualitative difference between having some expectation of kinship support from some category of relative and having none at all. Figure V shows the expected proportion of men having no living parents by age x. Clearly, mortality

Figure IV. Mean number of living brothers

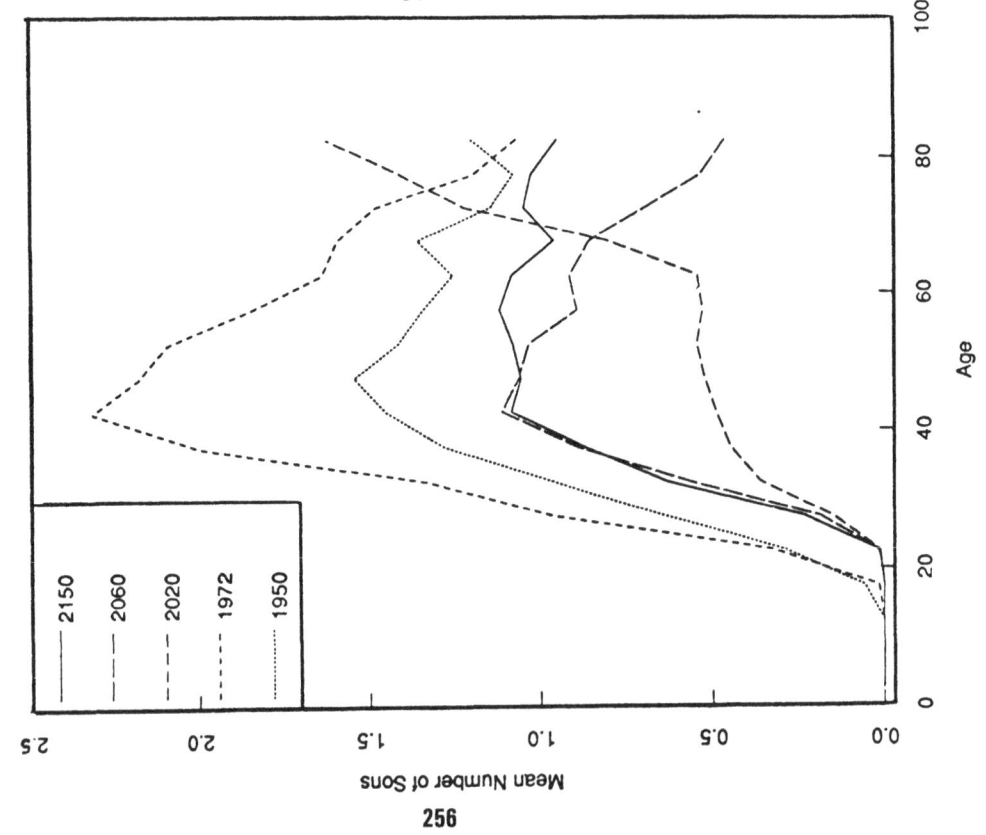

Figure III. Mean number of living sons

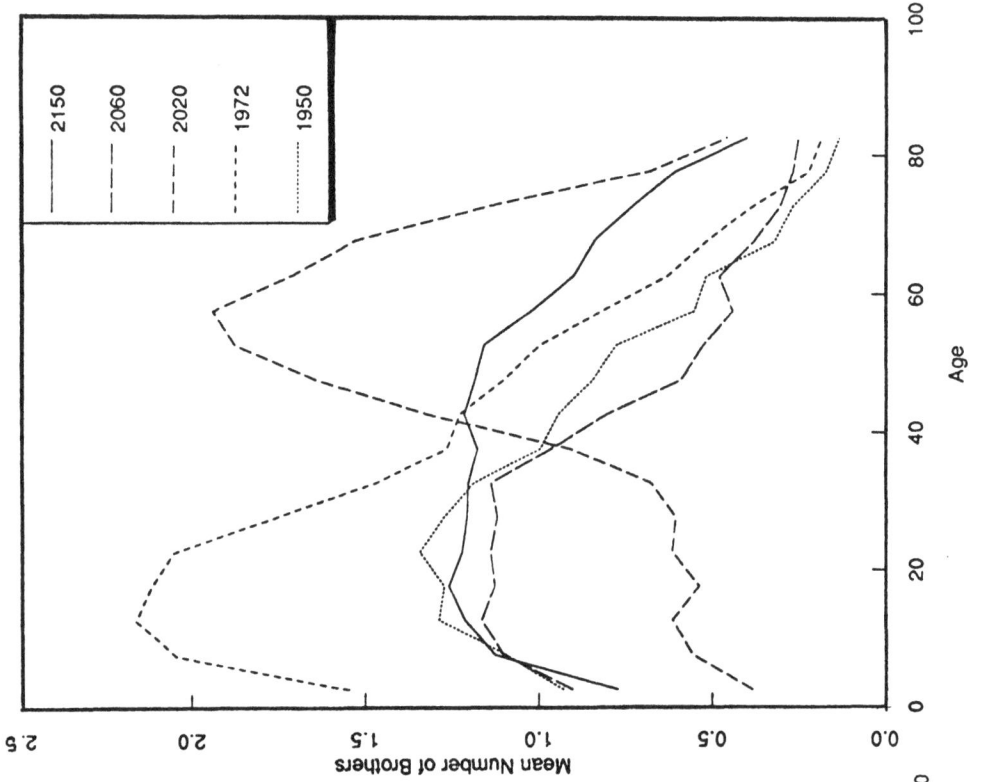

256

improvements are at work, and expectations of filial piety may endure for a longer period. In 2150 a man aged 60 has about one parent left, a status enjoyed by a man under age 40 in 1950. Differentiation of parents by sex would show the improvement to be more striking for mothers than for fathers.

The fraction of males having no living sons, a condition most undesirable in traditional Chinese culture, is shown in figure VI. Of particular interest are the age ranges over 60, for whose occupants the sunset of old age would be expectably enhanced by the presence of sons. In 1950 and 1972 only about a fifth or a quarter of men had no sons by age 65, or a quarter to a third by age 80. But in 2020 and 2060 the 65-year-old men have on average almost 0.5 living sons. In 2150 the proportion without sons is closer to the 1950 pattern in shape but shifted upward by about a percentage point because of the fertility differential. The crisis comes for men at all ages in 2020. An even more striking picture is that of the proportions of men having no surviving brothers who are thus left without the traditional basis of local political and economic solidarity (figure VII). After age 50, the situation is better in 2150 than in any previous time period except in 2020, the latter date reflecting the high fertility of the parents of men aged 50-70 in 2020.

We now examine a question of considerable interest for the socialization of children - the fraction of males at age x having no living grandparent at the five census points. But we do this in a different way, distinguishing among the four kinds of grandparents. The graphical convention employed designates the paternal grandparents with uppercase letters and the maternal ones with lowercase; for each of these the grandmother is indicated by M or m and the grandfather by F or f. We would expect an increase of grandparentless men with age. What might not be anticipated is that at any age, a man is more likely to have a maternal grandmother (m) alive than a paternal grandfather (F), with less distinction between the maternal grandfather (f) and the paternal grandmother (M). This is because men die younger than women and marry older; the two effects are intensified for the m and F and tend to cancel out for the M and f. This separation of grandparents is modest in 1950 (figure VIII) but becomes greatest by 2150 (figure IX), where we observe the best survivorship for any grandparent, a clear separation between M and f, and the greatest separation between F and m. Comparison across time periods shows, for example, that a man aged 25 in 2150 would enjoy the same expectation of having a maternal grandmother as a boy aged 5 in 1950, and that the difference in the expectation of having a paternal grandfather and maternal grandmother at age 20 is about 10 percentage points in 1950 but over 40 percentage points in 2150. It is particularly noteworthy that the greatest survival enhancement is for the maternal grandmother. She is according to some psychosocial theories a potentially more nurturant figure in a patrilineal and patriarchal society than are the other grandparents, especially the father's father, who can be expected to be an authority figure rather than a nurturant one.

We move now to an even more revealing statistic, the expectation of years of coexistence with a relative of particular type, for men aged x at the five census points. For example, figure X shows that a man aged 20 in 1950 could expect about another 19 years of coexistence with one or more parents, while a man of that age in 2150 could expect about another 30 years. Complementarily, figure XI shows that fathers about the age of 60 in 2150 could expect about

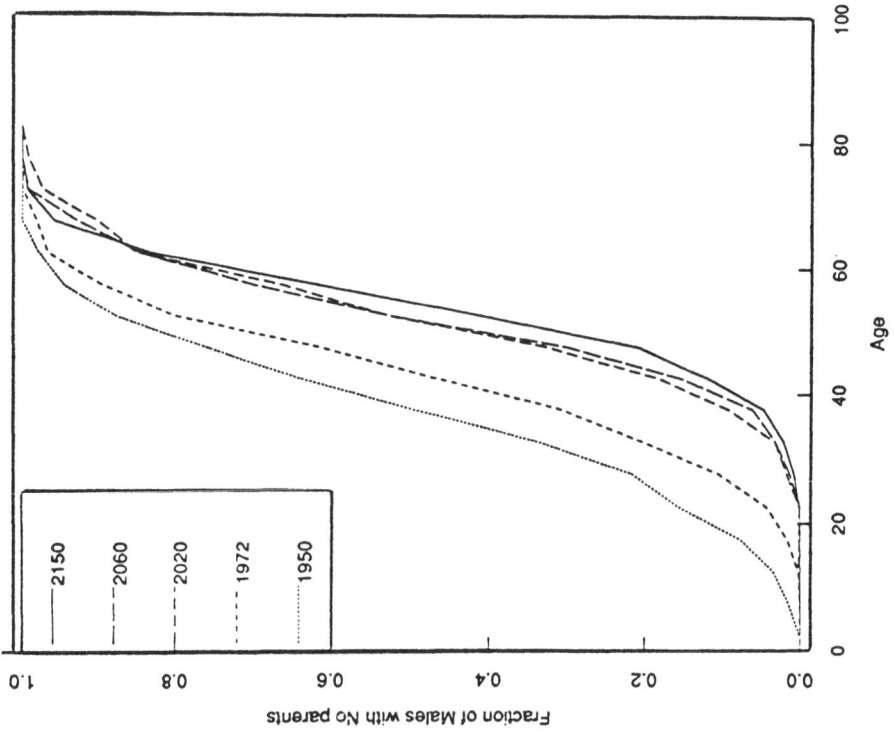

Figure V. Fraction of males with no living parents

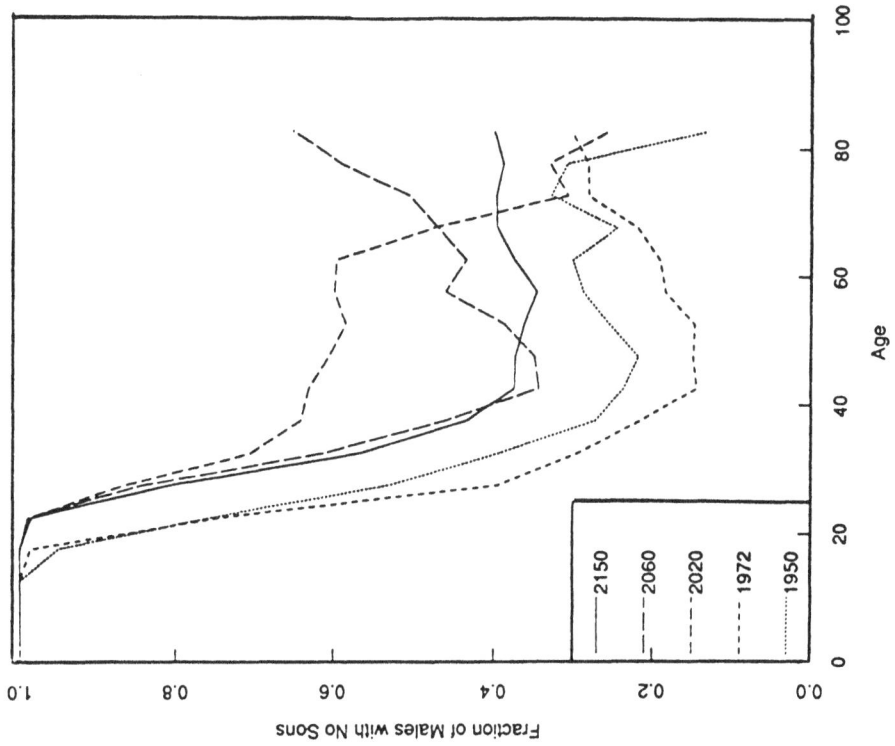

Figure VI. Fraction of males with no living sons

Figure VII. Fraction of males with no living
brothers

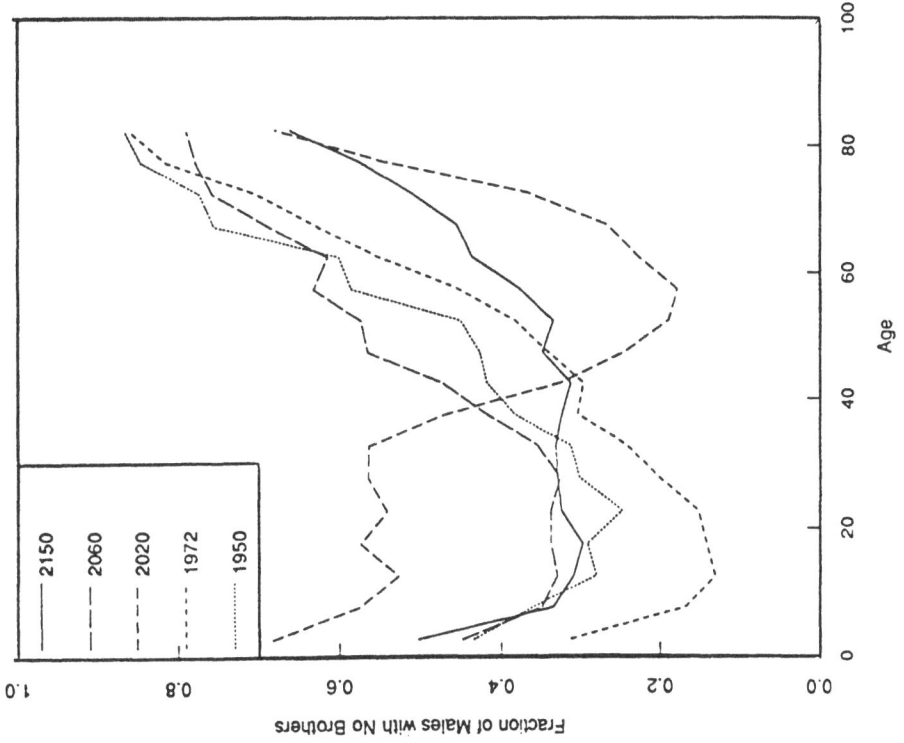

Figure VIII. Males without surviving
grandparents, 1950

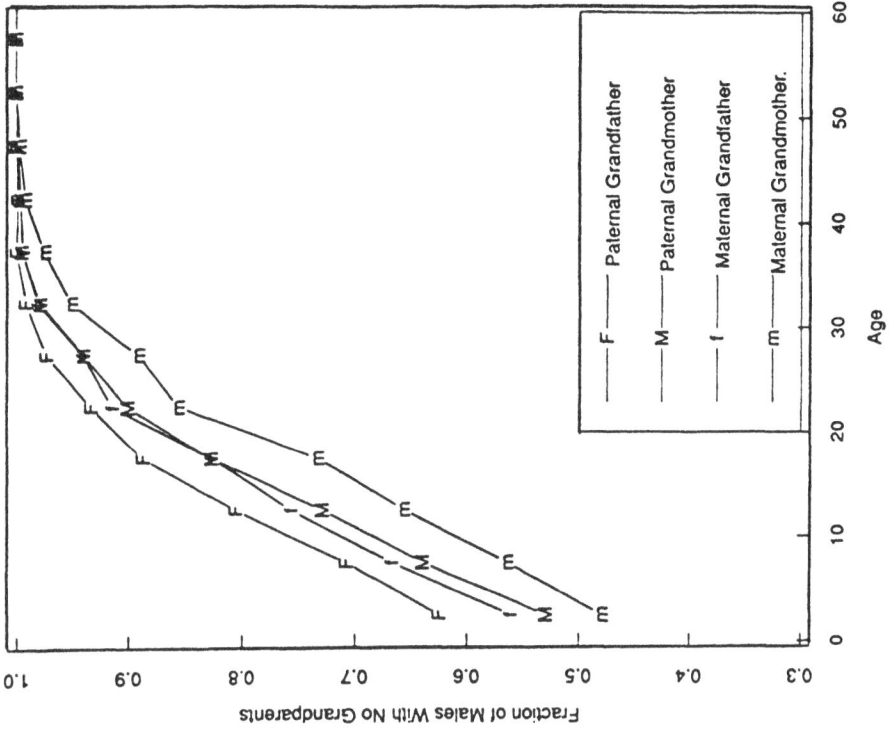

259

3.5 years more of coexistence with one or more sons than in 1950, the advantage persisting but narrowing as they age further. Thus, under the modern demographic regime the potential for filial support is generally greater in the later years of life than under the traditional demographic regime. It is the intermediate years that differ, with 1972 optimal and 2020 critical for support. In 1972 the high fertility of men aged 20–70, coupled with the gradually improving mortality of sons, created a larger expectation of filial coexistence. An analogous picture is given by figure XII for brothers. In 2150 men of practically all ages have a higher expectation of years of coexistence with one or more brothers than men at any other census date except 1972. Only in 1972 did men under age 40 have higher expectations, because of the higher fertility of the parents of men aged under 40, and only in 2020 did men over 40 have a higher expectation, revealing the higher fertility of their parents. The spousal pattern in figure XIII confirms earlier patterns; men at any age after most men are married in 2150 expect to coexist with their spouse longer than men at any other census date. The pattern is repeated in figure XIV for coexistence with one or more grandparents, except for the appearance of a small advantage in 2020 for men over 25.

We summarize these data by looking first at the mean number of living kin of any type and then at the proportion of males having no kin at all. The smallest number of living kin is experienced generally by men alive in 2020 and 2060, at virtually all ages, the picture being worst in 2060 (figure XV). The largest number of living kin is enjoyed by men of all ages alive in 1972.

At these time points we see the effects of rising and then falling fertility and of generally enhanced mortality, reflected analogously in the rates of population growth. The kinship rates for 1950 and 2150 are roughly intermediate between those of 1972 and 2060, although the expectation increases faster with age in 1950 and more slowly in 2150. For questions of old-age support, it is the higher ages that are of interest. Here we see that the average number of living relatives of men aged over 60 was better by as much as one kinsman in 1950 than in 2150, but that the difference is no larger than that. The probability of having no potential of support at all from any relative is shown in figure XVI. Here we can see that the worst conditions obtain for men of all ages in 2060 and are generally best for those alive in 2020, and that the probabilities for 1950 and 2150 are intermediate, close, and converge with age.

Conclusions from the Chinese simulations

The expectations of having kin are complexly determined by shifting patterns of nuptiality, fertility, and mortality. China exhibits rapid population increase due to varying combinations of diminished mortality and increased fertility, as well as a slowing of such growth from increased crisis mortality during the period 1958–1961 and a decrease in fertility after 1959. We would not expect the constitution of kinship networks, even at their simplest range, to be a function merely of the rate of growth of population unless the population in question were a textbook case of stability. Neither can we expect kinship networks to be very simple functions of mortality or fertility, even under conditions close to stability, because of the

Figure IX. Males without surviving grandparents, 2150

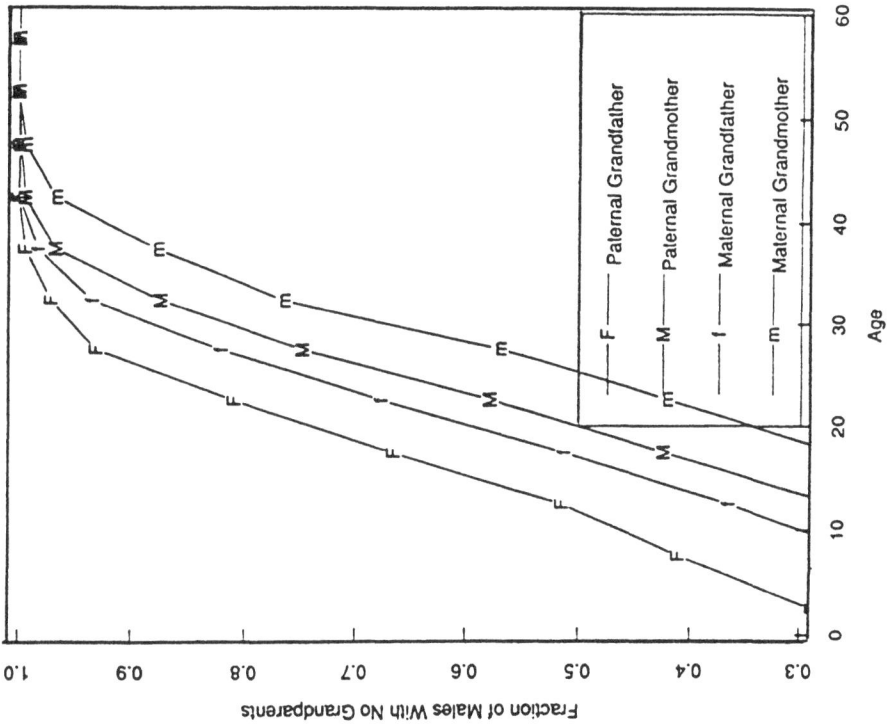

Figure X. Remaining years of coexistence with one or more parents

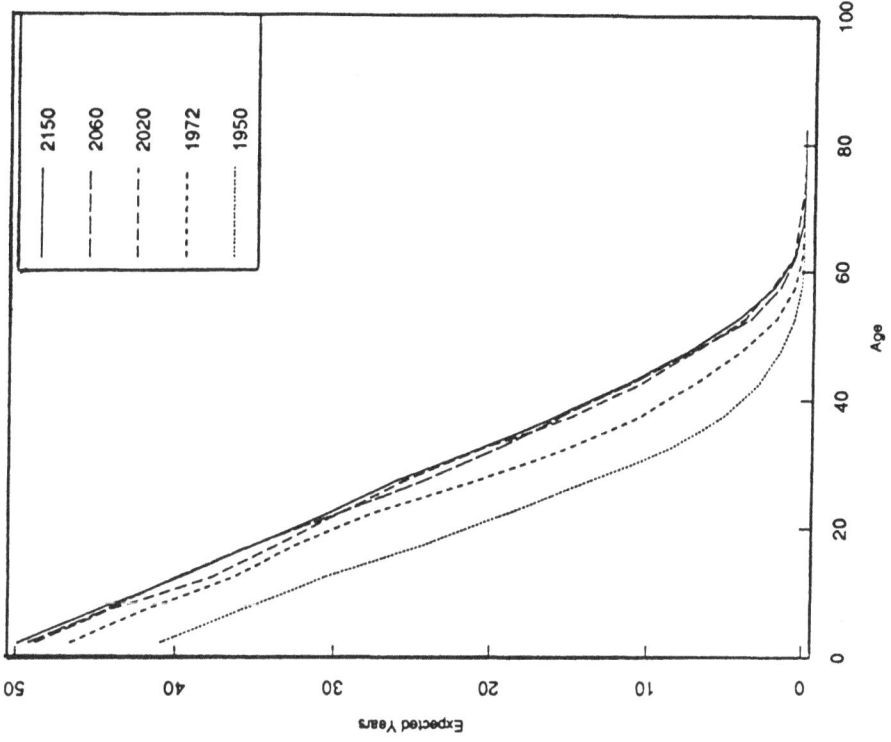

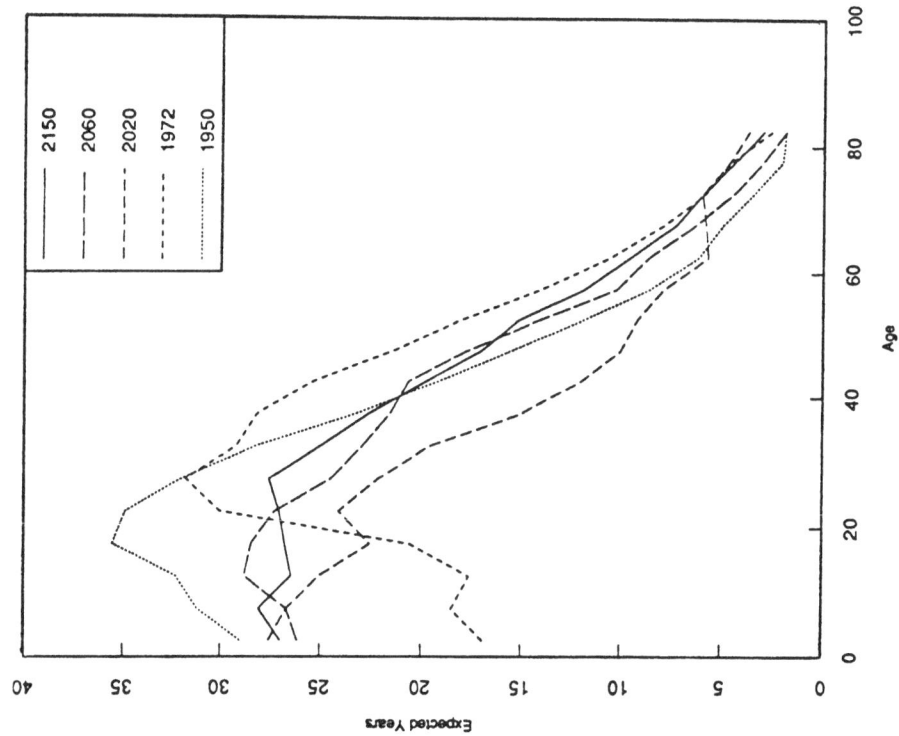

Figure XII. Remaining years of coexistence with one one or more brothers

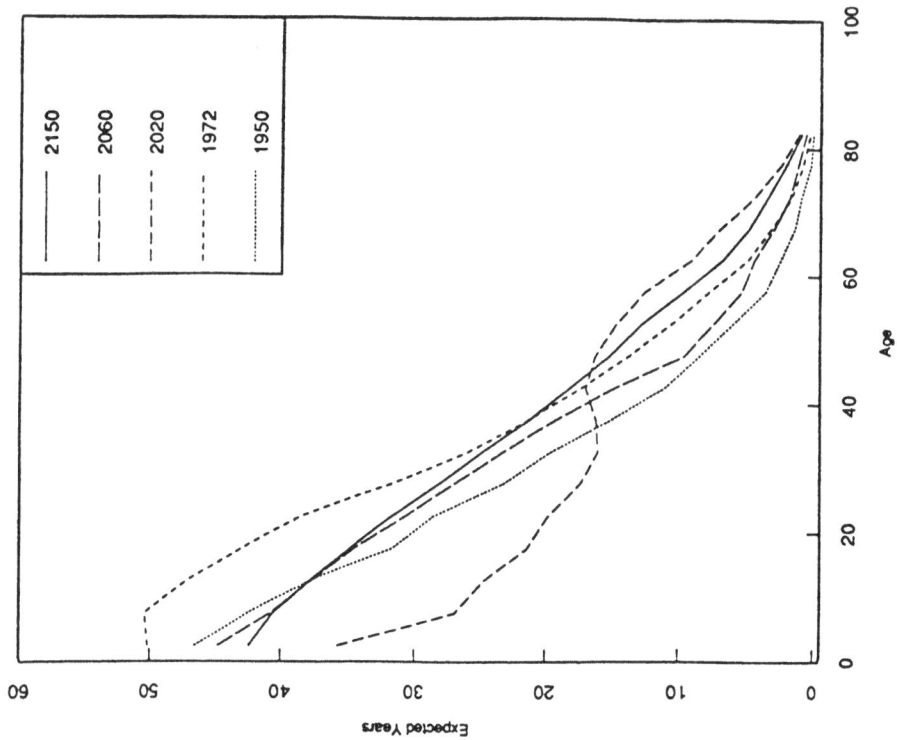

Figure XI. Remaining years of coexistence with one or more sons

262

Figure XIII. Remaining years of coexistence
with spouse

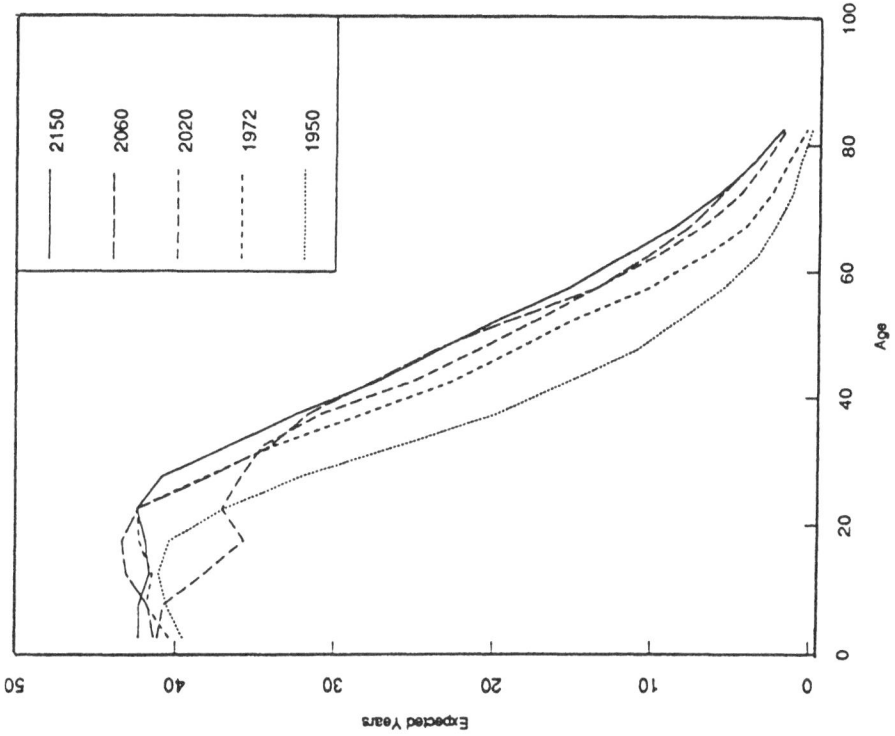

Figure XIV. Remaining years of coexistence with one
or more grandparent

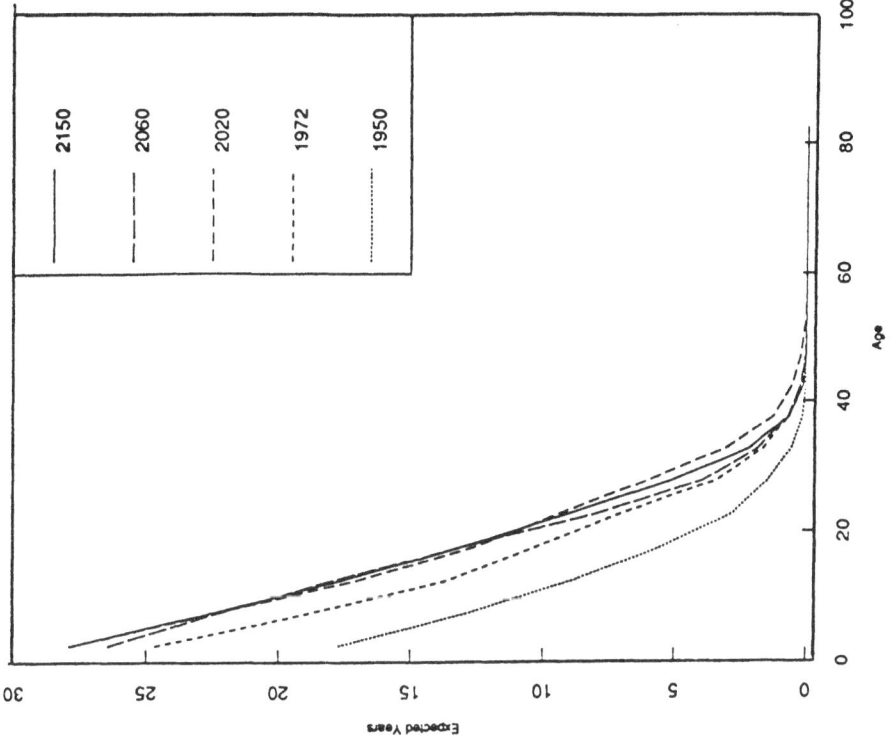

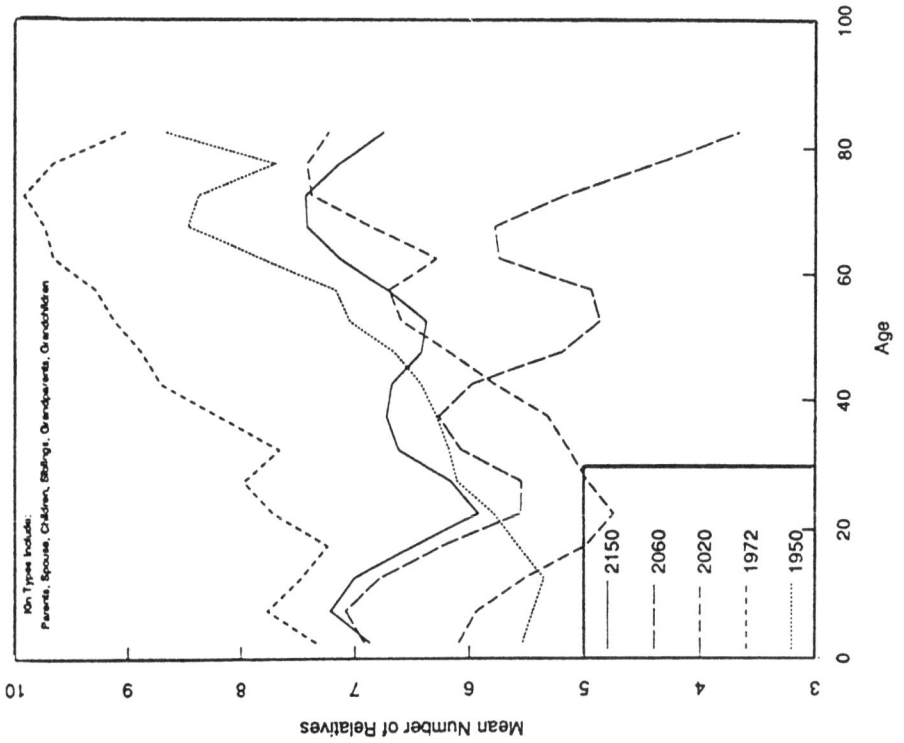

Figure XV. Mean number of living kin of any type

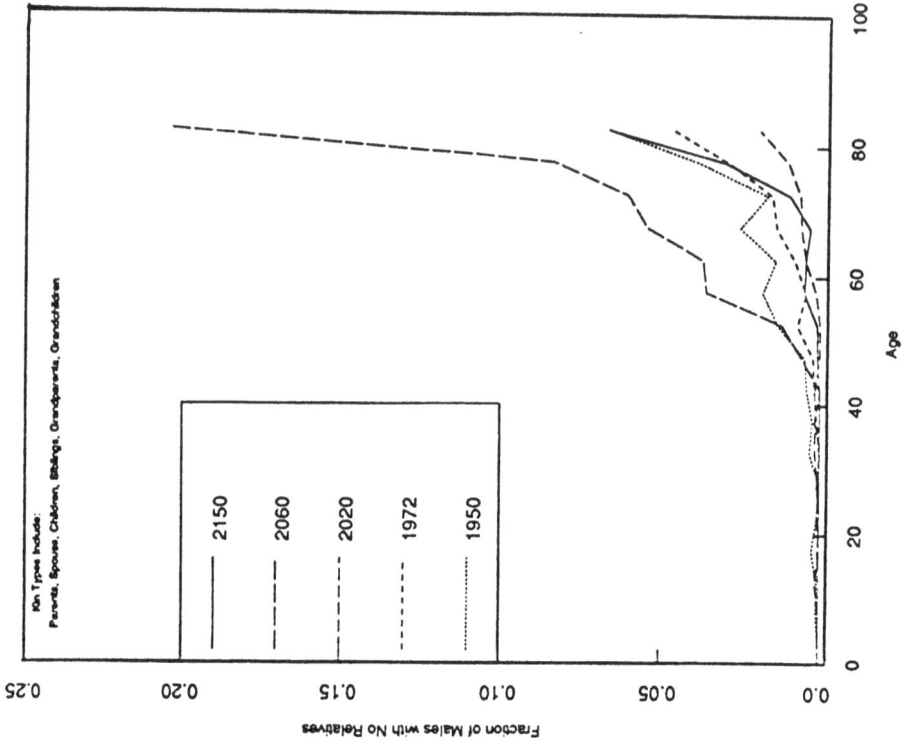

Figure XVI. Fraction of males with no living relations of any kind

264

simultaneous determination of linkages by demographic rates a generation or more apart. Under the chaotic changes of demographic regimes experienced in China, empirical reality defies simple analysis. We therefore constructed a simulacrum of similar chaotic changes in order to examine their results.

On the basis of the simulations we can say that with the declines in mortality characteristic of China, the probability of two- and three-generational networks improves substantially. The expected number of living parents for persons at the age of marriage changes from about 1.2 to about 1.9 and for persons aged about 40 from about .4 to about 1.3. Thus, middle-aged men in populations with the rates described are about three times as likely to have surviving parents in 2150 as in 1950.

The expectations of having a living grandparent show similar change, being dependent on the same mortality events. The expected number of living grandparents changes from about 1.4 to about 3.0 for persons aged 5; that ratio is roughly maintained over about the next decade of life, lessening thereafter as survivorship converges somewhat differently towards zero. About 4 in 100 men aged 40 in 2150 could expect to have a living grandparent (most likely a maternal grandmother). Children in populations with mortality rates characteristic of China would be likely to have about twice as many living grandparents in 2150 as in 1950. Fertility rates would make no difference to these chances, since it is the children who make up the sample. From the parental and grandparental scenarios we see that the traditional structures of kinship are best achieved by the most modern demographic regimes.

The expectation of having living sons is, of course, enormously affected by surges in fertility, as demonstrated by the population in 1972 and 2020, when fathers could expect almost one more son than those in 1950 and more than one more son than those in 2150. But fathers in 2150 could expect to have those sons for a longer time than in 1950 or 1972. These changes seem a fairly simple matter of the ratio of the two generations in the age structure at different time points. The differences are important for family organization and for both child and old-age dependency burdens. Again, it is evident that the traditional goal of many sons surviving and assisting in a father's ripe old age is least likely to be achieved in the oldest mortality regime. The mortality changes that are important are largely those that affect the sons, since dead fathers do not get into the sample. Fertility, is of course, an important factor, and the peak of expectation is reached under high fertility regimes even if accompanied by relatively high mortality of sons.

These results on the expected numbers of parents, grandparents, and sons show the same directions as those of Zeng (1986), although they are more specific and direct, involving particular kin types rather than family sizes or clusters and not being complicated by varying propensities in household formation. Unfortunately, for this reason we cannot compare our kinship network outputs directly with his or with empirical census data on household composition. Future work would permit us to produce directly comparable outputs, at least where families rather than households were the focus of analysis.

A reflection of these same demographic changes is seen in the expectations of having living brothers, rising from slightly over 1 at ages 10–20 for 1950, 2060, and 2150 to a peak of 2.16 at ages 15–20 for the population of 1972 and a peak of about 2 for men aged 55 in 2020. These expectations mirror the father–son distributions, downshifted by about 30 years. The lowest expectations of traditional fraternal solidarity are achievable in the oldest demographic regime (especially after age 40), the highest short–term expectations under the high fertility regime reflected in 1972 and 2020, and the most perduring expectations under the calmer regime reflected in the population of 2150.

For spouses, of course, we see what historical demography has shown us in many populations. The expectation of continuing conjugal bliss is achieved under the most modern rather than under the most traditional demographic regimes.

We see in these complex scenarios the combined effects of both fertility and mortality. Our expectations for the structure of population as demographic regimes change have always stressed the more important role of fertility. In this exercise, we are especially impressed instead by the strong role of mortality improvements. Where analytic focus is on the internal structure of populations and especially on linkages between persons across generations, mortality can be expected to have a major effect even under traditional fertility conditions. As both fertility and mortality rates decline, we should also expect the leverage of fertility to decrease and that of mortality to increase. We see both these tendencies at work in the Chinese simulations. It is particularly noteworthy to observe the role that mortality improvements play in the achievement of kinship networks regarded as traditional but unattainable under traditional demographic regimes. It seems to be demographic modernization that makes possible the structures that some traditional cultural norms have held as ideal. Indeed, we can contrast a traditional regime under which persons had early in life a larger number of relatives for a short time, to a more modern one characterized by later development of mature kinship networks and longer coexistence with fewer relatives. The policy implications of expectation of more person–years of coexistence between relatives are important. Social support costs are a function of the duration of dependency and, to the degree that socially acceptable pools of kinship support co–exist for longer periods of time, general insurance schemes are less necessary and less vulnerable. Similarly, under calmer demographic regimes with relatively low mortality, the expectations of individuals are less likely to be upset during their lifetimes, with a consequent gain in personal stability and security.

Notes

1/   This revised version of the paper originally prepared for the August 1988 conference presents new results based on the reprogramming of birth intervals, parity–specific rates, and computation of years of co–existence, which were noted as tasks yet to be done in the original paper. These new results were reported at the annual meeting of the Population Association of

America, Baltimore, 30 March, 1989. A more complete and technical report is to be found in Hammel and others (1989).

2/   The original programmes were written in Fortran. The programmes for this research were rewritten in Pascal by Mason, based on algorithm revisions for the processing of events by C. K. McDaniel. New post-processing routines were written.   The current programmes include improved algorithms for birth-spacing. Apart from these revisions, the basic logic of the original programmes and the mathematics for the timing of events are unchanged.

References

Barclay, George W. and others (1976). A reassessment of the demography of traditional rural China. Population Index, vol. 42, pp. 606–635.

Bongaarts, John and Robert G. Potter (1983). Fertility, Biology, and Behavior: an Analysis of the Proximate Determinants. New York: Academic Press.

Coale, Ansley (1984). Fertility in prerevolutionary China: defense of a reassessment. Population and Development Review, vol. 10, pp. 471–480.

_____ and Sheng Li Chen (1987). Basic Data on Fertility in the Provinces of China, 1940–82. Papers of the East–West Population Institute, No. 104. Honolulu: East–West Center.

Fitch, Nancy (1980). The household and the computer: a review. Historical Methods, vol. 13, pp. 127–137.

Giesbrecht, F. G. and G. Ranney (1968). Demographic microsimulation model. POPSIM I: manual for program to generate the initial population, closed core model. Technical Report No. 2. Project SU–285. Research Triangle Park, North Carolina: Research Triangle Institute.

Gilbert, J. and E. A. Hammel (1963). Computer analysis of problems in kinship and social structure. Paper presented at the 62nd Annual Meeting of the American Anthropological Association, San Francisco.

_____ (1966). Computer analysis of problems in kinship and social structure. American Anthropologist, vol. 68, pp. 71–93.

Goodman, Leo, Nathan Keyfitz and Thomas Pullum (1974). Family formation and the frequency of various kinship relationships. Theoretical Population Biology, vol. 5, pp. 1–27.

_____, Nathan Keyfitz and Thomas Pullum (1975). Addendum to: Family formation and the frequency of various kinship relationships. Theoretical Population Biology, vol. 8, pp. 376–381.

Hammel, E. A. (1965a). A transformational analysis of Comanche kinship terminology. American Anthropologist, vol. 67, No. 5, part 2, pp. 65–105.

_____ (1965b). An algorithm for Crow-Omaha solutions. American Anthropologist, vol. 67, No. 5, part 2, pp. 118–126.

_____ (1984). On the *** of investigating household form and function. In Households: Comparative and Historical Studies of the Domestic Group, R. M. Netting, R. R. Wilk and E. J. Arnould, eds. Berkeley: University of California Press.

_____ and R. Z. Deuel (1977). <u>Five Classy Programs: Computer Programs</u>
<u>for the Classification of Households</u>. Research Monograph No. 33.
Berkeley, California: University of California, Institute of
International Studies,

_____ and D. W. Hutchinson (1974). Two tests of computer
microsimulation. In <u>Simulation of Human Populations</u>, B. Dyke and
J. MacCluer, eds. New York and London: Seminar Press.

_____ and K. W. Wachter (1977). Primonuptiality and ultimonuptiality:
their effects on stem family household formation. In <u>Population Patterns</u>
<u>in the Past</u>, R. Lee, ed. New York: Academic Press.

_____ D. W. Hutchinson and K. W. Wachter (1976). Appendix: a
stochastic simulation and numerical test of the deterministic model, to:
the matrilateral implications of structural cross-cousin marriage. In
<u>Demographic Anthropology: Quantitative Approaches</u>, E. Zubrow, ed.
Albuquerque: University of New Mexico Press.

_____ K. W. Wachter and C. K. McDaniel (1979). Demographic
consequences of incest taboos. <u>Science</u>, vol. 205, pp. 972–977.

_____ (1980). Vice in the Villefranchian: a microsimulation analysis of
the demographic effects of incest prohibitions. In <u>Genealogical</u>
<u>Demography</u>, B. Dyke and W. Morrill, eds. New York: Academic Press.

_____ (1981). The kin of the aged in 2000 A.D. In <u>Aging</u>. Vol. 2<u>:</u>
<u>Social Change</u>, James Morgan, Valerie Oppenheimer and Sara Kiesler, eds.
New York: Academic Press.

_____ and others (1976). <u>The SOCSIM Demographic–sociological</u>
<u>Microsimulation Program</u>. Research Series, No. 27. Berkeley,
California: University of California, Institute of International Studies,

_____ and others (1989). Microsimulation as a tool in exploring social
and demographic interrelationships: with an example from China,
1750–2200, or how tradition is achieved by modernity. Working Paper,
No. 27. Berkeley, California: University of California, Graduate Group
in Demography and Program in Population Research.

Horvitz, D. G. and others (unpublished). POPSIM: a demographic
microsimulation model.

Howell, Nancy and V. A. Lehotay (1978). AMBUSH: a computer program for
stochastic microsimulation of small human populations. <u>American</u>
<u>Anthropologist</u>, vol. 80, pp. 905–922.

Kunstadter, P. and others (1963). Demographic variability and preferential
marriage patterns. <u>American Journal of Physical Anthropology</u>, vol. 22,
pp. 511–519.

Lachenbruch, P. A., J. Klepfer and S. Rhode (1968). Demographic microsimulation model POPSIM I: manual for programs to generate vital events, closed core model. Technical Report No. 3. Project SU-285, Research Triangle Institute, Research Triangle Park, North Carolina.

LeBras, Herve (1973). Parents, grandparents, bisaieux. Population, vol. 1, pp. 9-37. (Translated in Wachter and others, 1978)

Lee, Lily (1985). Postpartum amenorrhea: behavioral and sociodemographic correlates. Ph.D dissertation. Berkeley, California: University of California,

MacCluer, Jean W. (1967). Monte Carlo methods in human population genetics: a computer model incorporating age-specific birth and death rates. American Journal of Human Genetics, vol. 19, pp. 303-311.

_____ (1968). Studies in genetic demography by Monte Carlo simulation. Ph.D. dissertation. Ann Arbor, Michigan: University of Michigan,

_____ (1973). Computer simulation in anthropology and human genetics. In Methods and Theories in Anthropological Genetics, M. H. Crawford and P. L. Workman, eds. Albuquerque: University of New Mexico Press.

_____ J. V. Neel and N. A. Chagnon (1971). Demographic structure of a primitive population: a simulation. American Journal of Physical Anthropology, vol. 35, pp. 193-208.

Menken, Jane (1985). Age and fertility: how late can you wait? Demography, vol. 22, pp. 469-483.

Orcutt, M. H. and others (1961). Micro-analysis of Socio-economic Systems. New York: Harper.

Population and Economy (1982). Beijing.

Pullum, Thomas W. (1987). Some mathematical models of kinship and the family. In Family Demography: Methods and their Applications, John Bongaarts, Thomas Burch and Kenneth Wachter, eds. Oxford: Clarendon Press.

Reeves, Jaxk K. (1987). Projection of number of kin. In Family Demography: Methods and their Applications, John Bongaarts, Thomas Burch and Kenneth Wachter, eds. Oxford: Clarendon Press.

Ruggles, Steven (1987). Prolonged Connections: the Rise of the Extended Family in 19th Century England and America. Madison, Wisconsin: University of Wisconsin Press.

Smith, James E. (1987). Simulation of kin sets and kin counts. In Family Demography: Methods and their Applications, John Bongaarts, Thomas Burch and Kenneth Wachter, eds. Oxford: Clarendon Press.

Wachter, K. W. (1987). Microsimulation of household cycles. In Family Demography: Methods and their Applications, John Bongaarts, Thomas Burch, and Kenneth Wachter, eds. Oxford: Clarendon Press.

_____, E. A. Hammel and Peter Laslett (1978). Statistical Studies of Historical Social Structure. New York: Academic Press.

Watkins, S. C., J. A. Menken and John Bongaarts (1987). Demographic foundations of family change. American Sociological Review, vol. 52, pp. 346-358.

Willigan, J. Dennis and Katherine A. Lynch (1982). Sources and Methods of Historical Demography. New York: Academic Press.

Wobst, Martin (1975). The demography of finite populations and the origins of the incest taboo. American Antiquity, vol. 40, pp. 75-81.

Wolf, Arthur (1984). Fertility in prerevolutionary China. Population and Development Review, vol. 10, pp. 443-470.

Zeng, Yi (1986). Changes in family structure in China: a simulation study. Population and Development Review, vol. 12, pp. 675-703.

_____ (1988). Changing demographic characteristics and the family status of Chinese women. Population Studies, vol. 42, pp. 183-203.

PART FIVE

Normative problems

Chapter 10

The world distribution of income : evolution over the recent period and effects of population growth

- A. Berry*, F. Bourguignon** and C. Morrisson***

Introduction

The present paper draws on previous work by the same authors on the distribution of world income. In Berry and others (1984), we analysed several methodological problems in studying income distribution when taking into account income inequality within as well as among countries, including the use of the relevant national account concept in connection with personal incomes, the heterogeneity of data across countries, the purchasing power parity correction of nominal exchange rates, etc. However, sensitivity analyses showed that the main inequality measures or the Lorenz curve of world income distribution were not very sensitive to most of these issues. Whichever concept was used, allowing for the imprecision of national income distribution data and purchasing power comparisons, the world income inequality was extremely high, with a Gini coefficient ranging between .65 and .70; this was certainly much higher than in any single individual country in the world.

In the second paper (Berry and others, 1983), we analysed the evolution of the world distribution over the post-war period, from 1950 to 1977. The conclusion was that when accounting for socialist countries, including China, no unambiguous trend was emerging for the period as a whole, regardless of whether gross domestic product (GNP) or private consumption expenditures was taken to be the indicator of national economic welfare. Yet there was a clear worsening of the distribution when the analysis was restricted to non-socialist countries with consumption expenditures as national welfare indicator. It also appeared that most of the change in world inequality was essentially explained by the economic performances of a few large countries at one or the other end of the world income per capita spectrum.

---

* University of Toronto, Ontario, Canada.

** DELTA/ENS, Paris, France.

*** Organization for Economic Co-operation and Development (OECD).

Despite a growing concern about the possibility that the evolution of the world economy over the past decade may have substantially affected the level of world inequality, few studies have looked at that issue in recent years. Moreover, they have adopted a static point of view — i.e., the world distribution at one point of time (see Grosh and Nafziger, 1986; Yotopoulos, 1988) 1/ — rather than a dynamic one, the latter being the only relevant choice if the objective is to map changes in world economic activity and population growth into the world income distribution.

In the present paper, we first update our 1983 work by extending the period of analysis up to 1986, thus including the most severe and long-lasting world economic crisis since the Second World War. Second, we investigate the relative roles of economic and demographic factors in explaining the evolution of the world income distribution. Although our updated work is still preliminary because we have not yet included socialist countries, the results are interesting. Unlike what might be expected, the adjustment process presently under way in many developing countries has not produced a further unambiguous increase in the inequality of world incomes, but neither has it led to any improvement. This is true when GNP is taken as the welfare indicator in each country. With consumption expenditures, however, the distribution unambiguously worsened over the crisis years (that is, between 1973 and 1986). Concerning the role of demographic factors, on the other hand, we find that in accordance with the theory, they essentially have an ambiguous effect on the world distribution of income. Some inequality measures are affected positively and others negatively when population growth is slowed in the fastest–growing countries. However, it is shown that this conclusion crucially depends upon the assumption made about the relationship between population and economic growth. In particular, an unambiguous improvement in world distribution would take place with a demographic slowdown if the population elasticity of GNP were small enough. These are the issues we consider here after a brief review of the methodology and data problems.

Review of methodology and data

For each country i and each year t included in the analysis, we know total population P_{it}, total income — approximated either by GNP or private consumption expenditures and converted into constant US dollar purchasing power   and thus income per capita Y_{it}, as well as the percentage distribution of income by deciles, v^d_{it} (d = 1, 2 ... 10). To compute the world distribution, we consider each decile of a country's population as a homogenous group of individuals with size 0.1 P_{it} and identical income $10v^d_{it} Y_{it}$. All these elementary groups are then ranked by increasing income. The world Lorenz curve, as well as traditional inequality and poverty measures, are computed. The full detail of this procedure is given in Berry and others (1983 and 1984).

At this preliminary stage, socialist countries are excluded from the analysis because of the specific data problems they raise. The world thus consists of 115 countries, but 8 of them had to be removed from the sample because of data unavailability or inconsistency. 2/ All data on population, GNP, and consumption expenditures are from the 1980 World Tables, various recent issues of the <u>World Development Report</u>, and the <u>World Bank Atlas</u>. For some countries with missing data in the preceding sources we also have used the estimates reported by Summers and Heston (1984 and 1988). In our previous work we computed, for each country, income series expressed in 1970 United States dollar purchasing power, using 1970 nominal national income data, the 1970 nominal exchange rate, the purchasing power parity index estimated in Kravis and others (1978), and constant-price national income series. For the present paper, these series have been extended using growth rates calculated from the sources covering the recent period, the problem being that the base year in those recent figures was sometimes distinct from that in previous series. There may thus be a slight inconsistency for countries where the base year for constant-price national income series has been changed during the past 10 years. But given the sensitivity analysis performed in our previous work, we do not expect this problem to cause any substantial bias.

Distribution data, $v^d{}_{it}$, are in fact constant over time and, for all countries, they refer to the state of the income distribution around 1970. Considerable work has been done to make those distribution estimates comparable across countries. 3/ Although more recent estimates are available for most countries in the sample, this work could not be repeated. Besides, previous experiences with all countries for which comparable distribution data were available around 1960 and 1970 have shown that the world income distribution was not very sensitive to actual changes in national income distribution. Indeed, between 50 and 60 per cent of the world inequality arises from income differences across countries, and actual changes in national income distributions over time are generally very limited (see Berry and others, 1983). Note finally that, as before, we assume no difference between national distributions of income and consumption.

Changes in the world distribution of GNP and consumption, 1950-1986

Figure I shows the evolution of world inequality when GNP per capita is used as a proxy for mean individual income in each country. The three measures of inequality appearing on that figure show a clear ascending trend in inequality since the beginning of the 1960s, with two peaks in 1973 and 1986. The amplitude of the trend depends on the measure that is used. Between 1960 and 1986, the Gini coefficient increases by .025, whereas the Theil coefficient gains .074, and the mean logarithmic deviation more than .1. This overall increase in inequality is much larger than observed year-to-year variations and may thus be considered as extremely significant. It is also interesting to note that the increase in world inequality seems to have accelerated somewhat since the beginning of the 1970s, that is, precisely during the world economic crisis and subsequent adjustment process.

It is well known that inequality measures may lead to conflicting views about the evolution of inequality when the Lorenz curves of the selected distributions cross each other. It is only when the Lorenz curve of a distribution moves uniformly upward or downward that inequality may be said to have unambiguously decreased or increased. The evolution of the world

distribution of income illustrates that point. Table 1 shows the detail of
the distribution for selected years in the period under analysis. The
examination of decile cumulated shares – i.e., the Lorenz curve – reveals
that, unlike the apparent case in figure I, no unambiguous worsening of the
income distribution has taken place between 1973 and 1986, nor between 1950
and 1970. In fact, the only unambiguous deterioration of the distribution
over the whole period occurs between 1970 and 1973. It is permanent, however,
in the sense that the Lorenz curve for 1970 is above the Lorenz curve for any
subsequent year until 1986.

A closer look at the Lorenz curves reported in table 1 shows the
following evolution of the world distribution of income. From 1950 to 1970,
the top decile of the distribution, which consists of more than 90 per cent of
individuals living in industrialized countries (see table 3) loses part of its
more than 50 per cent share of world income in favour of the "intermediate"
deciles 7 to 9, made up of relatively poor dividuals in industrialized
countries, and of the richest deciles of developing countries.

However, most of this transfer actually took place between the very top
of the distribution, where the United States has experienced a rate of growth
slower than the rest of the world (see table 4), and the deciles immediately
below, which were strongly influenced by the above–average performance of
industrialized European countries. The same phenomenon explains the trend
between 1960 and 1970; there is no further gain in the seventh decile because
many Japanese who were in that decile in 1950 had moved to upper deciles by
1960. So the astonishing growth performances of Japan during the 1960s
benefited mostly deciles 8 and 9. The worsening of the income distribution
that took place between 1970 and 1973 is explained by the above–average growth
performances of all the richest countries during that period and the
below–average performances of the poorest countries; the income per capita
dropped by 2 per cent in the Indian sub–continent. This is reflected in table
1 by the increased share of the top two deciles. Between 1973 and 1979,
income growth is more or less uniformly low in all countries, so no important
change takes place during that period. The performance of the Indian
subcontinent is rather good during the 1980s in comparison with the rest of
the world, but so is that of developed countries. As a result, the shares of
the middle deciles have been squeezed, with an ambiguous effect on the
distribution of world income.

On the whole, it thus appears difficult to attribute to the world
economic disruptions that started at the beginning of the 1970s the main
responsibility for the increase in world inequality. The slowdown in economic
activity, and possibly the political troubles in the Indian sub–continent at
the beginning of the 1970s, 4/ as well as the record growth performance of the
richest industrialized countries at that time have produced an increase in
world inequality that has not been offset by compensating growth records in
poor or rich countries.

The worsening of the world distribution of income is even more pronounced
when individual incomes are approximated by consumption expenditures rather
than by GNP per capita. As can be seen in table 2, the world Lorenz curve
started to shift downward between 1960 and 1970 and continued to do so until

Table 1. World distribution of GNP: 1950–1986, selected years

Decile shares in world income (%)	1950 Shares	1950 Cum. shares	1960 Shares	1960 Cum. shares	1970 Shares	1970 Cum. shares	1973 Shares	1973 Cum. shares	1979 Shares	1979 Cum. shares	1986 Shares	1986 Cum. shares
Decile 1	.6	.6	.6	.6	.6	.6	.5	.5	.5	.5	.5	.5
2	.9	1.6	.9	1.5	.8	1.4	.8	1.3	.8	1.3	.8	1.3
3	1.4	2.9	1.4	2.9	1.2	2.6	1.2	2.4	1.2	2.4	1.2	2.5
4	1.9	4.8	1.9	4.7	1.7	4.2	1.6	4.0	1.6	4.0	1.6	4.1
5	2.6	7.4	2.5	7.3	2.3	6.5	2.2	6.2	2.2	6.2	2.2	6.3
6	3.9	11.3	3.9	11.2	3.6	10.2	3.5	9.7	3.6	9.8	3.3	9.6
7	6.2	17.6	6.5	17.7	6.4	16.6	6.3	16.0	6.2	16.0	5.7	15.3
8	10.6	28.1	11.0	28.7	11.6	28.2	11.5	27.5	11.3	27.3	10.6	25.9
9	19.8	47.9	20.0	48.7	20.8	49.0	21.0	48.4	20.8	48.1	20.8	46.7
10	52.1	100.0	51.3	100.0	51.0	100.0	51.6	100.0	51.9	100.0	53.3	100.0
Top 5%	34.8		34.0		33.9		34.2		34.5		35.5	
Summary inequality measures												
- Gini	.673		.670		.679		.685		.686		.694	
- Theil	.863		.850		.870		.890		.893		.924	
- Mean logarithm deviation	.936		.939		.994		1.032		1.029		1.043	
- Atkinson e=-1.0	.735		.738		.759		.773		.771		.773	
e=-1.5	.802		.805		.823		.836		.835		.835	
e=-2.0	.840		.843		.858		.870		.868		.869	
Poverty												
- Number of poors (10^3)	658		698		719		722		758		859	
- Proportion of poors (%)	41.4		36.2		30.4		28.8		26.8		26.42	
- Poverty gap (1970 US Dollar)	40.2		32.2		25.0		24.0		21.1		19.1	

1979. Between 1979 and 1986 a slight improvement took place in deciles 4 and 5, but it is so small that the evolution can still be considered as negative. The world distribution of consumption – the concept that is probably the closest to individual welfare – has thus been continuously worsening since 1960. Over the whole period, the Gini coefficient has increased by .03, an amount that might be considered as unbearable if such an evolution had taken place in a single country. In a previous paper, we argued that the relative worsening of the world distribution of consumption in comparison with that of GNP might not be a problem if it corresponded to increased investment efforts in the poorest countries which would lead to future higher growth performances. After updating our initial data base, we found that those investment efforts apparently failed to bring the growth rate of the poorest countries much above that of the richest. Perhaps this is where the effects of the present adjustment process in many developing economies upon the world income distribution became most apparent.

The preceding arguments show that the economic performances of the countries at the very top of the world distribution crucially determine the evolution of inequality. From a social welfare point of view, however, it may be argued that what happens at the top of the distribution is of less importance in comparison with the situation at the bottom, poverty being what really matters.

Poverty measures may be considered as inequality measures that are restricted to the part of the income distribution that falls below some arbitrarily chosen poverty limit. 5/ Two simple poverty measures are reported in tables 1 and 2. These are the head-count ratio, which is the share of the population below the poverty limit, and the poverty gap, which is the amount that should be spent per person in the whole population to eradicate poverty by bringing all individuals below the poverty limit up to that limit. The poverty limit is set to $US 200 at 1970 prices, a figure that has frequently been used in poverty measurement by the World Bank (see for instance Ahluwahlia and others, 1979). 6/ With that limit, tables 1 and 2 show that poverty has undoubtedly diminished over the period under analysis, with both GNP and consumption as welfare indicators. However, this decline has slowed considerably over the recent period. There may be two reasons for this evolution: first, the obvious fall in the growth rate of world economic activity; and second, more concentration in the distribution of world income. Comparing 1986 with 1973, it may be determined that the first cause is largely preponderant and that the change in the world distribution contributed to a drop rather than to an increase in the proportion of poors. Without that change, it can be estimated that with the GNP definition of income, the proportion of poors in the world population would have declined from 28.8 per cent in 1973 to 27.2 per cent in 1986, whereas the proportion of the poor in world population actually fell to 26.4 per cent. If 1970 is used as the base year, on the other hand, the change in the world distribution of GNP shows an increase in poverty, which otherwise would have fallen from 30.4 per cent to 24.3 per cent. 7/

Even though the proportion of the poor in the world population, or the poverty gap, declined throughout the period under analysis, population growth has substantially increased the absolute number of the poor and the absolute level of the poverty gap (obtained by multiplying the poverty gap reported in

Table 2. World distribution of consumption: 1950–1986, selected years

Decile shares in world income (%)	1950 Shares	1950 Cum. shares	1960 Shares	1960 Cum. shares	1970 Shares	1970 Cum. shares	1973 Shares	1973 Cum. shares	1979 Shares	1979 Cum. shares	1986 Shares	1986 Cum. shares
Decile 1	.8	.8	.8	.8	.7	.7	.6	.6	.6	.6	.6	.6
2	1.2	2.0	1.2	2.0	1.0	1.7	1.0	1.6	.9	1.5	1.0	1.6
3	1.7	3.7	1.7	3.6	1.5	3.2	1.4	3.0	1.4	2.9	1.4	2.9
4	2.4	6.1	2.3	6.0	2.1	5.3	1.9	4.9	1.9	4.8	2.0	4.9
5	3.2	9.3	3.1	9.1	2.8	8.1	2.6	7.5	2.6	7.4	2.6	7.5
6	4.5	13.7	4.5	13.5	4.1	12.2	4.0	11.5	3.9	11.4	3.8	11.3
7	6.6	20.3	6.9	20.5	6.8	19.0	6.7	18.2	6.5	17.9	6.1	17.4
8	10.9	31.3	11.3	31.7	11.9	30.9	11.7	29.9	11.5	29.3	10.9	28.3
9	19.4	50.6	19.3	51.1	19.7	50.6	20.1	50.0	20.0	49.4	19.8	48.1
10	49.4	100.0	48.9	100.0	49.4	100.0	50.0	100.0	50.4	100.0	51.8	100.0
Top 5%	32.9		32.3		33.9		34.2		34.0		34.9	
Summary inequality measures												
Gini	.641		.639		.653		.662		.667		.672	
Theil	.776		.766		.799		.824		.838		.865	
Mean logarithm deviation	.809		.809		.872		.914		.929		.940	
Atkinson e=-1.0	.683		.684		.712		.730		.736		.738	
e=-1.5	.756		.758		.783		.800		.805		.807	
e=-2.0	.801		.802		.824		.838		.845		.848	
Poverty												
- Number of poors (10^3)	767		857		925		958		1013		1092	
- Proportion of poors (%)	48.2		44.5		39.1		38.2		35.8		33.6	
- Poverty gap (1970 US Dollar)	48.6		41.7		34.9		33.8		30.0		28.3	

tables 1 and 2 by the size of the world population), 8/ which may be a matter of concern. Over the whole 1950-1986 period, the average annual growth rate of the world population has been 2 per cent. From the figures reported in tables 1 and 2, it can be calculated that given the evolution of the world mean income per capita and of the world distribution, population growth should have been 40 per cent lower (in all countries) in order for the absolute number of the poor not to increase when using the GNP concept of income. 9/ This "excess" growth of population is higher when the comparison is made between 1973 and 1986. The world population should have grown at an annual rate of .7 per cent in order to prevent a rise in the absolute amount of poverty, whereas it actually grew at 2 per cent. Note, though, that these calculations are somewhat artificial, since they are based upon the assumption of a proportional reduction of population growth in all countries. A selective drop in demographic growth among countries that contribute most to world poverty would lead to constant absolute poverty levels with a lesser reduction of world population growth. This issue will be analysed further in the next section.

Another aspect of world poverty is its country composition. Table 3 shows that there have not been very significant changes over the period under analysis, except for the growing participation of poor countries outside the Indian subcontinent, that is mostly African countries (see the country composition of the groups appearing in tables 3 and 4 in the annex). As is made clear by table 4, this results from both an income per capita growth consistently below the world average and population growth increasingly above it. Another consequence of this trend is that world poverty tends to concentrate in fewer countries.

Table 3 also shows the rather complex consequences of income-specific population growth rates upon the world distribution of income and poverty. Because they tend to grow faster than the world average, the share of poor and developing countries in the world population has continuously increased over the whole period (from 54 to 62 per cent). This purely demographic factor implies that with no heterogeneity in income per capita growth, the contribution of those countries to all deciles of the world distribution would necessarily have increased. However, as income per capita has grown at a slower pace in poor countries than in the rest of the world, their increased share in the world population concentrates in the lower deciles, whereas the opposite is true of the group of developing, and indeed newly industrialized countries. At the top of the distribution, on the other hand, population growth is slower than the world average, so that individuals living in rich countries tend to concentrate more and more in the top decile of the world population. The result is that the composition of the world "middle class"- i.e., deciles 7 to 9 - has been substantially modified over time, with the poor citizen of the industrialized countries being progressively replaced by the rich citizen of developing and newly industrialized countries.

The complexity of the role of demographic growth in shaping the evolution of the world income distribution is well illustrated by the simple growth rates reported in table 4. The distribution of income and the level of world inequality depends on the population size of the various countries and on the level of their per capita income relative to the world average. Population growth affects both factors. A faster demographic growth in poor countries

Table 3. Country composition of selected quantiles of the world
distribution of GNP: 1950, 1970, 1986

Countries	Poor 1950	Poor 1970	Poor 1986	Bottom 60 % 1950	Bottom 60 % 1970	Bottom 60 % 1986	Intermediate Deciles 1950	Intermediate Deciles 1970	Intermediate Deciles 1986	Top 10% 1950	Top 10% 1970	Top 10% 1986
Poor												
-Indian Sub-continent	46.7	49.8	48.5	42.8	44.2	46.3	8.7	9.5	9.7	.0	.0	.0
-Nigeria & Indonesia	13.8	15.3	12.3	11.6	12.4	12.7	1.6	1.4	2.2	.0	.0	.0
-Others	14.1	17.7	22.9	11.8	12.3	13.8	1.8	1.6	1.4	.0	.0	.0
Developing	12.3	11.5	11.2	13.7	16.0	16.0	9.2	10.8	14.7	3.3	3.4	3.6
Newly industrialized	5.9	3.8	1.6	8.1	8.4	5.2	6.3	10.1	17.4	2.7	4.0	4.9
Oil exporting (excl. Nigeria, Indonesia)	3.2	1.3	2.7	3.2	3.2	3.8	2.0	3.2	4.4	.6	1.7	1.2
Semi-industrialized												
- European	1.3	.0	.0	2.3	.8	.6	5.4	6.2	5.0	.2	1.6	1.2
- Others	.8	.6	.8	.9	1.0	1.2	4.3	4.6	4.1	1.2	1.0	1.1
Industrialized												
- USA	.0	.0	.0	.0	.0	.0	12.6	12.0	9.9	56.2	45.0	44.4
- Largest 5 West-Eur.	.7	.0	.0	2.5	1.7	.3	28.2	21.1	16.7	25.1	27.1	26.0
- Japan	1.2	.0	.0	2.6	.0	.0	11.2	12.2	8.7	2.8	8.3	10.2
- Others	.0	.0	.0	.5	.1	.0	8.6	7.2	5.9	7.9	8.0	6.6
Total	100	100	100	100	100	100	100	100	100	100	100	100

Table 4. Income and population growth for selected groups of countries

	Average annual growth rate of GNP per capita 1950-60	1960-70	1970-73	1973-79	1979-86	Average annual population growth rate 1950-60	1960-70	1970-73	1973-79	1979-86
Poor										
- Indian Sub-Continent	1.6	1.9	-.7	1.4	3.2	2.0	2.4	2.2	2.4	2.3
- Nigeria-Indonesia	1.8	2.2	1.0	3.4	.3	2.2	2.3	2.1	2.4	2.0
- Other	1.5	1.2	1.4	.6	-1.2	2.0	2.4	2.5	2.7	2.8
Developing	1.8	2.5	3.3	2.6	.2	2.7	2.8	2.7	2.6	2.6
Newly Industrialized	3.3	3.9	7.1	4.4	1.5	3.0	2.9	2.8	2.4	2.2
Oil exporting	4.9	4.5	5.4	3.5	-4.6	2.6	3.0	3.1	3.4	3.4
Semi-Industrialized										
- European	4.7	6.4	6.5	2.5	.7	.9	.9	1.1	1.1	.8
- Other	.8	2.7	2.2	.5	-2.0	2.3	1.9	1.8	2.0	2.0
Industrialized										
- USA	1.6	2.6	3.9	1.4	1.4	1.7	1.3	.8	1.2	1.0
- Largest 5 West- European	3.0	3.7	3.9	2.3	1.2	.9	.9	.6	.3	.3
- Japan	5.0	10.0	9.2	2.5	3.1	1.3	1.0	1.4	1.1	.7
- Other	2.7	3.8	3.5	1.5	1.4	1.1	1.0	.8	.6	.5
World	2.0	2.9	3.4	1.3	.4	1.9	2.1	2.0	2.0	2.0

increases their weight in the world population but, by reducing the mean world income per capita, it also increases their relative income. For instance, the .4 per cent increase in world income per capita shown in table 4 for the period 1979–1986 clearly does not correspond to the weighted average of income per capita growth in the various countries that make up the world. It also incorporates the reshaping of the world population structure due to heterogeneous demographic growth rates, which tends to reduce the world income per capita. 10/ The income per capita in poor countries thus becomes closer to the world average, which in some sense reduces inequality. At the other extreme, however, the income per capita in rich countries increases in relation to the world average, which should increase inequality. One may thus expect the effect of differences in population growth upon world inequality to be essentially ambiguous.

The effects of population growth upon world inequality

In this section, we investigate more closely the issue just mentioned of the ambiguous effect of heterogeneous population growth upon income inequality. We begin by proving that at constant national incomes per capita, any change in the structure of the population leads to a Lorenz curve that necessarily intersects the original one. It is well known that under these conditions, there will always be two well–defined inequality measures pointing to opposite evolutions of the level of inequality. We then move on to examine the crucial assumption of independence between income per capita and population growth.

Consider an income distribution defined on N groups, i, of n_i individuals with the same income y_i. Assume that these groups are ranked by increasing income per capita and consider the associated Lorenz curve (figure II). Each segment of that curve corresponds to a group i of individuals; its slope is given by:

$$s_i = y_i / \bar{y}$$

where $\bar{y}$ is the mean income for the whole population.

Consider now an increase in the population of group k with no change in the income y_k of that group. Assume that the income of that group is below the population mean, y. The rise in n_k thus produces a fall in y. It follows that the slope of all segments of the Lorenz curve increases, so that the curve shifts upward at the bottom and downward at the top. By continuity the new curve necessarily intersects the initial one. This result would still obtain if the income of group k were above the overall mean, y. In that case, the bottom of the Lorenz curve would shift downward and the top of the curve upward. Generalizing that argument to any number of elementary changes of the n_i's shows that any modification of the demographic structure of the population that modifies its mean income has an ambiguous effect upon the level of inequality. 11/ Since Lorenz curves intersect, some inequality measures will point to more inequality while others will point to less.

The previous result may seem odd. Indeed, it would appear <u>a priori</u> that reducing the percentage of poor in a given population is "good", while increasing it is "bad". This intuitive argument is valid when one considers social welfare as such and inequality is not considered. Reducing the proportion of the poor in a given population increases the mean income and modifies the distribution of income in an ambiguous way from the point of view of inequality. However, both the mean income and the distribution enter the social welfare function, so it can easily be seen that the positive effect of the increase in the former dominates the ambiguous effect of the latter. <u>12</u>/ It may also be noted, on the other hand, that changes in the demographic structure have a less ambiguous effect when poverty instead of inequality measures are considered.

In the present context of changes in world population and distribution of income, assuming independence between population growth and income per capita seems rather extreme. Indeed, a considerable part of the literature on population economics has been devoted to the measurement of the elasticity of income per capita with respect to population size, the extreme assumptions being, on one hand, the Malthusian one of an elasticity equal to -1 – i.e., no relationship between population and output – and, on the other hand, the optimistic view of Clark that this elasticity is close to 1 – i.e., the growth of income per capita is independent of population growth. <u>13</u>/ The argument above about the ambiguous effects of demographic changes upon the world inequality of income rests upon the latter assumption. It thus is of interest to examine whether it remains valid with a less extreme assumption about the relationship between population and economic growth.

Assume that the relationship between the size of a group i and its level of income per capita is given by :

$$y_i = a \, n_i^{\,\alpha-1} \tag{1}$$

where a_i is some constant specific of group or country i, and α is the income–population elasticity, reasonably assumed to be between 0 and 1. The effect of a small change in the population of a group k upon the Lorenz curve is analogous to what was seen before if that group belongs to the middle of the income distribution. In that case the overall mean income increases or decreases depending on the sign of $\alpha y_k - y$, <u>14</u>/ and the slopes of both end segments of the Lorenz curve move in the same direction -- as in figure II, for instance – so that the new curve necessarily intersects the old one. However, for $k = 1$, that is when the size of the poorest group increases, things are different. The overall mean income decreases with the effect of increasing the slopes of all subsequent segments of the Lorenz curve. But if the elasticity a is sufficiently small, the concomitant fall in the income of the poorest group may now cause a drop in the slope of the first segment of the Lorenz curve, a movement that is consistent with a downward shift of the whole curve. <u>15</u>/

We have thus proved that if the population elasticity of income is sufficiently low, a faster demographic growth among the poor may produce an unambiguous worsening of the world distribution of income by shifting the

Figure I. World inequality: 1950–1986

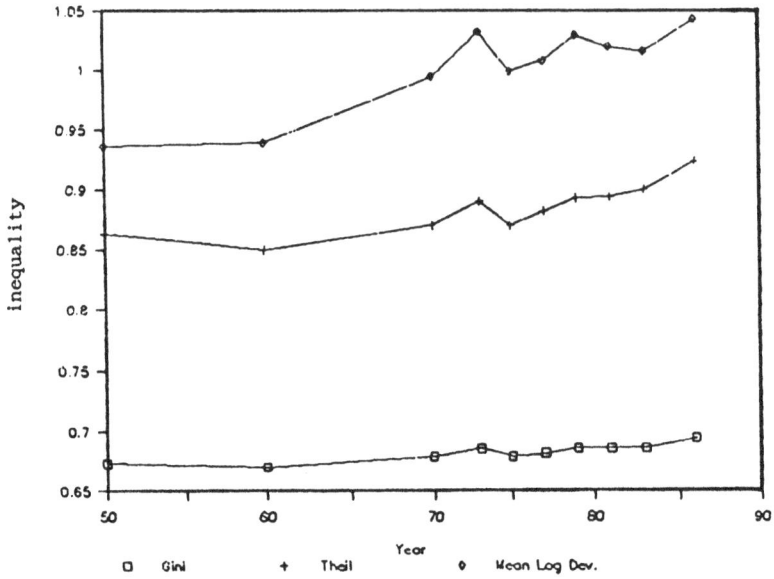

Figure II. Shift of the Lorenz curve resulting from an increase in the population of a group of individuals with income above the overall mean

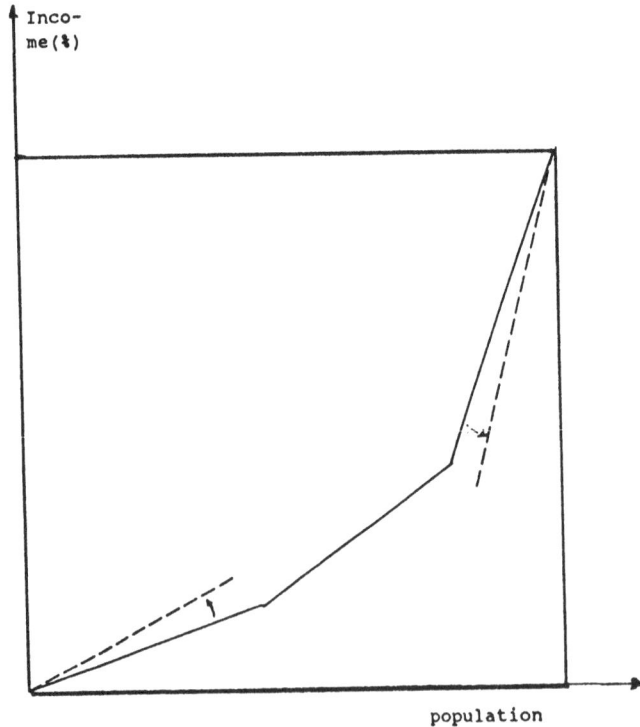

Lorenz curve uniformly downward, as in figure III, while this could not happen under the assumption that income per capita was independent of population size, as depicted in figure II.

Table 4 in the previous section shows that the fastest-growing countries, in terms of population, are developing and poor countries, so that world demographic growth corresponds to the case just described. In order to check the preceding argument and to measure the population elasticity of income, which ensures that population growth in poor countries will have an unambiguously negative effect on the world distribution of income, we now examine what that distribution would have been if demographic growth had been smaller, with alternative assumptions about the elasticity α. Table 5 summarizes the results we have obtained by limiting population growth to 2 per cent per annum - the actual average world growth rate - for all countries and over the entire 1950–1986 period. In other words, the demographic growth rate has been kept equal to the actual one for all countries with annual population growth below 2 per cent and brought down to that level for all others. Simultaneously, income per capita growth has been changed according to formula (1) with a taking the values 0, .5, and 1.

The results are as expected. The simulated deceleration of population growth in the fastest-growing countries produces a 14 per cent drop in world population in 1986. Compared with the actual distribution in that year and with income per capita assumed to be independent of population growth (a = 1), the effect of income upon world distribution is ambiguous, with the Lorenz curve shifting downward in its lower end and upward in its upper end, and with contradictory changes in the various summary measures used in this study. Poverty goes down when considering the proportion of the poor but not when using the poverty gap, which means that if there are relatively fewer poor in the population, those who remain so are poorer than before. This phenomenon reflects the fact that the fastest-growing populations are not in the poorest countries but in intermediate ones (see table 4). So the slower demographic growth in those countries eliminates the poor who were actually close to the poverty limit, whereas the number of the poor who were far below that limit falls more slowly. Of course, the total number of the poor decreases as a direct effect of the demographic slowdown.

In the other extreme case, where total income is independent of population (α = 0), the drop in population produces a proportional increase in income per capita so that the world distribution of income unambiguously improves, whereas poverty falls drastically. The middle case (α = .5) corresponds in fact to the threshold of the income-population elasticity, below which population growth deceleration leads to a uniform upward shift in the Lorenz curve. We thus conclude that in order for a slowdown in population growth among poor and developing countries to unambiguously improve the world distribution of income, given the present structure of per capita income in the world population, it is necessary that the relationship between income and population be such that 1 per cent less population produces at least .5 per cent more income per capita in all countries with above-average population growth rates.

Table 5.   The world distribution of GNP in 1986 in 1986 with reduced
population growth rates and alternative income–population
elasticities (α)

Decile shares in world income (%)	Actual distribution Shares	Actual distribution Cum. shares	α=1 Shares	α=1 Cum. shares	α = .5 Shares	α = .5 Cum. shares	α = 0 Shares	α = 0 Cum. shares
Decile 1	.5	.5	.5	.5	.5	.5	.5	.5
2	.8	1.3	.8	1.2	.8	1.3	.8	1.3
3	1.2	2.5	1.1	2.3	1.2	2.5	1.2	2.6
4	1.6	4.1	1.6	3.9	1.6	4.1	1.7	4.3
5	2.2	6.3	2.2	6.1	2.3	6.4	2.4	6.7
6	3.3	9.6	3.4	9.4	3.6	10.0	3.8	10.5
7	5.7	15.3	6.0	15.4	6.3	16.2	6.5	17.0
8	10.6	25.9	11.3	26.8	11.5	27.7	11.7	28.7
9	20.8	46.7	21.2	48.0	21.1	48.8	20.8	49.5
10	53.3	100.0	52.0	100.0	51.2	100.0	50.5	100.0
Top 5%	35.5		34.4		34.0		33.6	
Summary inequality measures								
Gini	.693		.690		.682		.675	
Theil	.924		.905		.880		.857	
Mean Logarithm Deviation	1.043		1.052		1.017		.986	
Atkinson e = -1.0	.773		.779		.769		.759	
e = -1.5	.835		.842		.833		.826	
e = -2.0	.869		.875		.868		.862	
Poverty								
- Number of poors (10^3)	859		724.9		642.1		581.3	
- Proportion of poors (%)	26.4		25.4		22.5		20.4	
- Poverty gap (1970 US Dollars)	19.1		19.2		16.8		10.9	
World Population (10^6)	3254.2		2846.9		2846.9		2846.9	
World Income per capita (1970 US Dollars)	1674.0		1804.0		1854.0		1911.7	

Figure III. Effect on the Lorenz curve of an increase in the
             number of the poor with a fall in their
             relative income

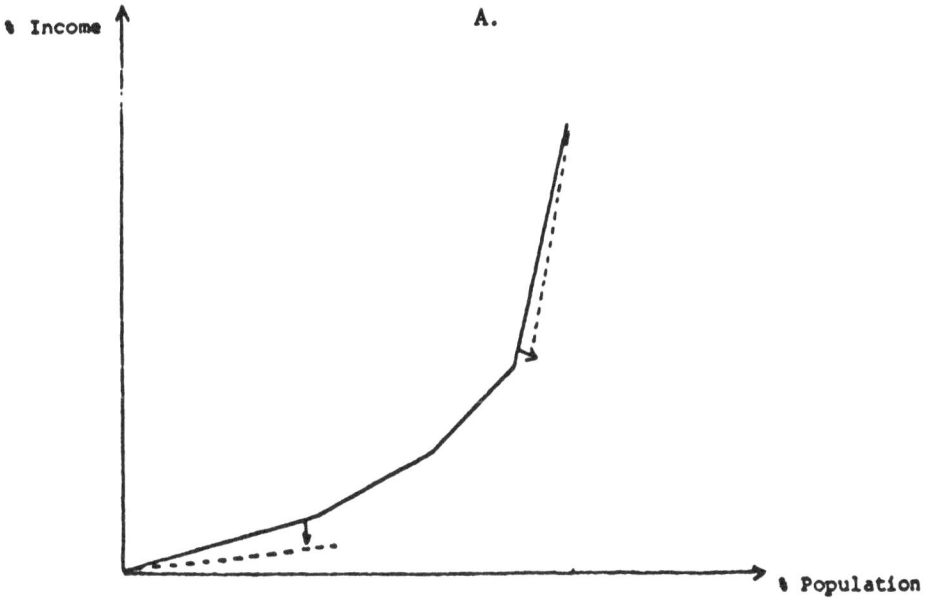

A.

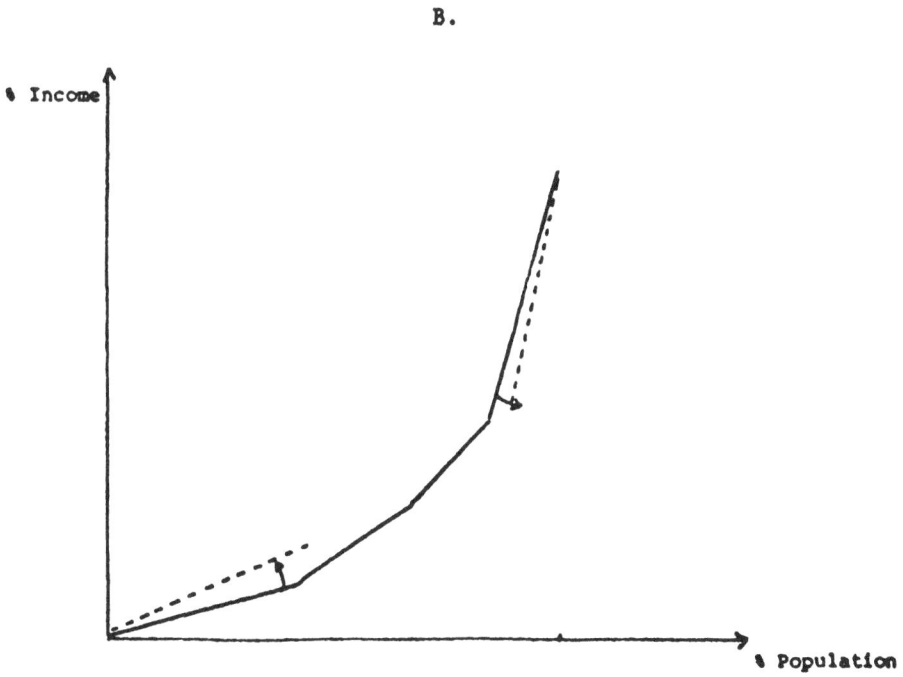

B.

Conclusion

We have shown in this paper that over the last decade, the world distribution of income among non-socialist countries cannot be said to have improved. As it had unambiguously worsened over the 1960s and early 1970s, the record for the entire post-war period is definitely negative. In 1986, world inequality was substantially higher than it had been 25 or 35 years earlier. Investigating the causes of that evolution, we have found no evidence of a strong immediate impact upon inequality due to the slowdown of the world economy in the recent past, although that slowdown has certainly contributed to a reduction in the rate of decline of world poverty. The long-run worsening trend in world distribution seems due to the vulnerability of poor countries affected by negative shocks that have not been compensated by subsequent better-than-average performances.

As far as population growth is concerned, it has been shown that its role in the evolution of the world distribution essentially depends on its impact upon the growth of income per capita. If it is assumed that in the long run, the elasticity of national income with respect to population is close to unity, then the heterogeneity of population growth across countries has had essentially ambiguous effects on the level of world inequality. On the other hand, if it is assumed that this elasticity is between 0 and .5, then the fact that the growth of world population has been concentrated in poor countries has had a substantial negative influence on world income distribution. The issue of the relationship between the increase in world inequality and the asymmetric growth of national populations thus brings us back to one of the fundamental issue in population economics, that of the link between output and population growth.

Notes

1/ Earlier studies include Andic and Peacock (1961), Beckerman and Bacon (1970), Kirman and Tomasini (1969), Whalley (1979), and Theil (1979).

2/ These are Cambodia, Cameroon, Cyprus, Gabon, Iceland, Kuwait, Lebanon and Qatar. Based on the pre-1977 period, we have determined that excluding these small countries had no significant effect on the measure of world inequality.

3/ On that point, see Berry and others (1981).

4/ The Indo-Pakistani War ended in December 1971 and the secession of Bangladesh became effective at that date.

5/ That limit itself may be defined as a range instead of as a precise value. Poverty measures then give rise to poverty "orderings" (see Atkinson, 1987; Foster and Shorrocks, 1988). We do not follow that direction here.

6/ Using the United States GDP deflator as an inflation index, this limit would presently be equivalent to approximately $US 500.

7/ The theoretical argument leading to these estimates is quite simple. Let $F_0(x)$ be the cumulative distribution of income in the base year, and assume that all incomes have grown in the same proportion, a, between that year and year t. If X is the poverty limit, the head–count ratio should thus have gone from $F_0(X)$ to $F_0(X/a)$. Comparing the actual proportion of the poor in year t, $F_t(X)$, with $F_0(X/a)$ then gives an estimate of the contribution of the change in the distribution to the change in poverty. The calculation is slightly more complicated for the poverty gap measure.

8/ In 1986, this amounts to between $US 62 and $US 110 billion in 1970 prices, approximately $US 150–275 billion at present prices, depending upon whether GNP or consumption is used as a proxy for individual incomes.

9/ The corresponding figure for the consumption concept of income is 50 per cent.

10/ Technically, it is easy to see that if Y is the world average income per capita, P the world population, Y_i the income per capita in country i, and p_i the population:

$$\delta Y = \sum v_i \ \delta y_i + \sum v_i \ \delta P_i - \delta P$$

where δ is the growth rate operator and v_i is the share of country i in world income. Because the δp_i are weighted by income shares rather than by population shares, the last two terms on the right do not sum to zero.

11/ It is straightforward to see that increasing the population of a group k with income $y_k = y$ necessarily shifts the Lorenz curve upward, generating more equality.

12/ On the relationship between inequality measures and social welfare, see Blackorby and Donaldson (1978).

13/ For a survey of this issue, see G. McNicoll (1984). See also World Bank (1984).

14/ By definition, $y = \sum w_i \ y_i$, where w_i is the population share of group i. Differentiating with respect to n_k yields:

$$dy = \sum y_i \ dw_i + w_k dy_k$$

with $dw_i = w_i \ w_k \ (dn_k/n_k)$ for $i \neq k$ and $dw_k = (w_k - w_k^2)(dn_k/n_k)$.

From the definition of the income–population elasticity above:

$$dy_k = (\alpha - 1)y_k \ (dn_k/n_k)$$

Rearranging leads to:

$$dy = (\alpha y_k - y) \ (dn_k/n_k)$$

15/ A simple calculation shows that the condition for the first segment of the Lorenz curve to move downward with an increase in n_1 is that:

$$\alpha \leq (n/n_1 - 1)/(n/n_1 - y_1/\bar{y})$$

This condition is thus necessary (but not sufficient) for a downward shift of the Lorenz curve.

Annex

COUNTRIES INCLUDED IN THE ANALYSIS*

Least developed countries

Indian subcontinent:

   Bangladesh, India, Pakistan, Sri Lanka

Oil-producing countries:

   Indonesia, Nigeria

Other poor countries:

   Afghanistan, Botswana, Burkina Faso, Burundi, Central African Republic, Chad, Ethiopia, Gambia, Lesotho, Madagascar, Malawi, Mali, Mauritania, Myanmar (formerly Burma), Nepal, Rwanda, Somalia, Togo, Uganda, United Republic of Tanzania, Zaire.

Developing countries

   Barbados, Bolivia, Chile, Colombia, Costa Rica, Côte d'Ivoire, Dominican Republic, Egypt, Ecuador, El Salvador, Fiji, Ghana, Guatemala, Guyana, Honduras, Jamaica, Jordan, Kenya, Liberia, Malaysia, Mauritius, Morocco, Nicaragua, Panama, Papua New Guinea, Paraguay, Peru, Philippines, Rhodesia, Senegal, Sierra Leone, Swaziland, Syria, Thailand, Trinidad, Tunisia, Turkey, Zambia.

Newly industrialized countries and territory

   Brazil, China (Taiwan Province), Hong Kong, Mexico, Republic of Singapore, Republic of Korea.

---

   * The following classification is self-explanatory except for a few cases. Nigeria and Indonesia have been distinguished from other oil-producing countries and classified together with poor countries, because of the level of their GDP per capita and its structure was close to that of other poor countries throughout most of the period of analysis. The same type of argument also explains why some countries are classified as least developed or developing (e. g., in terms of GDP per capita Ghana was much closer to other developing countries than poor countries during the fifties and the sixties). Nepal, on the other hand, could have been included in the Indian subcontinent, but we felt that for various reasons, including its demographic features, it was rather distinct from the countries in that group.

Oil-exporting countries

Algeria, Iran, Iraq, Libyan Arab Jamahiriya, Oman, Saudi Arabia, Venezuela.

Semi-industrialized countries

European:

Greece, Ireland, Israel, Malta, Portugal, Spain

Other:

Argentina, South Africa, Uruguay

Developed countries

Australia, Austria, Belgium, Canada, Denmark, Federal Republic of Germany, Finland, France, Italy, Japan, Netherlands, New Zealand, Norway, Sweden, Switzerland, United Kingdom, United States.

References

Ahluwahlia, M., N. Carter and H. Chenery (1979). Growth and poverty in developing countries. Journal of Development Economics, vol. 6, pp. 299-342.

Andic, S. and A. Peacock (1961). The international distribution of income. Journal of the Royal Statistical Society, vol. 124, pp. 206-218.

Atkinson, S. (1987). On the measurement of poverty. Econometrica, vol. 55, pp. 49-64.

Beckerman, W. and R. Bacon (1970). The international distribution of income. In Unfashionable Economics, P. Streeten, ed. London: Weidenfeld and Nicholson, pp. 56-74.

Berry, A., F. Bourguignon and C. Morrisson (1983). Changes in the world distribution of income between 1950 and 1987. Economic Journal, vol. 93, pp. 331-350.

_____, F. Bourguignon and C. Morrisson (1984). The level of world inequality: how much can one say? Review of Income and Wealth, vol. 29, No. 3, pp. 217-241.

_____ and others (1981). Data for the Analysis of the World Distribution of Income. Laboratoire d'Ecole Politique (LEP). Working Paper, No. 39, Paris: Ecole Normale Supérieure.

Blackorby, C. and D. Donaldson (1978). Measures of relative equality and their meaning in terms of social welfare. Journal of Economic Theory, vol. 18, pp. 59-80.

Foster, J. and A. Shorrocks (1988). Inequality and poverty orderings. European Economic Review, vol. 32, pp. 654-662.

Grosh, M. and E. W. Nafziger (1986). The computation of world income distribution. Economic Development and Cultural Change, vol. 34, pp. 347-359.

Kirman, A. and L. Tomasini (1969). A new look at international income inequalities. Economia Internazionale, vol. 22, pp. 437-461.

Kravis, I., R. Summers, and A. Heston (1978). Real GDP per capita for more than one hundred countries. Economic Journal, vol. 88, pp. 215-242.

McNicoll, G. (1984). Consequences of Rapid Population Growth: An Overview and an Assessment. Center for Policy Studies Working Paper, No. 105. New York: The Population Council.

Summers, R. and A. Heston (1984). Improved international comparisons of real product and its composition, 1950-80. Review of Income and Wealth, vol. 32, No. 2, (June) pp. 207-262.

_____ and A. Heston (1988). A new set of international comparisons of real product and prices: estimates for 130 countries, 1950–1985. <u>Review of Income and Wealth</u>, vol. 34, No. 1, (March) pp. 1–26.

Theil, H. (1979). World inequality and its components. <u>Economic Letters</u>, vol. 2, pp. 8–14.

Yotopoulos, P. A. (1988). A world distribution of income and of real poverty and affluence. Stanford University. Mimeographed.

Whalley, J. (1979). The worldwide income distribution: some speculative calculations. <u>Review of Income and Wealth</u>, vol. 25, No. 3, pp. 261–276.

Chapter 11

Evaluating externalities to child-bearing in developing countries : the case of India

● R. Lee with the assistance of N. Cohen*

Introduction

Externalities occur when some costs or benefits of children are passed on to others, rather than accruing to the parents. Many believe that such externalities underlie, or indeed constitute, the "population problem" and provide the rationale for governmental intervention in fertility decision-making. This paper discusses how such externalities may arise and evaluates them for contemporary India.

The problem

In many countries of the developing world, survey data reveal excess fertility--numbers of surviving children exceeding the number the parents say they want. In such circumstances, government policies designed to reduce the costs of fertility regulation may readily be justified, as for various reasons markets may do a poor job of meeting the demand for contraceptive information and services. For many people, costs of fertility regulation may readily be justified, as for various reasons markets may do a poor job of meeting the demand for contraceptive information and services. Many people, however, have argued that merely enabling couples to attain their private family size

*Graduate Group in Demography, University of California, Berkeley. This research was supported in part by a grant from the Rockefeller Foundation. Helpful comments were received from Gary Becker, Robert Willis and others at the University of Chicago Workshop on Population and Labor; from James Smith and others at the RAND Workshop on Population and Labor; from Allen Kelley, Eugene Hammel and others at the United Nations/INED Conference; and from Andy Foster. Marc Nerlove and Assaf Razin also made helpful comments on an earlier draft. The author is grateful to Dennis Ahlburg and Ken Reid for their advice on the Indian coal and iron industries. The views expressed are those of the author alone and responsibility for any errors of course rests with him.

objectives is too limited a goal and, if accomplished, could leave developing country populations doubling every generation. In a classic article Kingsley Davis (1967) wrote:

> "There is no reason to expect that the millions of decisions about family size made by couples in their own interest will automatically control population for the benefit of society....In underdeveloped countries...the elimination of unwanted births would still leave an extremely high rate of multiplication."

Becker (1981) has shown how reductions in the cost of fertility regulation might lead to substantial declines not only in excess fertility but also in the desired number of surviving children, by affecting the trade-off between the quality and quantity of children in the budget constraint. None the less, after all such adjustments to falling contraceptive costs had been made, and after excess fertility had been largely eliminated, the question still would arise: Should we expect that the privately optimal number of surviving children per family corresponds to the socially optimal one? And indeed this question is asked as well in developed countries, where contraceptive costs and excess fertility are typically quite low. [1]

The issue does not reduce to the question of whether rapid population growth impedes economic development. It might, but such a finding would not imply that parents would be better off with fewer children. [2] Parents may fully realize that children are costly, but because they derive satisfaction from children they may choose to bear them and to pay the cost, striking a balance between their enjoyment of children and their enjoyment of other costly things. The question we ask now is whether the child costs that parents consider in striking this balance represent a full accounting of children's costs and benefits, or whether there are spillover effects on other families. If such spill-overs occur, then the _laissez faire_ approach to population policy will not lead to the socially optimal outcome; it will be possible through public intervention in reproductive decision-making to improve the welfare of the typical parent.

Both popular and scholarly treatments of the subject argue that divergences between the private and public costs and benefits of children do lead to such spill-over effects. Divergences could arise in several ways. Society might place different values than the individual on the same outcomes, such as the income distribution across households at any given moment or across the sequence of generations, or the income distribution within the family. Or society may care about the size of the population itself for various reasons. Alternatively, even if society cares only for the welfare of a representative parent in the current generation, as assessed by that parent, the market and other institutions may fail to confront the parents with the full implications of their child-bearing. Such failures might arise through public provision for health and education of children or for old-age support, from public goods, from the effects of today's children on tomorrow's wages, or from commonly owned resources (see Nerlove and others 1987, chapters 6 and 7, on which this discussion is loosely based).

These possibilities are taken very seriously in the policy-oriented literature as well as by government planners. In 1984, an appeal to the social-private discrepancy was at the core of the World Bank's influential World Development Report: "Each individual family's decision to have another child seems rational. Yet added together, these separate decisions make all families, and especially children, worse off in the end. There is a gap between the private and social gains to large families." It is this gap (in addition to excess fertility) that is used to provide the basis for governmental intervention in fertility decision-making. Similarly, the recent National Academy of Sciences (NAS) report says: "A key policy question in considering population growth is whether a couple's child-bearing decisions impose costs on, or provide benefits for, other families" (1986).

Such a gap between public and private costs and benefits is also believed to occur in developed countries, where individual fertility no longer has implications for individual old-age support, although for society as a whole, old-age support still depends on the renewal of the labour force by child-bearing. A majority of Governments of developed countries have instituted explicitly pronatalist policies deriving from concern for the burden of supporting the elderly. At the same time, a majority of developing country Governments have officially adopted antinatal goals.

Contributions by economists

Over the past decade, a number of economists have turned their attention in a more sustained and seriously analytic way to the question of the social optimality of individual decision-making about family size. Some of these economists have done so within the context of a new theoretical approach, the so-called "New new home economics", distinguished by incorporation of the overlapping generations framework introduced by Samuelson (1958) and the altruistic utility function pioneered by Becker (e.g., 1981) and others. Among these are Becker (1988), Becker and Murphy (1988), Willis (1987), and, in a recent monograph on the subject, Nerlove, Razin, and Sadka (1987). These authors have spelled out conditions under which individual decisions will lead to optimal social outcomes even in the presence of diminishing returns to land, investment in human capital, intergenerational transfers, and public goods. Because the thrust of the literature has been to show that externalities need not arise in many situations where they had previously been expected, the general impression created is that externalities to child-bearing, at least of the sort traditionally considered, are rather unimportant. At a less technical level, a recent article by Ng (1986) argues that a laissez faire approach to population policy is most appropriate.

Where these economists have found externalities to arise, they have appeared in surprising places and have centred particularly on the possible failure of institutions to support optimal bequests. Nerlove and others argue that parents cannot affect their adult children's welfare efficiently through bequests because their children will share these with a spouse; consequently, parents leave smaller bequests than they would otherwise wish and have more children than they would otherwise wish. Becker and Willis have stressed that when institutional support to ensure negative bequests (child-to-parent transfers in later life) is lacking, parents will underinvest in their children's human capital and will again compensate by bearing too many children. In both cases, parental welfare would be increased by lower fertility and greater resources devoted to each child, in an appropriate institutional context. These are important insights, but they do not address the kind of externality trumpeted in the policy literature, and they bear no relation to problems arising from fixed natural resources. Nor is it clear that the sub-optimalities here result from child-bearing externalities; they seem rather to arise as by-products of market failures in other areas.

Other economists have shown that externalities can arise from patterns of intergenerational transfers, if a different parental utility function is assumed. Eckstein and Wolpin (1985) have shown that with a conventional parental utility function, 3/ individually chosen fertility may be non-optimal in an overlapping generations model. Lee (1988), Lee and Lapkoff (1988), and Ermisch (1988) have attempted to measure the net social cost or value of a child arising from intergenerational transfers in developing countries and have found evidence of similar positive externalities to child-bearing in the United States, the United Kingdom, and Japan.

Despite the theoretical attention devoted to the potentially important role of externalities and the policy importance attached to the topic, apparently no work at all has been done to estimate the likely magnitude of child-bearing externalities in developing countries. The NAS chapter on the subject concludes: "Current data and theory are inadequate to quantify the size of external effects" (1986). Yet some parts of the picture could now be sketched, allowing at least a partial and preliminary assessment of the magnitude of externalities and some clarification of the issues that must be resolved before further progress can be made.

Plan of this paper

Using a model developed by Nerlove, Razin and Sadka, I will begin by considering the base-line case of private ownership of land and no public sector and confirm that in this case, no child-bearing externalities arise even though child-bearing depresses the wages and raises the rents of the next generation. I will then consider whether externalities arise from various departures from the base-line case as follows: (a) public goods, the per capita cost of which is lower in a larger population; (b) commonly owned resources and public wealth, for which incremental births dilute the per capita value; (c) the effect of population size on technological progress; and (d) the age distribution of public taxes and transfers. In discussing these and other areas, I will abstract from some important aspects of the problem, aspects that would be covered in a fuller treatment. Specifically, I will not consider the problem of degradation (as opposed to congestion) of commonly owned resources. I will assume that all families are identical in tastes and economic circumstances. I will assume that the social welfare function is no different than the aggregation of welfares of currently existing parents as perceived by them, so that the objective is to maximize the utility of a representative couple of the current generation. Thus society is assumed to care about future generations exactly to the extent that contemporary adults do. These are important limitations, but we will see that despite them, a number of externalities may still occur.

For all items except intergenerational transfers, my theoretical analysis relies heavily on a simple two-period model developed by Nerlove, Razin and Sadka (1987), whose monograph I have found very helpful. However, I introduce a number of additional effects and assumptions. My analysis of intergenerational transfers builds on the treatment developed in Arthur and McNicoll (1978), Willis (1988), and Lee (1988); Willis's detailed consideration of the family, market, and public sector was particularly helpful. Ideally, the same model would be used for all parts; as it is, there is some inconsistency in the way the various potential sources of externalities are treated.

I will make the discussion concrete by using numbers drawn from India. Some of the preliminary findings are indeed provocative: some potential sources of externalities generally thought to be sizeable turn out to be very small; other potential sources previously overlooked, may be enormous. However, because population heterogeneity is so pervasive and important in India, perhaps I should instead say that I will be considering a country that is like India but in which everybody is identical in all respects except age and sex. Because I make no attempt to deal with heterogeneity, because I can claim no special knowledge of India, and because this analysis is preliminary and illustrative, it would be a mistake to draw any policy implications from it.

The base-line case: private ownership, no common property, no public sector

Background

It is often argued that when parents choose a number of children, they do not take into account the impact this number will have on the wages or per capita income of the next generation as a whole, when their children grow up and enter the labour market. Any such negative effect is therefore said to be an externality to child-bearing. The argument presumably applies either to the industrial sector, where capital per worker will be reduced, or to the agricultural sector, where land per worker will be reduced. The argument is believed to apply in the context of exclusively private ownership.

This plausible argument has repeatedly been demonstrated to be mistaken, for example, by Blandy (1974) and Willis (1987), and most formally by Nerlove, Razin and Sadka (1987). When ownership of resources is heterogeneous, the reason is simple: higher fertility does lead to lower wages, but it also leads to higher profits and rents and it would not be possible for the less numerous workers under a lower fertility regime to compensate the capitalists and landowners for their reduced profits and rents, and still to be better off. 4/ Therefore reduced fertility is not Pareto-preferable. If the workers themselves own the capital and land, as is here assumed to be the case, then all distributional effects of population growth vanish. Now the income of every member of the next generation can be raised by reducing fertility. None the less, as with working on Sunday, it does not follow that lower fertility would raise the utility of the parent generation. I will examine this case below, using the Nerlove, Razin and Sadka two-period model. (Nerlove, Razin and Sadka give a more rigorous, but more difficult, proof). In later sections, altered versions of this model will be used to consider other possible sources of externalities.

The Nerlove, Razin and Sadka two-period model with perfect foresight

Following Nerlove, Razin and Sadka, consider a couple whose utility depends on the current consumption by their family, c_1, on the number of children they have, n, and on the consumption by each of these children as adults in the second period, c_2. [5/] Parental satisfaction arises from the average consumption by their children as adults, not from the total. Each family owns a farm yielding output that depends on labour inputs according to the production function f(.), with land suppressed as an argument. They may leave a positive or negative bequest of b to the next generation. Storage of b is possible without gain or loss. Assume with Nerlove, Razin and Sadka that all families are identical in tastes and endowments and that all have perfect foresight about the fertility of other families, so that second-period wages, w_2, and rents, r_2, are known to first-period parents. For the individual couple, then, the problem is:

Max $U(c_1,c_2,n)$ (over c_1,c_2,n,b)

Subject to: $w_1 + r_1 - b = c_1$

$n*A(w_2) + A(r_2) + b = n*A(c_2)$

$A(w_2) = w_2$

$A(r_2) = r_2$

$A(c_2) = c_2.$

w_i and r_i refer to wages and rents (to the fixed family holding) in each period, and A(.) denotes the second-period value anticipated in the first period. The last three equations express the assumption of perfect foresight. We can combine the five constraints into a single one by first substituting actual values for anticipated values and then adding them (following Nerlove, Razin and Sadka), which eliminates the bequest, b. We then have:

$w_1 + r_1 + n*w_2 + r_2 = c_1 + n*c_2.$

Wages and rents in the second period, of course, depend on average fertility decisions in the first period, but from the point of view of the individual the effect of their own fertility on these is negligible. Thus, while first-generation parents can determine how many children will share the family farms, they cannot determine either the value of the farm or the wage rate their children will face.

The laissez faire decision

Each parent's first-order conditions for individually optimal fertility in this case are (suppressing the household index i):

$$U_n/U_{c1} = c_2 - w_2$$

$$U_{c2} = U_{c1}/n$$

The assumption of perfect foresight assures that the wages and rents expected to prevail in the second period will indeed do so.

The social planner's decision

Now suppose that there is a central planner whose objective is to maximize social welfare, which, by the homogeneity assumption, is no different than maximizing the utility of a representative individual. Suppose the planner can without cost choose the level of fertility for all couples, but cannot otherwise influence factor prices. Since a social planner would take second-period rents and wages as endogenous to his/her fertility decision, while individuals must take these as given, the planner may be able to improve on the laissez faire outcome.

We can explore this possibility by comparing the first order conditions for the individual parent with those for the social planner. The planner recognizes that second-period wages and rents depend on the choice of fertility, n. Thus if the production function is homogeneous, $w_2 = f'(n)$ and $r_2 = f(n) - n*f'(n)$. Aside from incorporation of these two relations, the planner's problem is identical to the individual's. The planner's first-order condition for fertility differs from the individual's by a term: U_{c1} $(dr_2/dn + n*dw_2/dn)$. But the term in parentheses is readily shown to equal $(-n*f'' + n*f'') = 0$. Therefore the form of the planner's first-order condition for fertility is no different than the individual's. The other first-order conditions are readily seen to be the same as well. Therefore the planner, in seeking to maximize the utility of the first generation parents, would make exactly the same choice of fertility as they, and no externality would occur.

Extensions: many periods, equilibrium, lack of foresight

We can easily extend this two-period model to a sequence of generations if we suppose that the children face the same fertility decision in the second period that their parents did in the first. 6/ In this case, under suitable conditions, an equilibrium population size will exist, such that parents will elect to have a number of children just sufficient for replacement (at equilibrium, n=2 for a two-sex model with no mortality before child-bearing). It is clear that this equilibrium population will be the same under either *laissez faire* or social planning, since the same fertility will be chosen every generation.

What has become of the externality that intuition led us to expect? Perhaps it was a casualty of the assumption of perfect foresight, which in combination with homogeneity implies that every parent knows that all other parents will be making the same fertility decision. Yet if we abandon it, then some other assumption about expectations for the second period must be put in its place, and none is particularly compelling. Let us suppose that parents myopically anticipate that current conditions will persist and that second-period wages and rents will equal those of the first period. If population is initially below equilibrium, then these anticipations will overstate the future reality, and consequently *laissez faire* fertility will exceed the optimal level. Indeed, this will be true whenever anticipations are unrealistically high. This is not an interesting or enlightening conclusion.

Now consider a long-run equilibrium towards which this process, arising from myopic expectations, converges. A moment's reflection indicates that it will be identical to the optimal equilibrium. For at the planner's equilibrium, wages and rents are by definition constant over time, so $w_1=A(w_2)=w_2$ and $r_1=A(r_2)=r_2$. At the optimal equilibrium, therefore, anticipations will be accurate, and behaviour must, therefore, be the same as under perfect foresight. The perfect foresight equilibrium, however, has already been shown to be the same as the optimal equilibrium. We therefore have the surprising result that although myopic expectations will not generally lead to optimal fertility decisions, if the intergenerational process converges, it must none the less converge to the optimal population equilibrium. Presumably, convergence will be slower in the myopic case, however. It appears that the "optimality of equilibrium" will hold for any expectations function that sets anticipated w_2 equal to the prior values of w, when these are unchanging. This includes functions that extrapolate past trends, taking a finite number of past values of w and r as arguments.

It, therefore, appears that no child-bearing externality occurs in the case of privately owned land. Higher fertility does, of course, reduce later incomes, but individuals will take this into account to the same degree as would a social planner seeking to maximize their utilities. I have not worked through a corresponding case for capital, but I suspect it would lead to the same conclusion.

Public goods and public wealth

Background

There are two potential sources of externalities to child-bearing that have symmetric effects and therefore may naturally be treated together, although they appear on the surface to be quite different. The first of these is public goods, that is, goods that can be consumed by any number of people without congestion or marginal cost. A positive externality to child-bearing may arise if there are public goods because the larger the population, the more thinly the cost of the public good can be spread over the population, reducing the individual tax burden and, perhaps, leading to a greater level of consumption of the public good by all. Examples of public goods include national defense, radio and television broadcasting, governmental research and development, 7/ weather monitoring and forecasting, a diplomatic corps, and so on.

Nerlove, Razin and Sadka show that it is possible to devise a non-distortionary tax such that public goods do not lead to a child-bearing externality. 8/ Rather than following the tax system assumed by Nerlove, Razin and Sadka, I will assume that a head tax is levied equally on all adults of each generation to pay for a public good- an assumption I believe to be closer to institutional realities. In other respects, my analysis is closely based on theirs.

The second source of externalities is any form of public wealth that is independent of the size of the population. Each birth automatically acquires rights to the average share of this wealth at the expense of the size of the share of others, an effect that will not be taken into account by the parent. 9/ One important example of such an asset is publicly-owned mineral wealth. Others are publicly-owned capital stock, taxes on foreign firms that extract minerals, public debt, and publicly-owned land. I will discuss each of these in more detail below. I will also argue in a later section that all common property resources, such as air shed and water shed, can be thought of in essentially the same way.

An example of this kind of reasoning and calculation is provided by Boskin and others (1985), who estimate the value of United States federal mineral rights and federal land. They derive a total value in 1981 of nearly a trillion dollars, or roughly $US 4,000 per capita, which they point out is approximately the level of the total national debt in 1981. The following statement is also of interest: "Saudi Arabia was able virtually to abolish taxation due to revenues from the sale of mineral rights, and Alaska used oil-based revenues to provide cash grants on a per capita basis to its citizens, thereby increasing their private wealth and consumption opportunities".

A model

The basic model of the previous section may now be altered to reflect these considerations. Suppose that the parental utility function now additionally incorporates satisfaction from consumption of a public good in period 1, P_1, and from their children's consumption of a public good in period 2, P_2. In each period, the Government chooses an optimal level of the public good and levies an equal tax, t_i, on all households to pay for it. In addition to revenues from taxes, the Government can sell the publicly held national wealth, which has value R. The Government has a balanced budget, and the net tax may be positive or negative.

For the individual, then, the problem is:

Max $U(c_1, c_2 n, P_1, P_2)$ (over c_1, c_2, n; P_is are given)

Subject to: $f(1) + f(n) = c_1 + nc_2 + t_1 + nt_2$.

The first-order condition for individually optimal fertility in this case is:

$$U_n/U_{c1} = c_2 + t_2 - f'(n).$$

The planner takes into account the fact that a larger population shares the revenues, R, and likewise shares the costs of providing P_2: $t_2 = (P_2 - R)/(nN)$. Optimizing with this additional constraint we get the first-order condition:

$$U_n/U_{c1} = c_2 - f'(n).$$

The term t_2 in the private first-order condition vanishes in that of the planner, because the planner sees that no matter how many children a woman has, their total tax obligation will remain the same, provided all other women have the same number of children. Consequently, an amount $t_2 = (P_2 - R)/(nN)$ should be subtracted from the individual's perceived marginal cost of children (where n is taken equal to the planner's optimal value) in order to internalize these two externalities. If $P_2 > R$, there is a net positive externality, and the social cost of children is lower than the private; higher fertility should then be encouraged. If, however, $P_2 < R$, then the social cost of children exceeds the private, due to the dilution of the population's claims on the revenues, R, and lower fertility should be encouraged.

Evaluation for India

Public goods. The cost of public goods, P, can be assessed through an inspection of the Indian Center and State budgets. Table 1 shows items in the Indian Government budget for 1981-1982 that I deem to represent public goods. Some, such as roads, I have counted at one half their value, since they have some public good aspects but are congestible and are therefore only quasi-public goods. "Water supply and sanitation" is one fairly large item that I have excluded, although it could be treated as roads are. The bottom line is a total of 129.3 rupees per capita, of which just under half is allocated to defense spending. This is equivalent to $US 14.20 (1981) and is 5.5 per cent of per capita income.

Table 1. Public–good type of expenditures (thousands of rupees), 1981 a/

Item	Amount	Weight[b]	Contribution
General Services			
Parliament	249631	0.5	124815
Pres/VP/Governor/Admin	45312	0.5	22656
Council of Ministers	112504	0.5	56252
Admin of Justice	1082912	0.5	541456
Elections	720753	0.5	360376
Audit	636342	0.5	318171
Subtotal	2847453		1423727
Aministrative Services			
Public Services Comm	98049	0.5	49024
Secretariat Gen Servs	1230797	0.5	615398
District Admin	1918437	0.5	959218
Stationery & Prntg	1205738	0.5	602869
External Affairs[c]	647480	1.0	647480
Subtotal	5100501		2873990
Defense	40421483	1.0	40421483
Social and Commun Serv			
Art and culture	428112	1.0	428112
Scientif Servs & Res	2630435	1.0	2630435
Information & Publicity	561896	1.0	561896
Broadcasting	747103	1.0	747103
Other[d]	181274	1.0	181274
Subtotal	4548820		4548820
Agric and Allied Servs			
Soil and Wtr Cons	1328607	1.0	1328607
Animal Husbandry	2045291	1.0	2045291
Dairy Dev	2907856	1.0	2907856
Fisheries	692792	1.0	692792
Forest	3515010	1.0	3515010
Subtotal	10489556		10489556
Industry			
Ind Res & Dev	986906	1.0	986906
Atomic Energy Dev	457999	1.0	457999
Subtotal	1444905		1444905
Water & Power Dev			
Wtr & Pwr Dev Servs	1850089	1.0	1850089
Irrig, Nav, Drng, Fld	15735962	1.0	15735962
Subtotal	17586051		17856051

Table 1   (continued)

Transport & communications			
Ports, Lt Hses & Shppg	1868132	1.0	1868132
Civil Aviation	1207386	0.5	603693
Rds & Brdgs	11384038	0.5	5917019
Rds & Wtr Trnspt Servs	2829064	0.5	1414532
Subtotal	17738620		9803376
Grand Total			88591909

Notes:

a/   Includes revenue, capital and net loans and advances, state and central.

b/   Items judged to be subject to congestion, but none the less to have some public good aspect, are weighted by .5; items judged to be pure public goods (not subject to congestion) are weighted by 1.0.

c/   This includes diplomatic and consular missions.

d/   This includes upkeep and capital expenditures for zoological and public gardens, and upkeep of shrines and temples.

If we wish to stick relatively closely to the model, we should now consider the value of this annual amount over the expected adult life span of a newborn. Under current mortality conditions this would be about 35 years. Without discounting, the externality would then amount to 35 times $US 14.20, or about $US 500. The present value at 2 per cent, 10/ calculated as of the date of birth and counting only years over the age of 20, would be approximately $US 225.

Public national wealth

Mineral rights. Suppose the current Government of India decided to auction off all publicly-owned mineral rights. What would these be worth per capita? Hotelling's Principle states that royalties on mineral rights, equal to the market price minus the cost of extraction, should rise over time at the rate of interest. Miller and Upton (1985) show that under certain simplifying assumptions, this implies that the current market value of the resource in situ can be computed as the amount of the reserves times the difference between the current pithead market price of the resource and the current cost of extraction. As a preliminary step, proven and expected reserves of many minerals and fuels were valued at Indian pithead prices, without taking costs of extraction into account. The results of this exercise are shown in table 2. Clearly, the dominant resource here is coal, which accounts for nearly 80 per cent of the total value and which is owned nearly 100 per cent by the Government. If we count only proven reserves, the per capita value is Rs. 9452 or $US 1,039 (1981). If we count all expected reserves, the per capita value is Rs. 33,385 or $US 3669 (1981). These are impressively large numbers, amounting to roughly four times and fourteen times, respectively, per capita income in India. I repeat, however, that costs of extraction are not included in these figures.

Our further empirical assessment focused on coal because of its apparent dominant importance, although iron reserves also warrant attention. A closer look revealed the following:

(a) The average market price of public sector coal in India in 1981 was Rs 142 per ton (FOR). However, India also imported coal, about 90 per cent of it from Australia in 1982. The price of this imported coal in India was 912 Rs/ton (FOB). It appears that roughly half the cost of this Australian coal is due to the cost of transport from Australia and insurance. I do not yet know why the Government sells its coal for so much less; for the moment I am assuming there is no difference in quality and only minor differences in price arising from the location.

(b) The cost of extraction in India in 1981 was Rs 156 per ton. The difference between price and cost of extraction could therefore be as high as Rs 750 per ton if we use the Indian price of Australian coal; more likely, a much lower figure would be appropriate.

(c) The expected coal reserves down to a depth of 600 metres (the depth to which it is currently economical to go) amount to 107 billion tons, 11/ which comes to 156 tons per capita in 1981.

Table 2. Estimated value of Indian mineral reserves, ignoring
costs of extraction, at 1981 prices

Mineral	Percent mined by public sector	Reserve as of 1. Jan. 1982 (in millions of tonnes)		Number of years total reserve would last (at 1981 rate of extraction)	Value of reserve (in millions of rupees)	
		Proven	Total = proven + indicated + inferred		Proven	Total
Phosphates	78	71	134	244	32278	60973
Bauxite	19	534	2654	1358	28466	141279
Building Stones[a]	n.d.	805	805	1992	384198	384198
Chromite	45	9	135	393	4475	65459
Coal	98	35826	127148[b]	1034	5088738	18074352
Lignite	100	2100	2100	351994	25610	25610
Copper ore	100	100	456	216	20311	92382
Dolomite	48	725	3947	1910	33465	182159
Fireclay	9	65	492	581	1740	13040
Fluorite	100	1	11	517	2710	18107
Gypsum	89	27	1249	1304	1022	45923
Ilmenite	100	n.d.	160	847	n.d.	160000
Rutile	100	n.d.	7	891	n.d.	21840
Iron ore	48	5442	17573	422	188682	3514000
Kaolin, Ballclay, other clays	4	90	1041	2063	11123	127943
Lead, Zinc	100	41	350	356	39937	250265
Limestone	23	7510	73198[c]	2256	204812	1996039
Magnesite	55	12	218	472	3112	53982
Manganese ore	43	17	127	83	2797	20885
Nickel ore	0	16	160	n.d.	5378[d]	51625[d]
Petroleum	100	470	470	31	377057	377057
Natural Gas	100	[e]	[e]	210	14460	14460
Quartz	13	11	503	2643	463	20324
Sulphur, Pyrites	n.d.	5	45	633	1543	13087

Notes:

a/   Not produced at present.

b/   1 January 1980.

c/   Detailed breakdown not available.

d/   1 February 1983.

e/   1 January 1983.

Table 2 (continued)

Notes:

f/ 579,000.

g/ Value of annual production is Rs. 2.24 million.

h/ 51.365 kgs.

i/ 85,335 kgs.

j/ Resources considered "quite satisfactory".

k/ Composite figures assume 28 per cent lead and 72 per cent zinc.

l/ Value of annual production is Rs. 35.563 million.

m/ Assumes average grade of 1.04 per cent.

n/ 419,850 cubic metres.

o/ Value of 1981 production is Rs. 1.08 million.

p/ There is no regular lease for mining tin ore; local people mine from pegmatites and pan alluvial beds, and sell to the Government.

q/ Used CIF price are ore.

Taking all these numbers at face value, the per capita value of the coal reserves in 1981 would be Rs. 117,000, or nearly $US 13,000. This is a staggering number, which will be greatly reduced if the Indian coal is of lower quality than the Australian and if transportation costs from pithead are substantial within India. 12/ In fact, the coal industries in many other countries, such as the United Kingdom and Taiwan (Province of China), are operated at a loss by the public sector, presumably as part of regional employment policies. Until we have further information on this score, we can only say that the per capita coal reserve has a value somewhere between 0 and $US 13,000 and is probably much closer to the zero end of the range. 13/

Capital stock. In India in 1981, the central government owned about 65 per cent of the nation's "productive" capital in the factory sector. In this sector, it hired 31 per cent of the employees, and paid 39 per cent of the wages. It used 30 per cent of the inputs to produce 38 per cent of the value added. Clearly the public sector looms very large in the Indian economy, and its productive assets may constitute a form of national wealth leading to externalities to child-bearing. In 1983–1984, public sector capital was valued at Rs. 537.7 billion, or about Rs. 785 per capita; this was $US 63 (1984). 14/

However, it is necessary to distinguish carefully among several different cases. First, suppose that the publicly-owned capital has been financed by the issue of bonds or shares that are held by private citizens. In this case, the Government is merely acting as a manager or entrepreneur and the public capitalist sector is, for our purposes, no different than the private. No child-bearing externalities arise. If the Government has raised money for the capital through foreign loans, the same is true. 15/ In fact, 66 per cent was financed by share capital and loans and another 12 per cent by credit or advances.

Second, consider the case in which the capital is financed through taxation. In the two-period case, we might suppose that the first generation of parents is taxed to accumulate capital for the second generation to use. It is easy to see that there is indeed an externality to child-bearing, since each child reduces the share of the others in the value of the capital stock. But here the two-period case is artificial; it would be more natural to think of a steady state in which every generation was taxed to accumulate capital. In this case, we might imagine that profits are used to offset taxes. I have not thought this through completely, but I suspect that in this case no externalities arise. In any event, the government documents do not indicate that a component of the public capital stock has been financed through taxes.

Finally, consider the case in which the capital stock has been financed through profits on prior capital. I believe that this gives rise to an externality to child-bearing equal to the per capita share of the value of the capital stock. Twenty-two per cent of the capital value is in this category, amounting to Rs. 168 per capita, or $US 13.50. This corresponds to a modest negative externality to child-bearing.

National debt. If public debt must be repaid by future generations this would lead to a positive externality to child-bearing, since with a larger population, the burden falls more lightly on each taxpayer. If, on the other hand, the debt can simply grow over time in proportion to the population, then there is no externality. I do not know which is the appropriate assumption.

Public debt in India, netting out the debt of states to the central government, was Rs. 667 billion in 1981, which comes to Rs. 973 per capita, or $US 107. 16/ Of this, 83 per cent is internal and 17 per cent external. However, I see no reason to distinguish between the two for present purposes. On the assumption of necessary repayment, this implies a sizeable positive externality to child-bearing of $US 107.

Public lands. The value of publicly-owned lands depends in part on the size of the population, since density raises rents. However, under normal conditions rents would rise less than in proportion to population size, so a birth would impose an externality here as well. For many purposes it is important to distinguish between publicly-owned land and common property resources. 17/ Here, however, they may be treated together. Fortunately, excellent work has been done recently to estimate the extent of these in India (Jodha, 1988; Chopra and others, 1988). Based on Chopra and others it appears that about 22 per cent of the geographic area is common property in the sense that there is some degree of public access, even though some of this land is privately owned. To this must be added the "reserved" category of publicly-owned forest land, another 7 to 11 per cent of land area. 18/ Thus, altogether perhaps 30 per cent of the land area is publicly owned or is considered a common property resource.

These lands must now be evaluated. On a per capita basis, I suggest the rough range of $US 10 to $US 200, with a best guess of $US 50. 19/ Although very rough, the calculations suffice to show that this item will not dwarf the others in the calculation. At present, I have no more precise estimate of the extent of these lands or of their value. 20/

National fisheries. According to World Bank data, the 1981 per capita annual value of fish consumption in India was Rs. 12, or $US 1.30. An unknown portion of this value is attributable to other inputs- labour, equipment, boats, and so on. Furthermore, the future trajectory of prices is unknown and, unlike the case of mineral resources, the value of the asset could increase at a rate greater or less than the rate of interest. As a rough approximation, I have simply discounted at 2 per cent an annual stream of $US 1.30 over the expected adult life span of a newborn, for a present value of $US 21. Alternatively, a perpetual stream would have a present value of $US 65.

From two periods to an infinite horizon

Departing somewhat from the formal model, we might wish to take into account the succession of generations and an infinite time horizon. To do this, some ad hoc adjustments are called for. First, what is the effect of an incremental birth on future population size? Is its initial effect, the reciprocal of the initial population size, also the long-run effect, taking into account future survival and reproduction?

Let us assume that this incremental birth and its progeny experience forever the same age–specific birth and death rates as the rest of the population. Then the long–run, asymptotic proportional effect on the population size is given by the ratio of the "reproductive value" of a birth to the "stable equivalent population" (see Keyfitz, 1987, pp. 141-150). This ratio is equivalent to the reciprocal of the reproductive value of the population as a whole, suitably adjusted for the chance that a birth will be female. For the Indian population of 1981, assuming the age pattern of fertility derived from vital registration data and a TFR of 4.8, and assuming life expectancy at birth of 52.5 years for both males and females, this calculation leads to an increase of 1 per cent in the denominator. [21/] That is, we should use $1/(1.012*N)$ for the long–run proportional change in population size resulting from an incremental birth. As it happens, this adjustment is negligibly small, but it could have been sizeable in other demographic circumstances.

We must also consider a suitable adjustment for the fact that R is measured as a stock and P as an annual flow. The present value of the flow of P over the years is P/i, where i is the real interest rate. We may take i = n = .02 for the golden rule case, or i = .04 or i = .10, resulting in figures for P/i of 50P, 20P, or 10P, respectively.

The bottom line

We can now evaluate the net externality from these sources. Assuming that the value of Indian coal is identical to that of Australian imports, the value of coal reserves alone would be about $US 13,000 per head, which is a negative externality to child–bearing. This dwarfs the minor contributions of the value of public capital, national debt, public lands, and other mineral resources. More complete information about the quality of coal and transport costs within India, could reduce this towards zero, however.

Several commentators have questioned counting the entire per capita value of mineral wealth as an externality to the child–bearing of the current generation. The matter can be settled rigorously only by using a model with an infinite time horizon. However, I suspect that the result would remain the same, for if this wealth were held privately, each generation of parents would have the option of consuming it themselves or dividing it among their children. The utility they derive from contemplating it in the hands of their children derives from the children's entire per capita share. If the children, in their turn, choose to pass it on to their children, that is their decision, and it in no way diminishes the utility of the original parents.

Discounting a perpetual stream of public good costs at .02, the population growth rate, we have P = $US 710; if only the years of adulthood of a newborn are counted, we would have about $US 225. These represent positive externalities to child–bearing. Therefore the net externality to childbirth from these sources is uncertain, but it is most likely a substantial negative amount. This section has led us to a strange conclusion. Are we really to argue that fertility in India is too high because people not take into account the value of the coal reserves.

The two tragedies of the commons: common property resources, congestion and fertility

Background

In 1968, Hardin published an influential article in <u>Science</u> titled "The tragedy of the commons". He explained the inefficiency of a public access resource: Herdsmen crowded too many grazing cattle onto the commons because the institutional structure did not guide them to the less intensive level of usage at which profits of all could be maximized. People, he suggested, were like cows on the commons, and we would all be better off with lower fertility than we individually would choose. Hence, he advocated "mutual coercion, mutually agreed on."

In my view, these child-bearing externalities arising from common property resources are probably the most serious of all those considered here. Examples of common property resources include air shed, water shed, public parks, the ozone layer, air traffic lanes, absence of noise pollution, climate to some degree, and so on. However, Hardin's main point remains strangely unexamined in much of the recent work by economists on the subject of externalities to child-bearing. Work has, on the whole, avoided the issue of common property resources and focused instead on the case in which all resources are privately owned and externalities do not occur, or on the inefficiency aspects of common property resources, rather than their implications for reproduction. In fact there are two "tragedies of the commons": the first is the tragedy of inefficient use of a public access resource; the second is the tragedy of the externality to child-bearing arising from freely admitting new members to the group with access to a congestible resource.

Recent discussions in the demographic literature have focused on the first of these, treating the tragedy as an externality arising from improper management, an externality relevant to population size because, as the National Academy of Science (NAS) report says, "Population growth can exacerbate the externalities inherent in common-property resources" (p. 79). The point is well taken, since the size of the externality arising from individual use does increase with the size of the population with access. However, this view invites us to think that if the resource were optimally managed, the population-related externality would vanish (see Willis, 1987, p. 671). 22/ But the second tragedy of the commons is that even an optimally managed common property creates an externality to child-bearing, since each birth dilutes the value of the right to access of all other citizens. With a larger population, the optimal usage per head is reduced, resulting in a welfare loss to all other members of the population, a loss not taken into account by the parent. To see this, consider the following simple model in which the size of the population is exogenous.

A congestible common resource

First consider the problem with a fixed population size. People derive satisfaction from a level of use, e_i, of the common resource, but their satisfaction is diminished by the amount of aggregate use of the resource, $Z=\sum_{i=1,N} e_i$. The _laissez-faire_ outcome will be that each individual uses the resource to an extent such that its marginal utility falls to 0, and accepts whatever level of Z the behaviuor of others imposes on him/her. (A small congestive effect on individuals arising from their own use can be ignored here.) The optimal level of use of the resource, however, will be less; a planner would maximize the individual utilities by choosing e (for identical individuals) such that $U_e = -U_Z N > 0$, thus taking into account that each unit of additional consumption of e by an individual imposes a cost U_Z on each of the N members of the population. It is clear that in the _laissez-faire_ case, population growth worsens the problem in this model, since Z, which yields disutility, increases monotonically with the population size, _ceteris paribus_, under these assumptions. But surely the problem can be dealt with much more effectively by appropriate public management of the resource than by the slow, cumbersome and uncertain route through population control, as Willis (1987, p. 668) points out.

However, the second "tragedy of the commons" lies in the distortion of child–bearing incentives in the _laissez-faire_ case, for each birth increases N and therefore increases the social cost of individual resource use, leading to reduced resource use per head and reduced utility per person. This cost of a birth will not be taken into account by the potential parent, and it is therefore an externality to child–bearing. Such externalities arising from common resources will lead to an excess of births under _laissez-faire_ reproduction.

A model: laissez–faire fertility and the planner's choice

The argument can be illustrated using the simple Nerlove, Razin and Sadka model. Suppose that in addition to c_1, c_2, and n, parents also care about their children's second–period enjoyment of a public access resource, arising from an amount of usage ei, an enjoyment diminished by the aggregate level of use, $Z=\sum_{i=1,N} n^i e^i$ over all N families. The _laissez-faire_ level of fertility will be chosen such that:

$$U_{ni} = U_{c1}{}^i (c_2{}^i - f'(n^i)).$$

A planner, however, would not take Z as given, but rather would recognize that total resource use depends not only on the choice of e, but also on the choice of n (Z=nNe). The planner, therefore, chooses an equal number of children for each of the N families such that:

$$U_n = U_{c1} (c_2 - f(n)) - U_Z Ne.$$

That is, the planner also takes into account that each additional child inflicts negative externalities of U_{ze}, even when use of the resource is chosen optimally for the given size of the population, and that any planned variation in fertility applies equally to all households and must therefore be multiplied by the number of households, N.

Can optimal resource management remove the child–bearing externality?

Suppose, however, that optimal management of the resource involves imposition of a user fee. In this case, perhaps, prospective mothers will take this into account as a marginal cost of a child and will suitably adjust fertility to an optimal level. On closer examination, we see that this is not the case. Consider a fee of p_2 for each unit of resource use in the second period. The budget constraint of each mother for the second period will now have added a term of the form ne_2p_2. But the fee will also generate revenue that will be used as an offset to taxes or distributed to the population; each child is automatically entitled to a share, and the per capita value of a share will be $av(e_2)p_2$. Therefore, each woman's budget constraint will also be modified by the addition of a term on the right equal to $n*av(e_2)*p_2$. Combining these on the cost side of the equation, we have: $n*p_2(e_2-av(e_2))$. If p_2 is correctly chosen, then this term does lead to the correct marginal incentive for efficient choice of resource usage per child but provides no incentive for reducing fertility. Indeed, the first–order condition for the woman's choice of fertility is completely unaltered, since in a homogeneous population no woman has a reason to expect her children's use of the resource to be different from the average usage in the population. Therefore, to avoid the second tragedy of the commons, an optimal user fee will not suffice, and it is necessary to alter child–bearing incentives directly.

Now consider the level of an optimal tax on child–bearing. Is it p_2e_2? From solution of the planner's problem, we see that the optimal tax on children would be $-(U_Z/U_C)(N-1)e_2$. The optimal user fee can readily be found to be $p_2=-(U_Z/U_C)(N-1)n$. We can see, then, that the optimal tax on children would not be p_2e_2, but rather $p_2e_2/n = p_1e_2$. The resource usage should therefore be evaluated at its first period level in setting the disincentive to child–bearing.

Boserup–Simon effects

It is often suggested that a larger, denser population stimulates technological progress in various ways (Boserup, 1965 and 1981; Simon, 1977 and 1986). If this is so, an externality to child-bearing occurs, since many of the proposed pathways through which additional population raises technological progress preclude capturing the gains privately. Virtually all analyses conclude that in the short and medium run, any benefits are swamped by the negative effects of diminishing returns; only over the long run will per capita incomes rise. However, in the short and medium run, the costs of higher fertility are in theory largely offset by the satisfactions of the parents who choose to bear both the children and their costs.

The model

Consider the same basic model used earlier, but now suppose that production in period t is expected to be $A_t f(n)$, where A_t is the level of technology. Furthermore, suppose that the growth in the level of technology between the periods depends on the size of the second-period population, so that $A_2 = A_1 g(N_2)$, where $N_2 = \sum_{i=1,N_1} n_i$.

Except for a negligibly small term, the first-order conditions for the individual parents are altered only by the addition of technology multipliers. However, the first-order condition for the planner is now:

$$U_n/U_{c1} = [c_2 - A_2 f(n)] - N_1 g'(N_2) A_1 f(n).$$

The terms in brackets correspond to the individual's first-order condition, while the final term represents an externality to child-bearing. The externality equals the effect of one additional person on second-period output on a single farm, $g'(N_2) A_1 f(n)$, times the number of farms affected, N_1.

Evaluation of the effect

In evaluating the effects, we should be aware of the possibility of double counting. Government expenditures on research and on infrastructure are two major channels through which productivity may be raised, and such expenditures have already been counted under public goods. 23/

Also, we should remember that the theoretical model we have used assumes that parents care about the level of consumption by their children but not about their children's utility. This implies that parents do not care about per capita consumption over an infinite time horizon but rather only over the lives of their children.

There have been very few serious attempts to estimate the growth-inducing effects of population size (see Lee, 1988; and Simon, 1977 and 1986), but fortunately for the present undertaking the most serious empirical study to date has been made for India by Robert Evenson (1988). He analyses Indian agricultural data for 1959–1975 for 14 states and the districts within four of these states.

Summarizing his analysis through impact multipliers, Evenson reports that a 10 per cent decrease in population would raise per capita incomes by 7.77 per cent through Malthusian forces but reduce it by 2.80 per cent through Boserupian forces, for a net gain of 4.97 per cent (p. 136, table 6.8). Under the crucial (and patently false) assumption of population homogeneity, the Malthusian effects are presumably of the sort analysed above in the benchmark case and reflect privately borne consequences of child-bearing; these therefore entail no externality. If we take the estimated Boserupian effect at face value, it implies that $N_1 g'(N_2) = .28$. If we are considering fertility variations in the neighbourhood of a net reproduction rate (NRR) of 2.0, then $A_1f(n)$ will be about 1.5 times the first–period–per–household income. This suggests that the annual value of the externality to child–bearing in the first period is about .16 times the average household income. Discounted and cumulated over the lifetime of the adult children, this would represent a very substantial amount. [24/]

However, closer examination of the Boserup effects incorporated in the model shows that they are not appropriately regarded as externalities to child–bearing. Evenson considers two kinds of effects: those operating on public expenditures at the level of states and those affecting farmer's decisions. Estimates in Evenson's table 6.2 indicate significantly negative impacts of population density on public sector investments in research, electrification, and provision of agricultural credit, which runs counter to Boserup's hypothesis; other effects are insignificant. The net positive effect reported above must therefore derive from the behaviour of farmers, where Evenson's table 6.3 shows substantial positive effects of population density on irrigation intensity and on the net cropped area, along with a negative effect on farm size. But these effects operate through individual investment and planning decisions and do not alter the productivity of given inputs; therefore, while they may appropriately be labeled "Boserup effects", they do not constitute externalities. Furthermore, the estimated effects of population density at both the public sector and the individual farmer level all represent costly investments, but the estimated gains are not counted net of these costs. We must therefore conclude that the detailed Evenson analysis, while providing much information on the consequences of population growth, provides no useful information about externalities to child–bearing.

Public sector taxes and transfers

Background

The modern state in both developed and developing countries provides heavily subsidized health and education services to the population as a whole. In addition, but to a much lesser extent in developing countries, the state provides old–age support through income transfers to the elderly. In this way, some costs of child–bearing, as well as benefits, have been moved from the family to the society, and perhaps externalities to child–bearing are thereby created. However, modelling and evaluating such externalities is not as straightforward as one might expect.

Consider the case of publicly–subsidized education. Recall the two–period model used earlier and suppose that second–period income per child, I, depends on the amount of education, E, each receives: $I=I(E)$. Suppose further that the Government imposes a head tax, t, per parent to pay for education. Then the first–order condition for the optimizing parent is $U_n/U_{c1} = c_2 - I(E)$, which ignores the cost of the publicly–funded education. The planner, however, will equate U_n/U_{c1} to $c_2 + p_E*E- I(E)$, where p_E is the price of a unit of education, and will choose a correspondingly lower level of fertility. [25/]

This argument suggests that there is a negative externality of p_E*E to each birth, equal to the public expenditure on education per child. The argument is easily extended to incorporate health costs of children and any other specifically child-related costs covered by the public sector. Such considerations led Blandy (1974) to suggest that a government should consider offering a bribe of p_E*E to parents to forgo a marginal child (although he subsequently concluded this would not be practical).

In a heterogeneous population in which some classes pay little or no tax, the argument has some merit. However, it then applies to <u>all</u> public services, not just to children, and it rests on different grounds than those claimed. In the hypothetically homogeneous population considered here, the argument makes no more sense than would bribing parents, in an amount equal to the average lifetime tax payments, to have an additional child. The first argument ignores the fact that children will grow up to become taxpayers and thereby repay their social debts; the second ignores the fact that taxpayers also receive costly government transfers and services. Both look at only one piece of a complex system of intergenerational transfers, rather than at the whole pattern. 26/

A two-period model is intrinsically unsuited to addressing these matters, so we now turn to models of populations with continuous age distributions and an infinite succession of generations. Such models can also consider transfers through the family and the private sector, as well as the public sector. Analysis will be confined to an examination of the public sector, assuming comparative golden rule steady states. 27/ The golden rule assumption implies that given the institutions and technology, the amount of capital per worker maximizes per capita consumption. This doubtless seems a strange assumption to make for a developing country that has little capital and is striving to increase capital per head. I make the assumption mainly for analytic convenience, and hope to be able to consider non-golden rule paths in the future. None the less, a large part of the economic problem of developing countries is that the structure of institutions and the lack of skilled labour make the rate of return on capital low even when capital is relatively scarce. I calculate that in India over the years 1974-1984, the real rate of interest on long-term government bonds was only 2.4 per cent per annum. This is close to the golden rule rate of return, which is the population growth rate (about 2 per cent per year) plus labour-augmenting technological progress.

Finally, the parental utility and social welfare functions are both different in this section. Parents are now assumed to care about their own consumption and that of their co-resident children; consumption by their non-co-resident children does not concern them. Parents are also assumed to care about the number of children they have. The social planner seeks to maximize per capita life cycle utility, including utility from child-bearing, across golden rule steady states. The fact that one steady state yields a higher life cycle utility than another does not necessarily mean that it is Pareto-preferable or that there is some externality present in one of the steady states; it may be that movement from one to the other involves loss of utility by some initial generations. Having raised these points, I will largely ignore them in the following discussion.

Intergenerational transfers: family, market and public sector

I will refer to any discrepancy between the labour earnings of an age group and consumption by that age group as an intergenerational transfer. This use of the term covers the net intertemporal market transactions of age groups as well as public and private (familial) non-market transfers. Public transfers include health, education, pensions, and taxes, and private familial transfers include costs of rearing children, old-age support provided to aged parents, and bequests.

Both Willis (1987) and Nerlove, Razin and Sadka have shown that with a nested altruistic utility function and no-public-sector transfers, no externalities arise from intergenerational transfers. The analysis here differs by including public-sector transfers and by assuming a different utility function. 28/

Familial transfers

Parents bear children until the marginal utility of a child (MUC), expressed in money units, equals the net within-family transfer to an incremental child, which is the net cost of a child (NCC): MUC=NCC. The NCC is measured as the present value at birth of all the expected outlays and income flowing from the other family members to the child, minus the reverse flows. This includes, for example, the period of child dependency, the later period when children produce more than they consume but are still co-resident, and any old-age support given to the elderly parents. Of course, it does not include the full costs or earnings of the child; the Government pays some of these costs (health and education) and the child eventually becomes a member of a separate household, at which point most of the child's consumption and earnings do not enter the accounting for the parents' household.

Market transfers

By a market intergenerational transfer, I mean net market borrowing or lending by households with a given age of head. 29/ Such transactions take place over the life cycle of the household subject to the constraint that their present value be zero.

Public sector transfers

I assume that the public sector budget is in balance at every instant, in the sense that current taxes exactly equal current expenditures on transfers. I assume, strictly for convenience, that taxes are proportional to labour income, at the rate t(n). (This rate is a function of the population growth rate, n, for reasons explained below.) In fact, in India only 15 per cent of total government tax revenues is from income taxes (only 8 per cent from personal income tax), and only a small fraction of the population pays such taxes. 30/ A further 3 per cent comes from taxes on property and capital transactions. The major share comes from indirect taxes on commodities and services, which account for 81 per cent, and the incidence of which must be very broadly, albeit unequally, distributed in the population. 31/ In any event, if labour income at age x is $y_1(x)$, then by this assumption, taxes paid at age x are $t(n)y_1(x)$.

Transfers received from the public sector include education, health services, and pensions, the three considered here. Denote the total money value of these services received at age x by $g(x)$. Then the balanced budget assumption implies that the quantity $[t(n)y_1(x)-g(x)]$, multiplied by the population age x in year s, say $N(x,s)$, and integrated over all ages, must equal zero. Under the steady state assumption, the population at age x is proportional to $e^{-nx}p(x)$, where $p(x)$ is the proportion surviving from birth to age x and the constant of proportionality is a function of time and need not concern us. The public sector balanced budget assumption can therefore be written:

$$\int e^{-nx}p(x)[t(n)y_1(x) - g(x)]dx = 0.$$

This equation can also be interpreted as stating that for a newborn, the present value of receipts of transfers and of taxes must be exactly equal, for under the golden rule assumption, the interest rate equals the population growth rate. But in this case, each child pays its way exactly; how can an externality arise? It can, because higher fertility makes the population age distribution younger. What matters here is the timing of an individual's interactions with the public sector and, in particular, whether the receipt of benefits on average precedes or follows the payment of taxes. In developed countries, the receipt of benefits is almost certainly at an older age, but in a less developed country it is likely that the receipt of benefits precedes payment of taxes, since public old-age support programmes are small while substantial expenditures are made on children's education. In this case, higher fertility and a younger population require a higher tax rate to provide a given age schedule of benefits, $g(x)$. Thus it appears likely that the age pattern of taxes and transfers in developing countries leads to a negative externality to child-bearing. This argument is developed more formally below.

The effect of an incremental child

To determine whether there is a net externality, we ask whether the life cycle utility of the representative individual would be higher or lower if fertility were exogenously raised slightly. (Of course, fertility is endogenous, but it is none the less subject to policy manipulation.) Now let the TFR be f, and consider the effect of an infinitesimal change in it, df, which is somehow exogenously imposed on each household. Within the household, this would lead to a change in the parents' consumption at every age, and the present value of such changes would equal the net cost to the parents of an incremental child (denoted NCC). Assuming that household fertility plans were initially optimal, 32/ the gain (or loss) in direct utility from the child should exactly equal the loss (or gain) in utility from the NCC, so the household welfare should be unaffected. However, there is no such offsetting change for between-household transfers. A general increase in fertility would change the age distribution of the population and thus alter the pattern of both market and public sector transfers. Any consequent effects are externalities.

To examine the magnitude of the between-household effect, first consider the effect of the change in f, df, on the population growth rate, n. This is given by the approximate accounting identity: $dn/df = 1/(f*\text{av age of child bearing}) = 1/(f*m)$. 33/ A change of one birth in the TFR would therefore induce a change of about .0075 in the population growth rate. 34/

For the public sector, the change in the tax rate when n changes can be found by differentiating the public sector budget constraint with respect to n and solving for dt(n)/dn, with the following simple result:

$$dt(n)/dn = t(n)[A_g - A_{y1}]$$

where A_g and A_{y1} are average ages of receiving benefits and paying taxes in the population. In other words, if the average age of paying taxes (A_{y1}) is greater than the average age of receiving government transfers (A_g), then the tax rate will be reduced when the population growth rate is increased. Expressed in terms of a change in current dollars of taxes due to a change in fertility, we have:

$$dT/df = (1/(f* \mu))*T*(A_g - A_{y1}) = .0075*T*(A_g - A_{y1}).$$

Here T=G is the present value of life cycle taxes (and government transfers), evaluated at r=n. dT/df is the present value of life cycle savings in taxes for a representative couple in a golden rule economy, when fertility is higher by one child. f is as usual the TFR and μ is the mean age at child-bearing.

A similar result can be derived for the market transfers:

$$dC/df = (1/(f* \mu))*C*(A_c - A_y) = .0075*C*(A_c - A_y).$$

Here C is the present value of consumption excluding in-kind public sector transfers of health and education, A_c is the average age of consuming in the population, and A_y is the average age of labour earning plus receipt of goverment income transfers, notably pension income.

Summary of inferences from analysis of model

If the economy is on a golden rule path, then, comparing steady states and abstracting from transitional costs, there is an externality to child-bearing equal to $.0075*[C*(A_c - A_y) + T*(A_g - A_{y1})]$, arising from intergenerational transfers both through the capital market and through the public sector. 35/ If the economy is not golden rule, then these expressions are more complicated.

Evaluation of public sector transfers in India: education,
health, pensions

Unfortunately, with the available data I am not able to calculate child-bearing externalities arising through market transfers.   To evaluate child-bearing externalities arising through the public sector, we must evaluate $T^*(A_g - A_t)$.   Attention will be restricted to three important age-differentiated in-kind transfers: education, health services, and pensions.   These were estimated for India in 1981, drawing on various surveys and government publications, as I now describe.

Health services were particularly difficult to estimate.   The age distribution of hospital days per year for one state agrees well with the shape of the age distribution of morbidity from another survey, as shown in figure I.   Taking the age-shape from these data, the level of the profiles was chosen to yield the actual total for Indian public sector health expenditures in 1981, when applied to the appropriate population age distribution.

Estimates for education were far more straightforward, since enrolment by age and expenditures by educational level were both available.   Again, the age-shape of the profile was estimated from these data, and the level was set to match government totals.   The resulting profile is shown in figure II.

The Government of India also pays pensions and, although they amount to only about one ninth the cost of health plus education, they have a substantial effect on the calculated average ages, due to the late age at which they are received.   Military pensions, including disability pensions, make up 40 per cent of total pensions. 36/ I have assumed that a third of these are provided to the disabled and are received equally by the entire population over age 20.   I assume that the remainder of the military pensions go equally to those over age 45 and that the general pensions go equally to the population over age 58, which is the official age of retirement from civil service.

Figure III plots age-specific expenditures on health, education, and pensions, weighted by the stable population age distribution with life expectancy = 50 years and growth rate = .02 (corresponding to a TFR of about 5).

As I explained earlier, I have had to assume that taxes are paid at an equal rate out of all earnings of labour, so that the schedule has the identical age-shape as the schedule of labour earnings by age.   The age-earnings schedule was taken from survey data on labour supply and wage rates in urban and rural areas in a sample of states.   The tax rate was set to generate exactly the revenues needed to pay for the government expenditures on education, health, and pensions.

Figure I. Estimates of value of publicly provided health services
by age of recipient (India, 1981, in rupees)

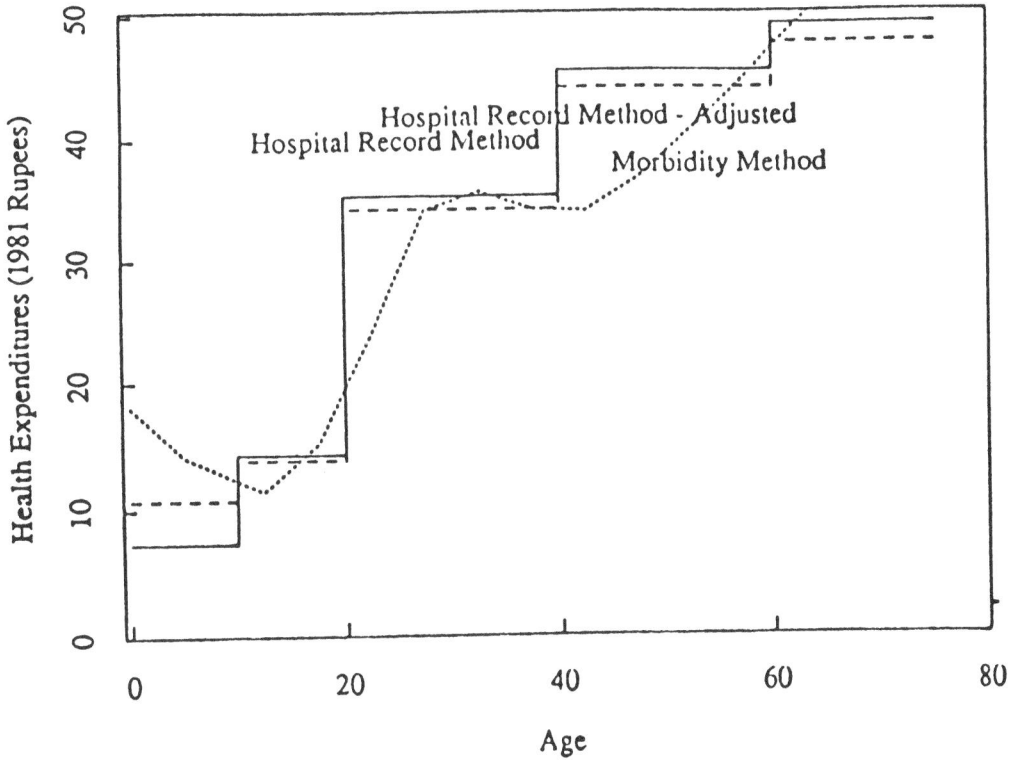

Note: The "morbidity method" assumes value of services received is
proportional to survey estimates of age-specific morbidity. The
"hospital record method" assumes that value of services received is
proportional to the propensity to occupy hospital beds. The "hospital
record method–adjusted" adjusts for non–hospital expenditures on maternal
and child health. The levels of the age–profiles obtained in these ways
were set to provide the governmental total expenditures on health
services as reported in the budget.

Figure II.   Estimated value of publicly provided education,
             by age of recipient (India, 1981, in rupees)

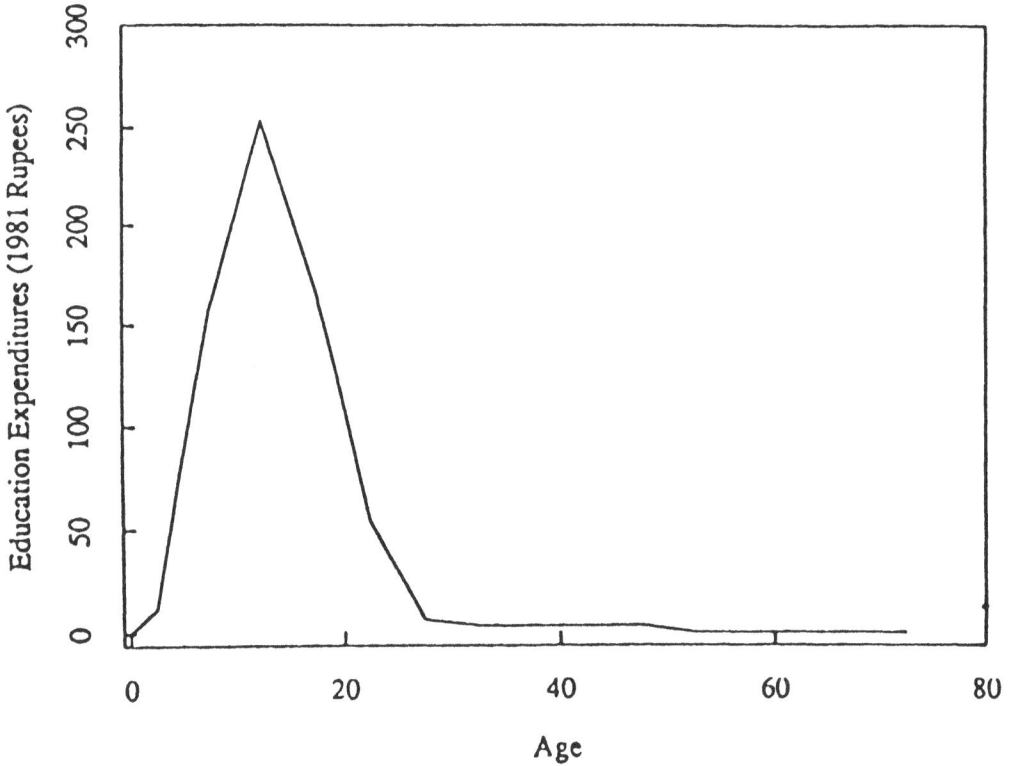

Note: The age profiles reflect age-specific enrolment rates, and governmental expenditures specific to each level. Adult education is included. The level of the age profile obtained in this way was set to provide the governmental total expenditure on education as reported in the budget, including spending by states and the central government.

Figure III. Estimated value of publicly provided health services,
education and pensions received at each age,
weighted by the stable age distribution
(for India, in 1981, in $US)

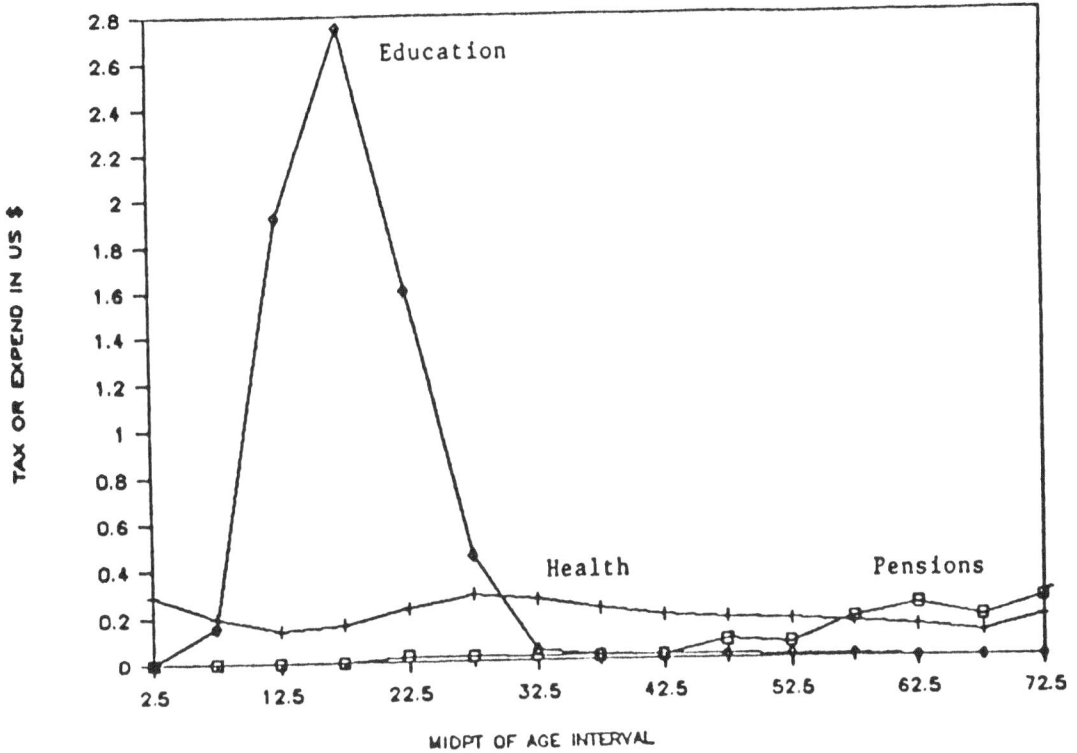

Note: The weights are the proportions of the population in each age group in a stable population, so the weights sum to unity. The stable population is a Coale-Demeny Model South Female with eo = 50 and n = .02.

Figure IV shows the unweighted age profiles of total public sector transfers and subsidies for health, education, and pensions, along with the age profile of labour earnings by age, averaged across sexes and urban-rural residence.

Finally, Figure V shows the same age profiles as figure IV, but now weighted by the stable population age distribution. It is quite clear from this figure that, in general, transfers are received from the public sector at an earlier age than taxes are paid to it. Although health expenditures and pensions add weight to the tail, the transfer schedule is clearly dominated by the early consumption of education services. The common belief that these public sector transfers give rise to negative externalities to child-bearing is therefore borne out by this analysis.

Table 3 shows the average age of receipt of each kind of transfer, along with the share of each and the average age of tax payment. The only surprise is that the average age of receiving educational expenditures is as old as 18; this must reflect the greater cost of higher education, and the fact that there is a certain amount of expenditure on adult education. Overall, the average age of receipt of transfers is 26 years and the average age of tax payment is 37 years, so there is a substantial gap.

Expenditures on education and health came to Rs 89.8 per head in 1981 by our estimates, or about $US 10 per capita; this was about 3.8 per cent of the per capita GDP. Receipt of these in-kind transfers is distributed over the life cycle. Discounting by 2 per cent per year and with due allowance for mortality, the present value of expected transfers is Rs. 2721, or about $US 310. This is a substantial amount, a bit more than one year's per capita income.

By the argument developed here, each child will also contribute taxes over its lifetime of a present value of $US 310. However, the different age distributions of taxes and transfers indicate that the typical individual can benefit from lower fertility to the tune of 310*10.6*(change in n), or by $US 33 for a reduction in n by .01. If each person had one less birth, n would decline by about .0075, so we can set the social cost per birth at .75*$US 33 = $US 25.

Other public sector expenditures

Overall, government spending accounted for roughly 20 per cent of the GNP in India in 1981. Of this amount, the transfers just discussed make up 3.8 per cent and expenditure on public goods an additional 5.5 per cent. The public goods can perhaps be assumed to benefit all ages equally. As for the other categories of expenditures, I have no basis for assigning them to one age or another. Let us consider two cases. First, suppose they are distributed in proportion to age-specific labour earnings; in this case marginal variations in fertility have no effect, since the average ages of receipt of benefits and payment of taxes are equal.

Figure IV. Estimated value of total age-specific transfers received at each age, and taxes paid at each age, not weighted by the stable age distribution, for India, 1981 (in $US)

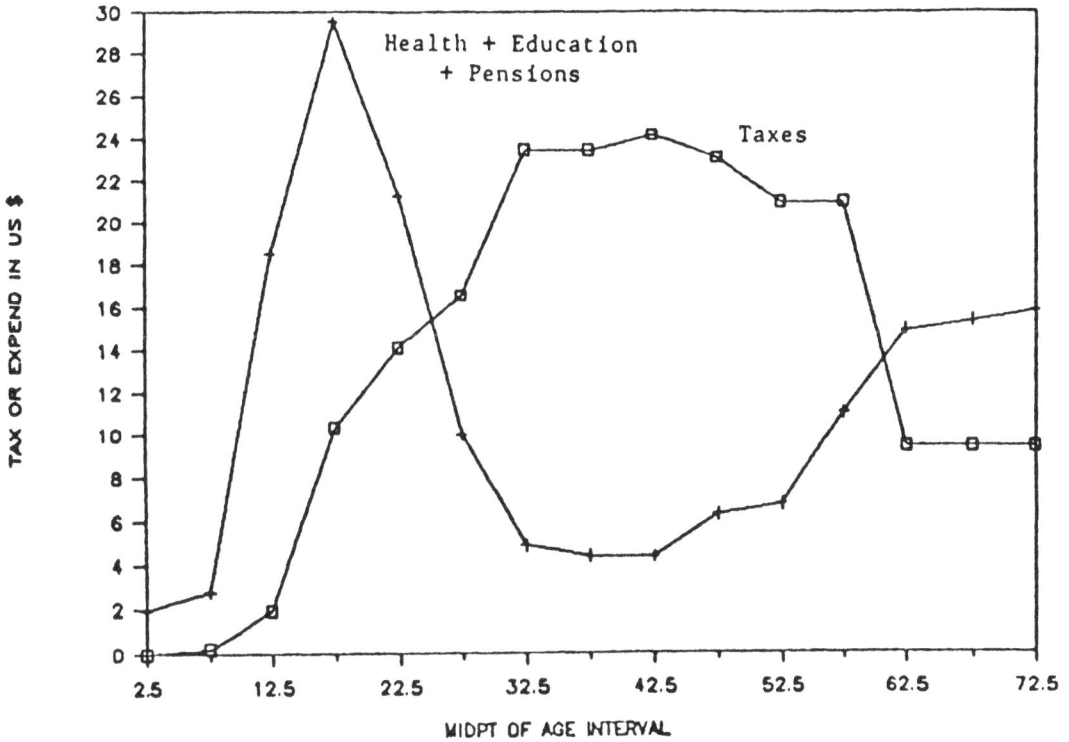

Note: Tax payments are assumed proportional to the earnings of labour by age, with the level set to make total taxes equal total age-specific transfers.

Figure V.   Estimated value of total age-specific transfers received at
            each age, and taxes paid at each age, weighted by the stable
            age distribution, for India, 1981 ($US)

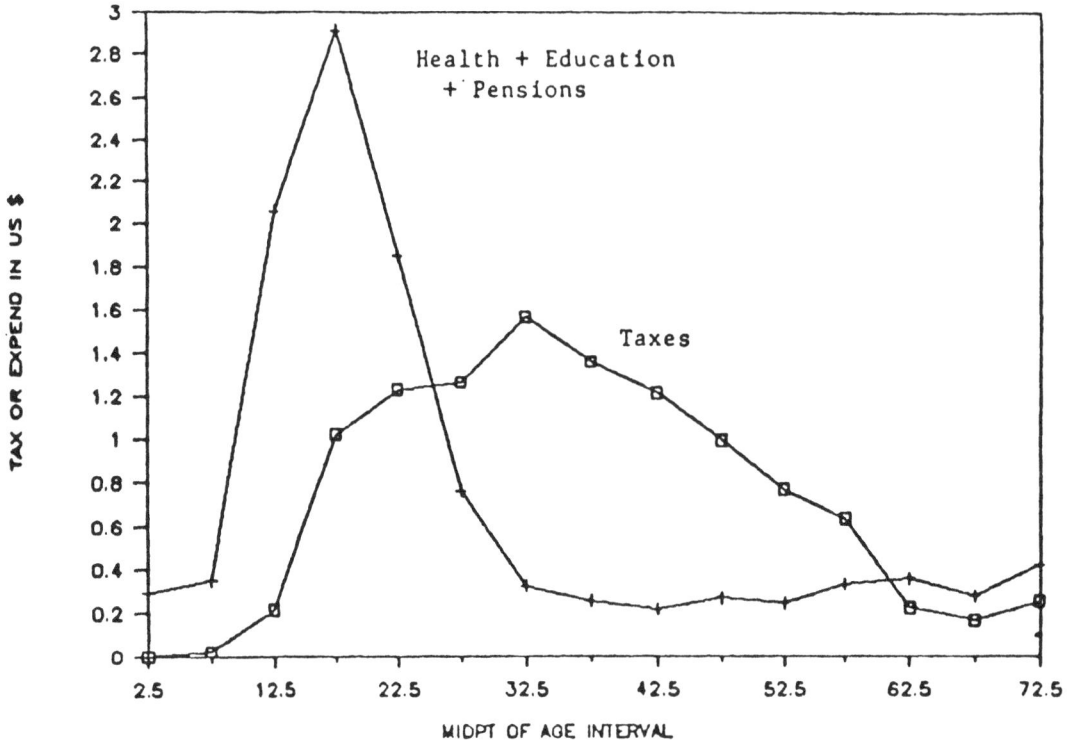

Note: The weights are the proportions of the population in each age
group in a stable population, so the weights sum to unity. The stable
population is a Coale-Demeny Model South Female with eo = 50 and n =
.02. Tax payments are assumed proportional to the earnings of labour by
age, with the level set to make total taxes equal total age-specific
transfers.

Table 3.   Integovernmental transfers through the public sector,
            India, 1981 (in $US)

Category	Amount ($)	Share (%)	Av Age (yrs) [a]
Public Expenditures (annual)			
Health	2.87	26	34
Education	7.00	64	18
Pensions	1.06	10	60
Total (A_g)	10.94	100	26
Taxes (A_t)	10.94	100	37
Diff in Av Ages of Receipt of Public Transfers and Payment of Taxes: .... -10.6			
Present Value at Birth of Expected Receipt of Services and Payment of Taxes (G): ...... 310$ (calculated as reciprocal of intrinsic birth rate times 10.94$)			
Externality to Childbearing : .... 14.65$ (Calculated as $(dn/df).G$.(Av Age Trans - Av Age of Taxes). $0.0075 \times 310\$ \times (-10.6)$)			

Note:

   a/ This is the average age of receipt of each type of public
transfers, weighted by the age distribution of the stable population, and
by the amount of expenditure going to each age group.

Second, suppose that benefits are distributed uniformly by age. In this case, when fertility varies marginally, the difference between the mean age of receipt of public services and of paying taxes to support them will give rise to a child-bearing externality of size: $T\#(A_{g\#}-A_t) = T\#(A_{g\#}-A_{y1})$, where the # indicates that the taxes and government services exclude those already considered under age-specific transfers. Note that expenditures on public goods are included in this total.

$A_{g\#}$ is simply equal to the mean age of the stable population, which, given the assumed vital rates, is 26 years. 37/ Coincidentally, this equals the mean age of receipt of the age-specific transfers, as calculated above. Using this line of reasoning, a case could be made that the child-bearing externality arising through all public sector activities leads to a negative externality of $US 131, which is to be set against the positive externality for public goods arising from the scale of the population, as opposed to its age distribution. 38/ Without further information and analysis concerning the non-age-specific expenditures, however, this number is highly conjectural. 39/ More work is clearly necessary.

Summary and conclusions

We can now draw together the various estimates for the different items, as shown in table 4. What are we to make of these calculations? First, I must caution once again that all numbers are rough and that the whole exercise is experimental. Second, recall that no number is proposed for externalities arising from common property resources, although I suspect that this should be the dominant item on the list. Third, recall also that I have assumed a homogeneous population. For all these reasons, it would be misleading to present a partial total of the figures.

But taking these numbers at face value, there are some striking and unexpected results. One is the relatively small role of public sector subsidies and transfers for health, education, and pensions. Although these have a present value of more than $US 300 over the individual life cycle, so do tax payments in support of these expenditures (under the assumptions of a golden rule economy and a balanced government budget). Externalities then arise only from age distribution changes and amount only to about $US 25 per newborn for these age-distributed transfers. (This number could be more than five times as large if we take the value of other government expenditures to be uniformly distributed over the life cycle). Of course, the assumption of a homogeneous population weighs heavily here, and there may be very large segments of the population that receive transfers in excess of their tax payments, and conversely. It must be remembered, however, that most taxes are indirect, so all segments of the population bear them to some degree.

Another unexpected result is the large positive externality found here from cost spreading for public goods. Again, the assumption of population homogeneity probably plays a critical role, since many large sectors of the population will pay far less than the average per capita tax.

Table 4. Summary of estimated externalites to child-bearing in
India (based on 1981 data and expressed in $US)

Item	Theoretical Amount	Rough Evaluation ('81 $)
Wages of Next Generation (under priv ownership)	0	0
Common Prop Res	$-N(eU_z)$	-?
Public Assets		
Mineral Rights	$-R(p-c)/N$	-(0 to 13000) [a]
Govt Debt	D/N	+107
Govt K	$-K_G/N$	-13 [b]
Govt Land	$-Lnd.p_L/N$	-(10 to 200) [c]
Fisheries		-(21 to 65)
Public Goods	-PV.(Pub Gds)/N	(225 to 710) [d]
Intergen Tranfers		
Public (Hlth, Ed, Pens)	$0,0075.G.(A_g - A_t)$	-25
Other Pub Expends	$0,0075.G.(A_g - A_t)$	-(0 to 100) [e]
Market	$0,0075.C.(A_C - A_{Y_1+M})$	?
Induced Tech Prog	$N_1 g'(N_2) A_l f(n)$	+?

Notes:

a/ The zero results from valuing Indian coal at its sale price,
which may represent a subsidy to public-sector industries; the 13,000
results from valuing it at the market price of Australian coal in India,
which may be of different quality. Both figures reflect extraction costs.

b/ This includes only the portion of the public-sector capital
stock which is financed by retained earnings; it excludes capital funded
by stock issue and bonds.

c/ Between 20 and 30 per cent of land in India may be publicly
owned, but much of this land is of little market value.

d/ The annual expenditure per capita is about $14; the figure in
the table, 710, is the present value of a perpetual stream discounted at
.02. For a higher interest rate, it would of course, be lower. The
present value is simply 14,20/i for discount rate i.

A third unexpected result is the potentially large negative externality created by the dilution of shares in the public wealth. Publicly-owned capital stock led to an unexpectedly small effect, while public debt was more important than anticipated—roughly equal to the loss from dilution of ownership of public land. What made the total effect for public wealth surprisingly large was the potentially very large per capita value of publicly-owned mineral resources, in which coal played the dominant role. At this writing, uncertainty remains about the market value of Indian coal, but it could be very high.

It seems frankly absurd to suggest that the value of Indian coal reserves provides the underlying rationale for governmental action regarding fertility. 40/ But would a similar assumption be inappropriate for parents in Saudi Arabia, for example, where enormous public mineral wealth is used to fund extensive public services with no income taxes? In any event, Indian coal here stands in for the many valuable common property resources for which quantification was impossible, but which are far more central to human life.

Before concluding, let me briefly discuss two issues that are often raised about this argument. First, homogeneity was strictly an assumption of convenience. People differ in many ways—by social class; by membership in subnational groups, including local economies; by tastes and values. These differences will lead to different kinds of externalities emerging at different levels of social organization. Future work might try to address these complexities. I conjecture, however, that the externalities discussed in this paper form a kind of base-line level to which other kinds may be added. I do not believe these considerations would lead to reductions in the numbers given.

Second, to what extent do the results depend on the particular theory of fertility employed? The result may appear to turn on the implicit assumption that fertility responds positively to wealth, but I believe that only a negative response to the cost of fertility is required, holding wealth constant£E. The correct conceptual experiment is not whether fertility would be higher in a country with more public wealth, but rather whether in a country with a given level of public wealth, fertility would be lower if ownership were instead private. 40/

This paper has made a start on setting forth a framework for evaluating externalities to child-bearing and has attempted an application to India. It would be a mistake, however, to take any of the estimated numbers too seriously. The assumptions, approach, and quantification all need to be more carefully considered. At a minimum, a more solid analysis would have to confront the valuation of non-market common property resources, to consider explicitly the effects of population heterogeneity, deal more carefully with the intertemporal aspects of the problem, and rethink the treatment of mineral wealth. These extensions might well alter the present results in important ways.

Notes

<u>1/</u>   I do not mean to suggest, however, that the issue of externalities to child-bearing arises only after excess fertility has been eliminated, as Blandy (1974) suggests. When fertility regulation is practised at all, no matter how imperfectly, a change in the pure demand for children will translate to some degree into a change in the total number of children born, including the excess births.

<u>2/</u>   As Demeny (1972) said, this would be like asserting that people would be better off if they all worked Sundays on the grounds that this would raise per capita income.

<u>3/</u>   By "conventional utility function" I mean one in which the parents care about the "quality" of their children, or about consumption by their children, but not directly about the utility that their children experience. When parents care about their children's utility, this leads to an infinitely regressing nested utility function, in which the utilities of all subsequent descendant generations forever enter.

<u>4/</u>   When ownership of factors of production is not homogeneous in the population and when (as is virtually always the case) there is no reason to expect redistributive policies to follow population growth, there will be externalities to child-bearing within social classes. For an empirical study of the effect of population growth on the per capita incomes of different social classes in India, see Evenson (1988). Results are as one would expect.

<u>5/</u>   We can view this as a two-sex model. If there are N first-period households, then there are 2*N parents. In the second period, if n is the total fertility rate, there will be nN second-period adults and nN/2 households. The net reproduction rate is then n/2. If, on the other hand, we view it as a single-sex model, then n is the net reproduction rate, there are N first-period parents and N first-period households, and there are nN second-period adults and households.

<u>6/</u>   In extending the model in this way we would be departing from the standard altruistic utility function, since here parental utility depends on the level of consumption by their children but not on the utility of their children. In this latter case the outcome is unaltered as shown by Nerlove, Razin and Sadka (1987).

<u>7/</u>   One might want to distinguish between public goods with consumption value and those with production value; research would then fall into the latter category. Many Boserup effects are of this sort: a larger population reduces the cost per head of public investments in research and infrastructural investment and thereby leads to a higher optimal level of such expenditures.

8/ They assume that at some initial time a fixed lump sum tax is levied on current and all future generations of each dynasty (family line). The key point here is that the amount of the tax is independent of the number of members alive in any generation. A woman's children must pay the same tax in aggregate, say $US 1,000, no matter how many children she chooses to have: If she has 10 children, each pays $US 1,000/10 = $US 100; if she has one child, it pays the full $US 1,000. Similarly for her grandchildren: if there are 100, each pays $US 10, while if there is only one, it pays the full $US 1,000 due from its generation, and so on to infinity. The Government must never redefine the dynasties responsible for the tax, for if it did, under the perfect foresight assumptions of this model, the original dynastic founder would know it, and her incentives would be altered in such a way as to create an externality. In the real world, of course, tax systems do not as a general principle distinguish among dynastic lines in levying lump sum taxes; every individual or household is taxed similarly. (I pass over the difficulty that a greater and greater proportion of the population will come to be descended from any given progenitor as dynastic lines intermingle through marriage).

9/ Parents, of course, do take into account this effect of child–bearing on their children's share of the parent's private wealth, or any bequest they choose to leave.

10/ This was the approximate real rate of return on long–term Indian government bonds over the preceding decade, and is also consistent with the golden rule assumption to be made in a later section. A good case could be made for using a higher discount rate, which would, of course, reduce this present value.

11/ Presumably the deeper coal has a higher cost of extraction, which is not reflected in these calculations.

12/ Furthermore, burning this quantity of coal, which equals 28 times the global annual consumption of coal in 1981, would probably have serious environmental consequences.

13/ The matter is even more complicated, since it will make a great deal of difference whether the coal is used, on the one hand, to substitute for Australian coal, the price of which includes the cost of transport, or is, on the other hand, exported, in which case transport cost must be deducted from the market value of the coal. Obviously the extent to which it can be used to substitute against costly imports is limited by the level of domestic demand for coal by Indian industry.

14/ Most of this was in the following three categories: plant and machinery (174 billion), capital work in progress and unallocated expenditure (113 billion), and working capital (139 billion).

15/ Robert Willis pointed out these issues to me.

16/ India's foreign exchange reserves in 1981 amounted to Rs. 48.2 billion; we were unable to obtain a figure for external holdings of rupees.

17/ Common property resources are generally taken to be those managed by non-market institutions, as opposed to those with unrestricted public access or those that are simply publicly-owned and managed in any of a variety of ways, including renting to private users.

18/ According to Chopra and others, land use surveys suggest that 22 per cent of land area is forested; satellite photographs suggest 14 per cent. Furthermore, about 50 per cent is believed to be "reserved" and is thus excluded from the count. Therefore, between 7 and 11 per cent should be added to the estimate of CPR area given above. Adding 8 per cent brings the total public ownership amount to 30 per cent of the land area.

19/ Frank Zimmerman, an anthropologist who has recently done field work in India, suggested that good quality irrigated land might sell for Rs. 10,000-20,000 per acre. Good quality dry land might sell for Rs. 10,000 per acre. With these figures as a benchmark, he suggested a range of Rs. 1,000 to 5,000 per acre for the average value of publicly-owned and common property land. This would amount to $US 35 to $US 170 per person, since there is about one third of an acre of such land per head. An alternative approach is to calculate an average per acre value for all private land, based on the assumptions that 40 per cent of agricultural income goes to land, that this can be capitalized at 2 per cent per year, and that the publicly-owned land is worth (at a maximum) one third this much per acre. This calculation results in a value of $US 200 per head for public land.

20/ For a discussion of the important role played by communal land holdings with common access in some villages in western Rajasthan, see Jodha (1985).

21/ A Coale-Demeny South Model life table was used for this calculation.

22/ Willis (1987) states: "It should be stressed, however, that the volume of auto emissions is not mechanically linked to the size of the population, and that policies attempting to reduce air pollution by reducing population generally would be exceedingly inefficient relative to alternative policies attacking emission directly." In later reference to common property resources, Willis suggests that: "If these resources are managed optimally through appropriate governmental intervention, no issues arise other than those discussed above with respect to diminishing returns to [privately-owned] land."

23/ When the population is larger, costs of such expenditures can be spread over more taxpayers, and so the public goods become cheaper per person; it is then optimal for the Government to provide more.

24/ The reasoning behind this calculation is as follows: Evenson's estimate implies that $d[A2/A1]/(dN2/N2) = .028/.1 = .28$, or equivalently, $dg/dN2 = .28/N2$. Multiplying this by $N1$ yields: $N1(dg/dN2) = .28(N1/N2)$. Now consider $A1f(n)$. From Evenson's estimate of the Malthusian effect, $f(n)=n.23f(1)$, so $A1f(2)=1.17A1f(1)$. The net externality, then, is $.28*.5*1.17*A1f(1)=.16A1f(1)$, where $A1f(1)$ is just first-period average household income. Therefore, the annual external effect on second-period income is 16 per cent of first-period household income.

25/   The planner will also choose an amount of education E such that $p_E = I'(E)$.

26/   In fact, it is not only transfers through the public sector that are affected by a birth, but also market transfers, since the population growth rate affects the market interest rate.

27/   Given the spirit of the analysis in the preceding sections, it could certainly be objected that the only possible steady state rate of population growth is zero or less. Presumably the insights gained from this comparative steady state analysis would also affect the choice of optimal trajectory to an eventual end point, as Samuelson (1976) suggested in a very similar context.

28/   Lee and Lapkoff (1988) and Lee (1988) give a fuller discussion of the model used here.

29/   My discussion here is based on Willis (1988) who gives a detailed analysis, including a parallel treatment of the production sector that invests in capital.

30/   In 1980–1981, it appears that only 1.15 million individuals were assessed income tax; of these, only 54,000 had incomes under Rs. 10,000. (This is more than four times per capita income in 1980.) Forty per cent of the individuals assessed were employees of the state or central government.

31/   Assuming that taxes are proportionate to age-specific consumption is not appropriate, since there is no reason to expect that an incremental child would lead to additional taxes, although it would certainly consume something. Incomes will on the whole be spent, and many investment expenditures may be taxed as well as consumption.

32/   They are assumed optimal in the sense that the disutility of the process of averting births equals the disutility of exceeding the number of births that would ideally be wanted (i. e., the "demand for children" in the Easterlin–Crimmins framework).

33/   Of course, a change of one whole child is not infinitesimal, and an infinitesimal change in number of children is not possible. However, if we relax for a moment the assumption of strict homogeneity of couples, then in a large population we should be able to find many couples which are nearly indifferent between their planned number of children and a number one child greater.

34/   Assuming the TFR is 4.5 children per woman and the average age of child-bearing is 30.

35/   As noted before, externalities arising from intergenerational transfers through the market sector represent the gain or loss per household, while those for the public sector represent gain or loss per individual, so they should not be added in this way without adjustment.

36/   Total government pension expenditures, at the state and central level, amounted to Rs. 6.621 billion, or Rs. 9.66 per capita. Of this total, Rs. 2.669 billion was for military pensions and Rs. 3.953 billion was for general pensions. No information was available on the ages of the pension recipients.

37/   That is, for a Coale-Demeny Model South Female population with $e_0=50$ and $n=.02$, the average age is 25.96 years; the median age is, of course, considerably lower (see Coale and Demeny, 1983).

38/   Because the average age of receipt of age-distributed services and transfers happened to be the same as for the stable population, the total figure is simply $(20/3.8)*25$.

39/   For example, how are we to view expenditures that enhance the performance of the economy? They will raise incomes and thereby raise consumption at every age—but probably more so at older ages, and perhaps in proportion to age-specific consumption.

40/   A reader noted: "If, with a stroke of a pen, coal rights were equally distributed to each citizen as a marketable, private asset, there would be no externalities. Yet little has happened, in real terms." But the transfer of ownership does not increase the wealth of the individual adults, because proceeds from the mineral rights were previously used to offset taxes, and the discounted value of the expected offsets must exactly equal the value of the stock shares. All that has happened is that adults receive a lump sum now in exchange for a perpetual stream of increased taxes. The only effect, then, is to lead them to take into account the fact that the more children they have, the smaller the share in the asset value each child will receive, which should lead them to reduce fertility. In the present arrangement, all children, regardless of number, will grow up to receive the per capita benefit of reduced taxes; that is, the "price of child" effect is not present when the mineral rights are publicly owned.

References

Arthur, Brian W. and Geoffrey McNicoll (1978). Samuelson, population and intergenerational transfers. International Economic Review, vol. 19, No. 1, pp. 241-246.

Becker, Gary S. (1981). A Treatise on the Family. Cambridge, Mass.: Harvard University Press.

_____ (1988). Family economics and macro behaviour. American Economic Review, vol. 78, No. 1, pp. 1–13.

_____ Gary S. and Kevin M. Murphy (1988). The family and the state. Journal of Law and Economics.

Bernheim, B. Douglas and Kyle Bagwell (1986). Is everything neutral? National Bureau of Economic Research, Working Paper, No. 2086. Cambridge, Mass.

Blandy, R. (1974). The welfare analysis of fertility reduction. Economic Journal, vol. 84, pp. 109-129.

Boserup, Ester (1965). The Conditions of Agricultural Progress. Chicago: Aldine Publishing Co.

_____ (1981). Population and Technological Change: A Study of Long-Term Trends. Chicago: University of Chicago Press.

Boskin, Michael J. and others (1985). New estimates of the value of federal mineral rights and land. American Economic Review, vol. 75, No. 5, pp. 923-936.

Chopra, K., G. K. Kadekodi and M. N. Murty (1988). Participatory Development: An Approach to the Management of Common Property Resources. New Delhi's Institute of Economic Growth.

Coale, Ansley and Paul Demeny (1983). Regional Model Life Tables and Stable Populations, 2nd ed. New York: Academic Press.

Cornes, Richard and Todd Sandler (1986). The Theory of Externalities, Public Goods, and Club Goods. Cambridge: Cambridge University Press.

Davis, Kingsley (1967). Population policy: will current programs succeed? Science, vol. 158, pp. 730-739.

Demeny, Paul (1972). The economics of population control. In Rapid Population Growth: Consequences and Policy Implications. Baltimore: The Johns Hopkins University Press, pp. 199-221.

_____ (1986). Population and the invisible hand. Demography, vol. 23, No. 4, pp. 473-488.

Eckstein, Zvi and Kenneth I. Wolpin (1985). Endogenous fertility and optimal population size. Journal of Public Economics, vol. 27, pp. 93-106.

Ermisch, John (1988). Intergenerational transfers in industrialized countries: effects of age distribution and economic institutions. Centre for Economic Policy Research Conference on Work, Retirement and Inter-generational Equity 1850-2050, St. John's College, Cambridge, 19-21 July 1988.

Evenson, Robert E. (1988). Population growth, infrastructure, and real incomes in North India. In Population, Food and Rural Development, Ronald Lee and others, eds. Oxford: Oxford University Press, pp. 118-139,.

Gale, David (1973). Pure exchange equilibrium of dynamic economic models. Journal of Economic Theory, vol. 6, pp. 12-36.

Government of India (1981). Combined Finance and Revenue Accounts of the Union and State Governments in India.

_____ (1983). Ministry of Finance. Budget Volume for 1981-82.

Hardin, G. (1968). The tragedy of the commons. Science, vol. 162, pp. 1,243-1,248.

Jodha, N. S. (1985). Population growth and the decline of common property resources in Rajasthan, India. Population and Development Review, vol. 11, No. 2, pp. 247-264.

Keyfitz, Nathan (1987). Applied Mathematical Demography. New York: John Wiley and Sons.

Lee, Ronald D. (1988). Induced population growth and induced technological progress: their interaction in the accelerating stage. Mathematical Population Studies, vol. 1, No. 3, pp. 265-288.

_____ and Shelley Lapkoff (1988). Intergenerational flows of time and goods: consequences of slowing population growth. Journal of Political Economy, vol. 96, No. 3, pp. 618-651.

Miller, Merton H. and Charles W. Upton (1985). A test of the Hotelling valuation principle. Journal of Political Economy, vol. 93, No. 1, pp. 1-25.

National Academy of Sciences Committee on Population Growth and Economic Development (1986). Population Growth and Economic Development: Policy Questions. Washington, D.C.: National Academy Press.

National Research Council (1986). Population Growth and Economic Development: Policy Questions. Working Group on Population Growth and Economic Development. Washington, D.C.: National Academy Press.

Nerlove, Marc, Assaf Razin and Efraim Sadka (1987). Household and Economy: Welfare Economics of Endogenous Fertility. New York: Academic Press.

Ng, Yew-Kwang (1986). The welfare economics of population control. Population and Development Review, vol. 12, No. 2, pp. 247-266.

Preston, Samuel (1986). Are the economic consequences of population growth a sound basis for policy? In World Population and United States Policy: The Choices Ahead, Jane Menken, ed. New York: W. W. Norton, pp. 67-95.

Samuelson, Paul A. (1958). An exact consumption-loan model of interest with or without the social contrivance of money. Journal of Political Economy, vol. 66, pp. 467-482.

_____ (1976). The optimum growth rate for population: agreement and evaluations. International Economic Review, vol. 17, pp. 516-525.

Simon, J. (1977). The Economics of Population Growth. Princeton: Princeton University Press.

_____ (1978). An integration of the invention-pull and population-push theories of economic-demographic history. In Research in Population Economics, J. Simon, ed., vol. 1. Greenwich, Conn.: JAI Press, pp. 165-187.

_____ (1986). Theory of Population and Economic Growth. Oxford: Basil Blackwell.

Starrett, D. (1972). On golden rule, the "biological rate of interest" and competitive inefficiency. Journal of Political Economy, vol. 80, pp. 276-291.

Willis, Robert (1987). Externalities and population. In Population Growth and Economic Development: Issues and Evidence, D. Gale Johnson and Ronald D. Lee, eds. Madison: University of Wisconsin Press, pp. 661-700.

_____ (1988). Life cycles, institutions and population growth: a theory of the equilibrium rate of interest in an overlapping generations model. In The Economics of Changing Age Distributions in Developed Countries, Ronald Lee and others eds. Oxford: Oxford University Press, pp. 106-138.

World Bank (1984). World Development Report 1984. Oxford: Oxford University Press.

PART SIX

Conclusions

Chapter 12

Recent findings on the consequences of rapid population growth in developing countries

● D. E. Horlacher and L. Heligman*

Since Second World War, considerable attention has been given to demographic growth in developing countries and its economic consequences. National and international research findings have demonstrated the complexity of the relationships between population growth and economic growth and the need for well-designed studies to quantify the size and direction of the interactions. Such studies are important for the formulation of integrated and consistent population and development policies.

Though academic research has failed to document the existence of clear, unambiguous relationships, the majority of popular writings in the post-Second World War era portrayed population growth as a major obstacle to achieving economic development in developing countries, a view that has received significant support among demographers. 1/ In a widely cited study, Ansley Coale and Edgar Hoover (1958) wrote that "to postpone fertility reductions in low income countries is to shrink the potential growth in income per capita for the indefinite future." In the decades since, this view has been greatly expanded. A recent statement signed by 40 heads of state representing more than half of the world's population warned that "if this unprecedented population growth continues, future generations of children will not have adequate food, housing, medical care, education, earth resources and employment opportunities (United Nations Population Fund, 1985).

A major exception to this general trend in the demographic literature is the more balanced view found in the second edition of Determinants and Consequences of Population Growth, (United Nations, 1971). During the 1980s, this view emphasizing the complexity of demographic-economic interrelations has re-emerged. 2/ Moreover, increasing attention has been paid to the socio-economic environment and to the institutional context through which population factors are exercising their influence on societies.

---

* Population Division, Department of International Economic and Social Affairs, United Nations Secretariat.

The views expressed in this article are those of the authors and do not imply the expression of any opinion on the part of the United Nations Secretariat.

This volume responds to and expands upon this new trend. This concluding chapter brings together not only the papers presented in this volume but all the papers presented at the Meeting, and discusses their findings in the context of a broader review of recent research on the consequences of population growth in developing countries (United Nations, 1987).

This paper is divided into nine sections. The first discusses prospects for continued population growth and its implication for age structures. The second section deals with inter-country relations between population and economic growth rates from a historical perspective and on the basis of current data. It also considers how population growth affects inter-country economic relations. The third section is devoted to such sectoral concerns as employment, savings rates, income distribution, and investment. The fourth section examines the impact of population growth on resources and the environment. The fifth and sixth sections consider possible benefits of population growth through economies of scale and hastening technical and institutional change. The seventh section deals with the impact of population growth on kinship structures; the eighth discusses a methodology for quantifying the externalities resulting from population growth; and the final section presents the conclusions of the group.

The demographic background

M. A. El Badry observes that when viewed from a historical perspective, rapid global population growth is both a recent and a unique phenomenon. Though there can be no question that for decades to come planners and policy makers will have to grapple with the consequences of this growth, it is unlikely that future generations will ever experience such unprecedentedly high growth rates on such a large geographic scale.

At the dawn of the Christian era the world's population was in the range of 250 million, representing the effect of an annual growth rate that averaged less than one twentieth of 1 per cent (Durand, 1977; Clark, 1968; Biraben, 1979). There was near stagnation in population growth during the first millennium of that era, with gains in some regions offset by losses in others. Between the years 1000 and 1780, the growth of the world's population resumed with average annual rates of about .13 or .14 per cent.

Population growth accelerated over the last two and a half centuries. In the early years of that period, rapid growth occurred in areas as diverse as Europe, North America, Latin America, and China. Near the beginning of the twentieth century the current geographical patterns of population growth began to appear. The decade of the 1950s was one of accelerated population growth in all regions of the world. By the early 1960s, however, the growth rate of the developed countries was declining, and in the second half of the decade the rate in the developing countries began its sustained decline.

The downward trend in growth rates continued in developing countries despite a significant decline in mortality, which has added almost 19 years to life expectancy at birth since mid-century. Mortality declines were more than matched by the dramatic declines in fertility, though they remain high in many countries in Africa and South Asia.

The medium variant United Nations projections indicate that world population will exceed 6 billion by the year 2000 (United Nations, 1988b). However, the annual growth rate of population will have fallen to 1.5 per cent and is expected to continue to fall.   An additional consequence of the fertility decline is that the population of countries throughout the world will continue to age.   And although aging is most advanced in the developed countries, it will be most rapid in those developing countries experiencing significant fertility decline.

An exploratory view of the long-term prospects for population growth was prepared by the Population Division of the United Nations Secretariat (United Nations, 1983), which made projections for eight major regions of the world to the year 2100.   The "high" variant calls for a population of 14.9 billion by the year 2100, while the lowest variant calls for less than half that amount, 7.2 billion.   According to the medium variant, world population would reach 9.5 billion by the middle of the next century.   It would then approach stabilization asymptotically, rising to 10.1 billion by 2075 and reaching 10.2 billion by the year 2100.   With differences in their rates of population growth, different demographic situations would be expected in the major developing areas, but in the second half of the next century there would be a gradual convergence to stabilization in all regions.

El-Badry's paper demonstrated that the historical record provides sufficient alterations in rates of population growth to justify an assessment of interrelationships between long-term demographic trends and trends in various aspects of socio-economic development.   He also demonstrates that there are sufficient differences in current rates of population growth to justify an assessment of interrelationships between growth rates and socio-economic indicators on the basis of cross-country analysis.

The projections reviewed by El-Badry also demonstrate that during the horizon for most prospective planning exercises, it is almost certain that population will continue to grow rapidly in many developing countries, and planners will have little choice but to adapt to this demographic reality. But for the very long run, population growth can be considered a policy instrument.   Though rapid population growth is unlikely to continue far into the next century, current policy decisions as to when and how rapidly to reduce rates of population growth will have a profound effect on the level at which world population is likely to stabilize.   Thus, long-term policy reviews should shift their focus from rates of population growth to the socio-economic implications of alternative levels of population size.

Inter-country relationships

The simplest and most direct way to assess the implications of these demographic trends for economic development would be to calculate the coefficient relating population growth to the growth of per capita income. The many cross-national studies of both the historical experience of Western Europe and the more modern experience of today's less developed regions have been unable to document a statistically significant relationship, either positive or negative, between economic change and population change.

The historical experience

David Weir noted that the long-term historical record of Western European experience can be divided into two distinct periods, the years before and after the onset of the industrial revolution.

Before the industrial revolution

During the period from 1250 to 1800, time-series evidence from France and England indicates a negative relationship between population growth rates and changes in economic circumstances. However, Weir notes that the number of economic cycles traced in these studies is small, leaving an enormous potential for coincidence between population and economic trends.

During this period, mortality change may have been an exogenous force (along with technological change) affecting real wages. Higher mortality reduced the quantity of labour and pushed up real wages; in the same way, lower mortality pushed down real wages. Rises (or declines) in real wages would lead to rises (or declines) in fertility, but this wage-fertility relationship was weak compared to the mortality-wage relationship. Hence, changes in population growth rates were dominated by the mortality component, and the observed negative relationship between population growth and real wages was due primarily to the positive relationship between mortality levels and real wages, presumably reflecting the impact of diminishing returns to labour.

This process was incorporated in an econometric model developed by Ronald Lee (1980). That model includes a constant elasticity of substitution production function that when fitted statistically produces an extremely low elasticity of substitution between land and labour (.16). This implies that an inflexible technology in agriculture is the basic source of the adverse effects of population growth on real wages.

Lee's finding implies that only half of the population growth taking place at that time could be absorbed in agriculture; population growth should therefore have resulted in increased rates of urbanization. However, other studies of that period have failed to confirm this implication of Lee's model, finding instead that the rate of urbanization is independent of the growth rate of population.

Lee's low elasticity of substitution also implies that population growth would be accompanied by an increase in total output and a decrease in the total wage bill (thus greatly increasing the absolute and relative share of income going to rents). However, the available evidence on movements of rents during this period also fails to confirm this implication of Lee's model. Finally, Weir finds that by taking price level effects into account, he can nearly eliminate any relationship between population and real wages during this period.

After the industrial revolution

Though data for the later period, the nineteenth century or the post-Industrial Revolution era, are available for a larger number of Western European countries, Weir finds that they provide no evidence demonstrating a statistically significant relationship between per capita income growth and population growth. The absence of such a statistical relationship may, of course, be itself a statistical artifact. But it is possible that the abatement of mortality epidemics in the years preceding the Industrial Revolution and the increasing importance of physical capital (the quantity of which could be altered by changes in the quality and quantity of labour) that characterized the post-Industrial Revolution period permanently altered the nature of the population-income relationship.

Though the statistical evidence of a historical relationship between population and per capita income is weak, Zdenek Pavlik (1989) maintained that changes in population size and growth are not neutral in their effect on general development. He asserted that under suitable economic and social conditions, population growth can have a favourable effect on general development, but without these conditions population growth can retard development.

In this context Pavlik questioned the relevance of the historical evidence, since the conditions (both internal and external) under which population growth is occurring in today's developing countries differs so markedly from those facing today's developed countries during their periods of rapid population growth. Developing countries at present are greatly influenced by coexisting developed countries that use the former as sources of raw materials and markets for finished goods. While the processes of development and urbanization in Europe were reasonably continuous and widely diffused, in today's developing countries they are discontinuous. New technology permits these countries to skip many evolutionary steps, but this often results in dualistic economies with coexisting modern and traditional sectors. Furthermore, unlike their counterparts in the past, today's developing countries have very limited opportunities for international migration.

The modern experience

During the greater part of the modern era, overall historical trends suggest a broad positive association between population growth and economic growth, as population has tended to grow faster in countries that have also experienced more rapid economic progress. Nevertheless, in cross-country analyses, Kuznets (1967), Easterlin (1967), and others found that levels and growth of per capita income were negatively associated with population growth when the experience of the more developed countries was contrasted with that of the developing countries. However, no significant association was found when the samples were stratified, that is, when the more and less developed countries were considered separately. In particular, among developing countries the growth of per capita income was apparently unrelated to rates of population growth.

Using more recent data, Bairoch (1981) recalculated the relationship between population growth and the growth of GNP per capita for the periods 1950–1960 and 1960–1970. He also found no significant correlation in either period between population growth and the growth of per capita GNP. Using data for the period 1970–1977, Rodgers (1984) found that when the growth of GNP per capita was the dependent variable, the coefficient of current population growth was not statistically significant. Dennis Ahlburg (1988) carried out a rank correlation analysis on data referring to the late 1970s for a sample of South Pacific countries and found that the rank correlation coefficient relating population growth and the growth of per capita GDP was not statistically significant.

Some recent cross–country analyses do, however, indicate that there may be a significant relationship between the growth of population and the growth of per capita income. Chesnais (1988) calculated correlations between rates of population growth and growth rates of per capita product for 77 developing countries, covering the periods 1960–1970 and 1970–1980. Though he found no significant correlation in the earlier period, he did observe a significant negative coefficient in the later period.

The United Nations (1988) subsequently undertook a comparable exercise in which developed and developing countries were considered both in toto and separately for the periods 1960–1983, 1960–1973, and 1973–1983. When the developed and developing countries were considered together for the period 1960–1983, a significant relationship was indicated. When developing countries were considered separately, the results were consistent with Chesnais's findings, namely, the regression coefficient was positive and not statistically significant in the period 1960–1973 and was negative and significant in the period 1973–1983.

Didier Blanchet describes his own correlations, which indicate that the experience of recent decades produces first a positive, then a negative, association between economic development and rates of population growth. He notes that other cross-national analyses of less developed countries provide no clearer picture of the interrelationship between population growth and economic growth. He confirms that analyses of data for the 1960–1975 period do not indicate a negative correlation between population growth and economic growth (whether total output or agricultural output is considered), while studies that incorporate data from the years 1975 through 1985 do show significant negative correlations.

Blanchet speculates that the appearance of a negative correlation between population growth and economic growth in the years since 1975 might indicate that nations have found it more difficult to cope with population growth in the context of the current world economic crisis. He emphasizes, however, that both the nonsignificant correlations between population growth and the growth in per capita income found in the earlier period and the significant negative correlations found in the more recent period could be due to random (or systematic) errors of measurement. Though random errors in measuring the growth of per capita income would not introduce a systematic bias in the measurement of the regression coefficient, random errors in measuring the growth rate of population would tend to bias the regression coefficient towards zero. He asserts, however, that random errors sufficiently large to explain the absence of a significant correlation are not likely.

A systematic measurement error may have been introduced by the fact that rates of growth of per capita income may reflect a growth in the proportion of the economy that is monetized (as well as a growth in real output). This may be systematically related to demographic increase, since a growth in population might promote urbanization, thus increasing the role of markets. However, Blanchet finds that the introduction of a control variable for urbanization does not alter the relationship between population growth and growth in per capita income.

Blanchet notes the extraordinary complexity of modeling the population-development interrelationships. Population growth rates in one time period are likely to be correlated with those of previous time periods; observed relationships could represent a confounding of long- and short-term effects working in opposite directions. Current population growth, consisting primarily of additional children, will primarily add to the denominator of per capita income. Past population growth, however, would be reflected in increases in the current labour force and thus induce more rapid output growth.

In Solow's growth model (1971), an increase in the population growth rate will have a short-term negative effect on the growth rate of income per capita, but in the long run it will have no effect, since economic growth rates will become constant at a lower level of gross domestic product (GDP). In the models of Boserup (1965) and Simon (1986), there will also be a negative impact in the short term. These economic constraints will stimulate more rapid technological progress, hence the long-term relationship may be positive.

The studies discussed by Blanchet implicitly assume a monotonic relationship between population growth and growth of income. However, as development proceeds, the rate of population growth tends to rise and then fall in accordance with the successive stages of the demographic transition. Thus, for a given country, the correlation over time would be positive in the first phase of transition and negative in the last phase. If the whole transition period were measured, the correlation coefficients would, therefore, tend towards zero.

To test whether the absence of a negative correlation between population growth and per capita income growth in the earlier period and the presence of the negative relationship in the later period can be explained by factors not included in the simple two variable model, Blanchet adds indicators of the terms of trade, education, and population density to the regression equation. Controlling for these variables does not change the results, nor are they changed by altering the dynamic specification of the model.

Blanchet further investigates this issue through construction of a multi-equation recursive model. He carries out a series of simulations using this model in which countries are hypothesized to move through three phases during the demographic transition. No exogenous event is assumed except for an increase in incomes, which initiates the process. In Phase I, increasing income implies rising population growth due at first to lower mortality and later to rising fertility. In Phase II, mortality decline slows and fertility begins to decline due to rising incomes; the result is an observed negative relationship between population growth and economic growth. In Phase III, fertility and mortality stabilize at low levels and become independent of income.

Starting with an initial assumption that the effect-coefficient of the population variable is close to zero, Blanchet finds that the relationship changes from being positive (Phase I) to negative (Phase II). Thus, Blanchet concludes that if the underlying mechanism is as postulated in the model, the currently observed negative coefficients might overestimate the true absolute value of the coefficient and previously observed coefficients might have underestimated the true absolute value.

Models are examined that relate, on the basis of cross-national data, the growth rate of GDP to the birth rate and to the death rate. Coefficients were estimated for both 1960–1970, when economic growth was strong in many developing countries, and 1970–1980, when economic growth was slow or stagnant. National crude death rates are found to be negatively related to economic growth in both periods. One possible interpretation of this association is that population growth due to mortality decline has a strong positive effect on GDP growth. However, the crude birth rate was positively related to economic growth for the earlier period and negatively related for the later period. It is hypothesized that during the 1960s, strong economic growth had a positive effect on fertility (a Malthusian response) -- households were able to accommodate more children under an environment of rising incomes. During the latter period, the mortality-induced population growth and poor economic conditions were incompatible -- families were unable to accommodate an increase in surviving children under difficult economic circumstances.

Similar results can arise if population growth and economic growth are not interdependent but are under the common influence of some other excluded factors. Blanchet suggests that generalized development could have the effect of constantly increasing per capita income while initially increasing rates of population growth and later reducing them. This could provide an alternative explanation for the significant negative correlations in the later period.

Finally, it should be recalled that even if the concerns reviewed by Blanchet are resolved, the relevance of international cross-sectional analysis for relationships between demographic and economic trends is questionable. To interpret such cross-sectional results as equivalent to changes over time would imply that all countries are moving along the same growth path.

International economic relations

Jean Coussy demonstrates that contradictory conclusions about the relationships between rapid population growth and foreign economic relations (e.g., extent and structure of foreign trade, terms of trade, trade balances, and effects of trade on welfare) can be reached, depending on the model(s) chosen to study those relationships. In particular, very different conclusions are derived from the extensive growth models of Meade (1955) and

Bauer (1981), the optimum population models of Sauvy (1963), the large-scale demo-economic models of Coale and Hoover (1958) and Enke (1976), the macro-economic world models of Meadows (1974) and the multiregional variants of Mesarovic and Pestel (1974), the neoclassical models of international specialization, the dependent models of Amin and Okediji (1971), and the dualistic development models of Ranis and Fei (1961).

Coussy maintains that the divergent implications of population growth for trade, financial, and immigration flows are generally not the result of differences in the quantitative estimates of the models' parameters but rather are due to the qualitative differences in their structures. He places these differences into four categories, which concern the effects of external economic and financial relations, the form of the production functions, capital formation, and the assumption that levels of consumption cannot be reduced below a specified level.

After examining alternative model structures, Coussy concludes that no general statement about the consequences of population growth for international economic relations is possible. Nations differ in their factor endowments, macro-economic production functions, institutions, and policy responses to the challenges and opportunities posed by population growth. He, therefore, speculates that it is "less the disparities in demographic growth than the differences between the reactions of the various societies to the same demographic growth that are decisive in the structuring of the international division of labour and the movements of capital".

Sectoral issues

Even if statistical correlations and formal economic-demographic models were to provide a definitive basis for assessing the economic implications of population growth, they provide little information on its mechanism. 3/ For this it is necessary to examine the various relationships between population growth and the variables that contribute to economic growth. In this section we will review findings on the impact of population growth on employment, savings rates, income distribution, and investment.

Employment

Planners and policy makers in developing countries are concerned that the capital stock will not expand rapidly enough to absorb into the modern sector the increase in the labour force resulting from rapid population growth. Although the proportion of the labour force employed in the modern sector is increasing in many countries (Bloom and Freeman, 1987), the empirical evidence suggests that rapid rates of population growth are indeed associated with slow absorption of labour (Oberai, 1978; and Squire, 1981). Though cross-national studies suggest that population growth is associated with slower absorption of the labour force into industrial and modern sector activities (Oberai, 1978; Squire, 1981; Chenery and Syrquin, 1975), this might be explained by market imperfections that tend to limit wage flexibility in the modern sector.

Empirical research suggests that population growth rates and the rate of unemployment are uncorrelated (Gregory, 1980). In most developing countries, those who do not find employment in the modern sector find work in other sectors rather than becoming unemployed. Furthermore, research findings indicate that employment in the informal sector is not only productive (Sinclair, 1978), it often teaches skills that are prerequisites for advancing into modern-sector employment. Oberai also observes that many informal-sector activities are a reservoir of entrepreneurship and innovation using resources efficiently and competitively.

The rapid growth of the rural labour force in developing countries could intensify rural underemployment, particularly in the face of a diminishing scope for expanding land area. High rates of population growth would add to a stock of agricultural labour that is already used at very low levels of average and marginal productivity, making labour absorption much more difficult in rural areas.

It is, of course, impossible to absorb these increases in the agricultural sector indefinitely. Achieving growth in rural incomes will ultimately require rapid growth in non-agricultural employment opportunities. Hence, the United Nations (1971) has observed that the transfer of agricultural labour to non-agricultural sectors is an essential prerequisite for, and a basic element of, the process of agricultural and overall development. These urban labour markets can adjust to growing relative supplies of urban labour in a variety of ways, e.g., (a) reduction in rural-urban migration, (b) increased unemployment, (c) reduced formal-sector wages, and (d) expansion of the informal sector. In developing countries the fourth option is very important.

Paiva (1989) asserted that the increase in the rate of population growth has expanded both the supply of non-wage labour in agriculture and the growth of the urban labour force. He noted that rapid population growth has increased the availability of labour and thereby the possibility of urban-industrial growth. A decline in mortality led to an excess of population in rural areas and to the intensification of rural-urban migration; the excess supply of labour kept the urban wage very low. Nevertheless, in the import substitution phase of Latin America development, modern employment growth failed to keep pace with the growth of the urban labour force. Since labour migration has made possible industrial expansion without increasing the real wage, it has a positive effect on economic growth.

Saving rates

The growth of modern-sector employment opportunities will depend in part on the growth of the capital stock. The rate of capital formation will in turn depend on savings rates. It has been suggested that slowing population growth may increase the propensity of households to save by altering the dependency ratio. 4/ Specifically, households with fewer young dependents relative to producers may be able to save a larger portion of their incomes. However, empirical studies have generally found only weak statistical associations between dependency ratios and household savings (Hammer, 1984). Though a cross-national empirical study by Leff (1969) found a significant negative effect of dependency on the national saving rate, researchers have called into question Leff's method and results (see Bilsborrow, 1979 and 1960; Ram, 1982 and 1984; Leff, 1969 and 1984; Kelley, 1988b).

In part, the weakness of the dependency effect could be explained by research findings indicating that the consumption requirements of children are but a small fraction of adult requirements (Rodgers, 1984a). Furthermore, because of indivisibilities, especially in housing, consumption requirements vary inversely with birth order. In countries where high fertility is concentrated in poor households with low propensities to save, the effect of family size on the average household saving rate will be small, regardless of the dependency ratio.

In a rapidly growing population there will be many young households saving for retirement relative to the number of elderly households drawing down accumulated assets. Thus, rapid population growth should increase the average household propensity to save. However, a recent model of intergenerational transfers suggests the opposite, namely, that a transition from high to low fertility would substantially increase the national saving rate (Mason, 1988).

Paulo Paiva (1989) suggested that if economic growth in Latin America were to depend on domestic savings, rapid population growth might hinder economic growth by increasing demands on government resources and by reducing household savings. However, he found little empirical evidence confirming a relationship between population growth and savings. With regard to the demand on government resources, he noted that although reduced rates of population growth would reduce pressures to allocate government resources to the younger segment of the population, this might be more than offset by the increased demands on government arising from the aging of the population.

Little is known of the effect of population growth on saving rates as it operates through the distribution of income. Neoclassical theory suggests that by increasing the supply of labour relative to that of capital, rapid demographic growth increases the savings rate by altering the distribution of income in favour of owners of capital and land who are generally wealthier and thus save a higher proportion of their income (Winegarden, 1978). However, there is little empirical evidence to support this hypothesis.

Income distribution

Pavlik (1989) warned that in assessing the impact of population growth on welfare, the choice of economic variables is crucial. Although the increase of income per capita is generally used as the measure of economic development, distributional measures may be of equal or greater significance. Among such measures are income differences across households and regions and the share of population having less than a minimum level of real income. He observed that gross national product per capita is often not highly correlated with these distribution measures, especially in dualistic developing economies in which the distribution of welfare is bimodal. The National Academy of Sciences (1986) found that slowing population growth would reduce income distribution inequality in the long run by increasing the rate of return of labour relative to other factors of production. Simulations with economic–demographic models have indicated, however, that the distribution of income is relatively insensitive to alterations in rates of population growth (Rodgers, 1984b).

Francois Bourguignon observes that population growth will alter the shape of the Lorenz curve in such a way that inequality is increased according to some measures and decreased according to others. He concludes, therefore, that it would not be possible to make an unambiguous statement unless we knew the elasticity of output with respect to population, and we do not know that. Bourguignon notes that the proportion of persons in poverty (having incomes of less than $US 200 at 1980 prices) fell between 1973 and 1986. Due to population growth, however, the absolute number of poor persons has substantially increased. If per capita consumption expenditure is used to indicate national welfare, average levels of welfare among non–socialist countries became more unequal during the 1950–1986 period. (The results are less conclusive if per capita gross national product is used to measure welfare.) He cautions that the role of population growth in explaining these trends is not obvious, since those countries with the fastest–growing populations tend to be neither the poorest nor the richest, but rather are countries with intermediate levels of income.

The share of the world's population living in the poorer developing countries increased throughout the period 1973–1976. Since their per capita income has grown at a slower pace than other countries, their increased population concentrates in the lower deciles. A faster demographic growth in poor countries (by reducing mean world income) would have increased their relative incomes; thus the per capita income in poor countries would have become closer to the world average. In a relative sense this would have reduced inequality. Hence, the effect of differences in population growth upon inter–country inequality is somewhat ambiguous.

Bourguignon observes that if the growth of per capita income were independent of the growth in population, any change in the national shares of world population would result in a new Lorenz curve that intersects the old one. This would imply that there was greater equality in some income ranges and less in others. In order for a reduction in population growth among poor countries to unambiguously improve the world distribution of income, a slowing of population growth by 1 per cent would have to increase per capita income by .5 per cent in all countries having greater–than–average population growth rates. That is, if the elasticity of income with respect to population were less than .5, a slower demographic growth among the poor countries could produce an unambiguous improvement of the world distribution of income. Although slower population growth in poor countries will reduce the proportion in poverty (given an elasticity of less than .5), those who remain in poverty will be poorer than before. This reflects the fact that the fastest growing populations are not in the poorest countries but the intermediate ones.

Bourguignon's analysis deals with national population size and its effect in the distribution of incomes among nations. Oberai observes that at the household level, family size is an important correlate of poverty. He notes that family size often peaks while children are still too young to work and the mother's ability to work is also limited because of child–care responsibilities. In that context he cites a study by Musgrove (1980) that assessed the separate effects of household size, family composition, and employment status on relative poverty in 10 cities in 5 Andean countries. Musgrove found that the higher the dependency burden in the family, the more likely the family is to be poor. He found that the presence of children not only increased family size, making poverty more likely; it often reduced adult employment by requiring at least one adult to stay home and care for the children. Oberai suggests that these may be temporary life–cycle effects. A family may not be poor before the children arrive nor after they are old enough to earn an income. Such transitory life–cycle effects may, however, impose severe hardships in countries where it is difficult to shift income between stages of the life cycle through borrowing and lending.

Paulo Paiva suggested that in the Latin American context, large family size (hence, implicitly high fertility and rapid population growth) had been deemed beneficial to agricultural households. The typical labour supply arrangement in agriculture was one in which labour was contracted not only with the worker but with his entire family, a system that avoided uncertainties about finding employment for children. As subsistence goods were not obtained through the market, the family standard of living would be maintained through the labour of the entire family.

Investment

While early economic–demographic simulation models tended to emphasize the negative impact of population growth on the capital–labour ratio, recent models emphasize the role of population growth as an incentive for capital formation (see Ahlburg, 1987; and Sanderson, 1980). By making labour more plentiful, population growth can raise the return to capital relative to the real wage rate, thus encouraging capital formation (Lee, 1980). The increased rate of return on capital resulting from population growth might also be expected to encourage direct foreign investment (Deardorff, 1987). However, the hypothesis that population growth raises the return on capital by increasing aggregate demand has not yet been verified empirically (Lee, 1983).

The creation of human capital is of primary importance for sustained economic development. Investments in health are an important aspect of human capital formation, and it is often asserted that rapid population growth rates reduce the quantity and quality of health care programmes. Rapid population growth is generally associated with short birth intervals and closely spaced children are subject to significantly higher mortality (see Cleland and Sathar, 1984; de Sweemer, 1984; Frenzen and Hogan, 1982; and Hobcraft, McDonald and Rutstein, 1985). Furthermore, a strong inverse empirical relationship has been found between the number of children in the household and child nutrition (see Evenson, Popkin and King–Quizon, 1979; and Heller and Drake, 1979). Though empirical studies do not indicate that family size per se reduces the survival prospects of infants and children (see Anker and Knowles, 1983; Kelley and da Silva, 1980; and Simmons, 1982), there are indications that large family size may adversely affect children's health.

The relationship between health and population growth has important implications for other facets of human capital formation, since low infant and child survival rates and poor health may discourage parents from investing in education and training (Preston, 1980). Inadequate birth-spacing also adversely affects maternal health, and the demands of pregnancy, lactation, and child care associated with high fertility reduce the return to the education of females, discouraging investment in this form of human capital.

Though there has been widespread concern that rapid population growth may strain public resources, leading to a dilution of health spending, the relationship between population growth and public spending on health appears to be weak (Golladay and Liese, 1980). Though numerous studies have been done to show that family planning has a beneficial impact on the health of mothers and children, there has been little effort to document the macro-level strains and constraints placed upon the health sector by rapid population growth. Furthermore, aggregate levels of health in developing countries may be largely independent of government health expenditures (see Mosley, 1983; and United Nations, 1985).

Joseph Potter presents evidence suggesting that lower fertility contributes to lower mortality. In particular, he asserts that there is ample evidence that high fertility in developing countries has negative consequences for the health of infants and young children and that this may affect their health and productivity throughout adult life. Reduction of population growth rates, therefore, might significantly improve the quality of human capital.

Oberai also asserts that rapid urban population growth frequently has deleterious effects on health and environmental conditions. He cites Boulier's (1977) finding that a reduction in births and increased spacing of children tend to improve maternal and infant health. Potter cautions, however, that the implications of reduced population growth for statistical measures of mortality and health are ambiguous. Though birth-spacing, birth order, and age of mother all affect child survival, studies indicate that birth order is the most important factor. Family planning programmes affect infant mortality measures less than might be expected because as average family size declines, first births (which exhibit high infant mortality) become a larger proportion of total births.

Resources and the environment

It has often been asserted that the increased material requirements of a rapidly growing population can be met by increasing production through the effective utilization of the increased supply of human resources that results from that same population growth. However, the conservation of the resource base and the protection of the environment might place severe constraints on the economic response to rapid population growth.

Resources

It is not possible to reach a definitive conclusion on whether population growth has yet or will lead to an increased scarcity of natural resources, due in part to the lack of consensus on how resource scarcity should be measured. The use of relative prices to measure scarcity could be justified if resource markets functioned perfectly, since prices would accurately reflect true economic scarcity. However, relative prices cannot be used to measure the scarcity of common–property resources, and market imperfections and price distortions, which are common in the case of private–property resources, may make it inappropriate to infer trends in scarcity from trends in resource prices. Unfortunately, quantitative measures such as per capita consumption, ratios of reserves-to-annual production, and unit extraction cost are also potentially misleading (Smith, 1978; and Brown and Field, 1979).

The immediate effect of the increased resource demand resulting from population growth would normally be higher resource prices, which would generally encourage exploration for new deposits and stimulate research on extractive technology. The development of renewable resources such as commercial forests should respond to price signals in a similar manner. As resource prices increase, consumers will tend to substitute towards less resource–intensive goods and producers will adopt fewer resource–intensive methods of production. Nevertheless, population pressure on resources may cause severe temporary dislocations due to lags in the adjustment process.

Increasing natural resource prices and improving technology might also lead to the conversion of common–property resources into private–property resources thereby promoting conservation and improved management. However, common–property resources in developing countries are being diminished in terms of area, maintenance and productivity. This has been attributed to many factors, but the role of population growth in this process has been particularly controversial since the writings of Hardin (1968). Although recent research findings of Runge (1981), Sandford (1983), and Repetto and Holmes (1988) indicate that population growth was of less significance than changes in the formal and informal norms governing the use of such common resources, this issue is still widely debated.

In a study of 80 villages from 20 districts in 7 states in the dry tropical regions of India, Narpat Jodha (1989) found that common property resources were especially important to the rural poor, providing them with the bulk of their fuel supplies and animal fodder and thereby partially ameliorating income inequalities in rural areas. His study showed that over a 30–year period, common-property areas in different states were reduced by an amount ranging from 31 to 55 per cent. In those lands that remained common, there was degradation in the composition of species of plants, trees and shrubs. The loss of area in the commons was due largely to government land distribution policies. Government policy also led to significant reductions in the private costs of using common–property lands, thus inducing excessive use of these lands. Government policies and programmes also resulted in abolition of traditional management systems that had formerly contributed to the conservation, development, and regulated use of common–property resources.

Jodha maintained that these government measures were not the result of population pressure, citing the fact that the larger share of privatized land went to those who already had more land than others. He did find, however, that the initial size of the common–property lands was negatively associated with the size of population and the number of households in the village. He observed that in the past increased population pressures had led to a shift from land–extensive to land–intensive farming and that the common property lands had borne the major burden of land–use intensification.

Thus, in the Indian context, population growth made only a small contribution to the degradation of common-property resources. The dominant factor was public policy, especially policies concerning land distribution that were formulated to encourage privatization. Though institutional reforms also contributed to the decline in common-property resources, they occurred independently of the pressure of population.

In many developing countries the task of meeting the nutritional requirements of growing populations will require an increase in the carrying capacity of their agricultural lands. But unless carefully managed, such efforts could actually lead to a reduction in the productivity of these lands. In order to meet rapidly increasing food requirements, humans have begun to cultivate marginal lands and to intensify cropping patterns, thereby increasing rates of soil erosion. This trend has in large part been the result of cultivators moving into hilly lands, reductions in followed areas in dry-land farming regions, shortening of the rotation cycles of shifting cultivators, and destruction of field terraces and tree shelter belts. The problems of desertification are largely the result of increasing population densities of humans and animals in extremely fragile ecosystems, under conditions where the use of land is held in common. The National Academy of Sciences study observed, however, that this adverse short-term effect of population pressure may foster the evolution of property rights that could promote conservation. Thus, population growth might eventually result in better land use as institutions adapt.

Environment

Barry Commoner attempts to demonstrate quantitatively that although population growth makes a small contribution to pollution, the dominant factor is the choice of technology. Other observers such as Paul Ehrlich (1968) have suggested that population growth is the dominant cause of environmental degradation. Commoner observes, however, that although statements of this sort are often supported by anecdotal data about environmental changes occurring in countries that have high rates of population growth, such data do not establish a causal relationship. He maintains that the role of population growth in degrading the environment can best be assessed by comparing its effects with those of other relevant factors. To do this he suggests a decomposition model in which the growth rate of pollution is essentially equal to the sum of the growth rate of population, the growth rate of output per capita, and the growth rate of pollution per unit of output.

When Commoner applies this model to data for 65 developing countries for the period 1970-1980, he finds that there was almost no growth per capita output, while population grew at about 2.5 per cent per annum. Since his pollution measures (motor vehicles in use and electricity production) increased at rates of approximately 8 to 10 per cent per annum, most of that growth was attributed to the growth of motor vehicles and electricity per unit of GDP. Thus, he concludes that in these instances, the influence of technology was more than double the influence of population growth. From these examples he generalizes that the choice of production technology has a much greater impact on the environment than either population growth or increased affluence and that assertions that environmental degradation is largely due to population growth are not supported by the evidence.

Commoner's decomposition analysis shows the effects of changing one factor assuming the other factors remain fixed. But if the population growth rate were to increase, it is quite likely that this would alter the growth rate of per capita GDP; that in turn would in all likelihood alter the growth rate of pollution per unit of GDP. Thus, the total effect of population growth on the environment would include not only the direct effects as measured in Commoner's decomposition model but also the indirect effects of population growth operating through its impact on per capita incomes and technology. In the examples cited by Commoner, it is likely that population growth would reduce per capita GDP growth and thus reduce the ratio of vehicles and electricity to GDP. Hence, the role of population growth as a contributor to environmental stress might well be even less than that shown in Commoner's calculations. Taking the indirect as well as the direct effects into account would reinforce Commoner's position that population growth is not the major factor in environmental degradation.

Economies of scale

Among the benefits of increasing population size may be a larger market that should permit greater specialization and division of labour and economies of scale, reduced costs per head of public goods of various kinds, and reduced costs per head of transportation, communication networks, and other forms of social infrastructure. The United Nations (1971) noted that low population density may impede efforts to increase the availability of infrastructure. This view has been supported by empirical studies confirming that regional population density can permit exploitation of scale economies in the provision of some types of facilities, such as roads and electric power (see Glover and Simon, 1985; and Frederickson, 1981). However, it is unlikely that further economies of scale can be gained from rapid demographic growth in those less-developed countries that already have very high rural population densities.

In so far as population growth increases demand, it can contribute to the realization of economies of scale. However, the question of whether population growth actually does increase total demand remains unresolved. Furthermore, if the product can be sold in international markets, the rate of growth of the national population may be irrelevant. Indeed, the possibility of scale economies has long been cited as a justification for international specialization and trade.

Paulo Paiva pointed out that recent Latin American experience demonstrates that during most of the period, population growth has not deterred economic growth. He observed that in the post-war development of Latin America, the period of export-propelled growth was followed by one of import-substituting industrialization (ISI). The latter approach depended for its success on the growth of large domestic markets that, in the view of Paiva, benefitted from the growth of the population.

It is generally asserted that demographic increase is one of the major factors contributing to the growth of cities. Initially there are economies of scale as cities grow, but once some minimum size has been reached, diseconomies of scale in the provision of public infrastructure are associated with further population increases; for example, transportation costs may start to increase at very low city sizes because population density tends to drive up land values (Lin, 1983).

Oberai observes that whether population growth at the city level is beneficial to overall development is a matter of considerable controversy. It is widely recognized that urban growth often gives rise to economies of scale. However, it also gives rise to diseconomies of scale, for example pollution and traffic congestion. Whether further city growth is desirable depends in part on the balance of economies and diseconomies of scale. Some (Richardson, 1973) suggest that there is no "optimum" size beyond which city growth is undesirable. Others (Gilbert, 1976) question whether the apparently high productivity of urban firms might reflect not scale economies but rather a transfer of the burden of urban diseconomies to other sectors of the society.

There remains some controversy concerning the significance of population growth as a cause of urbanization. Though reclassification plays a role, the major sources of urban growth are net migration and natural increase. The most recent evidence (United Nations, 1985) indicates that in general about two-thirds of the increase in the population of large cities in developing countries is due to natural increase. Nevertheless, the role of population growth in promoting rural-to-urban migration is difficult to isolate from other causal factors, which include among other things agricultural and industrial policies.

Oberai asserts that population growth pushes people from rural areas to the urban informal sector, where they find it hard to improve their welfare. He observes that while urbanization in developed countries was both a cause and a consequence of higher standards of living, urbanization in developing countries was largely the result of the push of rural populations to the cities. As a result of modern public health measures and imported medicines, death rates fell rapidly even as fertility rates remained high. This increased both rural-to-urban migration and the natural growth in the cities. Oberai asserts that the more rapid natural increase in the rural areas led to a growth in the rural labour force that could not be absorbed in the agricultural sector. Thus, population growth contributed to the acceleration of rural-urban migration.

Lawrence Adeokun (1989) suggested that in African countries characterized by a colonial history and plantation-based agriculture, indigenous demographic change and national economic growth were not always closely linked. For example, migration from agriculture to urban areas occurred for reasons other than rural population growth. The major reason for rural-to-urban movement was the spread of formal education, which estranged African youth from agricultural activities and encouraged rural-urban movement in spite of limited employment opportunities in non-agricultural sectors. Formal education led to the perception that agriculture was a traditional occupation; consequently, urban residence conferred higher status.

Technical and institutional change

Technical change

Given the diminishing importance of physical capital as a source of productivity growth, it may be that the major channel through which population growth affects productivity is its impact on invention–development of new techniques and innovation–application of new techniques to production (Simon, 1986). It is possible that the more populous a nation, the more likely its market will be capable of supporting a domestic capital–goods industry, and thus the more likely that indigenous technical change will take place. However, modern research and development often depends less on market conditions than on government decisions.

In many developing countries, technical innovations are largely imported from abroad, with the result that the effect of population growth on the pace and direction of technical change is severely limited. If rates of innovation are influenced by relative factor prices, advances in response to rapid population growth would move in a labour-intensive direction. However, this adjustment may be thwarted by institutional rigidities favouring capital–using technology.

In the agricultural sector, population size and growth affect not only the availability of land and the amount of labour expended on it, but also its productivity. Although the expansion of agricultural land in developing countries remained a significant factor in the growth of agricultural output, higher yields had become the predominant factor. In this regard, Boserup's 1965 study indicated that population growth and the pressure it exerts are important stimuli for increasing agricultural yields. In a more recent study, Boserup (1981) pointed out that population increase stimulates increased food supplies by forcing a shift towards more intensive land use. 5/

Ruttan and Hayami observe that the rate and direction of technical change responds to changes in relative factor prices and the growth of product demand, both of which are related to population growth. In this respect, the recent work of Pingali, Bigot and Binswanger (1987) has confirmed the validity of the Boserup hypothesis in the context of contemporary pre–industrial societies.

Ruttan and Hayami also report on their studies of induced technical change in industrial societies. In comparing the experiences of Japan and the United States they find that Japan, which had relatively high land prices, introduced land–saving innovations while the United States, which had relatively high wages, introduced labour–saving innovations. Hence, the alternative paths of technical change followed by each country appear to have been determined by relative resource endowments as reflected in relative factor prices.

Though technical advances are likely to be induced by population growth, they may not be sufficient to produce increased levels of per capita income. The evidence suggests that under pre-industrial conditions, technical advance is not sufficient to prevent a decline in productivity per unit of time worked. However, annual income per worker may be increased temporarily due to increased time worked per year. But in the long run, population growth will lead to stagnant or declining output per worker as the incremental technological response to population growth diminishes.

The National Academy of Sciences (1986) study pointed out that some investments in land improvement may require a certain minimum population density before they become profitable. Pingali and Binswanger (1987) attributed the failure of some large-scale irrigation schemes in sub-Saharan Africa to sparseness of population and a corresponding lack of demand. Preston (1986) suggested, however, that in developing countries having high agrarian density, additional population should not be necessary to induce adoption of technical improvements.

Institutional change

Ruttan and Hayami suggest that the ambiguity found in cross-national studies of interrelations between economic and demographic growth was partially due to the variety of national settings in which these interactions are played out. Demographic and economic change are separately and interactively affected by political and cultural structures, which are often referred to as the "institutional framework", that is, "the rules of a society or of organizations that facilitate co-ordination among people by helping them form expectations which each person can reasonably hold in dealing with others". They suggest that for a given technology and set of institutions, population growth is likely to reduce labour productivity. But it will also change demand and relative prices in ways that are likely to induce institutional changes that will at least partially offset the impact of diminishing returns.

Ruttan observes that in both premodern and modern societies, technical change has been both a cause and a consequence of institutional change and that population growth is interrelated with both types of change. For example, an increase in population (and the supply of labour) confronting an inelastic supply of land will induce pressure for the introduction of a technical change to increase the productivity of land. This technical change can lead to institutional (public policy) changes resulting in greater precision in the definition and allocation of property rights in land. Thus, population change, technical change, and institutional change are interrelated, and each is partially dependent on the other two.

Increases in output per worker over the long run have required not merely induced technical change but also institutional change, which develops science-based knowledge and delivers that knowledge in a usable form to rural areas. Thus, Ruttan observes that induced technical change is often dependent on prior institutional change that may have been the result _inter alia_ of population growth. Though technical change is itself a significant source of institutional change, population-induced changes in product demand and relative factor supplies can provide a powerful impetus to such institutional changes.

Alterations in rates of population growth have played a significant role in changing agricultural institutions. Ruttan describes a recent example of the evolution of systems for harvesting grain in Philippine villages that increased the efficiency of response to relative supplies of land and labour; this demonstrates clearly the interaction of population pressure, change in agricultural technology, and change in agrarian institutions.

Paiva noted that institutional change also alters the effects of population growth at the household level. A striking example is found in two contrasting economic periods in Latin America. During the first "export-propelled growth" period in which the economy was based on the export of staples, agricultural labour contracts were made with the family, not with the individual worker. This organization of employment favoured large families, since variations in food prices did not affect family living conditions (they received sufficient subsistence) and children's employment was assured. During the second phase, the "import-substituting industrialization" period, important institutional changes in the labour contract occurred, including the monetization of wages and individual contracts. Children were no longer assured of employment, nor were families assured of subsistence. The responses to these changes in the consequences of population growth at the household level were declining fertility and increased migration to urban areas where manufacturing was being supported by government policies.

Adeokun (1989) observed that political developments are an important aspect of institutional change and can obscure population and development interrelationships. Such political developments often include economic mismanagement, low bureaucratic morality, epidemic civil unrest, and rapid accumulation of international debt. Given these problems, population growth rates are often perceived by African policy makers as background variables that are already given excessive attention. According to Adeokun, there is little agreement with the proposition that the problems of the environment or even of socio-economic planning have their origins in excessive demands created by rapid population growth.

Adeokun observed that the institutional setting both responds to and intensifies a demographic change that does not promote economic betterment. Government policy makers may respond to the demands of an educated unemployed (or underemployed) elite living in urban centres through the development of policies to protect domestic industries and by providing incentives favouring industry over agriculture. Such urban-biased policies further hamper rural development and accelerate the rural-urban movement.

Pavlik maintained that for countries having a socialistic orientation, rapid population growth is never an obstacle _per se_ for socio-economic development, nor can rapid population growth _per se_ help development. The outcome will depend on the institutional setting. He warned, however, that although social organization and political systems can be of crucial importance at certain points in the history of a country, their influence on population change or on current population-development interrelationships should not be overstated. In particular, the period of socialistic orientation may have been too short in many developing countries to have a noticeable effect on the consequences of population dynamics. Pavlik suggested that there is no clear linkage between the socialistic orientation of a country and its relationships between rapid population growth and socio–economic development. Though socialist systems may confer many advantages on a developing country, those advantages are not always properly exploited. Among the institutional factors, history and tradition often play a much more important role than does the political system.

Kinship structure

Though international migration may play a role, most changes in rates of growth of national populations reflect changes in rates of fertility and mortality. Such changes cause variations not only in age structure but also in the structures of families and households. McNicoll (1984) observed that such changes are important proximate consequences of population growth considered at the household level.

Though the expectation of having kin is determined by patterns of nuptiality, fertility, and mortality, actual kinship networks are not a simple function of rates of population growth (except where such populations approximate a stable population). Under changing demographic regimes, kinship networks defy simple analysis. However, they can be investigated using stochastic micro–simulation. Eugene Hammel reports on the results of such an exercise using the Social Simulation Model (SOCSIM).

Hammel explores the consequences of population changes for the structure of kinship networks in China, where the marked fluctuations in fertility in recent decades make the application of stable population theory difficult. His simulations show that, due to the projected marked improvement in adult mortality, a person aged 55 will enjoy the same number and structure of kinship associations as a person aged 40 under the regime of 1980. A person aged 20 will have the same number of grandparents as a child aged 10 in the earlier period. Thus recent declines in mortality not only tend to increase rates of population growth, but also make it possible to achieve kinship networks that are regarded as traditional but, paradoxically, were not generally attainable under traditional mortality regimes.

Externalities

Ronald Lee (1988) observes that even if it could be demonstrated that population growth slows economic growth, this fact alone would not justify public intervention in family fertility decisions. It must be shown that the costs and benefits accrue not only to the family but also to the wider society and that these externalities are not fully taken into account as part of the decision–making process of individual families as they contemplate child–bearing. 6/

Economic research suggests that externalities to fertility–related household decisions arise because institutions fail to adjust adequately to current population growth or technical change. These externalities can arise from patterns of intergenerational transfers if the well–being of present and future children is only partially taken into account. However, little research has been done to quantify the externalities to child-bearing in countries of the less developed regions, in part because these externalities, if they exist, are difficult to measure.

Lee recognizes that in many developing countries, the average numbers of surviving children exceed the average number that parents desire and that this provides a powerful justification for programmes to aid couples in reducing family size and hence the rate of population growth. If such programmes are successful, the question that would then arise is, "Does the privately optimal number of surviving children per family correspond to a social optimum?"

Economically, rational parents may consciously choose to forgo certain material pleasures for the enjoyment of additional children. But their decision will be socially optimal only if those parents take into account all the costs and benefits of bearing children. If there are significant spillover effects on other families, then it is possible for public policy to increase total welfare by intervening in private decisions about family size. Thus, the key question for public policy is whether child-bearing decisions impose costs or provide benefits for other families.

Considerable theoretical work has been done on the role of externalities to child-bearing (Nerlove, Razin and Sadka, 1987) but little has been done to estimate the size of these externalities. Lee attempts such a quantification in five areas: (a) commonly used resources, (b) public goods, (c) public taxes and transfers, (d) the wage rate of the next generation, and (e) technical progress. To make his analysis more concrete, he uses numerical values corresponding to those of India. However, the illustrative country of his model differs from India in many important ways (e.g., everyone is identical except for age and sex). Thus, Lee abstracts from questions of redistribution of income between social classes and other population groups.

Lee points out that while higher fertility does lead to lower wages in future generations, it also leads to higher profits and rents. If workers also own capital and land, however, the effect on wages is not an externality to child-bearing. A positive externality to child-bearing does arise from the fact that the cost of public goods is not increased by having more children, but the burden of paying for them is shared more widely and is thus reduced for each individual. A negative externality will arise from diluting the public wealth (e.g., mineral reserves), which is independent of the size of population. Each newborn child acquires an equal claim on this wealth, thus reducing the claims of all others.

Externalities to child-bearing related to common property resources arise both from inefficient use of these resources and from freely admitting new members to the group having free access to the resources. Lee notes, however, that even an optimally managed resource creates an externality to child-bearing since each birth reduces the amount of resources available to others.

Governments provide subsidized health care and education to younger persons as well as special services and income transfers to the elderly. Lee points out, however, that subsidized education does not create an externality, since children grow up to be taxpayers and those who pay into a pension system ultimately retire. On average, each child pays for itself over its life cycle. However, in less developed countries transfers for education are likely to be larger than for old-age security; thus, the average age of receiving benefits will be less than the average age of paying taxes. This does create a negative externality to child-bearing.

In applying his externality analysis to data for India, Lee obtains several unexpected results. The costs of an additional birth to society as a whole arising from social expenditures for health, education, and pensions are positive but quite small. However, there are large beneficial externalities accruing to society from the wider sharing of the costs of public goods, for example communication, national defense, and government. The major negative externality to child-bearing was found to be a dilution of the publicly owned wealth; in the case of India, this wealth consists of underground coal reserves. After reviewing the results of this application of his methodology, Lee suggests that the assumptions, approach, and techniques of quantification will need to be more carefully considered before such models can be used as a basis for making public population policy.

Conclusion

The United Nations Expert Group Meeting on Consequences of Rapid Population Growth in Developing Countries reviewed a wide range of issues concerning population growth in relation to economic and social change. As a result of these deliberations, a consensus emerged that in the past, population growth may not have played a dominant role in either enhancing or retarding the economic progress of developing countries. Non-demographic factors such as technical and institutional adjustments, the choice of technologies, and specific public policies appear to be far more important. The group suggested that even under conditions of rapid population growth soundly conceived and efficiently implemented, institutional changes and public policies in the fields of agriculture, employment, education, health, resources, international trade and finance, income distribution, urban development, environmental protection, and natural resource management could successfully surmount most of the economic challenges facing the developing countries of the world.

However, the experts agreed that successfully meeting the challenges posed by rapid population growth and concomitant changes of the age structure that will inevitably occur during the next 40 years in the less developed regions will require that technical and institutional adjustments be implemented and human and financial resources be mobilized at rates that are unprecedented in all of human history. Reduced rates of population growth could make a significant contribution to this process by expanding the options and widening the time frame for institutional and policy adjustments. To ensure that population growth and structure will not close the door of economic opportunity for future generations in developing countries, population and development policies .should therefore be given a significant place as part of an overall strategy of economic and social development.

Notes

1/   Representative of this trend was the report of the National Academy of Sciences (1971).

2/   Among such studies are the papers prepared for Simon and Kahn, (1984), National Academy of Sciences (1986) and World Bank (1984). These studies are carefully reviewed in Kelly, (1988a). See also Horlacher and MacKellar (1988).

3/   The value of large-scale models as a means of assessing the consequences of demographic change was challenged by Brian Arthur and Geoffrey McNicoll (1975).

4/   Discussions of the impact of population growth on business saving can be found in Bilsborrow (1980).

5/   Boserup's model has been generalized by Robinson and Schutjer (1984).

6/   Ng (1986) argues that the existence of external costs to additional births does not necessarily justify limiting population growth. He suggests that the existence of externalities would justify efficient pricing (including taxes or subsidies) rather than efforts to limit population growth. The resulting rates of population growth would not be excessive if external costs were internalized by taxes or other charges.

References

Adeokun, L. (1989). Rapid population growth, migration and development in the African context. Consequences of Rapid Population Growth in Developing Countries, Proceedings sof a United Nations Expert Group Meeting, New York, 23–26 August 1988, (ESA/P/WP/110), pp. 267–286.

Ahlburg, D. (1987), The impact of population growth on economic growth in developing nations: the evidence from macroeconomic–demographic models. In Population Growth and Economic Development: Issues and Evidence, D. G. Johnson and R. Lee, eds. Madison, Wisconsin: University of Wisconsin Press, pp. 479–521.

_____ (1988). Is population growth a deterrent to development in the South Pacific? Journal of the Australian Population Association, vol. 5, No. 1, pp. 46–57.

Allen, J. and D. Barnes (1985). The causes of deforestation in developing countries. Annals of the Association of American Geographers, vol. 75, No. 2, pp. 163–184.

Amin, S. and F. O. Okediji. (1971). Land use agriculture and industrialization. In Population in African Development, P. Cantrelle, and others, eds. Liege: Ordina Editions.

Anker, R. and J. Knowles (1983). Population Growth, Employment, and Economic–Demographic Interactions in Kenya. New York: St. Martin's Press.

Arthur, Brian W. and G. McNicoll (1975). Large scale simulation models in population and development: what use to planners? Population and Development Review, vol. 1, No. 2, pp. 251–266.

Bairoch, P. (1981) Population growth and long–term international economic growth. International Population Conference, IUSSP, Manila, Leige: International Union for the Scientific Study of Population, vol. I, pp. 141–163.

Bauer, P. (1981). Equality, the Third World and Economic Debate. London: Weidenfeld and Nicholson.

Bilsborow, R. (1979). Age distribution and savings rates in less developed countries, Economic Development and Cultural Change, vol. 28 (Oct.), pp. 23–45.

_____ (1980). Dependency rates and aggregate savings rates revisited: corrections, further analyses and recommendations for the future, in Research in Population Economics, Vol. 2, Julian Simon and Jake De Vanzo, eds. Greenwich, Conn.: JAI Press, pp. 183–204.

Biraben, Jean-Noël (1979). Essai sur l'evolution du nombre des hommes. Population, vol. 34, No. 1, pp. 13–24.

Bloom, D. and R. Freeman (1987). Population growth, labour supply, and employment in developing countries. In Population Growth and Economic Development: Issues and Evidence, D. G. Johnson and R. Lee, eds. Madison: University of Wisconsin Press, pp. 105–147.

Boserup, E. (1965). The Conditions of Agricultural Growth: The Economics of Agrarian Change under Population Pressure. London: Allen and Unwin.

_____ (1981). Population and Technical Change: A Study of Long-Term Trends. Chicago: University of Chicago Press.

Boulier, B. L. (1977). Population policy and income distribution. In Income Distribution and Growth in the Less Developed Countries, C. R. Frank and R. C. Webb, eds. Washington, D.C.: Brookings Institution.

Brown, G. and B. Field (1979). The adequacy of measures for signalling the scarcity of natural resources. In Scarcity and Growth Revisited, V. K. Smith, ed. Baltimore: The Johns Hopkins University Press, pp. 218–248.

Chenery, H. and M. Syrquin (1975). Patterns of Development 1950–1970. New York: Oxford University Press.

Chesnais, Jean-Claude (1988). Population growth and development: an unexplained boom. Population Bulletin of the United Nations, No. 21/22 (United Nations publication, Sales No. F.87.XIII.5), pp. 17–31.

Clark, Colin (1977). Population Growth and Land Use, 2nd ed. 1977. New York: St. Martin's Press.

Cleland, J. and Z. Sathar (1984). The effect of birth spacing on childhood mortality in Pakistan. Population Studies, vol. 38, No. 3, pp. 401–418.

Coale, A. and E. Hoover (1958). Population Growth and Economic Development in Low-Income Countries: A Case Study of India's Prospects. Princeton, N.J.: Princeton University Press.

de Sweemer, C. (1984). The influence of child spacing on child survival. Population Studies, vol. 38, No. 3, pp. 47–72.

Deardorff, A. (1987). Trade and capital mobility in a world of diverging populations. In Population Growth and Economic Development: Issues and Evidence, D. G. Johnson and R. Lee, eds. Madison, Wisconsin: University of Wisconsin Press, pp. 561–588.

Durand, J. D. (1967). The modern expansion of world population. Proceedings of the American Philosophical Society, vol. 111, No. 3, pp. 136–159.

_____ (1977). Historical estimates of world populations: an evaluation. Population and Developent Review, vol. 3, No. 3, pp. 253-296.

Easterlin, R. A. (1967). The effects of population growth on the economic development of developing countries. Annals of the American Academy of Political and Social Science, vol. 369, pp. 98-108.

Enke, S. (1976). Economic consequences of rapid population growth. In Population, Public Policy and Economic Development, M. Keely, ed. New York: Praeger.

Ehrlich, P. (1968). The Population Bomb. New York: Ballantine Press.

Evenson, R., B. Popkin and E. King-Quizon (1979). Nutrition, Work, and Demographic Behavior in Rural Philippine Households: A Synopsis of Several Laguna Household Studies. Economic Growth Center Discussion Paper, No. 308. New Haven: Yale University.

Frederickson, P. (1981). Further evidence on the relationship between population density and infrastructure: the Philippines and electrification. Economic Development and Cultural Change, vol. 29, No. 4, pp. 649-758.

Frenzen, D. and D. Hogan (1982). The impact of class, education, and health care on infant mortality in a developing society: the case of Thailand. Demography, vol. 19, No. 3, pp. 391-408

Gilbert, A. G. (1976). The arguments for very large cities reconsidered. Urban Studies, vol. 13, pp. 27-34.

Glover, D. and J. Simon (1975). The effects of population density on infrastructure: the case of road building. Economic Development and Cultural Change, vol. 23, No. 3, pp. 453-468.

Golladay, F. and B. Liese (1980). Health Issues and Policies in the Developing World. World Bank Staff Working Paper, No. 412. Washington, D.C.: World Bank.

Gregory, P. (1980). An assessment of changes in employment conditions in less developed countries. Economic Development and Cultural Change, vol. 28, No. 4, pp. 673-700.

Hammer, J. (1984). Population Growth and Savings in Developing Countries. World Bank Staff Working Paper, No. 687. Washington, D.C.: World Bank.

Hardin, A. (1968). The tragedy of the commons. Science, vol. 162, No. 1, pp. 1,243-1,248.

Heller, P. and W. Drake (1979). Malnutrition, child mortality and the family decision process. Journal of Development Economics, vol. 6, No. 2.

Hobcraft, J., J. McDonald and S. Rutstein (1985). Demographic determinants of infant and early child mortality: a comparative analysis. Population Studies, vol. 39, No. 3, pp. 363-385.

Horlacher, D. and F. L. MacKellar (1988). Population growth versus economic growth? In World Population Trends and their Impact on Economic Developent, Dominick Salvatore, ed. New York: Greenwood Press, pp. 25-44.

Jodha, N. (1989). Population growth and common property resources: micro level evidence from India. Consequences of Rapid Population Growth in Developing Countries, Proceedings of a United Nations Expert Group Meeting, New York, 23-26 August 1988. (ESA/P/WP/110), pp. 209-230.

Kelly, Allen (1988a). Economic consequences of population change in the third world. Journal of Economic Literature, vol. 26, No. 4, pp. 685-728.

_____ (1988b). Population pressuress, saving and investment in the third world: some puzzles. Economic Development and Cultural Change, vol. 36, No. 3, pp. 449-464.

_____ and L. da Silva (1980). The choice of family size and the compatibility of female workforce participation in the low-income setting. Revue Economique, vol. 31, No. 6.

Kuznets, S. (1967). Population and economic growth. Proceedings of the American Philosophical Society, pp. 170-195.

Lee, R. (1980). An historical perspective on economic aspects of the population explosion: the case of pre-industrial England. In Population and Economic Change in Developing Countries, R. A. Easterlin, ed. Chicago: University of Chicago Press, pp. 517- 556.

_____ (1983). Economic consequences of population size, structure, and growth. IUSSP Newsletter, vol. 17, pp. 43-59.

Lee, R. D. (1980). A historical perspective on the economic aspects of the population explosion: the case of pre-industrial England. In Population and Economic Change in Developing Countries, Richard A. Easterlin, ed. Chicago: University of Chicago Press.

Leff, N. (1969). Dependency rates and saving rates. American Economic Review, vol. 59, No. 5, pp. 886-896.

_____ (1984). Dependency rates and savings. Another look. American Economic Review, vol. 59, No. 5, pp. 886-896.

Linn, J. (1983). Cities in the Developing World: Policies for Their Efficient and Equitable Growth. New York: Oxford University Press.

Mason, A. (1988). Population growth, aggregate saving and economic development. In World Population Trends and Their Impact on Economic Development, Dominick Salvatore, ed. New York: Greenwood Press, pp. 45-57.

McNicoll, G. (1984). Consequences of rapid population growth: an overview and assessment. <u>Population and Development Review</u>, vol. 10, No. 22, pp. 177–240.

Meade, J. (1955). <u>Trade and Welfare</u>. New York: Oxford University Press.

Meadows, D. L. and others (1974). Dynamics of Growth in the Finite World. Cambridge, Mass. Wright-Allen Press.

Mesarovic, M. and E. Pestel (1974). <u>Mankind at the Turning Point</u>. New York: Dutton.

Mosley, H. (1983). Will primary health care reduce infant and child mortality? A critique of current strategies, with special reference to Africa and Asia. Paper prepared for the IUSSP Seminar on Social Policy, Health Policy, and Mortality Prospects, Paris.

Musgrove, P. (1980). Household size and composition, employment and poverty in urban Latin America. <u>Economic Development and Cultural Change</u>, vol. 28, No. 2, pp. 249–260.

National Academy of Sciences (1971). <u>Rapid Population Growth: Consequences and Policy Implications</u>. In 2 vols. Baltimore: The Johns Hopkins University Press.

_____ (1986). <u>Population Growth and Economic Development: Policy Options</u>. Washington, D. C.: National Academy Press.

Nerlove, M., A. Razin and E. Sadka (1987). <u>Household and Economy: Welfare Economics of Endogenous Fertility</u>. New York: Academic Press.

Ng, Yew-Kwang (1986). On the welfare economics of population control. <u>Population and Development Review</u>, vol. 12, No. 2, pp. 247–266.

Oberai, A. S. (1978). <u>Changes in the Structure of Employment with Economic Development</u>. Geneva: International Labour Office.

Paiva, P. (1989). Rapid population growth and economic development in Latin America. <u>Consequences of Rapid Population Growth in Developing Countries</u>, Proceedings of a United Nations Expert Group Meeting, New York, 23–26 August 1988. (ESA/P/WP/110), pp. 431–460.

Pavlik, Z. (1989). Rapid population growth and socio-economic development in socialist developing countries. <u>Consequences of Rapid Population Growth in Developing Countries</u>, Proceedings of a United Nations Expert Group Meeting, New York, 23–26 August, 1988. (ESA/P/WP/110), pp. 61–100.

Pingali, P. and H. Binswanger (1987). Population density and agricultural intensification: a study of the evolution of technologies in tropical agriculture. <u>Population Growth and Economic Development: Issues and Evidence</u>, D. G. Johnson and R. Lee, eds. Madison, Wisconsin: University of Wisconsin Press, pp. 27–56.

_____, Y. Bigot and H. Binswanger (1987). Agricultural Mechanization and the Evaluation of Farming Systems in Sub-Saharan Africa. Baltimore: The Johns Hopkins University Press.

Postel, Sandra (1989). Halting land degredation. In State of the World 1989, Lester Brown and others, eds. New York: W. W. Norton, pp. 21-40.

Preston, S. (1980). Causes and consequences of mortality decline in less developed countries during the twentieth century. In Population and Economic Change in Developing Countries, R. Easterlin, ed. Chicago: University of Chicago Press.

_____ (1986). Are the economic consequences of population growth a sound basis for population policy? In World Population and U.S. Policy, J. Menken, ed. New York: W. W. Norton, p. 73.

Ram, R. (1982). Dependency rates and aggregate savings: a new international cross-section study, American Economic Review, vol. 72, No. 3, pp. 537-544.

_____ (1984). Dependency rates and savings; another look. American Economic Review, vol. 74, No. 1, pp. 231-237.

Ranis, G. and F. C. H. Fei (1961). The theory of economic development. American Economic Review (September).

Repetto, R. and T. Holmes (1984). The role of population in resource depletion in developing countries. Population and Development Review, vol. 9, No. 4, pp. 609-632.

Richardson, H. W. (1973). Economics of Urban Size. London: Saxon House.

Robinson, W. and W. Schutjer (1984). Agricultural development and demographic change: a generalization of the Boserup model. Economic Development and Cultural Change, vol. 32, No. 2, pp. 355-366.

Rodgers, G. (1984a). Poverty and Population. Geneva: International Labour Organisation, p. 31.

_____ (1984b). Population growth, inequality and poverty. In Population, Resources, Environment and Development: Report of an Expert Group on Population, Resources, Environment and Development, Geneva, 25-29 April 1983, Sales No. E.84.XIII.12, pp. 442.

Runge, L. F. (1981). Common property externalities: isolation, assurance, and resource depletion in a traditional grazing context. American Journal of Agricultural Economies, vol. 63, No. 4, pp. 595-606.

Sanderson, W. (1980). Economic-Demographic Simulation Models: A Review of Their Usefulness for Policy Analysis. Laxenburg, Austria: International Institute for Applied Systems Analysis.

Sandford, S. (1983). Management of Pastoral Development in the Third World. London: ODI–John Wiley and Sons.

Sauvy, A. (1963). Théorie générale de la population. Paris: P.V.F.

Simmons, G. and others. (1982). Post-neonatal mortality in rural India: implications of an economic model. Demography, vol. 19, No. 3, pp. 371–389 .

Simon, J. and H. Kahn, eds. (1984). The Resourceful Earth. New York: Basil Blackwell.

_____ (1986). Theory of Population and Economic Growth. New York: Basil Blackwell.

Sinclair, S. (1978). Urbanization and Labor Markets in Developing Countries. London: Croom Helm.

Smith, V. K. (1978). Measuring natural resource scarcity: theory and practice. Journal of Environmental Economics and Management, vol. 3, No. 2, pp. 150–171.

Solow, R. (1971). Growth Theory, An Exposition. New York: Oxford University Press.

Squire, L. (1981). Employment Policy in Developing Countries. New York: Oxford University Press.

United Nations (1953). The Determinants and Consequences of Population Trends: A Summary of Findings of Studies on the Relationships between Population Changes and Economic and Social Conditions. Sales No. 53.XIII.2.

_____ (1971). Determinants and Consequences of Population Trends, vol. 1. Sales No. E.71. XIII.5.

_____ (1985). Socio–Economic Differentials in Child Mortality in Developing Countries. Sales No. E.85.XIII.7.

_____ (1983). Long-range global population projections, as assessed in 1980. Population Bulletin, No. 14. Sales No. E.82.XIII.6.

_____ (1985). Migration, Population Growth and Employment in Metropolitan Areas of Selected Developing Countries (ST/ESA/SER.R/57).

_____ (1989a). World Population Trends and Policies: 1989 Monitoring Report. Sales No. E.88.XIII.3.

_____ (1989b). World Population Prospects, 1988. Sales No. E.88.XIII.7.

_____ (1990). World Population Monitoring, 1989. Sales No. E.89.XIII.12.

_____ (1989). Consequences of Rapid Population Growth in Developing Countries: Proceedings of a United Nations Expert Group Meeting New York, 23–26 August 1988 (ESA/P/WP.110).

United Nations Population Fund (1985). Population, vol. 11, No. 11, p. 1.

Winegarden, C. R. (1978). A simultaneous equations model of population and income distribution. Applied Economics, vol. 10, No. 4, pp. 319–330.

World Bank (1984). World Development Report. Washington, D.C.: World Bank.

Zhenghua, J. (1989). Population growth and regional development planning in China. Consequences of Rapid Population Growth in Developing Countries: Proceedings of a United Nations Expert Group Meeting, New York, 23–26 August, 1988 (present volume).

Contributors

ALBERT BERRY, University of Toronto, Ontario, Canada

DIDIER BLANCHET, Institut national d'études démographiques, Paris, France

FRANCOIS BOURGUIGNON, Ecole des hautes études en sciences sociales, Paris, France

GERARD CALOT, Institut national d'études démographiques, Paris, France

JEAN-CLAUDE CHASTELAND, Institut national d'études démographiques, Paris, France

NIGEL COHEN, University of California, Berkeley, California, United States of America

BARRY COMMONER, Center for the Biology of Natural Systems, Queens College, New York, United States of America

JEAN COUSSY, Ecole des hautes études en sciences sociales, Paris, France

MOHAMMED EL-BADRY, United Nations, New York, United States of America

EUGENE A. HAMMEL. University of California, Berkeley, California, United States of America

YUJIRO HAYAMI, School of International Politics, Economics and Business, Aoyama-Gakuin University, Tokyo, Japan

LARRY HELIGMAN, United Nations, New York, United States of America

DAVID HORLACHER, United Nations, New York, United States of America

RONALD D. LEE, University of California, Berkeley, California, United States of America

CARL MASON, University of California, Berkeley, California, United States of America

CHRISTIAN MORRISON, Organisation for Economic Cooperation and Development, Paris, France

A. S. OBERAI, International Labour Organisation, Geneva, Switzerland

JOSEPH POTTER, Harvard University, Boston, Massachusetts, United States
   of America

VERNON W. RUTTAN, University of Minnesota, Minneapolis, Minnesota,
   United States of America

GEORGES TAPINOS, Institut national d'études démographiques, Paris, France

KENNETH WACHTER, University of California, Berkeley, California, United
   States of America

DAVID WEIR, Yale University, New Haven, Connecticut, United States of America

FENG WANG, University of California, Berkeley, California, United
   States of America

YANG HAIOU, University of California, Berkeley, California, United
   States of America

For Product Safety Concerns and Information please contact our EU
representative GPSR@taylorandfrancis.com
Taylor & Francis Verlag GmbH, Kaufingerstraße 24, 80331 München, Germany

www.ingramcontent.com/pod-product-compliance
Lightning Source LLC
Chambersburg PA
CBHW080811280326
41926CB00091B/4153